# THE
# PRESBYTERIAN
# HYMNAL
## COMPLETE CONCORDANCE
## AND INDEXES

# THE PRESBYTERIAN HYMNAL

## COMPLETE CONCORDANCE AND INDEXES

Judith L. Muck

Westminster John Knox Press
Louisville, Kentucky

*Book and cover design by Jennifer K. Cox*

*First edition*
Published by Westminster John Knox Press
Louisville, Kentucky

This book is printed on acid-free paper that meets the
American National Standards Institute Z39.48 standard. ∞

PRINTED IN THE UNITED STATES OF AMERICA
97 98 99 00 01 02 03 04 05 06 — 10 9 8 7 6 5 4 3 2 1

**Library of Congress Cataloging-in-Publication Data**

Muck, Judith L., date.
    The Presbyterian hymnal : complete concordance and indexes /
Judith L. Muck. —1st ed.
        p.    cm.
    "Based on the Presbyterian hymnal . . . published by
Westminster/John Knox Press in 1990"—Pref.
    Includes bibliographical references.
    ISBN 0–664–25740–2 (alk. paper)
    1. Presbyterian hymnal—Concordances.    2. Hymns, English—
Concordances.    3. Presbyterians—Hymns—Concordances.
4. Presbyterian hymnal—Indexes.    5. Hymns, English—Indexes.
6. Presbyterians—Hymns—Indexes.    I. Presbyterian hymnal.
II. Title.
M2130.P8    1990 Index
264′.051023—dc21                                                97–5369

# CONTENTS

# PREFACE

The purpose of this book is to assist pastors and church musicians in selecting the most appropriate hymns for worship. It is based on *The Presbyterian Hymnal: Hymns, Psalms, and Spiritual Songs,* published by Westminster/John Knox Press in 1990. This concordance can also be used with the hymnal's ecumenical edition, titled *Hymns, Psalms, and Spiritual Songs,* published in the same year.

Finding hymns appropriate to a wide range of sermon topics is often a challenge. The topical index found in the back of the hymnal is limited in scope and breadth; it covers only a small number of possible subjects, and for those subjects there are usually several other hymns applicable than just the ones listed. The Topical Index in this book has double the number of subject headings and lists a greater number of hymns under them.

This book begins with a key word index, which is similar in format to a biblical concordance. The key word provides a means of searching for hymns appropriate to a topic that may not be found in the Topical Index. Many words have significant meanings in and of themselves. During the indexing process most of these key words were included in the index. The Key Word Index is also useful for locating hymns when one can remember only a word, phrase, or line from a hymn but cannot remember the first line. In most hymnal indexes, remembering the first line is essential in locating a hymn. The method used in selecting the key words is covered in the Introduction.

The Key Word Index and the Topical Index have been constructed to complement each other. It is hoped that between the two indexes worship leaders will be able to find those special hymns that will complete and enhance a congregation's worship experience.

The third and fourth indexes are of scriptural allusions. The third index leads from scripture to hymn, and the fourth index leads from hymn to scripture. These indexes should assist the searcher in identifying appropriate scripture to match a selected hymn, or in identifying an appropriate hymn to use with a scripture passage being read in a worship service.

I would like to acknowledge and thank the following persons:

Kinley Lange, Director of Music at First Presbyterian Church, Austin, Texas, and former Director of Music at Covenant Presbyterian Church, Austin, Texas, for the idea that inspired this work.

Dr. Donald Davis, Professor at the University of Texas Graduate School of Library and Information Science, Austin, Texas, for sponsoring this work as an independent study toward a master's degree in Library and Information Science.

Michael Rhoades, computer expert and member of Covenant Presbyterian Church, Austin, Texas, who helped conceptualize, and then developed and custom made the software program used to prepare the Key Word Index.

Terry Muck, my husband, for his encouragement while I did the work and his patience during the many hours it took to complete.

David, Paul, and Joe Muck, for their willingness to give up their computer time so their mother could finish this work.

# INTRODUCTION

## Key Word Index

In planning the compilation of the Key Word Index (or Concordance proper), I originally attempted to choose key words intuitively. The words selected were those that seemed likely to be of greatest use to the person seeking the best hymn for a given purpose. But after perusing several hymns and returning to them later, I found that totally different words might be selected the second or third time. This approach was much too subjective, and a more systematic approach was needed. The pattern on which the present Key Word Index was based, with adaptations, was *The Judson Concordance to Hymns,* compiled by Thomas B. McDormand and Frederic S. Crossman. Key words were selected according to the following guidelines.

1. The entire hymn was assessed for key words, including the first line.

2. Generally, the first common noun or the first verb of any phrase or line has been used as a key word. Only one word is listed for a given phrase or line. In a normal hymn, between 16 and 32 key words were chosen. This number should be enough to assist in hymn location and selection. No pronouns are used as key words.

3. Proper names, names of the Deity, and names descriptive of the Deity, such as Shepherd, Creator, Redeemer, Savior, Lamb, Sovereign, Father, King, Friend, Master, and Lord, are not used. The Topical Index should be consulted for references to these or related terms.

4. The verbal forms (infinitive, participle, and gerund) are not used as key words unless no identifying noun or verb was found. For example, in the phrase "To save our sinful race," the word "save" is in the infinitive form and is not used. Instead, the key word in this phrase is "race."

In the phrase "And a discerning mind," the word "discerning" is a present participle and is not used. The key word in this phrase is "mind." Again, in the phrase "Earth's scattered isles and contoured hills," the word "scattered" is a past participle and is not used. The key word in the phrase is "isles." And in the phrase "Through the moving of your presence," the word "moving" is a gerund and is not used. The key word in this phrase is "presence."

5. The verbs "praise" and "thank" are not included in the Key Word Index because of their common occurrence throughout the hymnal. The Topical Index should be consulted under the topics of "praise" and "psalms of praise."

6. Several verbs are not used as key words, except where no other identifying word is available. These verbs normally have very little descriptive use. The verbs that have been eliminated as key words are: be (been), become (became), behold (beheld), bid (bade), bring (brought), can, cause, do (did, done), feel (felt), find (found), give (gave), go (gone, went), hail, hark, have (had), hear (heard), is (are, was, were), keep (kept), know (knew), lay (lie, laid), leave (left), let, make (made), may, place, put, say (said), see (saw, seen), send (sent), set, show (shown), and take (took).

7. Nouns used as adjectives are not listed as key words. For example, in the phrase "Across the desert sands," the key word is

"sands" because "desert" is used as an adjective.

8. In the case of verbal phrases, only the main verb is used for listing purposes. For example, in the phrase "that I may teach transgressors your ways," the key word is "teach," and "may" is not used (see also rule 6).

9. When a thought unit runs into two inseparable lines, only one key word is used.

10. For listing purposes, a full line will not necessarily be printed, but only enough for recognition or to identify its usefulness.

11. A phrase is listed only once for a given hymn. The first stanza in which the phrase appears is the stanza referenced in the index.

The number of the hymn in which a phrase is found is given after the phrase, together with the stanza number; for example, 543–01.

## Topical Index

The Topical Index consists of subject headings chosen for their frequency of appearance in hymnals and in publications dealing with ministerial filing systems.

The selection of hymns for the various subjects was accomplished by personal perusal, comparison with other hymnal topical indexes, and consultation with clergy and church musicians.

Under each subject heading the first line of each applicable hymn is listed in the order of the hymn number.

## Indexes of Scriptural Allusions

The hymnal is a resource for the preparation of worship. A hymn is often an interpretation, translation, or response to a particular passage of scripture, a popular restatement of a doctrinal truth, or a burst of devotional piety. An appropriately selected hymn that echoes the other elements of worship may be what the worshipers take with them to their home, work, school, or recreation. The indexes are designed to assist the worship leader in selecting hymns that will most effectively complement the other elements of worship.

Two indexes are titled "Index of Scriptural Allusions." Each lists the hymns, psalms, and service music of *The Presbyterian Hymnal* along with related biblical passages. These indexes should assist the searcher in identifying appropriate scripture to match a hymn that is to be sung, or a suitable hymn to echo a scripture passage being used in the worship service.

For appropriate hymns related to scripture, the "Scripture to Hymn" index should be used. For appropriate scripture related to hymns, use the "Hymn to Scripture" index. At least one or two scripture passages have been noted for each hymn. Although these indexes are extensive, they are not exhaustive.

In the "Scripture to Hymn" index, scripture passages are listed as they appear in the Bible, from Genesis to Revelation, followed by corresponding hymns, listed by number and title.

In the "Hymn to Scripture" index, the hymns are listed numerically, with related scriptures given underneath. For some hymns, scripture passages have been set in italic type. These hymns, at least in part, allude directly to scriptural passages.

# I. Key Word Index

## ADORE (cont.)

| | |
|---|---|
| Gladly for aye we adore him | 482–03 |
| I do adore you, and will ever praise you | 093–04 |
| Joyful, joyful, we adore thee | 464–01 |
| Let us adore and worship still | 052–03 |
| O come, let us adore him | 041–refrain |
| O let all that is in me adore him | 482–03 |
| Of Christ whom we adore | 418–01 |
| Serving thee whom we adore | 420–05 |
| The Lord your God adore | 491–05 |
| The Trinity whom we adore | 083–05 |
| Thee we adore, O hidden Savior, thee | 519–01 |
| Then let us adore and give him his right | 477–04 |
| Thus we adore thee | 459–01 |
| We adore you! We believe | 461–04 |
| Where we find thee and adore thee | 489–02 |
| Whom with the Father we adore | 010–04 |
| Yes, Amen! Let all adore you | 006–03 |
| Your Lord and King adore | 155–01 |

## ADORED

| | |
|---|---|
| The God of gods by all adored | 215–01 |

## ADVENT

| | |
|---|---|
| New advent of the love of Christ | 007–03 |
| Whose advent has our freedom won | 010–04 |

## ADVERSARIES

| | |
|---|---|
| My adversaries taunt me | 190–10 |

## AFFECTION

| | |
|---|---|
| And with true affection | 114–02 |
| And with true affection | 115–02 |

## AFFIRM

| | |
|---|---|
| Affirm you God Incarnate still | 437–02 |

## AFFLICTION

| | |
|---|---|
| Affliction has broken down my strength | 182–02 |

## AGE

| | |
|---|---|
| Age to age and shore to shore | 481–02 |
| And every age shall know thy name | 209–01 |
| And shall from age to age endure | 220–04 |
| Calling age and youth | 465–02 |
| Comes around the age of gold | 038–04 |
| From age to age eternally | 004–04 |
| From age to age more glorious | 205–04 |
| From age to age the same | 260–02 |
| From age to age the tale declare | 075–02 |
| From age to age to all who fear | 600–03 |
| In an age of change and doubt | 461–04 |

| | |
|---|---|
| In every age and land | 443–01 |
| Showing God to every age | 331–01 |
| The age of grace begun | 072–04 |
| Though age is urging us to rest | 402–03 |

## AGENTS

| | |
|---|---|
| Though feeble agents, may we all fulfill | 415–03 |

## AGES

| | |
|---|---|
| A thousand ages in thy sight | 210–03 |
| But down the ages rings the cry | 035–02 |
| Come, great God of all the ages | 132–01 |
| God of past ages, be the God | 269–02 |
| God of the ages | 272–06 |
| God of the ages, whose almighty hand | 262–01 |
| O'er the ages long | 430–04 |
| That through the ages, all along | 125–03 |
| Through ages joined in tune | 470–01 |
| Through all the ages long | 487–04 |
| Through the ages long | 430–01 |
| Through the ages spoke your praise | 486–03 |
| While ages roll | 488–03 |
| While unending ages run | 416–04 |
| While unending ages run | 417–04 |
| You are, while endless ages run | 141–03 |

## AID

| | |
|---|---|
| Aid us in our strife | 122–03 |
| For I am thy God, and will still give thee aid | 361–02 |
| From whence shall come my aid | 234–01 |
| Our ever-present aid | 191–01 |
| Without our aid he did us make | 220–02 |

## AILMENT

| | |
|---|---|
| From every ailment flesh endures | 380–02 |

## AIM

| | |
|---|---|
| Aim your breath with steady power | 131–01 |

## AIR

| | |
|---|---|
| Filled all the swirling air | 128–01 |
| Let air and sea and sky | 487–03 |
| There's a Spirit in the air | 433–07 |
| Till the air, everywhere | 021–01 |

## ALARMS

| | |
|---|---|
| From war's alarms, from deadly pestilence | 262–03 |

**ALLEGIANCE**
To God your full allegiance yield    227–03

**ALLOY**
Pure, and free from sin's alloy    063–03

**ALPHA**
Alpha and Omega be    376–02

**ALTAR**
And make thee there an altar    069–02
From God's own altar brought    491–03

**ALTARS**
At your altars, O Lord of hosts    208–03

**AMEN**
Let the amen sound from his
     people again    482–03
The sweet amen of peace    447–02
The sweet amen of peace    448–02

**ANCESTORS**
When our ancestors called on you    168–02

**ANCHOR**
My anchor holds within the veil    379–02

**ANCIENT**
The ancient of eternal days    488–01

**ANGEL**
An angel clad in white they see    116–03
As Mary heard the angel    019–06
No angel in the sky can fully bear
     that sight    151–02
The angel answered quickly    019–05
The angel of the Lord came down    058–01
The angel of the Lord came down    059–01
The first Nowell the angel did say    056–01
What was the angel saying    019–03

**ANGELS**
And hear the angels sing    038–03
Angels adore him in slumber reclining    067–02
Angels and archangels may have
     gathered there    036–03
Angels, announce with shouts of mirth    012–05
Angels appeared that night    034–01
Angels descend with songs again    423–05
Angels, descending, bring from above    341–02
Angels, from the realms of glory    022–01

Angels, help us to adore him    478–04
Angels in bright raiment    122–01
Angels round the throne above    481–01
Angels sang about his birth    027–02
Angels sing praise, shepherds fear    033–02
Angels singing "Peace on earth"    051–03
Angels, teach us adoration    479–04
Angels we have heard on high    023–01
Born the King of angels    041–01
Come, with all thine angels, come    551–04
From angels bending near the earth    038–01
From angels in the air    308–01
Give the angels charge at last    551–03
Hark, the angels shout for joy    112–01
Hark! The herald angels sing    031–01
Heard the angels singing    027–02
Let angels prostrate fall    142–01
Let angels prostrate fall    143–01
Of angels praising God, who thus    058–05
Of angels praising God, who thus    059–05
Round us, too, shall angels shine    077–04
Swift are winging angels singing    037–01
Than all the angels heaven can boast    306–03
The angels hovered round and sang
     this song    057–03
The angels sing alway    308–01
The blessed angels sing    038–02
Thine angels adore thee, all veiling
     their sight    263–04
To hear the angels sing    038–01
We hear the Christmas angels    043–04
We hear the Christmas angels    044–04
Where the angels ever sing    123–03
Which now the angels sing    038–04
Whom angels greet with anthems
     sweet    053–01
With angels sing the
     Savior's birth    054–04
With the angels let us sing    060–04
Your holy angels bear me up    212–03

**ANGER**
Filled with anger God replies    159–02
God's anger is not permanent    181–01
Nor will he keep his anger forever    222–09
Or God's anger will appear    159–04
Slow to anger and abounding
     in steadfast love    222–08
Your anger always slow to rise    252–02

**ANGUISH**
Our human anguish everywhere    035–04

**ANNOUNCE**
Announce the gospel to the world 471–07

**ANNOUNCES**
Announces that the Lord is nigh 010–01

**ANOINT**
Come, anoint us with your power 317–02
You anoint my head 175–03
You anoint my head with oil 173–03

**ANOINTED**
All hail to God's anointed 205–01
My anointed I'll maintain 159–02

**ANSWER (N)**
Calm may my answer be, "Lord,
    I am here" 344–03

**ANSWER (V)**
Answer Jesus 382–03
God will hear and answer from
    on high 169–03

**ANSWERED**
I thank you that you have answered me 232–21
When the Lord has heard and
    answered every prayer 169–02

**ANTHEM**
Hark, how the heavenly anthem
    drowns 151–01
The joyful anthem rang 089–01

**ANTHEMS**
Supernal anthems echoing 451–04

**APATHIES**
Our apathies increase 291–03

**APOSTLES**
All apostles join the strain 460–03
Send them forth as bold apostles 523–01
The apostles saw their risen Lord 121–01

**APPAREL**
And bright apparel wearing 156–01

**APPEAR**
Appear before the God of grace 189–01

O Jesus, now appear 015–03
That with you we may appear 077–05
Until the Son of God appear 009–01

**APPEARED**
And that he appeared to Peter 598–00
And that he appeared to the women 598–00
Appeared a shining throng 058–05
Appeared a shining throng 059–05
There appeared a wondrous light 051–03

**APPEARING**
Joyful in your appearing 549–01

**APPEARS**
See, the gentle Lamb appears 051–01

**APPLE**
Dear as the apple of thine eye 441–02

**APPROACH**
Approach with joy his courts unto 220–03

**APPROACHES**
The Lord our God approaches 177–04

**ARISE**
Arise, keep silence now no more 475–02
Arise, O heirs of glory 015–02
Arise, thou sun so longed for 015–03
Arise, your light is come 411–01
Glorious now behold him arise 066–05
Sun of Righteousness, arise 462–01
Sun of Righteousness, arise 463–01
Then may I arise 541–04

**ARISING**
The Bridegroom is arising 015–01

**ARM**
Another arm save yours to lean upon 520–02
Be thy strong arm our ever sure
    defense 262–03
In this arm I rest me 365–02
No arm so weak but may do service
    here 415–03
Whose arm has bound the restless
    wave 562–01
Whose arm of strength does wondrous
    things 219–01

## ARMIES
When will armies wage no war 401–01

## ARMS
In his arms he'll take and shield thee 403–03
In your arms be shielded ever 493–03
Put unfailing arms around you 540–03
Redeeming God, your arms embrace 134–03
The virgin's tender arms enfolding 047–01
Who, from our mother's arms 555–01

## ART
And laughter's healing art 358–03

## ASCEND
If I ascend to heaven you are there 248–02

## ASCENDS
God ascends the throne with a joyful cry 194–02

## ASK
And to dare what you will ask 512–02
Ask and it shall be given unto you 333–02
Ask for nought beside thee 365–01
Ask of me and I will make 159–03
Ask the saved of all the race 027–01
Be near me, Lord Jesus; I ask thee
to stay 024–03
Be near me, Lord Jesus; I ask thee to
stay 025–03
Dost ask who that may be? Christ Jesus,
it is he 260–02
I ask you to cleanse me 167–03
Then freely ask for daily bread 349–04
We ask for sight, your rest restore 215–04
We ask you, Lord, come to our aid 497–01
What they ask of you to gain 416–03
What they ask of you to gain 417–03
You are here, we ask not how 154–02
You never said, "You ask too much" 390–04

## ASKED
And asked to be baptized 071–01
Till I asked my Lord if all was mine 315–01

## ASKING
You are asking—can it be 099–03

## ASS
The ass and oxen shared the roof with
them 057–02

## ASSIST
Assist me to proclaim 466–04

## ASSURANCE
Blessed assurance, Jesus is mine 341–01

## ATHLETE
Athlete and band 458–03

## ATOM
Stored in each atom, gathered from the
sun 266–03

## ATTACK
Attack the powers of sin 443–03

## ATTAIN
We may attain at last 081–04

## ATTEND
Attend me all my days 172–03
Spirit divine, attend our prayers 325–01

## AUGHT
Aught of joy or hope foretell 020–01

## AUTHOR
Author of liberty 561–04
Author of the new creation 317–02
The author of life and creation 120–02

## AVOID
And would avoid the burden of
this life 086–03

## AWAITS
Jesus anxiously awaits you 381–02

## AWAKE
Awake and hearken, for he brings 010–01
Awake from your slumbers 319–01
Awake, Jerusalem, arise 017–01
Awake, my soul, and sing 151–01
Awake, my soul, and with the sun 456–01
To serve thee, God, when I awake 542–03

## AWAKEN
Awaken us to action 291–03

## AWE
In awe and wonder to recall 507–01

## BEAR

| | |
|---|---|
| All who bear its daily stress | 413–01 |
| And all who bear us ill | 601–02 |
| And we are few who bear the insults hurled | 086–01 |
| And you shall bear a child | 019–04 |
| Bear the fruit repentance sows | 409–02 |
| Bravely bear and nobly strive | 321–03 |
| Cannot bear, cannot accept | 381–01 |
| Must bear the longest part | 468–02 |
| O bear me safe above, a ransomed soul | 383–04 |
| O God, we bear the imprint of your face | 385–01 |
| We bear our Lord's impression | 443–02 |
| Who will bear my light to them | 525–01 |
| Yea, whate'er we here must bear | 365–03 |

## BEARER

| | |
|---|---|
| Thou bearer of the eternal Word | 451–02 |

## BEARERS

| | |
|---|---|
| Burden bearers of the earth | 305–01 |

## BEARS

| | |
|---|---|
| Bears on the brow the seal of Christ who died | 371–02 |
| Soon bears us all away | 210–04 |

## BEASTS

| | |
|---|---|
| As beasts and cattle calmly graze | 450–02 |

## BEAT

| | |
|---|---|
| Yet with a steady beat have not our weary feet | 563–02 |

## BEAUTY

| | |
|---|---|
| All beauty speaks of thee | 278–03 |
| All the beauty and the splendor | 486–01 |
| And what we have of beauty in our race | 385–01 |
| For the beauty of the earth | 473–01 |
| In beauty and in power | 452–01 |
| In beauty glorified | 151–02 |
| O God of beauty, oft revealed | 412–04 |
| The beauty of thy peace | 345–04 |
| When sensing beauty or in love's embrace | 400–03 |
| Where beauty graces human life | 274–02 |
| Who brings you beauty, peace, and joy | 061–03 |

## BED

| | |
|---|---|
| As you lie on your bed | 160–04 |
| For his bed a cattle stall | 037–01 |
| Kneeling low by his bed | 046–03 |
| My bed is made in pastures green | 174–01 |
| To that lowly manger bed | 063–02 |

## BEGAN

| | |
|---|---|
| With thee began, with thee shall end the day | 539–02 |

## BEGGARS

| | |
|---|---|
| Making beggars of all kings | 159–04 |

## BEGGED

| | |
|---|---|
| I begged for help, to you I cried | 181–02 |

## BEGINNING

| | |
|---|---|
| As it was in the beginning | 567–00 |
| As it was in the beginning | 577–00 |
| As it was in the beginning | 579–00 |
| As it was in the beginning, is now, and | 578–00 |
| So from the beginning the fight we were winning | 559–02 |
| The beginning and the end | 598–00 |
| Who from the beginning was the mighty Word | 148–01 |

## BEGOTTEN

| | |
|---|---|
| I've begotten you this day | 159–03 |

## BEGUN

| | |
|---|---|
| Then when we'd first begun | 280–05 |

## BEHELD

| | |
|---|---|
| As each beheld the Son | 034–02 |

## BEHOLD

| | |
|---|---|
| To behold the Lamb of God | 409–03 |
| We may behold you as you are | 399–04 |
| With Mary we behold it | 048–02 |
| Your God behold, behold | 490–02 |

## BEING

| | |
|---|---|
| My inmost being thrills with joy | 165–03 |
| So come, O King, and our whole being sway | 457–02 |

## BELIEVE

| | |
|---|---|
| And bring us to believe | 358–01 |
| And we believe thy word | 428–05 |
| But we believe him near | 399–01 |
| On all who would believe | 128–03 |
| Only believe, and thou shalt see | 307–04 |

**BELIEVE** (cont.)

| | |
|---|---|
| To believe and to adore | 461–03 |
| We all believe in Jesus Christ | 137–02 |
| We all believe in one true God | 137–01 |
| We'd have nothing to believe | 109–02 |

**BELIEVERS**

| | |
|---|---|
| But believers want for nothing | 187–01 |
| When believers break the bread | 433–03 |

**BELIEVES**

| | |
|---|---|
| Faith believes nor questions how | 144–02 |

**BELLS**

| | |
|---|---|
| Hear the church bells ring | 039–01 |

**BELONG**

| | |
|---|---|
| Belong to you and you alone | 590–02 |
| For earth's mighty ones all belong to God | 194–02 |
| Little ones to him belong | 304–01 |
| To Christ the Lord belong | 490–04 |
| We belong to God, we belong to God | 400–refrain |

**BELONGS**

| | |
|---|---|
| Belongs to God, who founded it | 176–01 |
| Belongs to you, O Lord | 197–06 |
| Which alone to you belongs | 486–02 |

**BELOVED**

| | |
|---|---|
| For God's beloved there is sleep | 238–02 |

**BEND**

| | |
|---|---|
| And adoring bend the knee | 460–04 |
| Bend our pride to thy control | 420–03 |
| They bend on hovering wing | 038–02 |
| When I bend upon my knees | 336–03 |

**BENDS**

| | |
|---|---|
| But downward bends his burning eye | 151–02 |

**BENEDICTION**

| | |
|---|---|
| And your fullest benediction | 416–02 |
| And your fullest benediction | 417–02 |

**BENEFITS**

| | |
|---|---|
| For all the gracious benefits | 228–03 |

**BESEECH**

| | |
|---|---|
| O Lord, we beseech you, give us success | 232–25 |

**BEST**

| | |
|---|---|
| Like one who would not bring less than the best | 344–02 |
| We bring our best to you | 414–03 |

**BESTOW**

| | |
|---|---|
| Here bestow on all your servants | 416–03 |
| Here bestow on all your servants | 417–03 |

**BESTOWED**

| | |
|---|---|
| God hath bestowed on me | 228–03 |

**BESTOWING**

| | |
|---|---|
| Bestowing life and power | 128–03 |

**BESTOWS**

| | |
|---|---|
| He bestows favor and honor | 208–11 |

**BETRAYAL**

| | |
|---|---|
| Through betrayal, pain, and loss | 073–02 |

**BIDDEST**

| | |
|---|---|
| And that thou biddest me come to thee | 370–01 |

**BIDDING**

| | |
|---|---|
| Should on his bidding wait | 089–02 |

**BILLOWS**

| | |
|---|---|
| Yea, though the mighty billows shake | 191–02 |

**BIND**

| | |
|---|---|
| Bind my wandering heart to thee | 356–03 |
| Bind the festal procession with branches | 232–27 |
| Bind up the brokenhearted ones | 411–03 |
| O bind us in that heavenly chain | 295–04 |
| O come, Desire of nations, bind | 009–03 |
| So now bind our friendship up | 504–02 |

**BIRD**

| | |
|---|---|
| Bird and beast and all your creatures | 224–02 |
| Chanting bird and flowing fountain | 464–02 |
| Each little bird that sings | 267–01 |
| Like the first bird | 469–01 |
| The lone, wild bird in lofty flight | 320–01 |
| The spirit bird of hope is freed for flying | 105–02 |

**BIRDS**

| | |
|---|---|
| And hear the birds sing sweetly in the trees | 467–02 |
| Birds of the air fly here and yonder | 352–03 |
| Birds, though you long have ceased to build | 012–03 |

By you the birds are fed                560–02
When all the birds had fled             061–01

**BIRTH**
As at creation's birth                  452–05
At Bethlehem I had my birth             302–01
Bethlehem saw his birth                 046–02
Born to give us second birth            031–03
Born to give us second birth            032–03
By your lowly human birth               305–01
Give birth to happiness                 534–02
Him whose birth the angels sing         023–03
Jesus, Lord, at thy birth               060–03
Of Jesus' birth and peace on earth      308–01
Son of God, of humble birth             027–03
That hailed our Savior's birth          029–02
The Spirit brought to birth             130–02

**BIRTHING**
Everything comes to new birthing        296–01

**BIRTHMARK**
Birthmark of the love of God            494–02

**BITTERNESS**
Old bitterness depart                   347–02

**BLACKBIRD**
Blackbird has spoken                    469–01

**BLADE**
First the blade, and then the ear       551–02

**BLAST**
God of the trumpet blast                272–02
The deep-toned organ blast              278–03

**BLAZE**
That in thy sunshine's blaze its day    384–02

**BLED**
He bled and died to take away my sin    467–03

**BLEED**
Alas! and did my Savior bleed           078–01

**BLEND**
All blend their song, good news to bring 152–04
Let water's fragile blend with air      134–02

**BLESS**
All within me bless God's name          223–01

And bless God's holy name              222–refrain
And bless the sprouting grain           201–03
And bless the upright heart             186–05
And bless the work we've wrought        277–02
And bless you all my days               198–03
And God shall surely bless              534–02
And I will ever bless your name         252–01
As thou didst bless the bread by Galilee 329–02
Bless all the dear children in thy tender
  care                                  024–03
Bless all the dear children in thy tender
  care                                  025–03
Bless and keep you forever              596–00
Bless God's holy name                   597–00
Bless his holy name                     222–01
Bless the Lord, my soul and being       224–01
Bless the Lord, O my soul               222–01
Bless the Lord, O my soul               597–00
Bless the Lord of all, my soul          223–06
Bless the Savior, and forget not        223–01
Bless thou the truth, dear Lord, now
  unto me                               329–02
Bless us with life that has no end      271–02
Bless your Maker, all you creatures     223–06
For you shall bless the righteous, Lord 161–04
God bless your church with hope         418–03
God bless your church with life         418–02
God bless your church with strength     418–01
Hear and bless our prayers and praising 454–03
Lord, bless us all to whom this day
  brings joy                            532–05
Lord, you bless with words assuring     429–05
May God be gracious to us and
  bless us                              202–01
The Lord now bless from heaven above    242–02
Thus will I bless your name through all
  my days                               199–02
We bless the hand that brought you here 444–02
We bless you from the house of the
  Lord                                  232–26
We bless you now with one accord        243–01
You bless the earth with streams and
  rivers                                201–03

**BLESSED (N)**
With the blessed to retain              416–03
With the blessed to retain              417–03

**BLESSED (V)**
God, our God, has blessed us            202–06
Hath blessed us on our way              555–01
To Jesus, who had blessed them          089–01

**BLESSEST**

And gladly, as thou blessest us 428–02

**BLESSING**

Above all blessing high 491–02
All blessing and all blest 205–04
And have God's blessing 177–03
Blessing and honor and glory
 and power 147–01
Blessing and honor and glory
 and praise 147–03
Blessing, honor, glory, and might 594–04
Come, thou Fount of every blessing 356–01
For with blessing in his hand 005–01
Grant them the blessing of an open
 mind 532–02
Of blessing overflow 207–03
Rich in blessing 069–01
To each one a blessing gives 290–02
With blessing is the nation crowned 209–04
With thy tenderest blessing 541–02

**BLESSINGS**

And blessings they shall claim 600–02
And for these blessings 398–refrain
Blessings all mine, with ten thousand
 beside 276–03
For all the blessings of the light 542–01
From which earth's blessings flow 556–03
He comes to make his blessings flow 040–03
In blessings on your head 270–03
Praise God, from whom all blessings
 flow 542–04
Praise God, from whom all blessings
 flow 591–00
Praise God, from whom all blessings
 flow 592–00
Praise God, from whom all blessings
 flow 593–00
The blessings of his heaven 043–03
The blessings of his heaven 044–03
There are blessings you cannot receive 398–02

**BLEST**

Abundantly hath blest 228–01
And richly blest us all in you 444–02

**BLEW**

When you blew through your people 319–03

**BLIND**

And the blind, their eyes be opened 018–02

**BLINDED**

And when they were blinded 319–02

**BLINDNESS**

And blindness to your way 289–02
Blindness, treason, blood and gall 135–03

**BLISS**

And brighter bliss of heaven 441–05
From the best bliss that earth imparts 510–01
From the best bliss that earth imparts 511–01
Now ye hear of endless bliss 028–02
What bliss till now was thine 098–01

**BLOOD**

And precious is their blood in his sight 204–14
And with his blood our life hath bought 056–06
Born of his Spirit, washed in his blood 341–01
But that thy blood was shed for me 370–01
Christ's blood availed for me 466–03
Christ's blood can make the
 sinful clean 466–03
Cleansed by the blood of Christ, our
 King 492–01
For Christ alone, whose blood
 was shed 421–04
Than Jesus' blood and righteousness 379–01
The blood came trickalin' down 095–04
The blood of Christ outpoured 521–03
Through the blood of the slaughtered 563–02
Thy blood so precious shedding 395–01
Who still your blood and body give 156–03
Whose blood set us free to be people of
 God 594–01
With his own blood he bought her 442–01
With his own precious blood 441–01

**BLOSSOM**

And blossom as a rose 018–refrain
It shall blossom abundantly 018–01
We blossom and flourish like leaves
 on the tree 263–03

**BLOT**

And blot out all my guilt 196–05

**BLOW**

Blow through the wilderness 319–refrain
On me blow 352–01

**BLUR (N)**

A blur of mighty wings 071–01

**BLUR (V)**

When we blur your gracious image      285–02

**BOARD**

Seated at the heavenly board      508–03
Seated at the heavenly board      509–03
Thyself at thine own board make
     manifest      503–01
Your laden table board      239–02

**BOAST**

There are some who boast of the
     weapons of the world      169–04

**BOAT**

In my boat there's no money nor
     weapons      377–02
Lonely the boat, sailing at sea      373–01
My God is here in my small boat      373–03
Now my boat's left on the shoreline
     behind me      377–refrain
Tossing the boat, lost and afloat      373–02
Tossing the tiny lone boat      373–02

**BODIES**

Let all our bodies sway to God's music      484–02
Our bodies clamor to be freed      380–02

**BODY**

As Christ's new body takes on flesh
     and blood      495–04
Christ takes into his body      296–02
In the body and blood of our dear Lord      518–01
In the body and the blood      005–02
One body we, one body who partake      503–03
The body they may kill      260–04
"This is my body"; so thou givest yet      503–02
This my body, this my blood      429–03
Thy body and thy blood      505–02
We, as Christians, one body shall
     become      518–03
Where thy body lay      122–01

**BOND**

Their bond be strong against all strain
     and strife      532–03

**BONDAGE**

From bondage long ago      237–01
From the bondage of sorrow      319–04
No more shall they in bondage toil      334–03
Then shall all bondage cease, all fetters
     fall      329–02

**BONDS**

In friendship's bonds our souls unite      444–03
Then bound to all in bonds of love      347–04

**BONES**

And my bones waste away      182–02
That the bones you have crushed may
     thrill      196–05
They keep all their bones      187–06

**BORDERS**

Our borders to protect      255–02

**BORE**

Bore it up triumphant, with its human
     light      148–03
Bore the weight of human need      427–01
Faithfully he bore it spotless to
     the last      148–02
For he whom Mary bore was God the
     Son      057–04
He bore the shameful cross and death      083–03
He who bore all pain and loss      112–03
She bore for us a Savior      048–02

**BORN**

Alleluia! born of Mary      144–04
Born here among us, in Bethlehem      055–03
Born is God's Son, born today      052–02
Born of the Spirit, we are God's
     children      492–03
Born to reign in us forever      001–03
Born to reign in us forever      002–02
Christ is born in Bethlehem      031–01
Christ is born in Bethlehem      051–refrain
"Christ is born," their choirs
     are singing      021–01
Christ is born today      039–02
Christ the Savior is born      060–02
For Christ is born of Mary      043–02
For Christ is born of Mary      044–02
He was born in Bethlehem      039–01
Is born today for you      061–03
Jesus Christ is born today      028–01
Jesus Christ was born for this      028–02
Jesus Christ was born to save      028–03
Jesus, your King, is born      061–01
King of kings, yet born of Mary      005–02
Of her, Emmanuel, the Christ,
     was born      016–04
Singing, "Come, come, Christ
     is born"      034–refrain

**BORN** (cont.)

| | |
|---|---|
| The humble Christ was born | 029–03 |
| We're born into a guilty world | 195–03 |
| We're born, we live, but pass unseen | 211–02 |
| When Christ our Lord was born on Christmas night | 057–01 |
| You must all be born again | 493–02 |

**BORNE**

| | |
|---|---|
| Borne witness to the truth in every tongue | 264–03 |
| I have borne my people's pain | 525–02 |

**BORROWS**

| | |
|---|---|
| While all that borrows life from thee | 288–03 |

**BOSOM**

| | |
|---|---|
| Let me to thy bosom fly | 303–01 |
| When on thy bosom it has leant | 378–06 |

**BOUGHT**

| | |
|---|---|
| Thou hast bought us, thine we are | 387–01 |

**BOUND**

| | |
|---|---|
| A bound between what life requires | 283–03 |
| You set forth each ocean's bound | 224–02 |

**BOUNDS**

| | |
|---|---|
| From earth's wide bounds, from ocean's farthest coast | 526–06 |
| The sacred bounds that must be kept | 283–05 |

**BOUNTIES**

| | |
|---|---|
| May we thy bounties thus | 428–02 |

**BOUNTY**

| | |
|---|---|
| Father, whose bounty all creation shows | 375–03 |
| For thee the bounty of the Lord | 228–01 |

**BOW**

| | |
|---|---|
| Bow down and hear our cry | 291–01 |
| Bow thy meek head to mortal pain | 090–04 |
| Bow thy meek head to mortal pain | 091–04 |
| I bow down with tears of anguish | 355–02 |
| I will bow down before your throne | 247–01 |
| Lord of all, we bow before you | 460–01 |
| Then I shall bow in humble adoration | 467–04 |
| We bow before your holy name | 488–01 |

**BOWED**

| | |
|---|---|
| He bowed his head and died | 095–05 |

| | |
|---|---|
| Then gentle Mary meekly bowed her head | 016–03 |
| While others bowed to changeless gods | 330–02 |

**BOY**

| | |
|---|---|
| In Bethlehem a newborn boy | 035–01 |
| And of the sinless Boy | 308–02 |

**BOY-CHILD**

| | |
|---|---|
| That boy-child of Mary was born in a stable | 055–refrain |

**BRACE**

| | |
|---|---|
| And brace your heart and nerve your arm | 393–02 |

**BRANCH**

| | |
|---|---|
| The victor palm branch waving | 089–02 |

**BRANCHES**

| | |
|---|---|
| May all our branches thrive | 418–02 |
| To the branches of the Vine | 314–02 |
| Where tempting, fruited branches swayed | 283–02 |

**BRASS**

| | |
|---|---|
| As sounding brass, and hopeless gain | 335–01 |

**BREAD**

| | |
|---|---|
| Alleluia! bread of angels | 144–03 |
| Be known to us in breaking bread | 505–01 |
| Be known to us in breaking of the bread | 503–04 |
| Become to us the living bread | 500–01 |
| Bread is broken, the wine is poured | 514–01 |
| Bread of heaven, bread of heaven | 281–01 |
| Bread of heaven, on thee we feed | 501–01 |
| Bread of the world in mercy broken | 502–00 |
| Finest bread I will provide | 525–03 |
| For bread and breath each day anew | 590–01 |
| For the bread which you have broken | 508–01 |
| For the bread which you have broken | 509–01 |
| Give us today our daily bread | 571–00 |
| Here, as bread and wine are taken | 461–03 |
| In Christ's communion bread | 507–02 |
| May your Bread among us broken | 512–05 |
| On the true bread of heaven | 110–03 |
| One bread is ours for sharing | 517–03 |
| Renewed in bread and wine | 517–03 |
| That living bread, that heavenly wine | 505–02 |
| The bread and wine remove, but you are here | 520–04 |
| The bread of life is broken | 517–01 |

The bread of life to eat 521–refrain
This bread to break, this wine to taste 515–03
Through bread and wine made near 470–03
To share his bread, his loving cup 094–02
To share our daily bread 558–04
To share the bread and wine 517–01
Who living Bread to all doth
    here afford 519–02
With this true and living Bread 501–01
You give our daily bread 560–02
You, the Bread of heaven, are broken 305–02

**BREAK**
As thou didst break the loaves
    beside the sea 329–01
Break forth, O beauteous heavenly
    light 026–00
Break forth with shouts of holy joy 219–03
Break the bread and bless the cup 504–02
Break the bread of new creation 104–03
Break thou the bread of life,
    dear Lord, to me 329–01
Come, O Lord, break the sword 192–03
I will break their hearts of stone 525–02
Let us break bread together on our
    knees 513–01
You break ancient schemes 319–04

**BREAKS**
As Christ breaks bread and bids us
    share 507–03
Christ breaks the power of reigning sin 466–03
He breaks the bow and shatters the
    spear 193–09
Till your Spirit breaks our night 454–02

**BREAST**
All girt about your breast with gold 156–01
Close folded to his breast 089–01
In every human breast 412–02
Into every troubled breast 376–02

**BREATH**
Breath of life and voice of prophets 523–01
Eternal Spirit, give me breath 340–02
For us gave up his dying breath 083–03
I'll praise my Maker while I've breath 253–01
I'll praise the Lord with all my breath 226–02
Our breath, our pulse, our lives,
    our gifts 490–04
Then shall my latest breath 359–03
While I have breath to pray 362–02

**BREATHE**
Breathe and blow upon that blaze 131–03
Breathe, O breathe thy loving Spirit 376–02
Breathe on me, Breath of God 316–01
Breathe through the heats of our desire 345–05
Breathe your life, and spread your light 317–01
Let all that breathe partake 561–03

**BREATHES**
Breathes a life of gathering gloom 066–04
It breathes in the air, it shines 476–04

**BREEZES**
In cooling breezes, flowing wells 274–01
The breezes and the sunshine 560–01

**BRIDE**
To be his holy bride 442–01

**BRIDEGROOM**
Forth like a bridegroom comes the sun 166–03

**BRIER**
The brier and the thorn grow wild 337–02

**BRIGHTENS**
That brightens up the sky 267–02

**BRIGHTNESS**
And in the brightness of thy light 186–04
Eternal brightness, help me see 340–02
I may the eternal brightness see 301–04
Show the brightness of your face 203–01
Thou heavenly brightness! Light divine 069–02

**BRIM**
O brim the barreled lungs with joy 490–04

**BROKE**
And broke oppressive kingdoms down 153–02
I was defiant then, still God broke
    through 410–01

**BROKEN**
Christ has broken every chain 112–01
Has broken every barrier down 370–04

**BROKENHEARTED**
God is near to the brokenhearted 187–05

**BROOD (N)**
As her brood shelters under her wings 547–01

**BROOD (V)**

| | |
|---|---|
| Let me not brood upon my needs | 390–03 |
| O Holy Spirit, who did brood | 562–03 |

**BROODS**

| | |
|---|---|
| That broods on wrongs and will not let | 347–02 |

**BROOK**

| | |
|---|---|
| And hear the brook and feel the gentle breeze | 467–02 |

**BROTHER**

| | |
|---|---|
| Brother, sister, parent, child | 473–04 |
| Christ is the brother we still crucify | 385–03 |
| Makes him our brother of Bethlehem | 055–04 |

**BROTHERS**

| | |
|---|---|
| And we're brothers and sisters in God's love | 273–refrain |
| Brothers, sisters, in life, in love, we'll be | 518–04 |

**BROUGHT**

| | |
|---|---|
| Our Christ hath brought us over | 118–01 |

**BROW**

| | |
|---|---|
| The mighty victor's brow | 149–01 |

**BUD**

| | |
|---|---|
| Bring its bud to glorious flower | 420–01 |

**BUILD**

| | |
|---|---|
| And build its glory there | 453–04 |
| And finely build for days to come | 452–03 |
| As we build the church today | 132–02 |
| That build your rule o'er all the earth | 346–02 |
| Till, pledged to build and not destroy | 035–05 |

**BUILDERS**

| | |
|---|---|
| The weary builders toil in vain | 238–01 |

**BUILDS**

| | |
|---|---|
| Builds on the rock that nought can move | 282–01 |

**BUILT**

| | |
|---|---|
| And built the lofty skies | 288–01 |
| God built it on the deeps and laid its foundations | 177–01 |
| He built his throne up in the air | 153–01 |

**BULWARK**

| | |
|---|---|
| A bulwark never failing | 259–01 |
| A bulwark never failing | 260–01 |

**BURDEN**

| | |
|---|---|
| And the burden of the day | 092–01 |

**BURDENS**

| | |
|---|---|
| All whose burdens we can share | 136–02 |
| Gladly all our burdens bearing | 479–03 |
| Our mutual burdens bear | 438–03 |
| To ease another's burdens | 552–04 |
| Whatever burdens may bow us down | 094–02 |

**BURIED**

| | |
|---|---|
| They buried my body and they thought I'd gone | 302–04 |

**BURN**

| | |
|---|---|
| Burn brighter through the cold | 292–02 |
| O let it freely burn | 313–02 |

**BURNS**

| | |
|---|---|
| He burns the shields with fire | 193–09 |

**BURST**

| | |
|---|---|
| Burst in tongues of sacred flame | 131–02 |
| Christ hath burst his prison | 114–02 |
| Christ hath burst his prison | 115–02 |

**BURSTS**

| | |
|---|---|
| See, it bursts o'er all the earth | 020–02 |

# C

## CAGES
Our cages of despair 105–02

## CALL (N)
And when your last call comes serene
   and clear 344–03
By your call to heaven above us 508–02
By your call to heaven above us 509–02
Christ's clear call to work and worth 343–02
Faithful when we hear Christ's call 432–00
The call of our salvation 156–02
The Spirit's call obey 411–01
Your call to hear, your love to find 353–01

## CALL (V)
And when I call, in mercy hear 249–01
As often as I call to you 212–04
Call each by name 215–03
Call for songs of loudest praise 356–01
Call forth sunshine, wind, and rain 285–01
Call to mind the word of Jesus 413–02
Call us, O Lord, to thine eternal peace 539–04
Call us to rejoice in thee 464–02
Great God, in Christ you call our name 353–03
I call in supplication new 249–02
In the Christ's forsaken call 135–03
Lord, you call us to your service 429–02
So when you call your family, Lord 521–01
The Lord will hear when I call
   on the holy name 160–03
To call on you when you are near 399–03
To you I call, on you rely 249–01
What shall we call him,
   child of the manger 055–01
When I call, you give heed, O Lord,
   righteous God 160–01
You call from tomorrow 319–04
You call us your sisters and brothers 157–01
You know and call us all by name 156–02

## CALLED
And called his saints from everywhere 153–01
And, while smiling, have called out
   my name 377–refrain
Called the Twelve to share his last meal 547–02
God called you "My beloved Son" 070–02
I called and then you answered me 247–02
None ever called on thee in vain 295–03
Today we all are called to be 434–01

We all are called for service 435–02
We're called to probe for secret gifts 162–04
You called me by my name 522–01
You called once again 319–03
You called to each thing 319–01
You called to the deep 319–01
You have called us to be faithful 285–02

## CALLING
Our calling here fulfilling 277–02
The gracious calling of the Lord 345–02

## CALLS
Calls you one and calls you all 028–03
Jesus calls us in, sends us out 514–03
To God who calls us all to be 434–04

## CALM (N)
Calm of a call obeyed 452–02
In calm or strife 274–04
O calm of hills above 345–03
With a calm that conquers strife 343–04
With the holy calm around 545–01

## CALM (V)
You calm the tumult of the people 201–02

## CALMS
Calms every fear 544–01

## CAME
Among them came their Lord most dear 116–04
Among them came their Lord most dear 117–02
And to Elijah, fasting, came 087–02
From the Godhead forth you came 014–02
God's Spirit on you came 070–01
God's you are, from God you came 498–03
Lord, when you came to Jordan 071–01
When Jesus came to Jordan 072–01

## CAMELS
Took strong camels hurrying 065–03

## CANTICLE
My canticle divine 487–04

## CAPTAIN
Thou, Lord, their captain in the
   well-fought fight 526–02

## CAPTIVE

| | |
|---|---|
| Captive leading death and hell | 014–02 |
| Make me a captive, Lord | 378–01 |
| The captive to release | 428–04 |
| To help to set the captive free | 434–01 |
| To set the captive free | 205–01 |

## CAPTIVES

| | |
|---|---|
| Pledged to set all captives free | 420–04 |
| Still the captives long for freedom | 427–02 |
| The captives dream dreams | 319–04 |
| When will captives be set free | 401–01 |

## CAPTORS

| | |
|---|---|
| There are captors in derision | 246–02 |

## CARE (N)

| | |
|---|---|
| Care, anguish, sorrow melt away | 366–03 |
| Cumbered with a load of care | 403–03 |
| God's care is over me | 294–01 |
| God's care like a cloak | 480–02 |
| God's great care | 352–02 |
| God's watchful and unslumbering care | 234–02 |
| I see God's loving care | 294–02 |
| In care for others taught us how | 402–02 |
| Is ever in thy care | 288–03 |
| May your care and mercy lead us | 429–04 |
| Me in his dear care | 557–02 |
| Much we need thy tender care | 387–01 |
| My loving care shall never cease | 235–05 |
| Placed himself within God's care | 406–03 |
| The constant care which Israel knew | 152–03 |
| Thy bountiful care what tongue can recite | 476–04 |
| To God's care who cares for all | 545–03 |
| To know with us God's loving care | 499–03 |
| We to your guardian care commit | 265–02 |
| With a Shepherd's care enfold you | 540–01 |
| Within your care my soul is satisfied | 199–01 |
| Your watchful care is round me there | 284–03 |

## CARE (V)

| | |
|---|---|
| Should care for us at all | 162–02 |
| To care for all, without reserve | 421–05 |

## CARES (N)

| | |
|---|---|
| And, amid the cares that claim us | 429–05 |
| To her my cares and toils be given | 441–03 |

## CARES (V)

| | |
|---|---|
| Yet our Maker cares for them | 352–03 |

## CARING

| | |
|---|---|
| That by caring, helping, giving | 504–03 |

## CAROLINGS

| | |
|---|---|
| With glad, exuberant carolings | 490–01 |

## CARPENTER

| | |
|---|---|
| You, the carpenter of Nazareth | 305–01 |

## CARRY

| | |
|---|---|
| All because we do not carry | 403–01 |

## CAST

| | |
|---|---|
| And round it hath cast, like a mantle, the sea | 476–03 |
| Cast care aside, lean on thy guide | 307–03 |
| Cast out our sin and enter in | 043–04 |
| Cast out our sin and enter in | 044–04 |
| Do not cast me away from your presence | 196–06 |
| Praise God and cast on God your care | 455–05 |
| Till we cast our crowns before thee | 376–04 |
| Why are you cast down, O my soul | 190–05 |
| With you, Lord, I have cast my lot | 183–04 |

## CATCH

| | |
|---|---|
| We catch the vision of thy tears | 408–02 |

## CATTLE

| | |
|---|---|
| The cattle are lowing, the poor Baby wakes | 024–02 |
| The cattle are lowing, the poor Baby wakes | 025–02 |

## CAUGHT

| | |
|---|---|
| Caught from the Christ-flame | 528–02 |

## CAUSE

| | |
|---|---|
| Not just to serve your cause, but share | 414–03 |
| What better cause for praise | 255–04 |

## CAUSED

| | |
|---|---|
| That caused the Lord of bliss | 085–01 |

## CAUSES

| | |
|---|---|
| Sometimes it causes me to tremble | 102–01 |

## CAVERNS

| | |
|---|---|
| From the caverns of despair | 104–02 |

## CAVES

| | |
|---|---|
| Stirrings in the mind's deep caves | 131–01 |

## CEASE
Cease we fearing, cease we grieving 545–03
May we not cease to look to you 419–04
O never cease thy shining 064–refrain

## CELEBRATE
Celebrate this day of days 104–01
Celebrate with joy and singing 107–01
We celebrate with songs of praise 087–01

## CELEBRATION
Come, O come, in celebration 132–04

## CENTER
Center of unbroken praise 464–02

## CHAINS
From chains of fear or want or greed 332–04
Half-free, half-bound by inner chains 353–02

## CHALICE
As a chalice cast of gold 336–01
From thy pure chalice floweth 171–05

## CHALLENGE (N)
Like the challenge of her flight 314–01
Our challenge and our prod 274–04

## CHALLENGE (V)
Challenge us to do your bidding 132–03
May it challenge us anew 268–03

## CHALLENGED
Who challenged us, when we
    were young 402–02

## CHAMBERED
You are chambered on the deep 224–01

## CHAMPION
Their champion and their head 443–04

## CHANGE (N)
Beset by change but Spirit led 421–01
By the change of time or place 331–02
Change and decay in all around I see 543–02

## CHANGE (V)
You change my grief to joy-filled dance 181–04

## CHANGELESSNESS
Ever secure in his changelessness 062–03

## CHANGES
Amid the changes of this earthly life 532–03
Changes never cease 465–03

## CHANGEST
O thou who changest not, abide
    with me 543–02
Thou changest not 276–01

## CHANGETH
God changeth not, and thou art dear 307–04

## CHANGING
In all life's changing where you
    are leading 436–03

## CHANTING
And chanting clear and loud 089–02
Still chanting as ye go 145–02
Still chanting as ye go 146–02

## CHAOS
May we in chaos shine to light 418–03
The chaos of our days 255–04
Upon the chaos wild and rude 562–03

## CHARGE
This is my charge to witness faithfully 410–03

## CHARIOT
The chariot rode on the mountaintop 445–01

## CHARIOTS
The chariots of heaven the deep
    thunderclouds form 476–02

## CHARITY
Of tender charity and steadfast faith 533–02
With your charity our zeal 425–03

## CHART
It is the chart and compass 327–02

## CHARTER
Her charter of salvation 442–02

## CHASE
O chase the night of sin away 510–05
O chase the night of sin away 511–05

## CHASED
And chased my grief away 362–02

**CHASTENS**
He chastens and hastens his will
   to make known     559–01

**CHEER**
Cheer my eyes and warm my heart     462–02
Cheer my eyes and warm my heart     463–02
O come, thou Dayspring, come
   and cheer     009–02

**CHERISH**
Thee will I cherish     306–01

**CHERUBIM**
Cherubim and seraphim     460–02
Cherubim and seraphim falling down     138–02
Cherubim and seraphim thronged
   the air     036–03
Cherubim, with sleepless eye     005–04
O higher than the cherubim     451–02

**CHIDE**
Slow to chide, and swift to bless     478–02
Slow to chide, and swift to bless     479–02

**CHIEFS**
The chiefs from far before him knelt     061–02

**CHILD**
A child of grace has given     602–02
A little child shall lead them all     450–02
As a child and heir of heaven     493–01
Born a child and yet a King     001–03
Born a child and yet a King     002–02
But like a child at home     172–03
Child of blessing, child of promise     498–01
Child of God, your loving Parent     498–04
Child of joy, our dearest treasure     498–03
Child of love, our love's expression     498–02
Coming in need, Mary's Child     030–01
For a lost child to come back home     381–02
For that Child so dear and gentle     049–04
Gentle Mary laid her child     027–01
How happy is each child of God     239–01
I'm your child while I run this race     354–04
Jesus Christ her little child     049–01
Knew a child was born in Jewry     065–03
Let this child, your mercy sharing     493–03
No child unsought, unknown     412–01
O holy Child of Bethlehem     043–04
O holy Child of Bethlehem     044–04
O tiny child, your name shall be     601–04

Saint Joseph too was by to tend
   the Child     057–03
So give this child of yours, we pray     496–00
The Child of peace and sacrifice     034–refrain
This Child, now weak in infancy     026–00
This child of God, though young or old     499–03
This child so long foretold     603–01
This newborn child of lowly birth     054–02
To the child, the youth, the aged     427–04
Warm and safe the Child are holding     047–01
What Child is this, who, laid to rest     053–01
When a hungry child is fed     433–03
With this child we now draw near     493–01
Yes, it is true, Mary's Child     030–03
You are my own holy child     159–03
Your child will be God's child     019–05

**CHILDHOOD**
Since the childhood of our race     268–02

**CHILDREN**
All children of the living God     439–03
All children of the living God     440–03
All children of Zion, rejoice and
   give praise     257–01
And children sing your fame     162–01
And God's children free from pain     401–03
Are children given in days of youth     238–03
As God's children, Christ's body
   we will share     518–04
Bringing all of God's children into
   one community     273–03
Children of creative purpose     268–03
Come, my children, and listen     187–02
Frail children of dust, and feeble as frail     476–05
God's children everywhere     294–02
Here our children find a welcome     461–03
How do your children say Home     272–06
How do your children say Joy     272–06
Making all your children one     425–04
Much more to us, your children     560–02
Nor scorned that little children     089–02
O children of the forest free     061–03
Of those who saw their children die     035–02
Our children God does surely bless     255–01
Still your children wander homeless     427–02
Taking children on his knee     304–02
The children sang their praises     089–01
The little children sang     089–01
Thine erring children, lost and lone     426–01
Thy children 'neath the western sky     546–04
To their children's children ever     223–04

| | | | |
|---|---|---|---|
| We, your children in your likeness | 268–01 | Binding all the church in one | 416–01 |
| We're so blest to be your children | 140–02 | Binding all the church in one | 417–01 |
| Yes, children are a great reward | 238–03 | Blest as the church above | 325–04 |
| Your children strong, adored | 239–02 | For thy church that evermore | 473–05 |
| | | Give the church a stronger vision | 129–01 |

**CHILLS**

| | | | |
|---|---|---|---|
| It chills the body but not the soul | 315–02 | In church, or in trains, or in shops, or at tea | 364–03 |
| | | In the church a table | 300–03 |

**CHIME**

| | | | |
|---|---|---|---|
| Chime throughout the land | 039–01 | Jesus, with all your church I long | 351–04 |
| | | Lest the church neglect its mission | 429–01 |

**CHOICE**

| | | | |
|---|---|---|---|
| Calling us to make a choice | 409–01 | Let the church with gladness | 122–02 |
| | | Lord of all, of church and kingdom | 461–04 |

**CHOIR**

| | | | |
|---|---|---|---|
| A lusty, joyous choir | 219–04 | May the church still waiting for you | 508–03 |
| Choir and orchestra and organ | 486–03 | May the church still waiting for you | 509–03 |
| | | O make your church, dear Savior | 327–03 |

**CHOIRS**

| | | | |
|---|---|---|---|
| Angel choirs above are raising | 460–02 | On your church this day, this hour | 131–01 |
| Sent angel choirs instead | 061–01 | On your waiting church below | 524–01 |
| | | One church in all the earth | 443–02 |
| | | One church united in communion blest | 503–03 |

**CHOOSE**

| | | | |
|---|---|---|---|
| But we choose alien life | 437–01 | Place us in the church triumphant | 132–04 |
| By which alone we choose you | 007–03 | Shall be the church at rest | 442–04 |
| Choose old clothing, wrap him warmly | 065–02 | So has the church, in liturgy and song | 264–03 |
| Choose the paths you choose for them | 178–02 | So may those the church exalts | 523–03 |
| To choose and to command | 286–03 | Still the church is called to mission | 129–01 |
| You choose to be made at one with the earth | 311–04 | That in this church and congregation | 497–04 |
| | | The church, formed and re-forming | 128–03 |

**CHORUS**

| | | | |
|---|---|---|---|
| In unceasing chorus praising | 460–02 | The church from you, dear Savior | 327–02 |
| Let the mighty chorus roll | 256–02 | The church its voice upraises | 470–04 |
| | | The church of Christ in every age | 421–01 |

**CHOSE**

| | | | |
|---|---|---|---|
| God chose you, you are blest | 019–02 | The church of Christ is calling us | 414–02 |
| That the Lord chose such a birth | 014–01 | The church of Christ on earth | 130–02 |
| | | The church on earth can raise | 230–04 |
| | | The church our blest Redeemer saved | 441–01 |

**CHOSEN**

| | | | |
|---|---|---|---|
| Chosen of the Lord and precious | 416–01 | The church with psalms must shout | 468–02 |
| Chosen of the Lord and precious | 417–01 | Then let the servant church arise | 421–03 |
| You have chosen me to be | 323–01 | There let your church awaking | 443–03 |
| | | Through the church the song goes on | 460–03 |
| | | To the church in faith assembled | 314–02 |
| | | To your church in every place | 523–01 |
| | | Was not the church we love | 130–01 |

**CHURCH**

| | | | |
|---|---|---|---|
| A caring church that longs to be | 421–03 | We thank thee that thy church unsleeping | 546–02 |
| A pilgrim church through change and stress | 152–03 | | |

**CIRCLE**

| | | | |
|---|---|---|---|
| Amid your church abiding | 156–03 | Let earth's wide circle round | 487–03 |
| Amid your church appearing | 156–01 | Within the circle of the faith | 522–02 |

**CITADELS**

| | | | |
|---|---|---|---|
| And let the church on earth become | 325–04 | To storm the citadels of wrong | 402–02 |

**CITIES**

| | | | |
|---|---|---|---|
| And the great church victorious | 442–04 | For you our broken cities cry | 437–04 |

**CITIES** (cont.)

| | |
|---|---|
| Let all our cities shine forth peace | 431–03 |
| Our cities cry to you, O God | 437–01 |
| Our cities, Lord, wear shrouds of pain | 431–02 |
| Thine alabaster cities gleam | 564–04 |

**CITY**

| | |
|---|---|
| A city built compact and fair | 235–02 |
| A radiant city filled with light | 431–01 |
| And down in the city | 319–03 |
| Be the city of despair | 413–04 |
| In every city for your love and care | 424–01 |
| O holy city, seen of John | 453–01 |
| Once in royal David's city | 049–01 |
| Risen Lord, shall yet the city | 413–04 |
| Shall come the city of our God | 408–06 |
| Show us your Spirit, brooding o'er each city | 424–03 |
| That city rises fair | 453–04 |
| That city will rejoice | 191–03 |
| The city of our God | 437–04 |
| The city that has stood | 453–03 |
| Throughout the holy city | 259–02 |
| Unless the Lord the city shield | 238–01 |
| Zion, city of our God | 446–01 |

**CLAIM (N)**

| | |
|---|---|
| By your divine and urgent claim | 351–03 |
| Laying claim to every age | 512–01 |
| Responding to your claim | 522–01 |

**CLAIM (V)**

| | |
|---|---|
| And claim me as your own | 390–06 |
| And claim with Christians far and near | 499–04 |
| And claim you as my Lord | 207–02 |
| Claim the high calling angels cannot share | 415–02 |
| Claim the kingdom for your own | 006–03 |
| Must claim and test its heritage | 421–01 |
| Undivided God we claim you | 460–04 |

**CLAIMS**

| | |
|---|---|
| That claims us as God's own | 471–04 |

**CLASH**

| | |
|---|---|
| Able to clash and forgive | 436–02 |

**CLASHING**

| | |
|---|---|
| For not with swords' loud clashing | 447–02 |
| For not with swords' loud clashing | 448–02 |

**CLASP**

| | |
|---|---|
| Clasp my hands, or bow my head | 336–03 |

**CLASSROOMS**

| | |
|---|---|
| Classrooms and labs | 458–03 |

**CLAY**

| | |
|---|---|
| Where they laid his breathless clay | 097–04 |

**CLEANSE**

| | |
|---|---|
| And cleanse me from my sin | 196–01 |
| Cleanse us from evil within | 120–03 |
| Cleanse us, unclean, with thy most cleansing blood | 519–03 |
| Cleanse your heart and mind and soul | 409–01 |
| Come, cleanse us deep within | 195–01 |
| Lord, cleanse the depths within our souls | 347–04 |
| To cleanse us and redeem | 434–03 |

**CLEAR**

| | |
|---|---|
| First clear the cluttered heart | 349–01 |

**CLEARS**

| | |
|---|---|
| God gently clears thy way | 286–02 |

**CLIMB**

| | |
|---|---|
| Calvary's mournful mountain climb | 097–03 |
| Of the Hebrews' climb ashore | 494–03 |

**CLIME**

| | |
|---|---|
| Of every clime and shore | 412–03 |

**CLING**

| | |
|---|---|
| To you I cling, my joy, my God alone | 199–03 |

**CLOSE (N)**

| | |
|---|---|
| Swift to its close ebbs out life's little day | 543–02 |

**CLOSE (V)**

| | |
|---|---|
| I cannot close my heart to thee | 384–03 |

**CLOSENESS**

| | |
|---|---|
| Loving Spirit, in your closeness | 323–04 |

**CLOTHE**

| | |
|---|---|
| And clothe me round, the while my path illumining | 313–02 |

**CLOTHED**

| | |
|---|---|
| Clothed yourself with power and might | 213–01 |

**CLOUD**

| | |
|---|---|
| See the cloud and fire appear | 446–03 |
| Swift the cloud of glory came | 074–03 |

**COMFORT (V)** (cont.)

| | |
|---|---|
| Comfort, comfort you my people | 003–01 |
| Comfort those who sit in darkness | 003–01 |
| Comfort those who suffer | 541–03 |
| The Lord will comfort you greatly | 381–03 |
| To comfort and to bless | 428–03 |
| Will comfort, save, and cheer me | 174–03 |

**COMFORTS**

| | |
|---|---|
| Our comforts and our cares | 438–02 |

**COMING (N)**

| | |
|---|---|
| To make God's coming known | 601–04 |

**COMING (V)**

| | |
|---|---|
| You're coming soon to reign | 030–04 |

**COMMAND (N)**

| | |
|---|---|
| Gladly your command obeying | 493–01 |
| To heed my wise command | 184–04 |
| With no one in command | 349–02 |
| Your command is clear and plain | 493–02 |

**COMMAND (V)**

| | |
|---|---|
| Command, O Lord, calm to the sea | 373–04 |
| Whatever you command | 277–02 |

**COMMANDED**

| | |
|---|---|
| He commanded, and it stood firm | 185–09 |

**COMMANDMENTS**

| | |
|---|---|
| The commandments and obey | 223–05 |

**COMMANDS**

| | |
|---|---|
| Christ alone commands the height | 073–01 |
| Our Lord commands this in our midst | 241–03 |

**COMMISSION**

| | |
|---|---|
| A single, great commission | 435–01 |
| Lord, you give the great commission | 429–01 |

**COMMISSIONED**

| | |
|---|---|
| Commissioned from above | 130–01 |

**COMMIT**

| | |
|---|---|
| Commit your journey to the Lord | 188–03 |
| Then I shall not commit great wrongs | 167–04 |
| Today I come, commit myself | 522–01 |

**COMMITMENT**

| | |
|---|---|
| Commitment free from strife | 277–01 |
| In commitment and rejoicing | 132–04 |

| | |
|---|---|
| Ours a commitment we know never ends | 516–01 |

**COMMON**

| | |
|---|---|
| Lord, you make the common holy | 429–03 |

**COMMUNION**

| | |
|---|---|
| And mystic sweet communion | 442–05 |
| God is Oneness by communion | 135–02 |
| Her sweet communion, solemn vows | 441–04 |
| O blest communion, fellowship divine | 526–04 |
| Their high communion find | 439–02 |
| Their high communion find | 440–02 |

**COMMUNITY**

| | |
|---|---|
| Closer in community | 429–02 |
| God's true community must grow | 402–02 |
| In your community may find | 380–05 |
| Joined in community, breaking your bread | 436–04 |
| Joined in one community | 285–02 |
| The new community of love | 507–02 |

**COMPANION**

| | |
|---|---|
| Jesus is our strong companion | 104–02 |
| Jesus, our divine companion | 305–01 |

**COMPANY**

| | |
|---|---|
| A company of God's beloved | 241–01 |
| In closer, dearer company | 357–03 |

**COMPASS**

| | |
|---|---|
| In this fellowship's small compass | 512–02 |

**COMPASSION**

| | |
|---|---|
| As, O Lord, your deep compassion | 427–02 |
| Full of compassion, merciful | 252–02 |
| God of compassion, in mercy befriend us | 261–01 |
| Has the Lord's compassion been | 223–03 |
| In your compassion blot out my offense | 196–01 |
| Jesus, thou art all compassion | 376–01 |
| Our compassion to increase | 343–04 |
| So the Lord has compassion for those who fear him | 222–13 |
| The sweet compassion of thy face | 408–04 |
| Thou Christ of great compassion | 360–01 |
| Your compassion bids us bear | 427–03 |

**COMPASSIONS**

| | |
|---|---|
| Thy compassions they fail not | 276–01 |

**COMPELS**
Compels us from above                    435–01

**COMPLAINT**
From my complaint and my distress        168–01

**COMPLETENESS**
Sprung in completeness                   469–02

**COMPOSE**
To God compose a song of joy             219–01

**CONDEMNED**
And none will be condemned who
    trust in God                        187–07

**CONDESCEND**
To us he'll condescend                   150–02

**CONFESS**
All must alike confess thy might         240–02
I now confess to thee                    395–01
We all confess the Holy Ghost            137–03

**CONFESSION**
Baptized in one confession               443–02
But when I made confession               184–02

**CONFIDENCE**
And our confidence alone                 416–01
And our confidence alone                 417–01
Our confidence and joy shall be          026–00

**CONFINED**
We are not free when we're
    confined                            283–05

**CONFIRM**
Confirm thy soul in self-control         564–02

**CONFLICT**
And conflict turns parent from child     337–02
With many a conflict, many a doubt       370–02
Your Redeemer's conflict see             097–01

**CONFLICTS**
An earth where conflicts cease           434–03
In conflicts that destroy our health     380–04

**CONFOUNDED**
Let me not be confounded                 183–01

**CONFUSION**
Above this earth's confusion             278–01
And gave, for fierce confusion, peace    562–03

**CONGREGATION**
Let thy congregation escape
    tribulation                         559–03
The great congregation his triumph
    shall sing                          477–02

**CONQUER**
And conquer hate in every soul           035–05
The Lord's Messiah shall conquer         071–02

**CONQUERED**
For God has conquered and is King        226–02

**CONQUEROR**
And I shall conqueror be                 378–01

**CONQUERORS**
Make us more than conquerors             122–03

**CONSCIENCE**
And sends the laboring conscience
    peace                               253–03
Make my conscience wholly thine          321–04

**CONSECRATED**
Consecrated, Lord, to thee               391–01

**CONSIDER**
Consider all the worlds thy hands
    have made                           467–01

**CONSOLED**
Not to be consoled, but to console       374–03

**CONSPIRING**
And conspiring plots in vain             159–01

**CONSTELLATION**
O Lord of every shining constellation    297–01

**CONSUMMATION**
The final consummation                   443–04

**CONTEND**
As thou with Satan didst contend         081–02

**CONTINENT**
As o'er each continent and island        546–03

**CONTINUE**
May God continue to bless us 202–07

**CONTINUED**
And so it continued both day and night 056–02

**CONTROL**
And with their control be done 159–01
Even under God's control 223–06

**CONVERSE**
The Lord holds converse high
and sweet 075–02

**CONVERTED**
Are converted into the bread and wine
of God's love 518–01

**COOLNESS**
In that coolness find thirst healed 224–02
Thy coolness and thy balm 345–05

**CORE**
The folded mountain's potent core 287–02

**CORN**
Then the full corn shall appear 551–02

**CORNER**
In every corner of the earth 219–03

**CORNERSTONE**
Has become the chief cornerstone 231–22
Has become the chief cornerstone 232–22

**CORRUPTION**
And from corruption, thou, O Lord 165–04

**COST**
To live and love and not to count
the cost 532–05

**COUNSEL**
Counsel, aid, and peace we give 427–04
My counsel you shall know 184–04
The Lord brings the counsel of the
nations to nothing 185–10
Your counsel let us find 277–03

**COUNSELS**
Loving counsels guide, uphold you 540–01
The counsels of your sovereign will 227–01

**COUNT**
If thou shouldst count our every sin 240–01

**COUNTENANCE**
Your countenance is burning bright 156–01

**COUNTRY**
My country, 'tis of thee 561–01
My native country, thee 561–02

**COURAGE**
By the courage where the radiance 425–02
Courage in every endeavor 596–00
Courage that perseveres 279–03
Give us the courage clear 274–03
Let courage be our friend 430–03

**COURSE**
Set our course of pilgrimage 512–01
That in course the flower may flourish 012–02
To make its course complete 166–04

**COUNT**
That you should count us worthy,
Lord 521–02

**COURT**
Through pillared court and temple 089–01

**COURTS**
For the courts of the Lord 208–02
In your blest courts to worship 207–02
Within your courts they live 201–01

**COVENANT**
God's covenant with us is sealed 499–01
Lord of covenant and goodness 178–02
On Sinai you gave to us your
covenant of love 601–02
Praise God, whose loving covenant 600–05
Unto such as keep God's covenant 223–05
Your covenant of grace remains
the same 532–01
Your covenant remove 205–04

**COVET**
Taught by you, we covet most 318–01

**CRADLE**
And his cradle was a stall 049–02
Cold on his cradle the dewdrops
are shining 067–02

| | |
|---|---|
| O hear our cry, O Lord | 206–01 |
| O Lord, make haste to hear my cry | 249–01 |
| O that warning cry obey | 003–02 |
| The cry for justice and an end to strife | 086–03 |
| Their cry goes up: "How long?" | 442–03 |
| This be the parting cry | 359–03 |
| Who hears your sad and bitter cry | 054–03 |

**CRY (V)**

| | |
|---|---|
| All who cry for peace and justice | 413–01 |
| And cry, my Lord and God | 399–02 |
| Cry, Christ has died in vain | 453–02 |
| Cry out dominions, princedoms, powers | 451–01 |
| Cry out, we cannot understand | 035–03 |
| Let all cry aloud and honor the Son | 477–03 |
| O hear us when we cry to thee | 562–01 |
| Then against the Lord they cry | 159–01 |
| We hear you, O Christ, in agony cry | 311–03 |

**CRYING (N)**

| | |
|---|---|
| But little Lord Jesus, no crying he makes | 024–02 |
| But little Lord Jesus, no crying he makes | 025–02 |
| The crying of a homeless child | 348–01 |

**CRYING (V)**

| | |
|---|---|
| Someone's crying, Lord, kum ba yah | 338–02 |
| Those who are crying with no peace of mind | 400–04 |

**CRYSTAL**

| | |
|---|---|
| In crystal and in rose | 292–03 |
| The crystal of the snow | 292–01 |

**CUP**

| | |
|---|---|
| And my cup overflows | 170–04 |
| And my cup overflows | 175–03 |
| And when this cup you give is filled to brimming | 342–03 |
| Do not one cup, one loaf, declare | 521–03 |
| Is not the cup we bless and share | 521–03 |
| My cup is full, and more than full | 174–05 |
| My cup with blessings overflows | 172–02 |
| Salvation's cup my soul shall take | 228–04 |
| The cup of water given for thee | 408–04 |
| This blest cup of sacrifice | 501–02 |

**CURE (N)**

| | |
|---|---|
| Is there no cure, O Christ, for these | 380–04 |

**CURE (V)**

| | |
|---|---|
| Can cure the fever in our blood | 421–04 |
| Cure thy children's warring madness | 420–03 |

**CURSE (N)**

| | |
|---|---|
| Far as the curse is found | 040–03 |

**CURSE (V)**

| | |
|---|---|
| All who curse and all who bless | 413–01 |

**CURTAINS**

| | |
|---|---|
| Its curtains of darkness | 557–02 |

**CUT**

| | |
|---|---|
| They cut me down and I leap up high | 302–05 |

**CYMBALS**

| | |
|---|---|
| Praise God with clashing cymbals | 258–02 |
| Praise God with holy cymbals | 258–02 |

# D

**DANCE (N)**

| | |
|---|---|
| But I am the dance and I still go on | 302–04 |
| Endless dance of love and light | 135–01 |
| They came with me and the dance went on | 302–02 |

**DANCE (V)**

| | |
|---|---|
| But they would not dance and they would not follow me | 302–02 |
| Dance and spring, spring, spring | 300–refrain |

| | |
|---|---|
| Dance, then, wherever you may be | 302–refrain |
| Dance with joy to God | 484–refrain |
| So dance for our God and blow all the trumpets | 472–03 |
| That dance for joy in summer air | 475–03 |
| When I dance or chant your praise | 336–04 |

**DANCED**

| | |
|---|---|
| And I danced in the moon and the stars and the sun | 302–01 |

**DANCED** (cont.)

| | |
|---|---|
| I danced for the fishermen, for James and John | 302–02 |
| I danced for the scribe and the Pharisee | 302–02 |
| I danced in the morning when the world was begun | 302–01 |
| I danced on a Friday when the sky turned black | 302–04 |
| I danced on the Sabbath and I cured the lame | 302–03 |

**DANGER**

| | |
|---|---|
| And calmly every danger brave | 393–04 |
| And danger hovers near me | 174–03 |
| He, to rescue me from danger | 356–02 |
| What danger could I fear | 173–02 |

**DANGERS**

| | |
|---|---|
| Dangers do all assail | 373–01 |
| If dangers gather round | 277–03 |
| Through many dangers, toils, and snares | 280–03 |

**DARE**

| | |
|---|---|
| I dare not ask to fly from thee | 384–04 |
| I dare not trust the sweetest frame | 379–01 |
| Let us, if we dare to speak | 074–01 |
| So we dare to journey on | 409–03 |
| You dare to make us Christ to our neighbors | 436–01 |

**DARES**

| | |
|---|---|
| Who dares stand idle on the harvest plain | 415–01 |

**DARK**

| | |
|---|---|
| Dark descends, but light unending | 544–02 |
| For dark and light are both alike to thee | 539–03 |
| The dark of the grave prepares for your birth | 311–04 |

**DARKNESS**

| | |
|---|---|
| As the darkness clears away | 005–03 |
| As the darkness deepens o'er us | 545–04 |
| Bid darkness turn to day | 383–03 |
| Darkness veils your anguished face | 099–01 |
| E'en in darkness hope appears | 465–02 |
| I will make their darkness bright | 525–01 |
| If I should say, let darkness cover me | 248–04 |
| Lie in deepest darkness shrouded | 454–02 |
| Surely the darkness is not dark to you | 248–04 |
| The darkness deepens | 543–01 |
| The darkness falls at thy behest | 546–01 |

| | |
|---|---|
| The darkness of the tomb | 105–01 |
| Thou, in the darkness drear their one true light | 526–02 |
| Though the darkness hide thee | 138–03 |
| Through darkness and perplexity | 301–03 |
| Turn thou for us its darkness into light | 539–03 |
| When darkness veils his lovely face | 379–02 |
| With thee to bless, the darkness shines as light | 275–02 |

**DAUGHTER**

| | |
|---|---|
| Daughter and son | 458–04 |

**DAWN (N)**

| | |
|---|---|
| And till the dawn appeareth | 240–04 |
| Hail redemption's happy dawn | 051–refrain |
| Since that tremendous dawn | 130–02 |
| The dawn leads on another day | 546–03 |
| The dawn of hope for humankind | 330–01 |
| Until, in God's all-glorious dawn | 444–04 |
| With the dawn of redeeming grace | 060–03 |

**DAWN (V)**

| | |
|---|---|
| Dawn on our darkened day | 030–02 |
| Dawn on our darkness and lend us thine aid | 067–01 |
| Dawn upon this soul of mine | 321–01 |

**DAWNING**

| | |
|---|---|
| The dawning of forgiveness | 602–03 |

**DAWNS**

| | |
|---|---|
| Dawns upon our quickened sight | 427–03 |
| That dawns upon eternal love and life | 533–03 |
| Till dawns the morning glorious | 289–04 |

**DAY**

| | |
|---|---|
| And thus this day most glorious | 470–02 |
| And to life's day the glorious unknown morrow | 533–03 |
| As through this day your name we bless | 161–03 |
| Blest day to be hallowed forever | 120–refrain |
| By day, by night, at work, at prayer | 490–05 |
| By day the Lord commands his steadfast love | 190–08 |
| Christmas day is here | 039–01 |
| Day after day the tale is told | 166–01 |
| Day by day like us he grew | 049–03 |
| Day by day to the Lord | 225–02 |
| Day by day with strength supplied | 501–01 |
| Day is done, but love unfailing | 544–01 |
| Day unto day doth utter speech | 292–03 |

| | | | |
|---|---|---|---|
| Day when our Lord was raised | 120–refrain | This is the day that the Lord has made | 231–24 |
| For a day in your courts is better | 208–10 | This is the day that the Lord has made | 232–24 |
| From day to day God's praise record | 216–01 | This is the day the Lord hath made | 230–01 |
| From their bright baptismal day | 524–01 | Through this and every coming day | 535–00 |
| Give us each day our daily bread | 269–03 | Till God's day dawns gold | 348–03 |
| Give us this day our daily bread | 589–02 | Till the great and glorious day | 127–03 |
| Great day, the righteous marching | 445–refrain | To comfort and help us each day | 157–02 |
| Hail thee, festival day | 120–refrain | True day, all days illumining | 474–01 |
| Holy Jesus, every day | 063–04 | While all day long they say to me | 189–02 |
| In the day of need may your answer | | Who on this wedding day | 534–01 |
| be the Lord | 169–01 | With each new day, when morning | |
| In the day this world is fading | 531–04 | lifts the veil | 275–01 |
| In your day of wealth and plenty | 413–02 | | |
| Never silent day or night | 425–04 | **DAYLIGHT** | |
| Now the day is over | 541–01 | Lord Jesus Christ, as daylight fades | 548–03 |
| O day of God, draw nigh | 452–01 | | |
| O day of joy and light | 470–01 | **DAYS** | |
| O day of peace that dimly shines | 450–01 | Adored through all our changing days | 265–03 |
| O day of radiant gladness | 470–01 | All those who keep the holy days | 189–03 |
| O joyful be the passing day | 474–03 | And the days were hard and long | 246–02 |
| O let me from this day be wholly thine | 383–01 | And through these days of penitence | 081–03 |
| Of a future, perfect day | 401–03 | And weary days of toil partake | 238–02 |
| Of the day and of the night | 473–02 | Despite chaotic days | 418–03 |
| On that day long ago | 128–04 | Felt in the days when hope unborn | |
| On this blest day of light | 470–03 | had died | 563–02 |
| On this day angels sing | 046–04 | For all days are days of judgment | 413–03 |
| On this day earth shall ring | 046–01 | For lo, the days are hastening on | 038–04 |
| On this day of resurrection | 107–03 | For the living of these days | 420–02 |
| On this most holy day of days | 116–05 | Forty days and forty nights | 077–01 |
| One day the Rabbi Lord Jesus | 547–02 | I all my days could gladly spend | 076–05 |
| Our endless Sabbath day | 470–04 | I will praise my God all the days | |
| Our triumphant holy day | 123–01 | of my life | 254–refrain |
| Praise God both day and night | 258–04 | In his days may righteousness flourish | 204–07 |
| Praising my Savior all the day long | 341–refrain | Lord, who throughout these | |
| Promised day of Israel | 020–01 | forty days | 081–01 |
| Quite early in the day | 128–01 | My days of praise shall ne'er be past | 253–01 |
| Salvation's dawning day | 601–04 | Of days when war shall cease | 289–04 |
| Shining to the perfect day | 462–03 | Of sunny days of joy | 308–02 |
| Shining to the perfect day | 463–03 | Praise the Maker all your days | 479–01 |
| That Easter day with joy was bright | 121–01 | Still evil days bring burdens hard | |
| That he was raised on the third day | 598–00 | to bear | 342–02 |
| The day of march has come | 447–01 | The three sad days are quickly sped | 119–03 |
| The day of march has come | 448–01 | Through days of preparation | 447–01 |
| The day of resurrection | 118–01 | Through days of preparation | 448–01 |
| The day thou gavest, Lord, is ended | 546–01 | To bear thee through the evil days | 282–01 |
| This day and every day | 130–01 | We've no less days to sing | |
| This day at the creation | 470–02 | God's praise | 280–05 |
| This day for our salvation | 470–02 | When the forty days were o'er | 144–02 |
| This day God's people, meeting | 470–03 | | |
| This day our Lord victorious | 470–02 | **DEAD** | |
| This day the high and lowly | 470–01 | And keep on rising from the dead | 421–01 |
| This is the day of Jubilee | 445–02 | I am like the dead | 182–04 |

**DEAL**

| | |
|---|---|
| He does not deal with us according to our sins | 222–10 |

**DEALS**

| | |
|---|---|
| And with you so kindly deals | 223–02 |

**DEATH**

| | |
|---|---|
| And death cannot imprison | 105–refrain |
| And, doomed to death, must bring to doom | 007–02 |
| And for his death they thirst and cry | 076–03 |
| And from death set me free | 181–03 |
| And in whose death our sins are dead | 502–00 |
| And when from death I'm free | 085–03 |
| Brought it back victorious, when from death he passed | 148–02 |
| But he did not give me over to death | 231–18 |
| Death and darkness could not hold him | 109–01 |
| Death has lost its old dominion | 109–03 |
| Death has lost its sting and terror | 109–02 |
| Death hath lost its sting | 122–02 |
| Death in vain forbids him rise | 113–02 |
| Death may come, in love's safekeeping | 544–03 |
| Death of death, and hell's destruction | 281–03 |
| Death that gives birth to new living | 296–01 |
| Embraced by death he broke its fearful hold | 495–01 |
| From death and deep despair, from sin and guilt | 360–04 |
| From death thou hast delivered me | 228–05 |
| From death to life eternal | 118–01 |
| O Christ, o'er death victorious | 360–05 |
| O'er captive death and conquered sin | 090–02 |
| O'er captive death and conquered sin | 091–02 |
| O'er death and hell rose triumphing | 116–01 |
| O'er death and hell rose triumphing | 117–01 |
| One through death and resurrection | 135–03 |
| Save in the death of Christ my God | 100–02 |
| Save in the death of Christ my God | 101–02 |
| Straightway and steadfast until death | 070–03 |
| That death is swallowed up by death | 110–02 |
| That else in death had slept | 228–02 |
| Thou o'er death hast won | 122–01 |
| What fearful death he died | 103–03 |
| Where, O death, is now your sting | 113–03 |
| With his death and rising again | 296–01 |
| Your death has brought us life eternally | 371–03 |
| Your death is your rising, creative your word | 311–04 |
| Your death of anguish and your bitter passion | 093–03 |

**DEBT**

| | |
|---|---|
| How great our debt to you | 347–03 |
| The debt of love I owe | 078–04 |

**DEBTORS**

| | |
|---|---|
| As we to debtors show your grace | 590–02 |

**DEBTS**

| | |
|---|---|
| What trivial debts are owed to us | 347–03 |

**DECEIVE**

| | |
|---|---|
| You never will deceive me | 284–02 |

**DECISIONS**

| | |
|---|---|
| With bold new decisions | 319–04 |

**DECK**

| | |
|---|---|
| Deck yourself, my soul, with gladness | 506–01 |

**DECLARE**

| | |
|---|---|
| Declare the wonders of God's might | 475–04 |
| Let us now declare Christ's greatness | 107–01 |

**DECREE**

| | |
|---|---|
| God's decree unto the King | 159–03 |

**DEDICATE**

| | |
|---|---|
| Dedicate us to the task | 132–01 |

**DEDICATION**

| | |
|---|---|
| Here, in this day's dedication | 461–04 |

**DEED**

| | |
|---|---|
| Each evil deed or thought within | 240–01 |
| Most patiently in deed | 188–04 |
| Of the empty cultic deed | 336–02 |
| To witness with each deed | 552–03 |

**DEEDS**

| | |
|---|---|
| Behold what wondrous deeds of peace | 259–03 |
| Come, behold these mighty deeds | 192–03 |
| Deeds and words and death and rising | 331–03 |
| Let all your deeds and words compose | 490–05 |
| Praise God for almighty deeds | 258–03 |
| Through deeds that live our praise | 556–refrain |
| With deeds of love and mercy | 447–02 |
| With deeds of love and mercy | 448–02 |
| You, Lord, alone did wondrous deeds | 243–02 |

**DEEP**

| | |
|---|---|
| Deep calls to deep at the thunder of your cataracts | 190–07 |

Glorious is the breaking deep 213–03
The sea's dark deep and far-off land 320–02
Who bade the mighty ocean deep 562–01

**DEEPS**
He put the deeps in storehouses 185–07

**DEER**
As a deer longs for flowing streams 190–01
As deer long for the streams, O Lord 189–01
Gentle deer and the eagle and
    the mighty buffalo 273–02

**DEFEATS**
God defeats darkest night 300–02

**DEFEND**
And then defend our claim by force 283–04
May he defend the cause of the poor
    of the people 204–04

**DEFENDER**
The strong defender of my home 212–02
You alone, our strong defender 154–01

**DEIGN**
Come, risen Lord, and deign to be
    our guest 503–01

**DEIGNS**
Christ deigns to manifest today 075–04

**DEJECTION**
May we, whenever tempted to dejection 529–03

**DELIGHT (N)**
It brings you no delight 195–06
Take your delight in God and then 188–02

**DELIGHT (V)**
Delight to make their vows 534–01

**DELIGHTS**
Which of you delights in life 187–02

**DELIVER**
And deliver us from evil 571–00
But deliver us from evil 589–04
Deliver every nation 289–02
Deliver me from the hands of those
    who hate me 182–06
Deliver us, good Lord 291–02

**DELIVERANCE**
Deliverance from its ways 349–05
Give deliverance to the needy, and
    crush the oppressor 204–04
Who brings deliverance sure 197–02

**DELIVERED**
They are delivered from their distress 187–05
They are delivered from them all 187–06
When God delivered Israel 237–01

**DELIVERER**
Strong deliverer, strong deliverer 281–02

**DELIVERS**
For he delivers the needy when
    they call 204–12

**DEMANDS (N)**
And makes demands we do not want
    to pay 086–02

**DEMANDS (V)**
Demands my soul, my life, my all 100–04

**DENIED**
No longer Thomas then denied 117–05
'Twas I, Lord Jesus, I it was
    denied you 093–02

**DENY**
Could not deny that power 237–02

**DEPART**
And ne'er from us depart 139–03
But do not then depart 505–01
Depart in exultation 605–01

**DEPENDENCE**
You are mortal life's dependence 136–01

**DEPRIVE**
Nor deprive me of your holy spirit 196–06

**DEPTH**
From depth to height reply 487–03
God our King in depth and height 213–01
The great depth of Jesus'
    loving heart 381–01

**DEPTHS**
Out of the depths to thee I raise 240–01

**DEPTHS** (cont.)

| | |
|---|---|
| The depths of earth and mountains high | 214–03 |
| The depths of the ocean proclaim God divine | 554–02 |
| The hidden depths of many a heart | 426–03 |

**DESCEND**

| | |
|---|---|
| Descend to us, we pray | 043–04 |
| Descend to us, we pray | 044–04 |
| Descend with all your gracious powers | 325–01 |
| On us descend | 139–02 |
| Spirit of God, descend upon my heart | 326–01 |

**DESCENDANTS**

| | |
|---|---|
| May you and your descendants know | 239–04 |

**DESCENDED**

| | |
|---|---|
| Who descended from above | 524–01 |
| Who descended from his throne | 137–02 |

**DESCENDETH**

| | |
|---|---|
| As the Light of Light descendeth | 005–03 |

**DESCENDS**

| | |
|---|---|
| It descends to the plain | 476–04 |

**DESERT (N)**

| | |
|---|---|
| Crossing desert sought their King | 065–03 |
| In the desert all surrounding | 104–01 |
| In the desert far and near | 003–02 |
| The desert shall rejoice | 018–refrain |
| The desert writhes in tempest | 180–02 |

**DESERT (V)**

| | |
|---|---|
| I will not, I will not desert to its foes | 361–05 |

**DESERVE**

| | |
|---|---|
| 'Tis I deserve thy place | 098–02 |

**DESIGN**

| | |
|---|---|
| All I design or do or say | 456–03 |

**DESIGNS**

| | |
|---|---|
| The bold designs of farthest space | 134–01 |

**DESIRE (N)**

| | |
|---|---|
| Dear desire of every nation | 001–02 |
| Dear desire of every nation | 002–01 |
| It's my desire to live for you | 350–02 |
| May God give you all your heart's desire | 169–02 |

| | |
|---|---|
| My heart's desire is Zion's peace | 235–05 |

**DESIRE (V)**

| | |
|---|---|
| Nothing desire, or seek, but thee | 366–03 |

**DESIRED**

| | |
|---|---|
| And even more to be desired | 167–02 |

**DESIRES (N)**

| | |
|---|---|
| How strong, O Lord, are our desires | 380–03 |
| How thy desires e'er have been | 482–02 |

**DESIRES (V)**

| | |
|---|---|
| And desires long life to enjoy all things | 187–02 |

**DESOLATION**

| | |
|---|---|
| And desolation cease | 452–04 |
| God is one through desolation | 135–03 |

**DESOLATIONS**

| | |
|---|---|
| See what desolations he has brought on the earth | 193–08 |

**DESPAIR**

| | |
|---|---|
| And our despair he turned to blazing joy | 495–01 |

**DESTROYED**

| | |
|---|---|
| Dying, you destroyed our death | 582–00 |

**DESTROYS**

| | |
|---|---|
| As he destroys them he brings us | 296–02 |
| Destroys my inward peace | 390–02 |

**DESTRUCTION**

| | |
|---|---|
| Destruction through the night | 289–02 |
| Facing us with life's destruction | 268–02 |

**DEVIL**

| | |
|---|---|
| It's hard to dance with the devil on your back | 302–04 |

**DEVOTE**

| | |
|---|---|
| Would he devote that sacred head | 078–01 |

**DEVOTION**

| | |
|---|---|
| And our devotion dies | 126–02 |

**DEW**

| | |
|---|---|
| As dew on Zion's mountaintop | 241–03 |

**DEWFALL**

| | |
|---|---|
| Like the first dewfall | 469–02 |

## DIADEM

| | |
|---|---|
| A royal diadem adorns | 149–01 |
| Bring forth the royal diadem | 142–01 |
| Bring forth the royal diadem | 143–01 |

## DIE

| | |
|---|---|
| And did my sovereign die | 078–01 |
| Born that we no more may die | 031–03 |
| Born that we no more may die | 032–03 |
| God Most High, lest we die | 192–04 |
| I shall not die, but I shall live | 231–17 |
| So shall I never die | 316–04 |
| Thyself for all to die | 395–03 |
| Till the Lamb of God may die | 099–02 |

## DIED

| | |
|---|---|
| And say, "He died for all" | 394–03 |
| As thou hast died for me | 383–02 |
| Christ has died | 569–00 |
| For he who died on Calvary | 308–04 |
| For thou hast died for me | 151–04 |
| Jesus died, our souls to save | 113–03 |
| Jesus died to show God's love | 355–01 |
| Jesus has died and has risen | 106–02 |
| Jesus who died shall be satisfied | 293–02 |
| Of him who died for thee | 151–01 |
| On which the Prince of glory died | 100–01 |
| On which the Prince of glory died | 101–01 |
| Surely he died on Calvary | 096–refrain |
| That Christ died for our sins | 598–00 |
| When Christ, the great Redeemer, died | 078–03 |
| Yes, he died to save us | 299–06 |

## DIES

| | |
|---|---|
| Dies at the opening day | 210–04 |
| Nor dies the strain of praise away | 546–03 |
| Soon as dies the sunset glory | 545–02 |

## DIMENSION

| | |
|---|---|
| A new dimension in the world of sound | 264–02 |

## DIN

| | |
|---|---|
| And the pious, babbling din | 336–02 |

## DINE

| | |
|---|---|
| When Jesus bids us dine | 517–01 |

## DIRECT

| | |
|---|---|
| Direct, control, suggest this day | 456–03 |
| Now direct our daily labor | 422–02 |

## DIRECTION

| | |
|---|---|
| Give direction now, we ask | 132–01 |

## DISAPPEAR

| | |
|---|---|
| Everything false will disappear | 324–02 |

## DISBELIEVE

| | |
|---|---|
| Lord, disbelieve my unbelief | 390–06 |

## DISCARD

| | |
|---|---|
| Discard each vengeful hope that's fed | 349–04 |

## DISCERN

| | |
|---|---|
| We may discern the beauty of your will | 297–03 |

## DISCERNMENT

| | |
|---|---|
| Here for faith's discernment pray we | 154–02 |

## DISCIPLE

| | |
|---|---|
| Each disciple touching | 127–01 |
| If you would my disciple be | 393–01 |

## DISCIPLES

| | |
|---|---|
| And his disciples still gather there | 094–01 |
| As disciples used to gather | 504–02 |
| Be not so anxious, O disciples | 352–02 |
| Disciples, do not fret | 352–04 |
| Disciples of the Lord | 434–01 |
| How with the three disciples there | 075–02 |
| We may be disciples true | 504–03 |

## DISCIPLINE

| | |
|---|---|
| By faithful discipline prepare | 349–06 |
| Give us the discipline that springs | 079–04 |

## DISCONTENT

| | |
|---|---|
| But discontent with finite powers | 283–04 |

## DISCORD

| | |
|---|---|
| Our discord spreads a deadly cloud | 434–02 |

## DISCOVER

| | |
|---|---|
| May we discover gifts in each other | 436–04 |

## DISEASES

| | |
|---|---|
| All diseases gently heals | 223–02 |

## DISGRACE

| | |
|---|---|
| And wretched, dire disgrace | 103–02 |

## DISMAYED

| | |
|---|---|
| O be not dismayed | 361–02 |

**DISMISS**
Dismiss the fear that this world drifts 349–02
Lord, dismiss us with thy blessing 538–01

**DISPEL**
Dispel the gloom of error's night 412–03
Holy Ghost, dispel our sadness 317–01

**DISPELS**
God dispels our fear 365–02

**DISPERSE**
Disperse my sins as morning dew 456–02

**DISPLAY**
Display that wondrous hand 255–03
More and more thyself display 462–03
More and more thyself display 463–03

**DISQUIETED**
And why are you disquieted within 190–05

**DISTILLS**
And sweetly distills in the dew
and the rain 476–04

**DISTORTION**
Keep us clear of all distortion 285–03

**DISTRESS**
For I am in distress 182–01

**DIVISION**
Each proud division ends 507–03

**DO**
And do it when we ought 277–02
And do what thou wouldst do 316–01
And kind in everything you do 251–03
I shall be still, whate'er you do 284–01
'Tis all that I can do 078–04
We do it unto thee 428–05
Whate'er for thine we do, O Lord 428–05

**DOCTOR**
And one was a doctor, and one
was a queen 364–01

**DOING**
This is the Lord's doing 231–23
This is the Lord's doing 232–23

**DOINGS**
Thy wondrous doings heard on high 546–04

**DOMAIN**
Infinite your vast domain 460–01
O'er all the world's domain 289–04

**DOMINION**
All throughout God's vast dominion 223–06
May he have dominion from sea to sea 204–08
With dominion crowned we stand 163–05
Your high dominion will endure 252–03

**DONE**
All that God for us has done 481–03
For all you have done and still do 157–03

**DONOR**
Gracious donor of our days 422–01

**DOOM**
For lo! his doom is sure 260–03
His the doom, ours the mirth 046–02

**DOOR**
No door can keep them out 468–02
Their door be wide to stranger and
to guest 532–02

**DOORKEEPER**
I would rather be a doorkeeper
in the house of my God 208–10

**DOORS**
O everlasting doors, give way 176–03
With doors kept open wide 381–02

**DOUBT (N)**
Doubt and terror are withdrawn 020–03
To check the rising doubt, the
rebel sigh 326–03
When doubt obscures the victory
of your Son 086–04
Where all is doubt, may we sow faith 374–02
Without a doubt we'll know 398–refrain

**DOUBT (V)**
No more we doubt thee 122–03

**DOUBTED**
He doubted the disciples' word 117–03

**DOUBTETH**
It doubteth not nor feareth 240–04

**DOUBTS**
Away with gloomy doubts and
    faithless fear 415–03

**DOVE**
As peaceful as a dove and yet 070–01
Come as the dove and spread
    your wings 325–04
So when the dove descended 072–04

**DRAIN**
That drain their treasures dry 556–02

**DRAW**
And soon he will draw nigh 015–01
But, Jesus, draw thou nearer 388–02
But, Jesus, draw thou nearer 389–02
Draw us in the Spirit's tether 504–01
May I undisturbed draw near thee 489–03
O Comforter, draw near 313–01
Will draw all humankind to adoration 105–03

**DRAWING**
The King of kings is drawing near 008–01
Your Christ is drawing near 013–01

**DRAWN**
You have drawn me to your wonder 323–01

**DREAD**
From dread of war's increase 289–03

**DREAM (N)**
O beautiful for patriot dream 564–04
To make the dream come true 414–02
Too long a dream, whose laws are love 453–03

**DREAM (V)**
Dream the dream 430–02

**DREAMS**
In dreams of human art 412–04
May our dreams prove rich
    with promise 268–03
The dreams of wars you'll win 349–04
The dreams of young and stories
    of old 547–03
The flagging dreams of weary folk 152–02

**DRINK (N)**
Giving drink to every field 224–02

**DRINK (V)**
Drink the wine of resurrection 104–02
Here we drink of joy unmeasured 331–04
Let us drink wine together on
    our knees 513–02
We drink of thee, the fountainhead 510–03
We drink of thee, the fountainhead 511–03

**DRIVE**
Drive the gloom of doubt away 464–01

**DRIVEN**
We're driven to the quest 278–02

**DRIVES**
Drives all my fears away 172–02

**DROP**
Drop thy still dews of quietness 345–04

**DROPLETS**
Like the droplets of water that are
    blended in the sea 518–03

**DROPS**
But drops of grief can ne'er repay 078–04

**DROSS**
Thy dross to consume, and thy gold
    to refine 361–04

**DROVE**
And drove thee from my breast 396–02
And drove thee from my breast 397–02

**DRY**
Dry your tears, be unafraid 109–01

**DULLNESS**
The dullness of our mortal sight 125–02

**DUST**
Above the chanted "Dust to dust" 530–03
I lay in dust life's glory dead 384–04
Leave me not helpless in the dust 183–01
To dust and ashes in its
    heat consuming 313–02
Went down to dust beside you 007–02

## DWELL

| | |
|---|---|
| All who dwell in deepest sin | 525–01 |
| All you who dwell on earth below | 052–03 |
| And I will dwell in God's own house | 175–04 |
| And none shall dwell within your hall | 161–02 |
| Come dwell with us, make all things new | 431–03 |
| Come, O Spirit, dwell among us | 129–01 |
| Come unto us and dwell with us | 271–02 |
| From all that dwell below the skies | 229–01 |
| If I should dwell on ocean's farthest shore | 248–03 |
| Lord, who may dwell within your house | 164–01 |
| May dwell, but thy pure love alone | 366–02 |
| That all may dwell secure | 452–03 |
| That we may dwell in perfect unity | 457–04 |

## DWELLERS

| | |
|---|---|
| Dwellers all in time and space | 478–04 |
| Dwellers all in time and space | 479–04 |

## DWELLING

| | |
|---|---|
| In your high eternal dwelling | 213–04 |
| Wherein the Holy Spirit makes a dwelling | 313–03 |

## DWELLS

| | |
|---|---|
| Christ has come down, dwells with us | 033–03 |
| Dwells ever here | 544–01 |

## DYING (N)

| | |
|---|---|
| At our dying, Lord, may we | 406–03 |

## DYING (V)

| | |
|---|---|
| And when we're dying, it is in the Lord | 400–01 |

---

# E

## EAR

| | |
|---|---|
| Give ear, O God of Jacob | 208–08 |
| Lord, turn a gracious ear to me | 240–01 |
| No ear heard such delight | 017–03 |
| No ear may hear his coming | 043–03 |
| No ear may hear his coming | 044–03 |

## EARS

| | |
|---|---|
| And to my listening ears | 293–01 |
| But the fruitful ears to store | 551–03 |
| For the ears of the deaf shall hear | 018–02 |
| Have we ears to hear | 348–01 |
| O give us ears to listen | 128–04 |
| The ears of God hear their cry | 187–04 |
| Their ears are deaf, their hands are weak | 227–02 |
| To deaf ears and blinded eyes | 512–04 |
| We have ears to hear | 348–01 |

## EARTH

| | |
|---|---|
| All earth waits hopefully | 201–02 |
| All on earth your scepter claim | 460–01 |
| All the earth is seeking | 127–02 |
| All the earth find peace | 412–02 |
| And earth and heaven be one | 293–02 |
| And earth and seas with all their train | 253–02 |
| And earth repeat the loud Amen | 423–05 |
| And therefore, though the earth remove | 191–01 |
| And to the earth be peace | 058–06 |
| And to the earth be peace | 059–06 |
| And to the earth it gave great light | 056–02 |
| And upon the earth be peace and love to all | 064–refrain |
| Born for us on earth below | 051–01 |
| Born on earth to save us | 046–01 |
| Born on earth to save us | 046–04 |
| Born to raise us from the earth | 031–03 |
| Born to raise us from the earth | 032–03 |
| But over the earth their power shall prevail | 257–04 |
| By earth and heaven confessed | 488–01 |
| Came to earth from heaven's throne | 065–02 |
| Christ comes down to earth today | 065–01 |
| Christ our God to earth descendeth | 005–01 |
| Down to earth, as a dove | 300–01 |
| Drawn from earth to love you solely | 454–01 |
| Earth and all stars | 458–01 |
| Earth and heaven reflect thy rays | 464–02 |
| Earth and heaven ring with praises | 033–02 |
| Earth can breathe again | 514–refrain |
| Earth is poised, to swerve no more | 213–02 |
| Earth, kindling, blazed its loud acclaim | 124–01 |

Earth revolving day and night 290–01
Earth shall then its fruits afford 203–04
Earth stood hard as iron, water
    like a stone 036–01
Earth, tell it out abroad 118–01
Earth thy footstool, heaven thy throne 144–04
Earth to heaven and heaven to earth 481–02
Excellent in all the earth 163–06
For all the earth shall know the Lord 450–02
For the earth is our mother, where
    all things grow 273–02
For the earth shall be filled with the
    knowledge of God 337–01
Hail, the Lord of earth and heaven 113–04
He came down to earth from heaven 049–02
In earth and sky and sea 138–04
Jesus is Lord of all the earth 106–01
Joy of heaven, to earth come down 376–01
King of the earth, Mary's Child 030–04
Let all the earth fear the Lord 185–08
Let all the earth move with our feet
    and hands 484–02
Let earth make melody 219–06
Let earth receive her king 040–01
Let earth the song begin 118–03
Let the earth hear his voice 485–refrain
Lord Christ, when first you came
    to earth 007–01
Make known on earth your
    healing love 134–03
Maker of earth and sky 271–01
Now o'er earth is shed abroad 003–03
O come, Lord Jesus, bring to earth 437–04
O God of earth and altar 291–01
O God of earth and space 274–01
O thou of God to earth come down 306–01
On all the earth to shine 327–02
On earth as in heaven 571–00
On earth as it is in heaven 589–02
On earth is not his equal 260–01
Or earth received its frame 210–02
See, all the earth is God's, its people
    and nations 177–01
So on earth your will be done 425–refrain
Spirit of God, unleashed on earth 124–01
Thank you, God, for making planet
    earth 266–05
That earth, from sunrise to the sunset 201–02
That the Christ on earth shall reign 159–02
The Creator of earth and moon and sun 273–01
The earth and all that dwell therein 176–01
The earth God's mercy fills 200–03

The earth has yielded its increase 202–06
The earth is full of the steadfast love
    of the Lord 185–05
The earth is not too low 468–01
The earth, the sea; each place 162–04
The earth with its store of wonders
    untold 476–03
The Holy Child of earth and heaven 061–03
Thou fertile earth, that day by day 455–04
Thou on earth both Priest and Victim 144–04
Thou on earth our food, our stay 144–03
Though earth is bare 012–02
Though the earth be ever changing 192–01
Though the earth be shaking 365–02
Throughout the whole wide earth 439–01
Throughout the whole wide earth 440–01
Till earth and heaven ring 563–01
Till earth and sky and ocean ring 108–05
To bless the earth God sends us 200–01
To judge the earth with right and
    the people with truth 217–06
To make the earth a home 274–03
To spread through all the earth abroad 466–04
Upon the fruitful earth 205–02
When he came down to earth 046–02
When lo! above the earth 029–02
While earth rolls onward into light 546–02
Who made the earth and
    all the heavenly frame 236–03
Yet she on earth has union 442–05
You are on earth most blest 019–02
Yours on earth and yours forever 493–03

**EARTHQUAKE**
God of the earthquake 272–02

**EASE**
Our ease and comfort last 434–01

**EASES**
And eases from their anxious clutch 471–02

**EAST**
As far as the east is from the west 222–12
Far as east from west is distant 223–03
In Christ there is no east or west 439–01
In Christ there is no east or west 440–01
Shining in the east beyond them far 056–02

**EAT**
We eat and drink, receiving 517–02
What you daily eat and what you wear 352–02

**EBB**
In all life's ebb and flow    128–04

**ECHO**
Echo these praises and tell
   of God's power    147–02

**ECHOES (N)**
Echoes of mercy, whispers of love    341–02
In living echoes of thy tone    426–01

**ECHOES (V)**
Echoes through the desert still    409–01

**ECSTASY**
Known the ecstasy of winging    268–02

**EFFORTS**
Where our best efforts should be    436–03

**ELDERS**
Talking to the elders    299–02

**ELECT**
Elect from every nation    442–02

**EMBRACE**
May feel God's warm embrace    435–02

**EMBRACES**
Loving Savior, whose embraces    512–02

**EMPIRES**
Like earth's proud empires,
   pass away    546–05

**EMPTINESS**
Our emptiness and woe    325–02

**EMPTY**
And empty out this song    490–04

**ENABLE**
Enable with perpetual light    125–02

**ENCOUNTERS**
Lord, for today's encounters    358–04

**ENCOURAGE**
Now I know the Lord will encourage
   all beloved    169–03

**END (N)**
By guiding us on to the end of
   our days    554–01
End of faith, as its beginning    376–02
I am with you to the end    429–05
No end there is! We depart in peace    094–04
The end of sin and toil    015–02
To fulfill God's chosen end    343–01
To serve thee to the end    388–01
To serve thee to the end    389–01
We praise you now and to life's end    274–04

**END (V)**
Soon end in joyous day    286–02

**ENDEAVOR**
Each endeavor well begun    268–03

**ENDEAVORED**
All you endeavored done    419–04

**ENDING**
Glorious, beauteous, without ending    213–03

**ENDS (N)**
Let all the ends of the earth
   revere him    202–07
The ends of earth are in thy hand    320–02

**ENDS (V)**
When ends life's transient dream    383–04

**ENDUE**
Let Christ endue our will    405–03

**ENDURE**
To do and to endure    316–02

**ENDURED**
Who endured the cross and grave    123–02

**ENDURES**
Endures, and shall endure    278–01

**ENEMIES**
And his enemies lick the dust    204–09
Mighty enemies to still    163–02
Then enemies shall learn to love    450–02

**ENEMY**
Because the enemy oppresses me    190–09

**ENERGIES**
And with their fusioned energies 490–03
Whose energies have been ordained 287–03

**ENERGY**
Thank you, God, for priceless
 energy 266–03

**ENLARGE**
Enlarge the love they come
 to consecrate 532–01

**ENLIGHTEN**
Enlighten our minds, great Redeemer 120–04

**ENRICHMENT**
Of the enrichment in the days
 behind us 529–02

**ENSLAVE**
Enslave it with thy matchless love 378–04

**ENTER**
Come, enter in with shouts of joy 215–01
Enter every trembling heart 376–01
For Christ to come and enter there 010–02
For now, behold, to enter in 176–03
O enter then his gates with praise 220–03
That I may enter through them 231–19
That I may enter through them 232–19
Zion, let me enter there 489–01

**ENTERED**
Then entered in those wise men three 056–05

**ENTERS**
Jesus, enters in 365–03
Still the dear Christ enters in 043–03
Still the dear Christ enters in 044–03

**ENTRANCE**
I'd rather keep the entrance 207–02

**ENTREAT**
Soft and sweet, does entreat 021–02

**ENVY**
Bid envy, strife, and discord cease 009–03

**ENWRAPPED**
Enwrapped his beauty round 061–02

**EONS**
And over the eons 319–01

**EQUALITY**
Equality achieved 386–02

**ESCAPES**
Escapes its scorching heat 166–04

**ESSENCE**
While in essence only One 460–04

**ESTABLISH**
Establish, Lord, the work we do 211–05

**ESTABLISHED**
Hath stablished it fast by
 a changeless decree 476–03

**ESTABLISHES**
Establishes the world in peace 218–03

**ESTATE**
Both high and low estate combined 197–03
Why lies he in such mean estate 053–02

**ETERNITY**
And through eternity 310–05
And through eternity I'll sing on 085–03
And to eternity 139–04
For all eternity 175–04
Now and for eternity 132–04
Now and through eternity 129–03
Of thine eternity 316–04
Safe in your own eternity 530–01
Through all eternity 151–01
Through all eternity 395–03
Through all eternity 438–04
Throughout eternity 151–04
To guide us to eternity 141–02

**EVENING**
Are like an evening gone 210–03
The evening is advancing 015–01

**EVENTS**
Let no events our unity destroy 532–05

**EVERLASTING**
From everlasting thou art God 210–02
From everlasting you are God 211–01

## EVIL

| | |
|---|---|
| From evil God will keep you safe | 234–04 |
| God of love, all evil quelling | 544–03 |
| No evil shall come near | 212–02 |
| Nor evil live to see your face | 161–02 |
| Their own evil brings death to the wicked | 187–07 |
| To conquer all evil and stand for the right | 257–03 |
| What is evil in your sight I have done | 196–02 |

## EVILS

| | |
|---|---|
| To the evils we deplore | 420–05 |

## EXALT

| | |
|---|---|
| And shall exalt forever | 549–03 |

## EXALTED

| | |
|---|---|
| Be exalted in this hour | 192–04 |
| I am exalted among the nations | 193–10 |
| I am exalted in the earth | 193–10 |

## EXAMINE

| | |
|---|---|
| Examine how temptation breeds | 349–05 |

## EXAMPLE

| | |
|---|---|
| And make us in example strong | 497–02 |
| Christ's example, Christ's inspiring | 343–02 |

## EXECUTES

| | |
|---|---|
| Who executes justice for the oppressed | 254–07 |

## EXISTENCE

| | |
|---|---|
| Yours is every hour's existence | 136–01 |

## EXPANSES

| | |
|---|---|
| O'er white expanses sparkling pure | 292–02 |

## EXPRESSIONS

| | |
|---|---|
| There are sweet expressions on each face | 398–01 |

## EXTOL

| | |
|---|---|
| And extol our God and King | 309–02 |
| I will extol you every day | 252–01 |
| We all do extol thee, thou leader triumphant | 559–03 |
| You are my God, I will extol you | 232–28 |
| Your God extol, extol | 490–03 |

## EYE

| | |
|---|---|
| And with my eye upon you | 184–04 |
| Every eye shall then behold you | 006–02 |
| God's watchful eye ne'er sleepeth | 483–02 |
| Mine eye at times can see | 092–02 |
| No eye has known the sight | 017–03 |
| Though the eye of sinfulness | 138–03 |

## EYELIDS

| | |
|---|---|
| May mine eyelids close | 541–02 |

## EYES

| | |
|---|---|
| And give the eyes clear sight | 167–01 |
| And give us open eyes | 278–04 |
| And our eyes at least shall see him | 049–04 |
| Eyes will close, but you unsleeping | 544–03 |
| For now my eyes have seen | 605–01 |
| God gave us eyes to see them | 267–04 |
| God hath mine eyes from tears set free | 228–02 |
| Have we eyes to see | 348–02 |
| Her longing eyes are blest | 442–04 |
| In thy holy eyes | 541–04 |
| It is marvelous in our eyes | 231–23 |
| It is marvelous in our eyes | 232–23 |
| Look down with sad and wondering eyes | 090–03 |
| Look down with sad and wondering eyes | 091–03 |
| My eyes have seen the Savior, Christ the Lord | 604–00 |
| My eyes view thy glories | 557–02 |
| O Lord, with your eyes you have searched me | 377–refrain |
| Of newly opened eyes | 071–03 |
| The eyes of all are fixed on you | 251–02 |
| The eyes of the Lord are on the righteous | 187–04 |
| These eyes have seen salvation's dawn | 603–01 |
| To open their eyes | 319–02 |
| Upon the sinner's eyes | 602–03 |
| We have eyes to see | 348–02 |
| When, to their longing eyes restored | 121–01 |
| Where'er I turn my eyes | 288–02 |
| You, living Christ, our eyes behold | 156–01 |

**FAITH** (cont.)

| | |
|---|---|
| Their faith in Christ the basis of their love | 532–04 |
| Though dim our faith may be | 428–05 |
| Till faith is fully grown | 390–06 |
| To faith and hope and joy and peace | 332–04 |
| To keep the faith unbroken | 443–01 |
| We come, each one in faith | 515–01 |
| When faith has heard the Master's word | 308–03 |
| Who keeps faith forever | 254–07 |
| Who thee by faith before the world confessed | 526–01 |
| With faith like noontide shining bright | 474–03 |
| With faith that none can alter | 289–03 |

**FAITHFUL**

| | |
|---|---|
| Come, ye faithful, raise the strain | 114–01 |
| Come, ye faithful, raise the strain | 115–01 |
| He will give to all the faithful | 005–02 |
| O come, all ye faithful | 041–01 |

**FAITHFULNESS**

| | |
|---|---|
| And in thy faithfulness and love | 250–04 |
| Glorious in his faithfulness | 478–02 |
| Great is thy faithfulness, Lord, unto me | 276–refrain |
| Great is thy faithfulness, O God my Father | 276–01 |
| In faithfulness you hear my cry | 181–04 |
| In your faithfulness I hope | 178–03 |
| Thy faithfulness will I proclaim | 209–01 |
| To thy great faithfulness, mercy, and love | 276–02 |
| Where faithfulness is shown | 274–02 |
| With present faithfulness | 600–05 |
| Your faithfulness, O Lord, is sure | 251–01 |

**FALL (N)**

| | |
|---|---|
| Sweet the rain's new fall | 469–02 |
| Ye ransomed from the fall | 142–02 |
| Ye ransomed from the fall | 143–02 |

**FALL (V)**

| | |
|---|---|
| And will not let us fall | 419–01 |
| Fall afresh on me | 322–00 |
| Fall down on their faces and worship the Lamb | 477–03 |
| Lo, here I fall, my Savior | 098–02 |
| Peter, James, and John fall silent | 073–01 |
| Though it fall into the sea | 192–01 |
| To those who fall, how kind thou art | 310–03 |
| When I fall on my knees | 513–refrain |

**FALLEN**

| | |
|---|---|
| To lift the fallen, guide the feet that stumble | 424–02 |

**FALLS**

| | |
|---|---|
| Falls peace upon the soul | 308–03 |

**FAME**

| | |
|---|---|
| Their fame and might to thee belong | 209–04 |

**FAMILY**

| | |
|---|---|
| A larger family held dear | 499–04 |
| And in his family our proper kin | 385–03 |
| How happy is the family | 239–03 |
| Kneeling as one family | 547–03 |
| One family with a billion names | 134–04 |
| They and all their family | 178–02 |

**FAN**

| | |
|---|---|
| And fan our smoldering lives to flame | 124–03 |

**FARM**

| | |
|---|---|
| Of farm and market, shop and home | 414–01 |

**FASHIONED**

| | |
|---|---|
| Who fashioned and made us | 554–01 |

**FASHIONS**

| | |
|---|---|
| God, who fashions all that lives | 290–02 |

**FAST (N)**

| | |
|---|---|
| Consumed in fast and prayer with you | 087–04 |
| His holy fast and hungered sore | 083–02 |
| That this our fast of forty days | 079–05 |
| Who keep this holy fast of Lent | 079–01 |

**FAST (V)**

| | |
|---|---|
| For us didst fast and pray | 081–01 |

**FASTED**

| | |
|---|---|
| Himself has fasted and has prayed | 087–01 |

**FASTING (N)**

| | |
|---|---|
| With inward fasting, so that we | 079–04 |

**FASTING (V)**

| | |
|---|---|
| You were fasting in the wild | 077–01 |

**FATHER**

| | |
|---|---|
| As a father has compassion for his children | 222–13 |
| Like a father you protect me | 323–03 |

## FAULT

| | |
|---|---|
| That without fault or fear I may fulfill | 344–02 |

## FAULTS

| | |
|---|---|
| And by our faults obscure | 419–03 |
| From all my secret faults, O Lord | 167–03 |

## FAVOR

| | |
|---|---|
| Find favor now, and always win | 167–04 |
| For in thy favor they are strong | 209–04 |
| Look on me with thy favor | 098–02 |
| Who have found his favor | 027–01 |

## FEAR (N)

| | |
|---|---|
| All fear before thy presence flies | 366–03 |
| And all fear of want remove | 446–02 |
| And of fear to my friends | 182–03 |
| And with fear and trembling stand | 005–01 |
| Fear and distrust remove | 383–04 |
| Fear is all around me | 182–05 |
| From fear of every foe | 601–03 |
| From fear of rattling saber | 289–03 |
| Hungry and in fear | 348–01 |
| Let no fear of death appall us | 538–03 |
| Lord, should fear and anguish roll | 099–04 |
| To vanquish all our fear | 128–02 |
| Trembling with fear, deep in despair | 373–03 |
| What fear could now alarm me | 174–04 |
| With you I have no fear | 212–02 |

## FEAR (V)

| | |
|---|---|
| All those who fear God will be blest | 227–03 |
| And I shall fear no evil though | 175–02 |
| Because we fear the anger of the world | 086–01 |
| Fear not, for God is with you | 019–04 |
| Fear not, I am with thee | 361–02 |
| Fear not, said he, for mighty dread | 058–02 |
| Fear not, said he, for mighty dread | 059–02 |
| Fear not, the angel told her | 019–01 |
| Fear the Lord, you holy ones | 187–01 |
| Good Christian, fear; for sinners here | 053–02 |
| I fear no foe, with thee at hand to bless | 543–04 |
| I shall not fear the battle | 388–01 |
| I shall not fear the battle | 389–01 |
| Now ye need not fear the grave | 028–03 |
| Therefore we will not fear though the earth should change | 193–02 |
| We will not fear, for God hath willed | 260–03 |
| What shall we fear | 261–03 |
| Who would not fear God's holy name | 491–02 |
| Yet will I fear none ill | 170–03 |
| You need not fear King Herod | 045–02 |

## FEARFULNESS

| | |
|---|---|
| All fearfulness banished | 554–01 |

## FEARS

| | |
|---|---|
| Bid my anxious fears subside | 281–03 |
| From our fears and sins release us | 001–01 |
| From our fears and sins release us | 002–01 |
| From the fears that long have bound us | 420–02 |
| Our fears, our hopes, our aims are one | 438–02 |

## FEAST (N)

| | |
|---|---|
| And by thy feast to us the token | 502–00 |
| Feast after feast thus comes and passes by | 520–05 |
| I will set a feast for them | 525–03 |
| In the eucharistic feast | 144–04 |
| That you the wedding feast may share | 017–01 |
| The feast, though not the love, is past and gone | 520–04 |
| The Lamb's great bridal feast of bliss and love | 520–05 |
| The marriage feast is waiting | 015–02 |
| This is the feast of victory for our God | 594–refrain |
| Who at this blessed feast art pleased to be | 519–01 |

## FEAST (V)

| | |
|---|---|
| Here let us feast and, feasting, still prolong | 520–03 |
| Then let us feast this Easter Day | 110–03 |

## FED

| | |
|---|---|
| But it is fed and watered | 560–01 |
| To find, as all are fed | 507–02 |
| While we ourselves are fed | 558–04 |

## FEED

| | |
|---|---|
| And feed the starving multitude | 421–04 |
| Feed me till I want no more | 281–01 |
| Feed me with your very body | 323–02 |
| Feed us, gathered at this table | 512–03 |
| O feed me, Lord, that I may feed | 426–02 |
| Safe they feed upon the manna | 446–03 |
| You feed my soul and I am satisfied | 199–03 |
| You feed us, take us by the hand | 215–03 |
| You feed your creatures here below | 243–04 |

## FEEL

| | |
|---|---|
| O let me feel thee near me | 388–02 |
| O let me feel thee near me | 389–02 |

## FEET

| | |
|---|---|
| And beneath our feet casts down every foe | 194–01 |
| And find you kneeling at our feet | 353–03 |
| And keep my feet secure | 212–03 |
| And peaceful leave before your feet | 265–02 |
| And round his pierced feet | 151–03 |
| At his feet the six-winged seraph | 005–04 |
| At thy feet its treasure store | 391–06 |
| At your feet I cry, my Maker | 506–02 |
| At your feet may lowly kneel | 425–03 |
| At your feet their tribute pay | 203–02 |
| Feet firmly planted on the earth | 522–04 |
| He saw the feet, the hands, the side | 117–05 |
| Lest our feet stray from the places | 563–03 |
| My feet from stumbling kept | 228–02 |
| O beautiful for pilgrim feet | 564–02 |
| Set our feet on lofty places | 420–04 |
| Silently washing their feet | 367–05 |
| So may we with willing feet | 063–02 |
| Take my feet, and let them be | 391–02 |
| The wandering and the wavering feet | 426–02 |
| There, adoring at his feet | 097–03 |
| To guide the faltering feet | 552–02 |
| To his feet thy tribute bring | 478–01 |
| To the feet of the holy Child | 062–01 |
| Trembling at his feet we saw | 074–02 |
| We at his feet may fall | 142–04 |
| We at his feet may fall | 143–04 |
| Where God's feet pass | 469–02 |
| Where you have set your feet may I place mine | 344–01 |
| Your glorious feet have sought and found | 156–02 |

## FELL

| | |
|---|---|
| Fell reverently upon their knee | 056–05 |

## FELLOWSHIP

| | |
|---|---|
| But one great fellowship of love | 439–01 |
| But one great fellowship of love | 440–01 |
| Our fellowship declaring | 517–03 |
| The fellowship of kindred minds | 438–01 |
| The fellowship of living wine and bread | 520–03 |

## FERVOR

| | |
|---|---|
| Give us all new fervor, draw us | 429–02 |

## FIELD

| | |
|---|---|
| Field and forest, vale and mountain | 464–02 |
| Field and fountain, moor and mountain | 066–01 |
| From each field shall in that day | 551–03 |
| In some far outlying field | 425–02 |

## FIELDS

| | |
|---|---|
| Be glad, you fields, and all your fruit | 217–05 |
| Henceforth in fields of conquest | 447–01 |
| Henceforth in fields of conquest | 448–01 |
| In fields where they lay a-keeping their sheep | 056–01 |
| Through the silent fields of space | 268–01 |
| While fields and floods, rocks, hills, and plains | 040–02 |

## FIERCE

| | |
|---|---|
| Nor shall the fierce devour the small | 450–02 |

## FIGHT (N)

| | |
|---|---|
| Firm to the fight I stand | 179–02 |
| Fought the fight, the battle won | 113–02 |

## FIGHT (V)

| | |
|---|---|
| Fight as the saints who nobly fought of old | 526–03 |
| Fight the good fight with all thy might | 307–01 |

## FIGHTINGS

| | |
|---|---|
| Fightings and fears within, without | 370–02 |

## FILL

| | |
|---|---|
| And fill my life with joy | 181–04 |
| And fill the world with joyful praise | 229–02 |
| And fill the world with love divine | 010–03 |
| Come and fill our hearts anew, Holy Spirit | 140–04 |
| Come and fill us with your power | 192–04 |
| Come, O Spirit, fill your church | 127–03 |
| Fill all our lives with love and grace divine | 262–04 |
| Fill and nerve this will of mine | 321–03 |
| Fill me, radiancy divine | 462–03 |
| Fill me, radiancy divine | 463–03 |
| Fill me, use me | 322–00 |
| Fill me with joy and strength to be thy member | 069–02 |
| Fill me with life anew | 316–01 |
| Fill my cup, let it overflow | 350–refrain |
| Fill my cup to overflowing | 173–03 |
| Fill our hearts with joy and peace | 538–01 |
| Fill the heavens with sweet accord | 460–02 |
| Fill the seas and spread the plain | 285–01 |
| Fill the whole world with heaven's peace | 009–03 |

Fill us with the light of day — 464–01
Fill us with your light divine — 203–01
Fill your church, its breadth and length — 131–02
Fill your daughters and your sons — 127–03
Fill your weak spirit with alarm — 393–02
Forever fill your home — 239–04
Jesu, Jesu, fill us with your love — 367–refrain
May the Spirit fill our praise — 433–06
O fill me with thy fullness, Lord — 426–04

**FILLED**
But still they're filled with pain and sin — 211–03
Filled it with the glory of that
   perfect rest — 148–03
Filled the new-made world with light — 244–02
That filled the earth with food — 288–02

**FILLS**
Fills all the world today — 308–01
God fills their hearts with new hope
   and joy — 225–04
That fills the heavenly dwelling place — 548–01
With sweetness fills my breast — 310–01

**FIND**
But if, forgetful, we should find — 419–02
But what to those who find? Ah, this — 310–04
More than all in thee I find — 303–03
Though we, who fain would find thee — 278–02
To love them as we find them — 358–02
To them that find thee, all in all — 510–02
To them that find thee, all in all — 511–02
We find in Jesus living — 517–02

**FINGERS**
Creating God, your fingers trace — 134–01
Thy fingers spread the mountains
   and plains — 271–01

**FINISH**
Come, finish your salvation — 007–04
Finish, then, thy new creation — 376–04

**FINISHED**
Don't you hear him say,
   "It is finished" — 096–04
"It is finished!" hear him cry — 097–03

**FIRE (N)**
Come as the fire and purge our hearts — 325–03
Fire by night and cloud by day — 129–02
Fire who fuels all fires that burn — 131–02

In the fire the tares to cast — 551–03
Let the fire and cloudy pillar — 281–02
Pure, warm, and changeless be,
   a living fire — 383–02
Thou fire so masterful and bright — 455–03

**FIRE (V)**
Fire our hearts afresh with yearning — 136–03

**FIRST**
He is the first and the last — 598–00
The first, the last, beyond all thought — 488–03

**FIRST-BEGOTTEN**
First-begotten from the dead — 154–01

**FIRSTBORN**
Christ, the firstborn of the living — 109–03
Firstborn from the dead — 346–01
Firstborn of everything — 346–01

**FIRSTFRUITS**
So we today our firstfruits bring — 414–01
To offer God the firstfruits — 558–01
To thee our firstfruits give — 428–02

**FISHED**
You, who have fished other oceans — 377–04

**FIT**
And fit us for heaven to live with
   thee there — 024–03
And fit us for heaven to live with
   thee there — 025–03
Can fit us for this hour — 130–03
Fit us for these sacred arts — 486–04
Fit us for the work of building — 132–01

**FIX**
Fix in us thy humble dwelling — 376–01
Fix on God's work thy steadfast eye — 286–04

**FIXED**
Where their Lord has fixed his eyes — 073–01

**FLAME**
And flame diffuses, glory, glory, glory — 180–02
As urgent as a flame — 070–01
Come, O Spirit, with your flame — 127–02
Flame and fire your bidding keep — 224–01
Like sacrificial flame — 325–03
O for the living flame — 491–03

**FLAME** (cont.)

| | |
|---|---|
| The flame shall not hurt thee; I only design | 361–04 |
| Wind-sped flame and hovering dove | 523–01 |

**FLAMES**

| | |
|---|---|
| Then will flames the chaff devour | 409–02 |

**FLEE**

| | |
|---|---|
| Flee from woe and danger | 021–02 |
| Flee to thee from day to day | 144–03 |
| To thee, O Lord, I flee | 250–02 |

**FLESH**

| | |
|---|---|
| All flesh to you will bow | 201–01 |
| And all flesh shall see the token | 003–03 |
| Both flesh and spirit in thy presence fail | 519–01 |
| Come, Christ Jesus, flesh and spirit | 132–02 |
| Flesh or spirit to assail | 077–03 |
| Let all mortal flesh keep silence | 005–01 |
| My flesh in hope shall rest | 165–03 |
| My Lord should take frail flesh and die | 076–01 |
| O Word made flesh, be seen in us | 437–02 |
| Pleased in flesh with us to dwell | 031–02 |
| Robed in flesh, our great High Priest | 144–04 |
| Veiled in flesh the Godhead see | 031–02 |
| Whose flesh and blood are ours, whatever skin | 385–03 |
| Word made flesh, Love crucified | 523–02 |
| Word of the Father, now in flesh appearing | 041–02 |

**FLIGHT**

| | |
|---|---|
| If I should take my flight into the dawn | 248–03 |

**FLING**

| | |
|---|---|
| Fling wide the portals of your heart | 008–02 |
| Fling wide the prison door | 411–02 |
| Fling wide your gates, O Zion | 013–03 |

**FLOCK**

| | |
|---|---|
| In the Shepherd's flock and fold | 461–03 |

**FLOCKS**

| | |
|---|---|
| All flocks and grains and hills and meadows | 201–03 |
| Flocks were sleeping | 037–02 |
| O'er silent flocks by night | 029–01 |
| The flocks in pastures graze | 200–04 |
| Watching o'er your flocks by night | 022–02 |

**FLOOD**

| | |
|---|---|
| The surging flood, in proudly swelling roll | 236–02 |

**FLOODED**

| | |
|---|---|
| Is flooded with your resurrection power | 105–01 |

**FLOODS**

| | |
|---|---|
| Floods and earthquakes, drought and famine | 401–02 |

**FLOOR**

| | |
|---|---|
| Burning clean the threshing floor | 409–02 |

**FLOW**

| | |
|---|---|
| Let them flow in ceaseless praise | 391–01 |
| Now flow in us, fount of our being | 120–05 |

**FLOWER**

| | |
|---|---|
| Both flower and flaming star | 412–01 |
| Each little flower that opens | 267–01 |

**FLOWERET**

| | |
|---|---|
| It came a floweret bright | 048–01 |

**FLOWERS**

| | |
|---|---|
| Bring flowers of song, bedeck the way | 111–02 |
| Fair flowers of Paradise extend | 151–03 |
| For now the flowers of Nazareth | 308–02 |
| The flowers and fruits that in thee grow | 455–04 |
| You flowers so fragrant and so fair | 475–03 |

**FLOWS**

| | |
|---|---|
| And often for each other flows | 438–03 |
| Ever flows their thirst assuage | 446–02 |
| From whom flows all rhythm in our dance | 484–02 |
| It flows throughout our common bond | 241–02 |

**FLUNG**

| | |
|---|---|
| Flung the suns in burning radiance | 268–01 |

**FLY**

| | |
|---|---|
| But ever fly to you | 233–01 |
| We fly forgotten, as a dream | 210–04 |

**FOCUS**

| | |
|---|---|
| Focus us and make us whole | 285–02 |

**FOE**

| | |
|---|---|
| For still our ancient foe | 260–01 |
| God of the foe | 272–05 |

O'er every foe victorious 205–04
What foe have I to fear 179–01

**FOES**
By foes derided, by your own rejected 093–01
Foes mock us night and day 206–03
Foes who would oppress me 365–02
In spite of foes who'd harm me 174–04
May his foes bow down before him 204–09
May my fierce and spiteful foes 178–03
My foes are ever near me 388–02
My foes are ever near me 389–02
That he his foes from thence might free 076–04
Though fierce and angry foes assail 212–03
To overcome our foes 277–03
When cruel foes against us rose to strive 236–01

**FOLD**
Wandering from the fold of God 356–02

**FOLDS**
God folds the mountains out of rock 287–01

**FOLK**
And Christian folk throughout
  the world will ever say 016–04
Reconciling folk on earth 343–02
So every folk and nation 435–02
So folk of every nation 128–04
Till all God's folk are freed 552–01
We are his folk, he doth us feed 220–02

**FOLLOW**
And follow where thy feet have trod 408–06
And follow where you are guiding 284–01
And humbly follow after me 393–01
Come, Christian, follow where
  our Savior trod 371–01
Follow the Star of Bethlehem 050–refrain
Follow the star, seeking him 052–03
Follow to the judgment hall 097–02
Let us follow, never faltering 343–02
Nor follow where he trod 399–02
Shall surely follow me 170–05
Shall surely follow me 175–04
To all who follow thee 388–04
To all who follow thee 389–04
We follow all and heed your call 017–02
We follow and rejoice 521–01
We follow, not with fears 447–03
We follow, strengthened by your grace 274–04
We follow thee 275–03

We'll follow you now and forever 157–02

**FOLLOWED**
And they followed the right,
  for Jesus' sake 364–02
From Olivet they followed 089–02

**FOLLOWERS**
To lead the followers forward 552–02

**FONT**
Standing round the font reminds us 494–03

**FOOD**
Be our immortal food 505–02
Food and raiment you freely bestow 352–01
Food you bring forth from our labor 224–03
For thou art our food indeed 501–01
Of this blessed food from heaven 506–02
To share this heavenly food 521–02
Toiling for your daily food 305–01
Who gives food to the hungry 254–07
With food celestial feedeth 171–02

**FOOT**
God will not let your foot be moved 234–02

**FOOTSTEPS**
Our footsteps God shall safely guide 601–05
Our wandering footsteps guide 269–03
Where evil footsteps lead the way 249–04

**FORBID**
Forbid it, Lord, that I should boast 100–02
Forbid it, Lord, that I should boast 101–02

**FORCE (N)**
Creative force of art 274–02

**FORCE (V)**
Force me to render up my sword 378–01

**FORCES**
By social forces swept along 335–02
You, Lord, have made the atom's
  hidden forces 297–02

**FOREBEARS**
Shown our forebears in distress 479–02

**FORERUNNER**
Forerunner in the way 602–02

## FORETASTE

Giving sweet foretaste of the festal joy 520–05
O what a foretaste of glory divine 341–01

## FORETOLD

Isaiah 'twas foretold it 048–02

## FORGE

And forge us into one 291–03

## FORGET

And do not forget all his benefits 222–02
And forget not all God's benefits 597–00
Oh, let me ne'er forget 293–02
We forget thee 563–03
When we forget the cross that held
    your Son 086–03
You'll forget your flocks 050–02
You'll forget your herds 050–02

## FORGIVE

And forgive us all our debts 589–03
As we forgive our debtors 589–03
As we forgive those who sin against us 571–00
Father, what they do, forgive 429–04
Forgive me, Lord, through Christ,
    I pray 542–02
Forgive our foolish ways 345–01
Forgive our greed and carelessness
    of power 266–03
Forgive our haste that tampers unaware 266–04
Forgive our reckless plundering
    and waste 266–02
Forgive our sins as we forgive 347–01
Forgive our spoiling and abuse of them 266–01
Forgive us, Lord, our sins and debts 590–02
Forgive us our sins 571–00
You graciously forgive 201–01

## FORGIVEN

Has freely been forgiven 184–01

## FORGIVES

Christ forgives and so I sing 355–02
God forgives all your transgressions 223–02
Who forgives all your iniquity 222–03

## FORGOTTEN

Why have you forgotten me 190–09

## FORM (N)

In painful form their message bring 152–02

The very dying form of One 092–02
Our mortal form for mortals' sake 083–01

## FORM (V)

Form me of your flesh and bone 323–02

## FORMED

Formed thee for a blest abode 446–01
God formed the creatures with a word 288–02
Till Christ is formed in every heart 412–05
Was formed, and still abides 214–04
You formed the earth above the sea 243–02

## FORMS

Whose forms are bending low 038–03

## FORSAKE

Do not forsake what you have made 247–05
I'll never, no, never, no, never forsake 361–05
O faithful God, forsake me not 183–04
When I forsake his ways 172–01

## FORSAKEN

Lord, why have you forsaken me 168–01
Why has God forsaken me 406–01
Why have you forsaken me 099–03

## FORSOOK

God never yet forsook at need 282–03

## FORTRESS

A mighty fortress is our God 259–01
A mighty fortress is our God 260–01
My fortress that withstands each shock 183–03
The fortress of our living faith 348–03

## FOUND

Is found alone with thee 186–04
O may I then in him be found 379–04

## FOUNDATION

Built upon a firm foundation 129–01
Christ is made the sure foundation 416–01
Christ is made the sure foundation 417–01
How firm a foundation, ye saints
    of the Lord 361–01
Lord, you laid the earth's foundation 224–02
O Christ, the great foundation 443–01
Sure foundation, cornerstone 132–02
The church's one foundation 442–01
You have laid your throne's
    foundation 213–02

**FRUIT** (cont.)

| | |
|---|---|
| In fruit and grain and tree | 274–01 |
| Unblemished, wholesome, bearing fruit | 418–02 |

**FRUITS**

| | |
|---|---|
| May the fruits of thy salvation | 538–02 |
| The ripe fruits in the garden | 267–03 |
| Through all our living, we our fruits must give | 400–02 |

**FRUSTRATES**

| | |
|---|---|
| He frustrates the plans of the peoples | 185–10 |

**FULFILL**

| | |
|---|---|
| God shall fulfill that promise | 602–01 |

**FULFILLED**

| | |
|---|---|
| So shall they be fulfilled in thee | 282–03 |
| 'Tis now fulfilled what God decreed | 068–02 |

**FULFILLS**

| | |
|---|---|
| For God fulfills our needs | 258–03 |
| Fulfills its purpose here | 534–03 |

**FULLNESS**

| | |
|---|---|
| And fullness of peace forever | 204–refrain |
| Christ, you are the fullness of God | 346–01 |
| In its fullness undiminished | 154–03 |
| Till you know him in his fullness and believe | 398–02 |
| With the fullness of your grace | 317–02 |

**FURROWS**

| | |
|---|---|
| Furrows be glad | 012–02 |

**FUSES**

| | |
|---|---|
| And fuses elemental powers | 287–01 |

**FUTURE**

| | |
|---|---|
| A future yet unknown | 330–01 |
| Let us, Lord, the future see | 132–04 |
| Of future, present, past | 522–02 |
| Our future is secure | 255–01 |
| The future, all to us unknown | 265–02 |

# G

**GAIN (N)**

| | |
|---|---|
| And every gain divine | 564–03 |
| Gain through powers your grace conferred | 422–03 |
| My richest gain I count but loss | 100–01 |
| My richest gain I count but loss | 101–01 |
| Was all for sinners' gain | 098–02 |

**GAIN (V)**

| | |
|---|---|
| They shall gain and keep its truth | 073–02 |
| What they gain from you forever | 416–03 |
| What they gain from you forever | 417–03 |

**GALE**

| | |
|---|---|
| In every high and stormy gale | 379–02 |
| Straight into the gale | 373–01 |

**GALES**

| | |
|---|---|
| Gales that heave the sea in waves | 131–01 |

**GARDEN**

| | |
|---|---|
| Of the wet garden | 469–02 |
| See him in the garden | 299–04 |
| The garden of the world has come to flower | 105–01 |

**GARDENER**

| | |
|---|---|
| We see you, the gardener, a tree on your back | 311–01 |

**GARNER**

| | |
|---|---|
| In God's garner evermore | 551–03 |

**GATE**

| | |
|---|---|
| This is the gate of the Lord | 231–20 |
| This is the gate of the Lord | 232–20 |

**GATES**

| | |
|---|---|
| Now heaven's gates are reopened | 296–03 |
| The gates wide open stand | 015–02 |
| Through gates of pearl streams in the countless host | 526–06 |
| Within thy gates, O Zion blest | 235–01 |

**GATHER**

| | |
|---|---|
| Gather thou thy people in | 551–04 |

## GATHERED

So gather round once again, friends 547–03
They shall not gather with the just 158–04
We gather here to bid farewell 444–01
We gather together to ask
   the Lord's blessing 559–01

## GATHERED

All is safely gathered in 551–01
He gathered the waters of the sea as
   in a bottle 185–07
On Pentecost they gathered 128–01
We are gathered all to hear you 454–01

## GATHERS

And gathers in one house of faith 471–01
Gathers round its head sublime 084–01

## GAVE

O God who gave yourself to us 414–03
Whom God the Father gave us 133–02

## GAVEST

Lord, willingly thou gavest 395–03

## GAZE

Or gaze upon the skies 288–02
To gaze on thee unveiled,
   and see thy face 519–04

## GAZED

Therefore I gazed on you 198–02

## GEMS

Gems of the mountain and pearls
   of the ocean 067–03

## GENDER

Oblivious to gender, wealth 471–03

## GENERATIONS

All generations praise continually 016–02
All generations shall tell forth 252–01
While generations rise and die 252–03
Your God, O Zion, to all generations 254–10

## GENTLENESS

Thou hast the true and perfect
   gentleness 457–04

## GIFT

A gift from God in very truth 238–03
A lasting gift Jesus gave his own 094–02
And have the gift to all inspire 335–01
By your gift of peace restored 508–02

By your gift of peace restored 509–02
Ever remembering God's great gift 062–01
Every gift that you impart 427–01
For this better gift we yearn 531–01
Gift of the Father, to human mother 055–04
God's gift from highest heaven 360–02
God's gift of love to all the earth 052–02
In the gift of Christ your Son 425–01
Let the gift of thy salvation 420–05
Lord, we bring our gift of music 486–04
The wondrous gift is given 043–03
The wondrous gift is given 044–03
This gift so great, so rare 605–02
To each the gift of truthfulness impart 532–03
Whate'er the gift may be 428–01
With gift of the finest wheat 521–refrain
With your strengthening gift of power 524–02

## GIFTED

And you gifted your people 319–02

## GIFTS

All perfect gifts bestowing 277–01
And holy and precious the gifts 062–refrain
Bearing gifts we traverse afar 066–01
For all your gifts we bring
   our praise 279–refrain
For the gifts to every nation 553–01
Gifts of blessing to bestow 524–01
Gracious gifts from God unfold 343–02
Large gifts supporting everything
   that lives 266–01
Lay their gifts before him 046–03
Of your gifts at Pentecost 318–01
Our varied gifts united 435–01
The gifts at Pentecost 130–02
The Spirit and the gifts are ours 260–04
Through the gifts that here you give me 506–03
To waste God's other gifts on force 287–02
Vainly with gifts would
   his favor secure 067–04
Who dost thy sevenfold gifts impart 125–01
With countless gifts of love 555–01
With gifts of fox and beaver pelt 061–02
With thee are found the gifts of life 271–02
With the Spirit's gifts empower us 429–refrain

## GILD

Gild the spot that gave them birth 020–02

## GIRD

Gird on thy mighty sword 139–02
Gird our lives that they may be 420–04

## GIVE

| | |
|---|---|
| All that you so freely give | 429–04 |
| And give us, Lord, within | 277–01 |
| Back to God we humbly give you | 498–03 |
| Give ourselves to him, of Bethlehem | 055–06 |
| Give we now to God above | 107–02 |
| Give what is best | 359–02 |
| Here, Lord, I give myself away | 078–04 |
| I will ever give to thee | 281–03 |
| In what you give us, Lord, to do | 419–04 |
| Myself to thee entirely give | 366–01 |
| O what can we give you, Lord Jesus | 157–03 |
| There's nought I can give thee | 557–03 |
| We give thee but thine own | 428–01 |
| What can I give him poor as I am | 036–04 |
| You give yourself to us, O Lord | 521–05 |

## GIVEN

| | |
|---|---|
| And Spirit now be given | 555–03 |
| Are to our Jesus given | 155–02 |
| God given for us, in Bethlehem | 055–02 |
| Still let thy Spirit unto us be given | 360–02 |
| That to you it shall be given | 493–01 |
| To Zion shall be given | 441–05 |
| Who unto us the Christ has given | 054–04 |

## GIVER

| | |
|---|---|
| Giver of grace for our needs all-availing | 261–01 |
| Giver of immortal gladness | 464–01 |
| Giver of salvation | 127–03 |
| Giver of steadfastness | 279–03 |
| To God, the giver of all good | 414–01 |

## GIVING (N)

| | |
|---|---|
| For in our giving we receive | 374–04 |
| God, whose giving knows no ending | 422–01 |

## GIVING (V)

| | |
|---|---|
| When we are giving, or when receiving | 400–02 |

## GLADDEN

| | |
|---|---|
| And gladden hearts of those who know | 259–02 |

## GLADNESS

| | |
|---|---|
| And gladness fills my breath | 165–03 |
| And gladness with thy children dwell | 235–04 |
| As with gladness men of old | 063–01 |
| For gladness breaks like morning | 447–03 |
| For gladness breaks like morning | 448–03 |
| For the Lord of gladness | 365–03 |
| Holier gladness ours shall be | 077–04 |
| In gladness and in woe | 145–02 |

| | |
|---|---|
| In gladness and in woe | 146–02 |
| Of triumphant gladness | 114–01 |
| Of triumphant gladness | 115–01 |
| The Passover of gladness | 118–01 |
| To the gladness of the sun | 425–03 |
| With Easter gladness | 529–03 |
| With gladness and mirth, we praise your great name | 257–02 |
| With gladness day and night | 158–02 |

## GLEAM

| | |
|---|---|
| Pure gleam of God's unending glory | 550–01 |
| Where the white gleam of our bright star is cast | 563–02 |

## GLIMPSED

| | |
|---|---|
| Was glimpsed by them alone | 330–01 |

## GLIMPSES

| | |
|---|---|
| Glimpses of truth thou hast for me | 324–01 |

## GLOOM

| | |
|---|---|
| Gloom around you and within | 099–02 |
| In the gloom to know you nigh | 099–04 |
| Leave behind all gloom and sadness | 506–01 |
| When Satanic gloom assails | 348–03 |
| Where all is gloom, may we sow hope | 374–02 |

## GLORIES

| | |
|---|---|
| But makes thy glories known | 288–03 |
| Glories stream from heaven afar | 060–02 |
| Praise the Lord, God's glories show | 481–01 |
| The brightest glories earth can yield | 441–05 |
| The glories of his righteousness | 040–04 |
| The glories of my God and King | 466–01 |
| When shall we its glories see | 014–03 |
| Your glories shine in radiant skies | 243–03 |

## GLORIFIED

| | |
|---|---|
| You glorified your name and Word | 247–02 |

## GLORIFY

| | |
|---|---|
| Glorify your holy name | 129–03 |

## GLORY (N)

| | |
|---|---|
| All glory and power, all wisdom and might | 477–04 |
| All glory be to God on high | 058–06 |
| All glory be to God on high | 059–06 |
| All glory be to God on high | 133–01 |
| All glory, laud, and honor | 088–refrain |
| All glory to our Lord and God | 083–05 |
| All glory to our risen Head | 119–03 |

## GLORY (N) (cont.)

| | |
|---|---|
| With the glory present there | 163–03 |
| Your glory all the light we need | 431–03 |
| Your glory lights eternal day | 431–01 |

## GLORY (V)

| | |
|---|---|
| For none can glory in thy sight | 240–02 |
| Glory in thy perfect love | 376–03 |
| In the cross of Christ I glory | 084–01 |
| May we increasingly glory in learning | 516–03 |

## GLOW (N)

| | |
|---|---|
| By morning glow or evening shade | 483–02 |
| Touched by fading glow of sun's gold | 547–03 |

## GLOW (V)

| | |
|---|---|
| Glow within this heart of mine | 321–02 |

## GLOWS

| | |
|---|---|
| Glows with thy fire divine | 316–03 |
| Lo! it glows with peace and joy | 084–02 |

## GO

| | |
|---|---|
| And safe shalt thou go on | 286–04 |
| "Go now, you are my Son" | 071–02 |
| Go to dark Gethsemane | 097–01 |
| Nor let me go astray | 301–03 |
| Then from your Spirit where, Lord, shall I go | 248–02 |
| While others go and come | 172–03 |
| You will always go with me | 173–02 |

## GOALS

| | |
|---|---|
| Our goals are pleasure, gold, and power | 437–01 |
| Till our goals and yours are one | 268–03 |
| Toward the goals of Christ, your Son | 422–02 |

## GODLY

| | |
|---|---|
| So let the godly seek you | 184–03 |

## GODS

| | |
|---|---|
| Above all gods enthroned | 214–03 |
| All other gods are merely idols | 217–03 |
| Before the gods my praise express | 247–01 |
| Handmade gods of wood and clay | 290–03 |
| The heathen gods are idols vain | 216–03 |
| The idol gods of heathen lands | 227–02 |
| To be feared more than all gods | 217–03 |
| To gods of silver and of gold | 227–02 |
| Yet you have made us less than gods | 162–03 |

## GOES

| | |
|---|---|
| Your Lord goes on to Galilee | 116–03 |

## GOLD

| | |
|---|---|
| And gold and incense bring | 205–03 |
| Bring we the gold of our faithfulness | 062–03 |
| Glowing gold I bring the newborn babe so holy | 064–02 |
| Gold and myrrh and frankincense | 065–03 |
| Gold I bring to crown him again | 066–02 |
| Gold or with silver | 557–03 |
| May God thy gold refine | 564–03 |
| Than gold, the finest gold | 167–02 |
| Their gold, and myrrh, and frankincense | 056–05 |

## GOOD

| | |
|---|---|
| For the good we all inherit | 553–03 |
| From you alone all good proceeds | 243–02 |
| Lord of all good, our gifts we bring to you | 375–01 |
| No good will you deny | 207–03 |
| What good is gained by my disgrace | 181–03 |
| Who in all good delightest | 088–04 |

## GOODNESS

| | |
|---|---|
| Behold the goodness of our Lord | 241–01 |
| Filled with his goodness, lost in his love | 341–03 |
| Finds goodness and delight | 158–02 |
| For the goodness of our Lord | 298–02 |
| Goodness and mercy all my life | 170–05 |
| His goodness we'll adore | 150–03 |
| In goodness, love, and peace | 601–03 |
| In your goodness, show favor to Zion | 196–10 |
| Surely goodness and kindness wait for me | 173–04 |
| Thy bounteous goodness nourish us in peace | 262–03 |
| Thy goodness faileth never | 171–06 |
| Whose goodness faileth never | 171–01 |
| Your goodness all our hopes shall raise | 265–03 |
| Your goodness and your mercy, Lord | 175–04 |

## GOODS

| | |
|---|---|
| Let goods and kindred go | 260–04 |

## GOOD WILL

| | |
|---|---|
| Good will to all from highest heaven | 058–06 |
| Good will to all from highest heaven | 059–06 |

## GOSPEL

| | |
|---|---|
| And the gospel go unheard | 429–01 |
| Indwelling God, your gospel claims | 134–04 |
| Keep us faithful to the gospel | 461–04 |
| Let your gospel, heard and heeded | 512–01 |
| We would be faithful to thy gospel glorious | 360–05 |

## GRACE

| | |
|---|---|
| Amazing grace, how sweet the sound | 280–01 |
| And grace my fears relieved | 280–02 |
| And grace will lead me home | 280–03 |
| And keep us in God's grace | 555–02 |
| But God's grace beyond compare | 290–04 |
| By God's surprising grace | 435–02 |
| By grace we make you known | 443–02 |
| By grace we were invited | 443–02 |
| By your grace shall understand | 131–03 |
| For grace and joy abounding | 013–02 |
| For so it is that sovereign grace | 197–06 |
| For the grace of yesteryears | 129–02 |
| Fresh anointing of your grace | 523–01 |
| From Christ the grace we need | 517–02 |
| From grace more grace receiving | 470–03 |
| Full of grace forever | 596–00 |
| God of grace and God of glory | 420–01 |
| God's grace for human good | 453–03 |
| God's grace unbound, for all, for me | 499–02 |
| Grace and glory bless the whole world | 033–03 |
| Grace and truth and love divine | 336–01 |
| Grace, grace alone prevaileth | 240–02 |
| Grace in human form declare | 331–03 |
| Grace to cleanse, and power to free | 387–02 |
| Grace to cover all my sin | 303–04 |
| Grace, which like the Lord the giver | 446–02 |
| How precious did that grace appear | 280–02 |
| How rich in grace are you, O Lord | 252–02 |
| I also come to ask for grace | 390–01 |
| In godly grace and fear | 437–02 |
| Let that grace now, like a fetter | 356–03 |
| Lord, give us grace that we | 442–05 |
| Lord of all grace | 199–01 |
| May thy rich grace impart | 383–02 |
| My grace, all-sufficient, shall be thy supply | 361–04 |
| Now by God's grace Christ is my all in all | 410–01 |
| O give me grace to follow | 388–04 |
| O give me grace to follow | 389–04 |
| O to grace how great a debtor | 356–03 |
| Plenteous grace with thee is found | 303–04 |
| Praise God for the grace and favor | 479–02 |
| Praise him for his grace and favor | 478–02 |
| Responding to God's grace | 434–02 |
| That by thy grace our souls are fed | 502–00 |
| The grace of Christ renewed in us | 152–04 |
| The grace of life is theirs | 534–01 |
| The Lord whose grace and power are known | 227–03 |
| The Lord's redeeming grace proclaim | 216–01 |
| Thy grace and love in me reveal | 008–03 |

| | |
|---|---|
| Thy grace has made us strong | 447–01 |
| Thy grace has made us strong | 448–01 |
| Thy unction grace bestoweth | 171–05 |
| Till by God's grace our warring world | 450–01 |
| 'Tis grace has brought me safe thus far | 280–03 |
| To feast upon your grace | 207–01 |
| Turn to me in grace and mercy | 178–03 |
| 'Twas grace that taught my heart to fear | 280–02 |
| Until by your most costly grace | 340–03 |
| Unto God, whose grace unbounded | 506–01 |
| What but thy grace can foil the tempter's power | 543–03 |
| Who would God's grace receive | 128–03 |
| With all its grace, is given | 149–04 |
| With every grace endued | 442–02 |
| With grace to fortify | 405–03 |
| With your grace our spirits shower | 317–02 |
| With your grace our triumphs hallow | 425–03 |
| With your grace unlimited | 512–03 |
| Your grace and blessing day by day | 496–00 |
| Your grace surrounds us all our days | 279–refrain |
| Your saving grace bestow | 212–05 |

## GRACES

| | |
|---|---|
| Armored with all Christlike graces | 420–04 |
| For it is God who has given us graces | 484–01 |

## GRAIN

| | |
|---|---|
| Then the harvest grain | 480–01 |
| To bless the springing grain | 200–02 |
| Wholesome grain and pure may be | 551–02 |
| With grain the fields are covered | 200–04 |

## GRAINS

| | |
|---|---|
| Like the grains which become one same whole loaf | 518–03 |

## GRANT

| | |
|---|---|
| But you alone can grant us grace | 347–01 |
| God, grant us strength to do | 277–02 |
| Grant a peaceful life | 373–04 |
| Grant, O God, an age renewed | 465–04 |
| Grant, O thou blessed Trinity | 079–05 |
| Grant, O unchanging Unity | 079–05 |
| Grant that knowledge, still increasing | 425–03 |
| Grant that we all, made one in faith | 380–05 |
| Grant that we not faint nor fail | 077–03 |
| Grant them courage and compassion | 523–02 |
| Grant them the joy which brightens earthly sorrow | 533–03 |

## GRANT (cont.)

Grant them the peace which calms
   all earthly strife 533–03
Grant unto us communion with thee 271–02
Grant unto us thy pardoning grace 079–02
Grant us a faithful life 277–01
Grant us in all our thoughts
   to honor thee 392–01
Grant us, Lord, the tears which heal 406–02
Grant us new courage, sacrificial,
   humble 424–02
Grant us thy peace, Lord, through
   the coming night 539–03
Grant us thy peace throughout
   our earthly life 539–04
Grant us thy peace upon
   our homeward way 539–02
Grant us wisdom, grant us courage 420–01
Grant us your Spirit's true illumination 297–01
Grant you peace, perfect peace 596–00
Lord, grant us what we cannot mine 287–03
May the Lord God grant you success 169–02
O grant that nothing in my soul 366–02
O grant to us the grace we find in thee 457–04
So God grant us for tomorrow 343–04
Then grant that we like them be true 087–04
You grant the homeless sheltered space 226–02

## GRANTED

For it is God who has granted
   us wisdom 484–03

## GRANTS

And grants his name to know 149–03
And grants the prisoner sweet release 253–03
Who grants us liberty 602–01

## GRAPES

Grapes in bunches cut down
   when ripe and red 518–01

## GRASP

Here grasp with firmer hand
   eternal grace 520–01
Too high to grasp, too great
   to understand 248–01

## GRASS

And like the green grass fade 188–01
As grass which sprouts yet fades
   at dusk 211–02
Grass for their bed; all is still 052–01
Grass you cause to grow for cattle 224–03
On the first grass 469–02

## GRASSES

You meadow grasses bright
   and slender 475–03

## GRATITUDE

Is old as gratitude 558–01
My gratitude bringing 557–03
With gratitude and humble trust 414–03

## GRAVE

Forgotten in the grave 165–04
God of the empty grave 272–03
Is risen from the grave 308–04
My grave cannot confess your name 181–03

## GRAVECLOTHES

Kept the folded graveclothes 122–01

## GREAT

The great and small for you are one 226–02

## GREATNESS

Your greatness is beyond our thought 252–01

## GREED

Till greed and hate shall cease 412–02

## GREET

Greet one who comes in glory 013–01
I greet thee, who my sure
   Redeemer art 457–01
Yea, Lord, we greet thee 041–02

## GREETS

Lovingly he greets us 122–02

## GRIEF

But through all grief distressing 483–03
From human grief and burdened toil 408–03
Lamb of God, your grief I see 099–01
Never was grief like thine 076–05
Of our deepest grief and loss 406–01
Still in grief we mourn our dead 427–02
Where neither grief nor pain
   shall dwell 431–01
With grief and shame weighed down 098–01

## GRIEFS

And griefs around me spread 383–03

## GRIEVES
Come and see; from all that grieves you 021–02

## GROANED
When Jesus groaned, a trembling fear 312–00

## GROUND
| | |
|---|---|
| All other ground is sinking sand | 379–refrain |
| All seated on the ground | 058–01 |
| All seated on the ground | 059–01 |
| And from the ground there blossoms red | 384–04 |
| For the ground will become a pool | 018–04 |
| Ground of being, life and love | 136–01 |

## GROW
| | |
|---|---|
| Grow to laugh and sing and worship | 498–04 |
| May it grow and purify | 107–02 |

## GROWTH
| | |
|---|---|
| By children's growth in strength and grace | 238–04 |
| Silent growth while we are sleeping | 553–01 |

## GUARD (N)
Be thou our guard while life shall last 210–05

## GUARD (V)
| | |
|---|---|
| And guard us from the devil's ways | 590–02 |
| Guard my first springs of thought and will | 456–02 |
| Guard the nest that must be filled | 012–03 |
| Guard thou each sacred hour from selfish ease | 392–03 |
| Guard thou the lips from sin, the hearts from shame | 539–02 |
| Guard us from harm without | 120–03 |
| O guard my thoughts, I now implore | 249–04 |
| The Lord will guard the righteous well | 158–05 |

## GUARDIAN
| | |
|---|---|
| Thou guardian of my soul | 388–03 |
| Thou guardian of my soul | 389–03 |

## GUARDS
The guards a useless watch maintain 238–01

## GUESS
For none can guess God's grace 313–03

## GUEST
As your guest in heaven receive me 506–03

## GUESTS
| | |
|---|---|
| Nay, let us be thy guests; the feast is thine | 503–01 |
| We come as guests invited | 517–01 |

## GUIDANCE
| | |
|---|---|
| Great Creator, give us guidance | 268–03 |
| The guidance of your light to use | 068–03 |

## GUIDE (N)
| | |
|---|---|
| Be thou my guide | 383–03 |
| Be thou our guide | 275–02 |
| God the Spirit, guide and guardian | 523–01 |
| He is our guide and friend | 150–02 |
| If thou wilt be my guide | 388–01 |
| If thou wilt be my guide | 389–01 |
| The Lord will be my guide | 175–01 |
| To bless the Lord, my guide | 165–01 |
| Using as our guide the star, so brightly beaming | 064–01 |
| Who, like thyself, my guide and stay can be | 543–03 |
| Your Spirit be their guide in every move | 532–04 |

## GUIDE (V)
| | |
|---|---|
| And guide the nations upon the earth | 202–04 |
| And guide them in the homeward way | 357–02 |
| And guide us when perplexed | 555–02 |
| Beside us to guide us, our God with us joining | 559–02 |
| Go with us, Lord, and guide the way | 535–00 |
| God guide you, keep you, lead you on | 444–04 |
| Guide me, O thou great Jehovah | 281–01 |
| Guide my feet while I run this race | 354–01 |
| Guide our thoughts and change our ways | 433–06 |
| Guide the church to true commitment | 132–01 |
| Guide thou our ordered lives as thou dost please | 392–03 |
| Guide us to justice, truth, and love | 450–01 |
| Guide us to thy perfect light | 066–refrain |
| Guide where our infant Redeemer is laid | 067–01 |
| Jesus, Savior, guide our steps | 465–01 |
| To guide, to strengthen, and to cheer | 083–04 |
| You guide us as a shepherd leads | 206–01 |

## GUIDES
| | |
|---|---|
| And guides in paths of righteousness | 174–02 |
| And guides us through the shades of night | 328–02 |

**GUIDES** (cont.)
God guides the feet of pilgrims 602–03
It guides you to abundant life 393–04
Still guides, O Christ, to you 327–02

**GUILE**
Who have no guile upon their tongues 164–02

**GUILT**
O see, in guilt I was born 196–03
Take all my guilt away 383–01
To turn from guilt and dull despair 353–05

Whose guilt has been forgiven 184–01
Whose guilt is wholly covered 184–01

**GUILTY**
Who was the guilty 093–02

**GUNS**
The guns and nuclear might 259–03
When will guns and bombs be silent 401–01

**GUSTS**
Gusts that bend the saplings low 131–01

# H

**HABIT-BOUND**
Is habit-bound and slow 351–02

**HABITATION**
Round each habitation hovering 446–03
The holy habitation of the Most High 193–04

**HALL**
To come into the banquet hall 017–02
To gain the everlasting hall 028–03

**HALLOW**
Hallow all our lives, O Lord 508–02
Hallow all our lives, O Lord 509–02

**HAMMER**
Don't you hear the hammer ringing 096–02

**HAMMERS**
Loud pounding hammers 458–02

**HAND**
And by God's hand the rising land 214–04
And graven on thy hand 441–02
And strong shall be my hand 378–02
And your right hand will guard me
  evermore 248–03
As with a mother's tender hand 483–03
But now at God's right hand
  Christ stands 110–01
By God's almighty hand 560–01
From God's attentive hand 349–02

God near at hand 272–06
God's hand is there, firmly in control 373–05
Hand we link with hand 465–01
His hand the wonders wrought 293–01
How wise, how strong God's hand 286–03
In you the upper hand 188–05
Is ever found at thy right hand 165–05
Joining hand in hand agree 318–04
Looking to my God's right hand 449–01
Lord, your right hand shall save my life 247–05
My hand will save 525–01
O God of Bethel, by whose hand 269–01
Out of so good and so beloved a hand 342–03
Precious Lord, take my hand 404–01
Shadowed beneath thy hand may
  we forever stand 563–03
Take my hand, precious Lord 404–01
The Bridegroom is at hand 015–02
The clean of hand, the pure of heart 176–02
The hand that shaped the rose
  hath wrought 292–01
The right hand of the Lord does
  valiantly 231–15
The right hand of the Lord is exalted 231–16
Thy hand we see 275–01
Upheld by my righteous,
  omnipotent hand 361–02
Whose hand brings victory 219–01
With a mighty hand God brings
  nations low 194–01
With God at my right hand 165–02
With God at my right hand 179–02

With thy hand to direct us 261–03
With your almighty hand 289–01
You hand can turn my griefs away 284–02
Your hand, in sight of all my foes 172–02
Your hand was heavy on me 184–02
Your mighty hand will rest
    upon me still 248–03
Your open hand is bountiful 251–02
Your right hand holds me fast 198–05

**HANDMAID**
Behold, I am your handmaid 019–06

**HANDS**
Behold his hands and side 151–02
Hands, eyes, and voice to serve
    your great design 375–02
Hands of the world stretch out 515–02
Into our hands you've placed all things 162–04
My hands, my feet, I show to thee 117–04
New hands for holding on 358–04
O wounded hands of Jesus, build 007–04
Place in my hands the wonderful key 324–01
Safely within your hands 279–05
Sustaining God, your hands uphold 134–02
Take my hands and let them move 391–02
Thy hands have set the heavens
    with stars 271–01
When the hands on them are laid 524–02
Who come with clean hands upraising 177–02
With hands that touch and heal 381–03
With lifted hands at close of day 249–03
With lifted hands your homage pay 242–01

**HANGS**
Hangs my helpless soul on thee 303–02

**HARBINGER**
The harbinger of day 602–02

**HARM (N)**
And safe from harm remain 164–03
From harm and danger keep
    thy children free 539–03
He will bring no harm to you 045–02
Keep me, O keep me safe from harm 542–01

**HARM (V)**
Nor harm their neighbor's life 164–02

**HARMONY**
A harmony of peace 434–03

For all to live in harmony 274–03
For the mystic harmony 473–03
To the nations' harmony 401–02

**HARPS**
As harps and cymbals swell the sound 017–03
To touch their harps of gold 038–01

**HARSHNESS**
No harshness hast thou
    and no bitterness 457–04

**HARVEST**
And shall take the harvest home 551–03
Far richer than their harvest of grain
    and wine 160–07
Lord of harvest, grant that we 551–02

**HARVESTS**
For the harvests of the Spirit 553–03
In the harvests we are sharing 553–02

**HASTE**
Make haste to heal these hearts of pain 408–05

**HASTEN**
Come, then, let us hasten yonder 021–03
Early hasten to the tomb 097–04
Hasten to your quiet home 020–03
I'll hasten to God's throne 362–01
Lord, hasten to bring in your kingdom
    on earth 337–02
To hasten or control 388–03
To hasten or control 389–03

**HATE (N)**
And armed with cruel hate 260–01
Where hate and fear divide us 289–01
Where there is hate, may we sow love 374–01

**HATE (V)**
And those who hate good will be
    brought to ruin 187–07
I hate the sins that made thee mourn 396–02
I hate the sins that made thee mourn 397–02

**HATRED**
Bid hatred, greed, injustice cease 431–03
When hatred and division 289–04

**HAUNTS**
In haunts of wretchedness and need 408–02

## HAVEN
Safe into the haven guide 303–01

## HAY
The little Lord Jesus, asleep on the hay 024–01
The little Lord Jesus, asleep on the hay 025–01

## HEAD
Christ the head and cornerstone 416–01
Christ the head and cornerstone 417–01
Cover my defenseless head 303–02
Low lies his head with the beasts
   of the stall 067–02
My head thou dost with oil anoint 170–04
O sacred head, now wounded 098–01
O sacred head, what glory 098–01
See, from his head, his hands, his feet 100–03
See, from his head, his hands, his feet 101–03
The head that once was crowned
   with thorns 149–01
The little Lord Jesus laid down
   his sweet head 024–01
The little Lord Jesus laid down
   his sweet head 025–01
When my head is bowed in sorrow 363–03
Who art one Savior and one living head 503–04
With your head against my breast 045–01
You are head of the church,
   which is your body 346–01

## HEAL
And heal our strife-torn world 289–01
Believing you can heal 390–01
Heal the sick, and lead the blind 303–03
Heal the sick and preach the word 429–01

## HEALED
Healed the sick and freed the soul 427–02

## HEALER
Jesus, healer, bring your balm 465–03
O Christ, the healer, we have come 380–01

## HEALING (N)
A healing for our strife 241–02
Find healing in the wounds he bore 103–01
Healing flows within your streams 192–02
Risen with healing in his wings 031–03
Risen with healing in his wings 032–03
With healing of division 314–03

## HEALING (V)
Healing all the sick ones 299–03

## HEALS
Who heals all your diseases 222–03

## HEALTH
Be thou my health and life 301–02
For he is thy health and salvation 482–01
Jesus, the health of the world 120–04
To pray for health, to plead for friends 380–01
With special health they reach fourscore 211–03

## HEAR
All ye who hear 482–01
Can't you hear him 382–02
Don't you hear him calling his Father 096–03
May hear, so calm and plain 118–02
O let me hear thee speaking 388–03
O let me hear thee speaking 389–03
The Holy Scripture hear 470–03

## HEARING
His own "All hail!" and, hearing 118–02

## HEART
A humbled, contrite heart
   you will not spurn 196–09
A pure heart create for me, O God 196–06
All my heart today rejoices 021–01
And everyone of tender heart 455–05
And from my stricken heart with tears 092–02
And give the heart delight 167–01
And let your foolish heart be still 393–03
And so to you my heart shall sing 181–04
And the heart of the Eternal 298–02
Be joyful in the Lord, my heart 483–04
But, above all, the heart 468–02
Daystar, in my heart appear 462–01
Daystar, in my heart appear 463–01
Each heart is manifest to thee 079–02
Enfolded in a faithful heart 287–03
Every heart be quaking 365–02
For the heart and mind's delight 473–03
For the mystery's heart is love 406–04
Generous of heart and mind 531–02
Give me the heart to hear your voice
   and will 344–02
Give to me, Lord, a thankful heart 351–01
Glad of heart your carols raise 479–01
God of the loving heart 272–06
Heart and life renewing truly 493–02
Heart of my own heart, whatever befall 339–03
Heart with the flame of your own
   love ablaze 375–02
Her heart with joyful hope is springing 017–02

Here's my heart, O take and seal it 356–03
In each new heart that hears 034–03
In every heart 274–02
In every heart may grow 308–02
In God's own heart and home
   they dwell 225–03
In heart and soul may dwell with thee 079–04
In my heart you have poured
   the fullness of joy 160–07
In whose heart are the highways
   to Zion 208–05
In-a my heart, in-a my heart 372–01
Let all, with heart and voice 150–01
Let every heart prepare him room 040–01
Let my heart add its Amen 336–04
Long my heart hath panted 365–01
Moving in my heart I will pray 315–refrain
My glad heart upraise 557–01
My grateful heart inspires my tongue 165–01
My heart an altar, and thy love
   the flame 326–04
My heart and my flesh sing for joy
   to the living God 208–02
My heart awaking cries 487–01
My heart is weak and poor 378–03
My heart pours out its praise 600–01
My heart restores its borrowed ray 384–02
My heart shall bloom forever 011–03
My heart shall raise 359–03
My heart still trusteth in God's might 240–04
My heart to thee; here, Lord, abide 008–03
My heart, which in the Lord rejoices 475–01
My heart with rapture fill 184–03
My heart with rapture thrills 561–02
Near to the heart of God 527–01
Nor leave my sinful heart to stray 249–04
O deep within my heart now shine 069–02
O let my heart no more despair 362–02
On heart and will and brain 437–03
Sent from the heart of God 527–refrain
Set your heart on things above 409–02
So let the Israelites in heart 240–04
Take heart, take hope,
   the Lord is King 152–refrain
Take my heart, it is thine own 391–05
Take thou ourselves, O Lord, heart,
   mind, and will 392–04
The unforgiving heart 347–02
Then on, ye pure in heart 145–04
Then on, ye pure in heart 146–04
Thou and thou only, first in my heart 339–02
Thy heart has never known recoil 408–03
To God's great heart of love and light 444–03

To my heart O enter thou 489–02
Until my heart is pure 316–02
Until my very heart o'erflow 426–04
Until we know by heart 358–03
We come, with all our heart and mind 353–01
We find your loving heart, O God 515–01
When my heart is almost breaking 363–02
Who makes the woeful heart to sing 306–02
Whose heart is true again 184–01
With heart and hands and voices 555–01
With heart and life and voice 089–03
With heart and mind, with strength
   and will 162–03
With heart, and soul, and voice 028–01
With heart and soul and voice 491–01
With hopeful heart through all
   thy ways 282–01
With ready heart and willing 277–02
With the cleansing of my heart 336–01
Within each clouded heart 278–04
Within my heart appear 313–01
Yet is this heart by its
   old foe tormented 342–02
Yet what I can I give him:
   give my heart 036–04
Your heart may fill with grace 349–06
Your heart will find true peace 188–02

**HEARTS**

All hearts are knit in holy love 295–04
And faithful hearts are raised on high 075–05
And hearts are brave again, and arms
   are strong 526–05
And in our hearts believing 517–02
And let us all our hearts prepare 010–02
And lift to God our grateful hearts 444–01
And our hearts confess him King
   of glory now 148–04
And to our inward hearts convey 474–02
Come, Spirit, come, our hearts control 335–03
Comes in our hearts to dwell 521–04
Dismissing selfish hearts 600–03
Do all our inmost hearts possess 121–02
Give them hearts for love alone 525–02
Have we hearts to love 348–04
Hearts unfold like flowers before thee 464–01
In Christ shall true hearts everywhere 439–02
In Christ shall true hearts everywhere 440–02
In our hearts and lives abound 538–02
In our hearts keep watch and ward 508–04
In our hearts keep watch and ward 509–04
In these cold hearts of ours 126–01
In whom all hearts find rest 412–02

**HEARTS** (cont.)

| | |
|---|---|
| Lest, our hearts drunk with the wine of the world | 563–03 |
| Let all our hearts open up to the Lord God | 484–01 |
| Let loving hearts enthrone him | 053–03 |
| Let not our slothful hearts refuse | 068–03 |
| Let our hearts and souls be stirred | 454–01 |
| Let your hearts be true and humble | 003–03 |
| Make our hearts an altar pyre | 131–03 |
| Make our hearts your habitation | 317–02 |
| Nor cause their hearts to fear | 184–03 |
| Our hearts be pure from evil | 118–02 |
| Our hearts from envy find release | 450–01 |
| Our hearts in Christian love | 438–01 |
| Our hearts to bear the covenant sign | 500–02 |
| Our hearts with love redeem | 195–04 |
| Our humble, thankful hearts | 560–03 |
| Set our hearts at liberty | 376–02 |
| Shall our hearts forget his promise | 144–02 |
| Take our hearts, of Love's own making | 544–01 |
| Take thou our hearts, O Christ | 392–02 |
| That make our hearts rejoice | 291–02 |
| Till their hearts be satisfied | 525–03 |
| To God your hearts and voices raise | 116–05 |
| To you with grateful hearts ourselves we give | 375–03 |
| We bring our hearts before your cross | 007–04 |
| We have hearts to love | 348–04 |
| While aching hearts in every land | 035–03 |
| Who with their hearts still seek you, Lord | 233–02 |
| With ever joyful hearts | 555–02 |
| With grateful hearts our faith professing | 497–01 |
| With grateful hearts rejoice | 214–02 |
| With grateful hearts the past we own | 265–02 |
| With hearts and hands uplifted | 015–03 |
| With hearts renewed, in all our work | 195–07 |
| Yet in our hearts we would confess | 380–02 |
| Yet our hearts are one in God | 465–02 |
| Your Spirit place within our hearts | 195–05 |

**HEAT**

| | |
|---|---|
| From the burning of the noontide heat | 092–01 |

**HEAVEN**

| | |
|---|---|
| Abba, as in highest heaven | 425–refrain |
| All in heaven above adore you | 460–01 |
| And Christ, our Lord, by heaven adored | 308–04 |
| And heaven and nature sing | 040–01 |
| And I came down from heaven and I danced on the earth | 302–01 |

| | |
|---|---|
| Are more felt than up in heaven | 298–01 |
| Bring us to heaven, where thy saints united | 459–02 |
| Christ by highest heaven adored | 031–02 |
| Come from heaven and stir our hearts | 127–01 |
| Come to us from heaven above | 355–01 |
| From heaven above to earth I come | 054–01 |
| From heaven he came and sought her | 442–01 |
| Glistening heaven sends forth great light | 065–01 |
| He comes from heaven above | 013–02 |
| Heaven and earth are embracing | 296–03 |
| Heaven and earth are full of thy glory | 580–00 |
| Heaven and earth are full of your glory | 568–00 |
| Heaven and earth are full of your glory | 581–00 |
| Heaven and earth, awake and sing | 256–01 |
| Heaven and earth shall flee away | 036–02 |
| Heaven and earth with loud hosanna | 154–04 |
| Him whom heaven and earth adore | 063–02 |
| Is our Lord in heaven above | 049–04 |
| Let heaven rejoice, let earth be glad | 230–01 |
| Like those in heaven, shall call you Lord | 004–03 |
| Living Bread come down from heaven | 512–03 |
| O Spirit, sent from heaven | 128–04 |
| Our Father in heaven | 571–00 |
| Our Father, Lord of heaven and earth | 590–01 |
| Our Father, which art in heaven | 589–01 |
| Our God, heaven cannot hold him | 036–02 |
| Sunlit from heaven | 469–02 |
| That hath made heaven and earth of nought | 056–06 |
| The angel Gabriel from heaven came | 016–01 |
| The God of heaven thunders | 180–01 |
| The Lord who heaven and earth has made | 242–02 |
| The Spirit sent from heaven | 470–02 |
| There a heaven on earth must be | 489–02 |
| Till glorious from thy heaven above | 408–06 |
| Till in heaven we take our place | 376–04 |
| To raise us up to heaven | 602–02 |
| To read in heaven the Lord's command | 068–02 |
| Way of life, to heaven lead it | 493–04 |
| Who heaven and earth has made | 234–01 |
| Who made heaven and earth | 254–06 |
| Whom heaven and earth adore | 555–03 |

**HEAVENS**

| | |
|---|---|
| Behold throughout the heavens | 029–01 |
| For as the heavens are high above the earth | 222–11 |
| For the Lord made the heavens | 217–04 |

Hear through the heavens the sound
   of the name 147–02
In the heavens with radiant signs 163–01
Lamb of God, the heavens adore you 017–03
Let all the heavens hear how
   our hearts rejoice 484–01
Let the heavens be glad,
   let the earth rejoice 217–05
Now let the heavens be joyful 118–03
Stretching out the heavens
   like tent cloth 224–01
The heavens above declare
   God's praise 166–01
The heavens and earth, by right divine 209–03
The heavens are not too high 468–01
The heavens declare 557–02
The heavens shall join in glad accord 209–02
The heavens shout your handiwork 162–02
The highest heavens in which
   God reigns 230–04
The shining heavens the Lord support 216–03

**HEAVINESS**
Of heaviness, why so downcast 189–04

**HEED**
As we heed Christ's ageless call 422–03
Give ye heed to what we say 028–01
If you take good heed
   to the angel's words 050–02
They know and heed his voice 521–01
We hear, and henceforth heed,
   thy sovereign call 392–04
When once we heed your call 419–01
Who heed the call to service 552–01

**HEEDED**
All I require is heeded 174–01

**HEIGHT**
From the height which knows
   no measure 317–01
Height and depth beyond description 136–01
In its height and depth and greatness 427–03

**HEIGHTS**
Heights and depths of life did share 331–03
O ye heights of heaven adore him 309–02
The heights and depths of earth 215–02

**HEIR**
Heir of salvation, purchase of God 341–01

**HEIRS**
Heirs of salvation trusting the promise 492–01

**HELD**
I am known and held and blest 323–04

**HELL**
And still are with me if in hell I lie 248–02

**HELP (N)**
A very present help in trouble 193–01
All my help from thee I bring 303–02
An ever present help and stay 483–03
Ever-present help in need 137–01
God, our help and constant refuge 192–01
Happy are those whose help is
   the God of Jacob 254–05
Help can be found 373–03
Help of the helpless, O abide with me 543–01
Hither by thy help I'm come 356–02
Holy Zion's help forever 416–01
Holy Zion's help forever 417–01
In the help we give our neighbor 553–02
Looking for help all around 373–03
May our Lord send help from the high
   and holy place 169–01
My help and my God 190–05
My help is from the Lord alone 234–01
My help, my life, my tower,
   my battle sword 183–03
Our ever-present help 274–04
Our God, our help in ages past 210–01
Our only help is in God's holy name 236–03
Secure and safe with God's sure help 191–04
That one will be your help and shield 227–03
The help of God to whom you pray 168–03
The Lord shall send all help and grace 239–03
Unless our help shall come from you 431–03
We have no help but yours,
   nor do we need 520–02

**HELP (V)**
And help all those who call on you 251–03
And help us see your light 130–03
And help us, till all sense of time is lost 532–05
But when we help them, or when we
   feed them 400–04
Called to portray you, help us to live 436–02
Cannot help us when we pray 290–03
God will help it when the morning
   dawns 193–05
Help me in my affliction 183–02

**HELP (V)** (cont.)

| | |
|---|---|
| Help me live the best I can | 350–01 |
| Help me the slow of heart to move | 357–02 |
| Help me to keep in vision still | 351–02 |
| Help me to sing God's praises high | 475–04 |
| Help me to tear it from thy throne | 396–03 |
| Help me to tear it from thy throne | 397–03 |
| Help our feeble lips to praise you | 129–03 |
| Help then, O Lord, our unbelief | 399–03 |
| Help us accept each other | 358–01 |
| Help us bear each other's burdens | 343–03 |
| Help us by your Spirit's pleading | 454–03 |
| Help us face each crucial hour | 129–01 |
| Help us form the church eternal | 132–02 |
| Help us in our varied callings | 523–04 |
| Help us live in peace as true members of your body | 346–03 |
| Help us love as sister, brother | 136–02 |
| Help us, O Lord; descend and bring | 230–02 |
| Help us renew the face of the earth | 266–01 |
| Help us thy name to sing | 139–01 |
| Help us to bear the cross | 277–03 |
| Help us to give ourselves each day | 414–03 |
| Help us to know him risen from the dead | 086–04 |
| Help us to praise | 139–01 |
| Help us to share, consider, save, and store | 266–05 |
| Help us to shed abroad thy deathless love | 392–02 |
| Help us to spread thy gracious reign | 412–02 |
| Help us to treasure all that will remind us | 529–02 |
| Help us witness to your purpose | 429–01 |
| Help us work your purpose out | 461–04 |
| Lord God, help your holy band | 246–03 |
| Lord, help keep our hearts and minds | 346–02 |
| Lord, help us to be wise in guiding | 497–02 |
| So, help me in my unbelief | 522–04 |
| You help the needy in distress | 226–02 |

**HELPER**

| | |
|---|---|
| Heaven-sent Helper of Bethlehem | 055–05 |
| My helper in the past | 198–05 |
| Our helper he amid the flood | 260–01 |

**HELPERS**

| | |
|---|---|
| When other helpers fail and comforts flee | 543–01 |

**HELPLESSNESS**

| | |
|---|---|
| From tender childhood's helplessness | 408–03 |

**HELPS**

| | |
|---|---|
| God helps the stranger in distress | 253–03 |

**HEN**

| | |
|---|---|
| As the hen tends her young, so for them | 547–02 |
| Mother hen prepares for night's rest | 547–01 |

**HERALD**

| | |
|---|---|
| Before him goes the herald | 602–02 |
| The herald of Messiah's name | 087–03 |

**HERESIES**

| | |
|---|---|
| By heresies distressed | 442–03 |

**HERO**

| | |
|---|---|
| And like a hero runs its course | 166–03 |

**HEROES**

| | |
|---|---|
| O beautiful for heroes proved | 564–03 |

**HID**

| | |
|---|---|
| And hid no sin from you | 184–02 |

**HIDE**

| | |
|---|---|
| And I shall hide within the veil of night | 248–04 |
| Hide me, O my Savior, hide | 303–01 |
| In you, O Lord, I hide me | 184–03 |

**HIGH**

| | |
|---|---|
| Dayspring from on high, be near | 462–01 |
| Dayspring from on high, be near | 463–01 |
| For us he went on high to reign | 083–04 |
| Laughing and enthroned on high | 159–02 |
| Singing evermore on high | 112–01 |

**HIGHEST**

| | |
|---|---|
| Hosanna in the highest | 581–00 |
| To God in the highest, hosanna and praise | 554–02 |

**HIGHWAYS**

| | |
|---|---|
| Afoot on dusty highways | 360–03 |

**HILL**

| | |
|---|---|
| And on Zion's holy hill | 159–02 |
| From hill to valley flow | 205–02 |
| Hill and vale, and tree and flower | 473–02 |
| Let every hill and valley | 013–01 |
| On hill and wood and field | 292–01 |
| On Zion's holy hill | 176–02 |
| Or on your holy hill | 164–01 |
| Than what lies past Calvary's hill | 073–03 |

## HILLS

| | |
|---|---|
| All the hills were ringing | 027–02 |
| And joyful are the hills | 200–03 |
| And the hills bow down in greeting | 003–02 |
| And the hills, in righteousness | 204–03 |
| Before the hills in order stood | 210–02 |
| Hills and valleys, field and woodlands | 033–01 |
| I to the hills will lift my eyes | 234–01 |
| Over the hills and everywhere | 029–refrain |
| The hills and the mountains | 554–02 |
| Though hills amid the seas be cast | 191–02 |

## HINDRANCES

| | |
|---|---|
| In hindrances more sure | 419–03 |

## HINTS

| | |
|---|---|
| Hints of the music vast | 278–03 |

## HOARD

| | |
|---|---|
| Yet we hoard as private treasure | 429–04 |

## HOIST

| | |
|---|---|
| Hoist me up upon your shoulder | 323–03 |

## HOLD (N)

| | |
|---|---|
| Lay hold on life, and it shall be | 307–01 |
| Where tyrants' hold is tightened | 443–03 |

## HOLD (V)

| | |
|---|---|
| Hold in mind eternity | 429–05 |
| Hold me with thy powerful hand | 281–01 |
| Hold my hand lest I fall | 404–02 |
| Hold my hand while I run this race | 354–02 |
| Hold my life within your own | 323–02 |
| Hold thou thy cross before my closing eyes | 543–05 |
| Hold us, when death appears | 279–05 |
| Hold us, who wait before thee | 527–refrain |
| Hold you silent and alone | 099–01 |
| I will hold your people in my heart | 525–refrain |
| Like them shall be all those who hold | 227–02 |
| On all we hold most dear | 534–03 |
| You hold me that I shall not fall | 284–01 |

## HOLDS

| | |
|---|---|
| And holds us safe in every strife | 226–02 |
| Still holds the freshness of thy grace | 408–04 |
| To one who holds us always dear | 282–02 |

## HOLINESS

| | |
|---|---|
| And holiness shall whisper | 447–02 |
| And holiness shall whisper | 448–02 |
| Holiness shall live with you | 213–04 |
| In holiness of heart | 412–04 |
| Majestic in your holiness | 162–05 |
| Spirit of holiness | 139–02 |

## HOMAGE

| | |
|---|---|
| Here our humblest homage pay we | 154–02 |
| Our full homage to demand | 005–01 |

## HOME

| | |
|---|---|
| A home for us and ages yet unborn | 266–05 |
| A home where trust and care | 534–02 |
| A home within the wilderness | 092–01 |
| And home, rejoicing, brought me | 171–03 |
| And our eternal home | 210–01 |
| And take me home | 467–04 |
| Each home with Christian graces fill | 497–03 |
| For their eternal home | 155–03 |
| From a distant home the Savior we come seeking | 064–01 |
| Our heart's true home when all our years have sped | 275–03 |
| Ours to use for home and kindred | 422–03 |
| Please come home, please come back home | 381–03 |
| Safely to arrive at home | 356–02 |
| To bless your home with love | 239–03 |
| To thy final harvest home | 551–04 |
| To thy home above | 122–03 |
| Until you bring me home | 351–04 |
| Virgin's Son, make here your home | 014–01 |
| Where you with us will make your home | 431–01 |

## HOMELESS

| | |
|---|---|
| Giving to the homeless a home | 225–04 |
| The homeless crouch in rain and snow | 431–02 |
| Where the homeless find a home | 433–05 |

## HOMES

| | |
|---|---|
| When our homes are filled with goodness in abundance | 407–04 |

## HONESTY

| | |
|---|---|
| Here in honesty of preaching | 461–02 |

## HONEYCOMB

| | |
|---|---|
| And sweeter than the honeycomb | 167–02 |

## HONOR (N)

| | |
|---|---|
| All honor and blessing with angels above | 477–04 |
| And honor, blessing, and glory are his | 594–02 |
| Cloaked with honor, grand and glorious | 224–01 |

**HONOR (N)** (cont.)

| | |
|---|---|
| Crowned with honor in thy sight | 163–04 |
| Honor, glory, and dominion | 309–03 |
| Honor, glory, praise, thanksgiving | 107–02 |
| In God alone my honor rests | 197–02 |
| Of honor and the sword | 291–02 |
| The honor of your name | 233–04 |
| Withhold the honor due | 011–03 |

**HONOR (V)**

| | |
|---|---|
| But honor those who fear the Lord | 164–02 |
| Honor the Lord with wild acclaim | 218–03 |

**HONORS (N)**

| | |
|---|---|
| Honors peculiar to our King | 423–05 |
| The honors of thy name | 466–04 |

**HONORS (V)**

| | |
|---|---|
| Who honors God above | 239–03 |

**HOOK**

| | |
|---|---|
| God of the pruning hook | 272–05 |

**HOPE (N)**

| | |
|---|---|
| Alive with hope for all | 330–04 |
| And only hope since I was born | 168–04 |
| And to one hope she presses | 442–02 |
| Bright with hope is burning | 021–03 |
| Can we new hope in it find | 052–02 |
| Eternal hope, lift up my eyes | 340–01 |
| From hope to hope, from strength to strength | 444–04 |
| Give us hope and hear our cry | 192–04 |
| Great hope we find within your law | 233–03 |
| He then is all my hope and stay | 379–03 |
| Hope and confidence and peace | 343–04 |
| Hope and faith and love rise glorious | 545–04 |
| Hope and health, good will and comfort | 427–04 |
| Hope in believing | 529–01 |
| Hope in God; for I shall again praise him | 190–05 |
| Hope of all the earth thou art | 001–02 |
| Hope of all the earth thou art | 002–01 |
| Hope of new tomorrows | 300–02 |
| Hope of the world | 360–01 |
| Hope of the world, Mary's Child | 030–04 |
| Hope to spring up from the ground | 109–03 |
| In cheerful hope, with heart content | 282–02 |
| In hope that sends a shining ray | 357–04 |
| Let your great Spirit give me hope | 522–03 |
| May the God of hope go with us every day | 432–00 |

| | |
|---|---|
| My hope is built on nothing less | 379–01 |
| My hope, my heart's delight | 011–01 |
| New hope for changing days | 330–03 |
| O hope of every contrite heart | 310–03 |
| Of patient hope, and quiet, brave endurance | 533–02 |
| On thee alone my hope relies | 250–01 |
| One same hope we will sing together as we walk along | 518–04 |
| Or hope had us forsaken | 082–refrain |
| Our hope and expectation | 015–03 |
| Our hope for years to come | 210–01 |
| Our hope is in no other save in thee | 457–05 |
| The hope and peace which from thy presence flow | 519–03 |
| The hope of peace shall be fulfilled | 450–02 |
| When hope and courage falter | 289–03 |
| Who my own hope has proved | 197–01 |
| Whose hope is in the Lord their God | 254–05 |
| Yet seeking hope for humankind | 353–02 |
| You, the hope of all the nations | 192–04 |
| Youth's hope is dimmed by ignorance | 431–02 |

**HOPE (V)**

| | |
|---|---|
| And I hope by thy good pleasure | 356–02 |
| Hope and be undismayed | 286–01 |
| When they hope though even hope seems hopelessness | 407–02 |

**HOPES**

| | |
|---|---|
| Hopes deceive, and fears annoy | 084–02 |
| How happy they whose hopes rely | 253–02 |
| The hopes and fears of all the years | 043–01 |
| The hopes and fears of all the years | 044–01 |
| Through all our hopes and prayers and dreams | 450–01 |
| Who by our own false hopes and aims are spent | 360–01 |

**HORIZON**

| | |
|---|---|
| As each far horizon beckons | 268–03 |

**HORNS**

| | |
|---|---|
| Up the horns of the altar | 232–27 |

**HORROR**

| | |
|---|---|
| But far greater is war's horror | 401–02 |

**HOSANNAS**

| | |
|---|---|
| Hosannas languish on our tongues | 126–02 |

## HOST

| | |
|---|---|
| And all the twinkling, starry host | 306–03 |
| And all their host by the breath of his mouth | 185–06 |
| And the angel host all shouted | 486–01 |
| Praise God above, ye heavenly host | 542–04 |
| Praise God above, ye heavenly host | 593–00 |
| Praise him above, ye heavenly host | 592–00 |
| Praised by all the heavenly host | 137–01 |
| With the angelic host proclaim | 031–01 |

## HOSTS

| | |
|---|---|
| Angel hosts, his praises sing | 309–02 |
| Heavenly hosts sing: "Alleluia" | 060–02 |
| Lo! the hosts of evil round us | 420–02 |
| Praise God, all ye hosts above | 256–01 |
| Though hosts encamp around me | 179–02 |
| While angel hosts from heaven come winging | 047–02 |

## HOUR

| | |
|---|---|
| And hour by hour fresh lips are making | 546–04 |
| Come in this most solemn hour | 524–02 |
| Even the hour when wings are frozen | 012–03 |
| For the facing of this hour | 420–01 |
| In this glad hour | 139–03 |
| Or our most triumphant hour | 268–02 |
| The hour I first believed | 280–02 |
| This is the hour of banquet and of song | 520–03 |
| To match our present hour | 452–01 |
| Who comes in this accepted hour | 230–03 |

## HOURS

| | |
|---|---|
| Look now! for glad and golden hours | 038–03 |
| Silent through those three dread hours | 099–02 |
| The hours are all God's own | 230–01 |

## HOUSE

| | |
|---|---|
| And for the house of God, the Lord | 235–05 |
| And in God's house forevermore | 170–05 |
| And make this house your home | 325–01 |
| God from the house of David | 602–02 |
| How to God's house I led the throng | 189–03 |
| In David's house, who reigned as king | 601–01 |
| In the house of the Lord will I live | 173–04 |
| In the house there is bread | 300–03 |
| Make your house fair as you are able | 012–01 |
| O may your house be my abode | 172–03 |
| That in this house have called upon thy name | 539–02 |
| The house of Israel | 219–02 |
| The house of thine abode | 441–01 |
| Unless the Lord the house shall build | 238–01 |
| Within God's house, the house of prayer | 228–06 |
| Within their house no foes are feared | 238–04 |
| Within thy house forever | 171–06 |

## HOUSEHOLD

| | |
|---|---|
| Household of the one true God | 132–04 |

## HUMANKIND

| | |
|---|---|
| As though all humankind around one table stood | 515–03 |
| Close-binding humankind | 439–02 |
| Close-binding humankind | 440–02 |
| To you and humankind | 058–02 |
| To you and humankind | 059–02 |

## HUMANITY

| | |
|---|---|
| All humanity stands in awe of God | 194–01 |
| And clothed in Christ's humanity | 421–03 |
| Humanity reduced to little worth | 385–02 |
| In his humanity we find our own | 385–03 |
| O God, you give humanity its name | 532–01 |

## HUMBLE

| | |
|---|---|
| And humble us, and call us friends | 353–04 |

## HUMBLENESS

| | |
|---|---|
| In humbleness O may we walk | 418–03 |

## HUNDREDS

| | |
|---|---|
| There are hundreds of thousands still | 364–03 |

## HUNG

| | |
|---|---|
| He hung there in our place | 103–02 |
| Hung our harps upon the willow | 246–01 |
| Of him who hung upon the tree | 308–04 |

## HUNGER (N)

| | |
|---|---|
| As hunger stretches out its hand | 431–02 |

## HUNGER (V)

| | |
|---|---|
| Who hunger for acceptance | 358–04 |

## HUNGRY

| | |
|---|---|
| For the hungry and despairing | 553–02 |
| God of the hungry | 272–04 |
| Still the hungry cry for bread | 427–02 |
| To feed the hungry, quench their thirst | 434–01 |
| To go to feed the hungry | 552–01 |

## HUNTERS

| | |
|---|---|
| And wondering hunters heard the hymn | 061–01 |

## HURT (N)

| | |
|---|---|
| Where there is hurt, may we forgive | 374–01 |

## HURT (V)

| | |
|---|---|
| Where no one shall hurt or destroy | 337–02 |

## HYMN

| | |
|---|---|
| A hymn of glory let us sing | 141–01 |
| Hark, the glad celestial hymn | 460–02 |
| Hymn and chant and high thanksgiving | 309–03 |
| Let our vesper hymn be blending | 545–01 |
| Of thine eternal hymn | 278–03 |
| Our common hymn outpouring | 549–02 |
| This our hymn of grateful praise | 473–refrain |

## HYMNS

| | |
|---|---|
| As hymns bring gladness to our days | 328–02 |
| Her hymns of love and praise | 441–04 |
| Hymns of praise then let us sing | 123–02 |
| Hymns of triumph sing | 122–02 |
| In evening hymns we lift our voices | 550–02 |
| New hymns throughout the world shall ring | 141–01 |
| O Jesus Christ, may grateful hymns be rising | 424–01 |
| To thee our morning hymns ascended | 546–01 |
| With hymns and psalms of praise | 490–01 |
| With hymns of victory | 118–01 |

# I

## IDOL

| | |
|---|---|
| The dearest idol I have known | 396–03 |
| The dearest idol I have known | 397–03 |
| Whate'er that idol be | 396–03 |
| Whate'er that idol be | 397–03 |

## IDOLS

| | |
|---|---|
| Idols are mere vanity | 290–03 |
| With their idols and lies | 319–02 |

## IGNORANCE

| | |
|---|---|
| Of ignorance and fear | 412–03 |

## ILL

| | |
|---|---|
| And keep them safe in childhood's ill | 497–03 |

## ILLS

| | |
|---|---|
| Ills have no weight, and tears no bitterness | 543–04 |
| Of mortal ills prevailing | 260–01 |

## ILLUMINE

| | |
|---|---|
| Illumine me, Spirit divine | 324–refrain |
| Illumine you with peace and grace | 242–02 |

## ILLUSIONS

| | |
|---|---|
| When weary with illusions | 278–01 |

## IMAGE

| | |
|---|---|
| In God's image, woman, man | 494–01 |
| Thine image to our hearts is born | 474–04 |
| We, created in your image | 285–01 |
| O image of the light sublime | 548–01 |
| Your full image to proclaim | 523–04 |
| Your image we see in simple and wise | 311–01 |

## IMMORTALITY

| | |
|---|---|
| Or immortality endures | 253–01 |

## IMPART

| | |
|---|---|
| Glorious Lord, yourself impart | 454–03 |

## IMPARTS

| | |
|---|---|
| So God imparts to human hearts | 043–03 |
| So God imparts to human hearts | 044–03 |

## IMPELS

| | |
|---|---|
| Impels us on to seek your face | 068–03 |

## IMPLANTED

| | |
|---|---|
| Implanted in the soul | 488–03 |

## IMPRISON

| | |
|---|---|
| Imprison me within thine arms | 378–02 |

**IMPULSE**
At the impulse of thy love          391–02

**IMPUTE**
Will not impute their sin           184–01

**INCARNATION**
For me, dear Jesus, was your
    incarnation                     093–03

**INCENSE**
Incense owns a Deity nigh           066–03
So bring him incense, gold,
    and myrrh                       053–03

**INCLINE**
Incline to me a gracious ear        249–01

**INCREASE**
Increase our faith and love
    that we may know                519–03

**INDIFFERENCE**
Indifference walks unheeding by     431–02

**INFANCY**
With us from infancy                279–01

**INFANT**
As you were once an infant here     496–00
Holy Infant, so tender and mild     060–01
Holy the Infant and holy
    the mother                      062–refrain
Infant holy, Infant lowly           037–01

**INFIRMITY**
Thou knowest our infirmity          079–02

**INHABITANTS**
Let all the inhabitants of the world
    stand in awe of him             185–08

**INHERIT**
Let us all in thee inherit          376–02

**INHERITANCE**
Our inheritance comes from
    God the Lord                    194–01
Thou mine inheritance, now
    and always                      339–02

**INJUSTICE**
Injustice stalks our earth          437–01

**INNOCENTS**
And innocents the price must pay    035–03
Where innocents are frightened      443–03

**INSIGHT**
With insight and with clarity       332–02

**INSPIRE**
Inspire our hearts grown cold
    with fear                       124–03
Inspire our worship, grant the glad
    surprising                      424–01
Inspire thy heralds of good news    412–05
Inspire us from above               278–04
Inspire us gratefully to sing       152–03
Inspire your church with love
    and power                       437–03
Which inspire your heavenly song    023–02

**INSPIRED**
Inspired each person there          128–01
While inspired by your own Spirit   486–03

**INSPIRER**
Inspirer of all thought             274–02

**INSPIRES**
For it is God who inspires and
    uplifts us                      484–02

**INSTRUCT**
Instruct, inspire, unite            130–03

**INSTRUCTION**
Instruction, guidance, holy law     255–05

**INSTRUMENT**
Let every instrument and voice      218–02
Let every instrument be tuned
    for praise                      264–04
Lord, let me be your instrument     350–01

**INSTRUMENTS**
And instruments of praise employ    328–04
Instruments of peace, committed     401–02
Our instruments can probe
    and sound                       287–02

**INSULT**
In every insult, rift, and war     108–04

**INTEGRITY**
Prove its integrity     390–05
With renewed integrity     429–01

**INTELLECT**
Take my intellect, and use     391–04

**INTERCESSOR**
Intercessor, friend of sinners     144–03

**INTERPOSED**
Interposed his precious blood     356–02

**INTERPRETER**
You are your own interpreter     270–04

**INVITATION**
We have come at your own invitation     516–01

**IRON**
Strong as iron smashing clay     159–03

**IRRIGATE**
Come irrigate dry souls     237–03

**ISLES**
Earth's scattered isles and
    contoured hills     152–01

# J

**JEERED**
Those who jeered and mocked
    and sold you     006–02

**JOIN**
And join in the hymn of all creation     594–03
Come, Christians, join to sing     150–01
Come join, O church, in song     430–01
Join hands, disciples of the faith     439–03
Join hands, disciples of the faith     440–03
Join me in glad adoration     482–01
Join me to make God's glory known     475–03
Join the saints and angels praising     074–01
Join the triumph of the skies     031–01
Join to sing the glad refrain     006–01
Join with all nature in manifold witness     276–02
Join with children's songs of praise     256–02
O come, then, let us join
    the heavenly host     057–04
We join the heavenly company     156–03
We join to thank you for the life
    remembered     529–01
We'll join the everlasting song     142–04
We'll join the everlasting song     143–04
Whom thou forevermore dost join in one     533–01

**JOINED**
Ever joined to thee in love
    that cannot falter     069–02

**JOURNEY**
All along the pilgrim journey     363–01
In the church's pilgrim journey     129–02
We journey in its light     447–03
We journey in its light     448–03
We journey on, believing     470–03

**JOURNEYS**
Does its successive journeys run     423–01

**JOY (N)**
An Easter of unending joy     081–04
And give us joy to see your face     087–04
And joy in life always     239–01
And thus with joy we meet our Lord     507–04
As we with joy your throne surround     017–03
As with joy they hailed its light     063–01
Beyond my highest joy     441–04
For in you my joy is found     224–04
For joy cries out to you     201–02
For joy I am singing     557–03
For the joy of ear and eye     473–03
For the joy of human love     473–04
Give me again the joy of your help     196–07
I come with joy to meet the Lord     507–01
In Christ our joy shall be made
    complete     094–03
Into joy and laughter lead     498–02
Into joy from sadness     114–01

| | |
|---|---|
| Into joy from sadness | 115–01 |
| I've got joy like a fountain | 368–02 |
| Jesus, thou joy of loving hearts | 510–01 |
| Jesus, thou joy of loving hearts | 511–01 |
| Jesus, our only joy be thou | 310–05 |
| Joy and peace shall never end | 104–02 |
| Joy of every longing heart | 001–02 |
| Joy of every longing heart | 002–01 |
| Joy to the world! the Lord is come | 040–01 |
| Joy to the world! the Savior reigns | 040–02 |
| Joy without ending | 459–02 |
| Joy, your wondrous gift bestowing | 506–02 |
| Lord, show us your joy | 160–06 |
| My joy, my treasure, and my crown | 366–02 |
| Now with joy is ringing | 021–01 |
| O joy of all the meek | 310–03 |
| O joy that seekest me through pain | 384–03 |
| Of joy a boundless store | 165–05 |
| Oh! what joy to be with Christ Jesus | 547–02 |
| Oh! what joy to feel her warm heart beat | 547–01 |
| Oh! what joy to pray close together | 547–03 |
| Once earthly joy I craved | 359–02 |
| Our joy that hath no end | 118–03 |
| Our joy when Christ appears | 552–02 |
| Shall be the joy of all the earth | 054–02 |
| So may we with holy joy | 063–03 |
| The joy of all below | 149–03 |
| The joy of all who dwell above | 149–03 |
| The joy of Israel | 603–02 |
| The joy we had, the brightness of your sun | 342–04 |
| The lasting joy of Christian love | 534–01 |
| The lasting joy of such a love | 534–02 |
| Their joy the joy of heaven | 149–04 |
| There with joy your praises render | 506–01 |
| Thy joy and crown eternally | 307–01 |
| Till with joy the heaven rang | 486–01 |
| To cope in joy and stress | 552–04 |
| To sing in joy, to cry in grief | 515–02 |
| Unto joy and sorrow grown | 551–02 |
| Unto Zion we come with joy | 018–06 |
| What joy shall fill my heart | 467–04 |
| When our joy fills up our cup to overflowing | 407–03 |
| With heartfelt joy our Maker's praise | 475–02 |
| With joy and praise to worship there | 235–02 |
| With joy and strength for duty | 278–04 |
| With joy I heard my friends exclaim | 235–01 |
| With joy we will sing forth your praise | 157–01 |
| With joy, with justice, love, and praise | 108–05 |

| | |
|---|---|
| Yet joy comes with the morning sun | 181–01 |
| You are a present joy, O Lord | 141–02 |
| You are our joy, and you our rest | 265–03 |

**JOY (V)**

| | |
|---|---|
| I joy to call thee mine | 098–01 |
| Who joy in God with perfect love | 075–04 |

**JOYS**

| | |
|---|---|
| And from worldly joys abstain | 077–02 |
| Earth's joys grow dim, its glories pass away | 543–02 |
| Here all our joys and sorrows share | 499–03 |
| Joys that through all time abide | 084–04 |
| With our neighbors' joys and cries | 512–04 |

**JUDGE (N)**

| | |
|---|---|
| Come today, our judge, our glory | 413–04 |
| For Christ, the Judge, shall come | 155–03 |

**JUDGE (V)**

| | |
|---|---|
| For God will judge with righteousness | 219–06 |
| For you judge the peoples with equity | 202–04 |
| May he judge your people with righteousness | 204–02 |

**JUDGED**

| | |
|---|---|
| While we are judged unequal by the state | 385–02 |

**JUDGMENT**

| | |
|---|---|
| And we for judgment there must stand | 133–02 |
| Come with your timeless judgment now | 452–01 |
| God's judgment passed on social ills | 152–02 |
| Have such kindly judgment given | 298–01 |
| That mortal judgment has on you descended | 093–01 |
| Your judgment, Lord, is right | 195–02 |

**JUDGMENTS**

| | |
|---|---|
| The judgments of the Lord are true | 167–02 |
| Thy judgments are a mighty deep | 186–01 |
| Your judgments in the earth | 452–05 |

**JUST**

| | |
|---|---|
| The just who do God's will | 176–02 |

**JUSTICE**

| | |
|---|---|
| And justice for all who are oppressed | 222–06 |
| And may thy justice still protect | 186–05 |
| Bring justice to our land | 452–03 |

## JUSTICE (cont.)

| | |
|---|---|
| Dispensing justice far and near | 600–03 |
| For justice and for peace | 291–03 |
| Has justice for its cornerstone | 209–02 |
| Justice shall flourish in God's time | 204–refrain |
| May justice be our aim | 418–03 |
| May the God of justice speed us on our way | 432–00 |
| Of your justice, grace, and mercy | 285–01 |
| Should you not justice know | 405–02 |
| The God of justice comes to save | 219–06 |
| Thy justice like mountains high soaring above | 263–02 |
| To work for equal justice | 552–01 |
| Where justice fused with mercy rules | 274–03 |
| With justice and with praise | 386–01 |

## JUSTIFIED

| | |
|---|---|
| That you may be justified when you give sentence | 196–03 |

# K

## KEEP

| | |
|---|---|
| Keep, O keep us, Savior dear | 077–05 |
| No longer keep us closed and life-denying | 105–02 |
| Still keep us calm and fearless | 277–03 |

## KEEPER

| | |
|---|---|
| Your faithful keeper is the Lord | 234–03 |

## KEYS

| | |
|---|---|
| The keys of death and hell | 155–02 |

## KIN

| | |
|---|---|
| Are surely kin to me | 439–03 |
| Are surely kin to me | 440–03 |
| Your kin in Christ commit you now | 444–03 |

## KINDLE

| | |
|---|---|
| And kindle it, your holy flame bestowing | 313–01 |
| And that shall kindle ours | 126–04 |
| Kindle a flame of sacred love | 126–01 |
| Kindle every high desire | 321–02 |
| Kindle our sinking hearts to flame | 351–03 |
| Kindle them with your own fire | 131–03 |
| O kindle, Lord most holy | 011–01 |

## KINDNESS

| | |
|---|---|
| And kindness dwell in human hearts | 412–02 |
| And kindness ours to share | 418–03 |
| Let me thy kindness know | 250–01 |
| Such great kindness! Such great mercy | 355–01 |
| There's a kindness in God's justice | 298–01 |
| Your kindness from of old has stood | 243–01 |

## KINDRED

| | |
|---|---|
| Let every kindred, every tribe | 142–03 |
| Let every kindred, every tribe | 143–03 |

## KINGDOM

| | |
|---|---|
| And my kingdom thus inherit | 493–02 |
| Boundless shall your kingdom be | 014–03 |
| Breaking the kingdom of death | 120–refrain |
| Eternal is your kingdom, Lord | 252–03 |
| For the kingdom, the power | 571–00 |
| For thine is the kingdom | 589–05 |
| God's kingdom cannot fail | 155–02 |
| God's kingdom shall endure | 259–02 |
| His heavenly kingdom brings | 443–04 |
| His kingdom is forever | 260–04 |
| His kingdom is glorious, he rules over all | 477–01 |
| His kingdom stretch from shore to shore | 423–01 |
| How God's earthly kingdom shall come | 337–01 |
| Let your kingdom come, O Lord | 508–04 |
| Let your kingdom come, O Lord | 509–04 |
| Lord, in your kingdom whatever our place | 516–02 |
| Now thy gracious kingdom bring | 001–03 |
| Now thy gracious kingdom bring | 002–02 |
| Ordaining, maintaining his kingdom divine | 559–02 |
| Sent you the kingdom to proclaim | 070–02 |
| Since the kingdom now is here | 003–02 |
| The heavenly kingdom comes | 447–02 |
| The heavenly kingdom comes | 448–02 |
| Thy kingdom come | 589–01 |
| Thy kingdom stands, and grows forever | 546–05 |

To see your kingdom come                                351–04
To seek the kingdom of your peace                       007–03
Whose are the kingdom, the crown,
   and the throne                          147–01
Within the kingdom of God's might                       483–02
Your kingdom come                                       571–00
Your kingdom come                                       590–01
Your kingdom, power, glory know                         252–03

**KINGDOMS**

All kingdoms and nations shall yield
   to their sway                           257–04
Though the kingdoms of earth may fall   062–03
While kingdoms slept, the Lord
   came down                               034–01

**KINGS**

All kings on earth who hear
   your words                              247–03
May all kings fall down before him      204–11
May the kings of Sheba and Seba
   bring gifts                             204–10
May the kings of Tarshish and
   of the isles render him tribute          204–10
We three kings of Orient are                            066–01

**KISS**

Kiss God's feet in trembling awe                        159–04

**KNEE**

Every knee to you shall bow                             113–04
On bended knee                                          359–01
There to bend the knee before                           063–02

**KNEEL**

Come kneel before the radiant boy                       061–03
Kneel at the feet of our friends                        367–05
Kneel in awe and wonder                                 021–03
Lowly we kneel in prayer
   before thy throne                       533–01
Where anyone may kneel                                  390–01
Yea, let us kneel before the Lord                       214–05

**KNEELS**

Kneels at the feet of his friends                       367–01

**KNEES**

All knees must bend, all hearts
   must bow                                004–03
Let us praise God together on
   our knees                               513–03
Loving puts us on our knees                             367–04

**KNELT**

Where Jesus knelt to share with thee    345–03

**KNIT**

O knit my thankful heart to thee        366–01

**KNOCK**

Knock and the door shall be opened
   unto you                                333–02

**KNOCKING**

Somebody's knocking at your door   382–refrain

**KNOCKS**

Knocks like Jesus                                       382–01

**KNOW**

And I know it's the Spirit of the Lord   398–01
Be still, and know that I am God        193–10
For we know that deeper, richer         401–03
I know that I shall not be left         165–04
I know you will not leave me            284–02
Know that the Lord is God indeed        220–02
The Bible that we know                  330–04
To know you, my eternal God             340–03

**KNOWLEDGE**

All our knowledge, sense, and sight     454–02
How weak our knowledge of ourselves     380–03
Knowledge and truth                     458–04
Such knowledge is too wonderful
   for me                                  248–01

# L

**LABOR**
Come, labor on 415–01
To labor, love, and give 414–02

**LACK**
And if you lack for knowledge 394–02
I nothing lack if I am his 171–01

**LADY**
Most highly favored lady, Gloria 016–refrain

**LAKE**
Of lake and woods and hill 308–03

**LAKESHORE**
You have come up to the lakeshore 377–01

**LAMB**
Shepherd, take your lamb and feed it 493–04

**LAME**
And the lame will dance with gladness 018–03

**LAMP**
A lamp of purest gold 327–03
A lamp within my breast 011–01
One lone bright lamp lights the stall 065–02

**LAMPS**
And lamps are lit, and children nod 550–02
See that your lamps are burning 015–02
We see the lamps of night 549–02
Your lamps prepare and hasten there 017–01

**LAND (N)**
And every land is thine 412–05
And the dry land springs of water 018–04
But not to overtake the land 283–01
For everyone in every land 294–02
From the land of Jordan and of
   Hermon, [and] from Mount Mizar 190–06
Go down, Moses, way down in
   Egypt's land 334–refrain
In a strange and bitter land 246–03
In every land and nation 259–03
In every land begin the song 229–02
In this free land by thee our lot is cast 262–02
Land of the noble free 561–02
Land of the pilgrims' pride 561–01

Land where my fathers died 561–01
Long may our land be bright 561–04
Now, on land and sea descending 545–01
Sweet land of liberty 561–01
Through every land, in every tongue 229–01
To every land the strains belong 229–02
True to our God, true to our native land 563–03
When Israel was in Egypt's land 334–01
Within a weary land 092–01

**LAND (V)**
Land me safe on Canaan's side 281–03

**LANDS**
All lands, make melody 219–03
All lands will bow rejoicing 013–03
Far out from settled lands 330–01
In barren lands and dry 198–01
Scattered are the lands 465–02
To make all lands thine own 412–01

**LANGUAGE**
And gave to each a language
   and a name 385–01
To understand their language 128–02
What language shall I borrow 098–03

**LANTERN**
A lantern to our footsteps 327–01

**LAP**
On Mary's lap is sleeping 053–01

**LAPS**
That laps at every shore 471–05

**LASTS**
So it lasts without an end 223–04

**LAUD**
Haste, haste to bring him laud 053–refrain
In laud and jubilee and praise 116–05
Laud and honor to the Father 416–04
Laud and honor to the Father 417–04
Laud and honor to the Son 416–04
Laud and honor to the Son 417–04

**LAUGH**
All those who see me laugh and say 168–03

## LAUGHTER
Laughter and quick-dried tears 279–01

## LAW
And in the keeping of your law 167–03
Be my law, and I shall be 321–04
By law God enforces 544–02
Established is your law 488–02
God's law is perfect and gives life 167–01
God's law so hard and high 405–03
How blest the one who in God's law 158–02
Law and prophets sing before him 074–04
O thou from whose unfathomed law 292–03
The law and prophets there have place 075–03
The loving God who gave the law 087–02
Who never from your law depart 233–01
With a law and a land 319–02

## LAWS
Your laws its mighty energies fulfill 297–02

## LEAD
And I'll lead you all in the dance,
    said he 302–refrain
And I'll lead you all, wherever
    you may be 302–refrain
And lead me in the everlasting way 248–05
And lead the way 183–04
And lead us all our days 195–03
And lead us in those paths of life 325–02
And lead us not into temptation 589–04
Give to those who lead your people 523–01
God will forever lead 234–04
I will go, Lord, if you lead me 525–refrain
It will lead to the place where
    the Christ was born 050–01
Lead all people to your way 132–02
Lead me all my journey through 281–02
Lead me home 404–01
Lead me on, help me stand 404–01
Lead me on to the light 404–01
Lead on, O God of might 447–03
Lead on, O God of might 448–03
Lead on, O King eternal 447–01
Lead on, O King eternal 448–01
Lead their praises, Alleluia 451–02
Lead us by faith to hope's true
    promised land 275–02
Lead us from night to never-ending day 262–04
May thy good Spirit lead 250–03
O lead me, Lord, that I may lead 426–02
O lead us, Lord, in righteousness 161–03

Shall lead his church victorious 443–04
Willing to lead and be led 436–04
You lead me by the proper path 284–02

## LEADERS
For leaders, long ago 330–04
For leaders of our years 552–02
Therefore leaders of the earth 159–04

## LEADETH
He leadeth me the quiet waters by 170–01

## LEADS
And he leads his children on 049–04
And leads me, for his mercy's sake 172–01
And he leads to victory o'er the grave 393–04
Because he leads us in a harder way 086–02
God gently leads the chosen band 483–03
Leads forth in beauty all the
    starry band 262–01
That leads me to the Lamb 396–01
That leads me to the Lamb 397–01

## LEAF
Its leaf is green, its fruit is sure 158–03

## LEAN
But wholly lean on Jesus' name 379–01

## LEARN
And daily learn, refreshed, restored 419–01
Learn and live a shepherd's care 523–02
Learn from Christ to bear the cross 097–02
Learn from Jesus Christ to die 097–03
Learn from Jesus Christ to pray 097–01
Learn to listen for God's call 498–04
May we learn the art of sharing 343–01
Shall learn to sing your praise 195–05
When we learn how to make peace
    instead of war 407–04

## LEARNED
When I had not yet learned
    of Jesus Christ 410–01

## LEAVE
And so to you I leave it all 284–03
Leave, ah! leave me not alone 303–02
My Savior, leave me not forlorn 168–04
When we are strong, Lord, leave us
    not alone 275–03
Wherefore to you I leave it all 284–01

**LIFE-BESTOWER**

**LIFT**

**LIVE** (cont.)

| | |
|---|---|
| Live into hope the blind shall see | 332–02 |
| Live tomorrow's life today | 433–02 |
| Long as I live and troubles rise | 362–01 |
| May he live while the sun endures | 204–05 |
| May live eternally | 442–05 |
| Now live your children gloriously | 530–01 |
| Now we live, salvation's our song | 296–03 |
| Now we shall live forever | 106–03 |
| So in Christ we live again | 109–02 |
| Soon gone, and then we live no more | 211–03 |
| Than live in the tents of wickedness | 208–10 |
| That I will live each night and day | 174–05 |
| That we may live eternally | 119–04 |
| Thine wholly, thine alone, I'd live | 366–01 |
| Those who live by war shall one day collapse and fall | 169–04 |
| To God that all may live | 414–02 |
| We cannot live without you | 461–04 |
| We'll live and speak his praise | 507–05 |
| Who live each day believing | 552–03 |
| Who live to share with others | 552–02 |
| With thee, O Master, let me live | 357–04 |
| You live in a palace, exist in a shack | 311–01 |
| You live to show God's praise alone | 475–03 |
| You will live, because I live | 109–02 |

**LIVED**

| | |
|---|---|
| Lived on earth our Savior holy | 049–02 |
| They lived not only in ages past | 364–03 |

**LIVES (N)**

| | |
|---|---|
| And let our ordered lives confess | 345–04 |
| And our lives reflect thanksgiving | 298–02 |
| By our lives of dedication | 107–02 |
| Filling all our lives with love and joy and peace | 432–00 |
| How blest are those whose lives are cheered | 238–04 |
| In purer lives thy service find | 345–01 |
| Lives of justice, truth, and love | 409–02 |
| Of lives made fair and free | 412–04 |
| Our lives are fragile, like a dream | 211–02 |
| Our lives are kept from shame | 233–04 |
| Our lives, Lord, are now dedicated | 157–03 |
| Our lives may be our gift to you | 535–00 |
| Our lives shall sing your praise | 195–07 |
| Our lives the book our cities read | 437–03 |
| Our lives will spread your peace | 347–04 |
| Take thou our lives and use them as thou wilt | 360–04 |

| | |
|---|---|
| That through our lives your love may shine | 211–04 |
| Threatening lives | 373–05 |
| Thus firm our lives are bound | 233–03 |
| Till our lives, our deeds and ways | 131–03 |
| To touch the lives of others | 435–02 |
| Whose lives are blameless still | 164–01 |

**LIVES (V)**

| | |
|---|---|
| And he lives forever | 299–07 |
| And lives, where even hope has died | 108–04 |
| I know that my Redeemer lives | 153–03 |
| Jesus lives again | 514–refrain |
| Lives again our glorious King | 113–03 |
| Lives in glory now on high | 112–03 |
| Now he lives forever | 299–06 |
| One who lives forevermore | 109–01 |
| Who lives and loves and saves | 601–05 |

**LIVETH**

| | |
|---|---|
| For the Lord now liveth | 122–02 |

**LIVING (N)**

| | |
|---|---|
| And for our own, our living and our dead | 528–03 |
| And our living and our dying | 073–03 |
| Lord of the living, in your name assembled | 529–01 |

**LIVING (V)**

| | |
|---|---|
| May all we're doing show that you're living | 436–05 |
| When we are living, it is in Christ Jesus | 400–01 |

**LOAD**

| | |
|---|---|
| And ye, beneath life's crushing load | 038–03 |
| Bowed beneath oppression's load | 003–01 |
| Joined with my God to lift my neighbor's load | 410–02 |

**LOAF**

| | |
|---|---|
| Common loaf and sung shalom | 135–02 |

**LOAVES**

| | |
|---|---|
| Loaves abound | 514–refrain |

**LODES**

| | |
|---|---|
| Among the lodes of buried ore | 287–02 |

**LODGE**

| | |
|---|---|
| Within a lodge of broken bark | 061–02 |

## LONELY

| | |
|---|---|
| To tend the lonely in distress | 428–03 |

## LONG

| | |
|---|---|
| And long to feast upon thee still | 510–03 |
| And long to feast upon thee still | 511–03 |
| I long to feel your healing touch | 390–04 |
| O Lord, you are my God, for you I long | 199–01 |
| Yet long these multitudes to see | 408–04 |

## LONGING (N)

| | |
|---|---|
| Toward thee longing doth possess me; turn and bless me | 069–02 |

## LONGING (V)

| | |
|---|---|
| For God is longing to restore | 434–03 |

## LOOK

| | |
|---|---|
| As you look on your creation | 224–04 |
| But look for hearts to understand | 374–03 |
| Do not look among the dead for | 109–01 |
| Look on Calvary's summit | 296–01 |
| Look on the face of your anointed | 208–09 |
| Look on the heart by sorrow broken | 502–00 |
| Look on the tears by sinners shed | 502–00 |
| May we not look for love's return | 374–04 |
| Nor look to understanding hearts | 374–03 |
| That I might look upon your power | 198–02 |
| When I look down from lofty mountain grandeur | 467–02 |
| When unto you I look and pray | 249–03 |

## LOOKED

| | |
|---|---|
| Looked all around me, it looked so fine | 315–01 |
| They looked up and saw a star | 056–02 |

## LOSE

| | |
|---|---|
| Lose wonder from our hearts | 558–02 |
| Lose your shyness, find your tongue | 433–02 |

## LOST (N)

| | |
|---|---|
| To God the lost to bring | 428–04 |
| To seek and save the lost | 130–02 |

## LOST (V)

| | |
|---|---|
| To regain what we have lost | 136–03 |

## LOT

| | |
|---|---|
| Where'er our changeful lot is cast | 510–04 |
| Where'er our changeful lot is cast | 511–04 |

## LOVE (N)

| | |
|---|---|
| A love not changed by time of death or dread | 528–03 |
| A love that shows our gratitude | 556–refrain |
| According to your steadfast love | 195–01 |
| And all but love will cease | 386–05 |
| And all-discerning love hath sent | 282–02 |
| And by his love sweet blessing gives | 153–03 |
| And Christ's great love confess | 552–04 |
| And God's love made them strong | 364–02 |
| And have not love, my words are vain | 335–01 |
| And love beyond degree | 078–02 |
| And love itself cannot unwind | 419–02 |
| And love, joy, hope, like flowers | 205–02 |
| And perfect love and friendship reign | 438–04 |
| And praise your love and faithfulness | 247–01 |
| And show how grandly love intends | 353–04 |
| And striving so my love profess | 335–02 |
| And the best, is love | 318–04 |
| And unto all your love be shown | 211–05 |
| As we, by love, for love were made | 353–01 |
| Be your love with love requited | 506–03 |
| Blest Savior, then, in love | 383–04 |
| But by your gracious love alone | 353–03 |
| But not be given by love within | 335–02 |
| But yet in love he sought me | 171–03 |
| By a mother's love embraced | 547–03 |
| By our love to grow more like you | 512–02 |
| By the love that passes knowledge | 425–04 |
| By your love I am invited | 506–03 |
| Came to light holy love | 300–01 |
| Come down, O Love divine | 313–01 |
| Come, Holy Sun of heavenly love | 474–02 |
| Did e'er such love and sorrow meet | 100–03 |
| Did e'er such love and sorrow meet | 101–03 |
| Ever descending the love that we share | 147–03 |
| Ever shining forth in love | 256–01 |
| Filled with deathless love | 465–04 |
| Filling us with your love | 398–refrain |
| For all who love the Lord | 552–03 |
| For all your love imparts | 560–03 |
| For his steadfast love endures forever | 232–29 |
| For love of friends and kindred dear | 235–05 |
| For love so deep, so high, so broad | 083–05 |
| For love so unbounded | 557–01 |
| For love that knows no end | 517–02 |
| For the love of God is broader | 298–02 |
| For the love which from our birth | 473–01 |
| For thy love so boundless | 557–03 |
| From those that know thee may thy love | 186–05 |
| Gives us love to tell, bread to share | 514–03 |

So that when thy love shall call us 538–03
Springing from eternal love 446–02
Such lavish love outpouring 174–05
Take away the love of sinning 376–02
Take my love; my Lord, I pour 391–06
Thanks for the love by which our life
   is fed 528–03
That all may know Christ's love 435–01
That God's love shall be made known 129–01
That love, that life which cannot die 111–03
That theirs may be the love
   which knows no ending 533–01
The God of love 488–01
The love of Christ our Lord 517–03
The love of Christ proclaim 371–refrain
The love of Jesus, what it is 310–04
The love that cannot cease to bear 035–04
The love that made us, makes us one 507–03
The love, the word, the tide 471–06
Their Creator's changeless love 545–02
Then be God's love in Christ
   proclaimed 491–04
There your love the world may see 136–02
Therefore give us love 318–02
Through great love has come
   the victory 107–01
Through his own redeeming love 049–04
Through love, immersed in living 071–03
Through thy deathless love 122–03
Thy love divine hath led us in the past 262–02
Thy love to tell, thy praise to show 426–04
To fill with love the growing mind 497–04
To share Christ's love in living 552–03
To show God's love aright 048–02
Unto love and grace divine 498–01
What love and power and peace can fill 351–02
What wondrous love is this 085–01
When reached by love that never ends 380–01
When we know that love for simple
   things is better 407–03
Where love and truth abound 274–02
Where love is, God abides 534–02
Where love is lived and all is done 386–01
While love is making all things new 353–05
Whom love, and love alone, can know 412–02
With love enough for all 034–01
With thy love our bosoms fill 387–03
Your constant love gives more 199–02
Your love and peace to show 418–02
Your love forever will endure 247–05
Your love has set us in the generations 529–02
Your love is everlasting 243–01

Your love is more than life 198–03
Your love shall be our strength and stay 488–03
Your love will keep us ever 243–01
Your love with neighbors too 414–03
Your love you share with us always 157–01
Your steadfast love shall welcome all 161–03
Your steadfast love you show to all 252–02

## LOVE (V)

All who love and serve your city 413–01
And make me love thee as I ought
   to love 326–01
Close by me forever and love me, I pray 024–03
Do justly; love mercy 405–01
Hast thou not bid us love thee,
   God and King 326–02
How I love you! Look upon me 355–refrain
I love the Lord, who heard my cry 362–01
I love thee, Lord Jesus, look down
   from the sky 024–02
I love thee, Lord Jesus, look down
   from the sky 025–02
I love thy church, O God 441–02
I love thy kingdom, Lord 441–01
I love thy rocks and rills 561–02
Indeed, you love truth in the heart 196–04
Jesus Christ, how much I love you 355–refrain
Love and adore 139–04
Love him who with love is yearning 021–03
Love me still and cleanse within 355–refrain
May all that love thee prosper well 235–04
Or saying we love only you 157–03
Prone to leave the God I love 356–03
That I may love what thou dost love 316–01
These are the ones we should love 367–03
Those who love the Father 365–03
When we love though hate at times
   seems all around us 407–02
Where humble Christians love
   and serve 437–02
Who love to do Jesus' will 364–03

## LOVED

As he loved so long ago 304–02
For the Lord they loved and knew 364–01
For those he loved until the end 094–01
Loved and visited by thee 163–04
So loved he the world that he gave us 485–01
They loved their Lord so dear, so dear 364–02
Thou hast loved us, love us still 387–03
You have loved and protected us
   since time first begun 273–01

## LOVELINESS

| | |
|---|---|
| And laid a silent loveliness | 292–01 |
| Till all shall know the loveliness | 412–04 |

## LOVER

| | |
|---|---|
| Jesus, lover of my soul | 303–01 |

## LOVERS

| | |
|---|---|
| Lovers and pioneers | 279–02 |

## LOVES (N)

| | |
|---|---|
| Love divine, all loves excelling | 376–01 |

## LOVES (V)

| | |
|---|---|
| Come unto Christ, who loves you so | 381–03 |
| He loves beyond the uttermost | 094–04 |
| He loves righteousness and justice | 185–05 |
| Jesus loves me! This I know | 304–01 |
| The Lord loves the righteous | 254–08 |
| Yes, Jesus loves me | 304–refrain |

## LOVING

| | |
|---|---|
| May the loving which we dare | 512–05 |

## LOVING-KINDNESS

| | |
|---|---|
| With your wonted loving-kindness | 416–02 |
| With your wonted loving-kindness | 417–02 |

## LURE

| | |
|---|---|
| Lure us away from thee to endless night | 360–03 |

## LUST

| | |
|---|---|
| While lust and greed for gain | 453–02 |

## LUTE

| | |
|---|---|
| Praise God with the lute and the harp | 258–01 |

## LYRE

| | |
|---|---|
| Praise the Lord with the lyre | 185–02 |

# M

## MADE

| | |
|---|---|
| And twice to me made known | 197–05 |
| God made them every one | 267–03 |
| The Lord God made them all | 267–refrain |
| You made us for yourself alone | 437–01 |

## MAGNIFY

| | |
|---|---|
| Most gracious, magnify the Lord | 451–02 |

## MAID

| | |
|---|---|
| To a maid engaged to Joseph | 019–01 |
| 'Twas gentle Mary maid, so young and strong | 057–02 |

## MAJESTY

| | |
|---|---|
| Robed in awesome majesty | 006–02 |
| Robed in majesty and light | 213–01 |
| Thy sovereign majesty | 139–04 |
| To him all majesty ascribe | 142–03 |
| To him all majesty ascribe | 143–03 |
| Your majesty surrounds the earth | 162–01 |

## MAKE

| | |
|---|---|
| And make me pure within | 301–01 |
| And you will make it plain | 270–04 |
| Christ is able to make us one | 514–02 |
| Lord, make us more faithful | 536–04 |
| Lord, make us more holy | 536–01 |
| Lord, make us more loving | 536–02 |
| Lord, make us more patient | 536–03 |
| Make and keep me pure within | 303–04 |
| Make each of us more ready | 558–04 |
| Make it known he goes before | 109–01 |
| Make me, Lord, as fit to hold | 336–01 |
| Make you straight what long was crooked | 003–03 |
| O make me thine forever | 098–03 |
| To make us strong and pure | 443–01 |
| Will you not make me whole | 390–04 |

## MAKER

| | |
|---|---|
| Our maker, defender, redeemer, and friend | 476–05 |

## MAN

| | |
|---|---|
| As man or woman, you alone define | 385–01 |
| The Man of God's own choosing | 260–02 |
| Were not the right Man on our side | 260–02 |

## MANGER

| | |
|---|---|
| A manger his cradle in Bethlehem | 055–refrain |
| And he is in the manger now | 028–01 |
| And in a manger laid | 058–04 |
| And in a manger laid | 059–04 |
| And thus that manger poor became a throne | 057–04 |
| At that manger rude and bare | 063–03 |
| Away in a manger, no crib for his bed | 024–01 |
| Away in a manger, no crib for his bed | 025–01 |
| Brightly does your manger shine | 014–04 |
| Down in a lowly manger | 029–03 |
| In a manger Christ the Lord sleeps | 033–01 |
| In a manger for his bed | 049–01 |
| Lowly in a manger | 027–01 |
| Lying in a manger | 299–01 |
| Manger shall his cradle be | 065–02 |
| To grace a manger stall | 034–01 |

## MANIFESTS

| | |
|---|---|
| To whom he manifests his love | 149–03 |

## MANKIND

| | |
|---|---|
| Dear Lord and Father of mankind | 345–01 |
| Redeemer of mankind | 395–02 |

## MANNA

| | |
|---|---|
| Daily manna still provide you | 540–02 |
| Life-imparting heavenly manna | 154–04 |
| Of Massah with its manna and the waters sweet | 215–04 |
| Thy hungering ones with manna sweet | 426–02 |

## MAR

| | |
|---|---|
| And though they mar that image, love them still | 297–03 |

## MARCH (N)

| | |
|---|---|
| All beautiful the march of days | 292–01 |
| At last the march shall end | 145–03 |
| At last the march shall end | 146–03 |

## MARCH (V)

| | |
|---|---|
| Ever singing, march we onward | 464–03 |
| Let us march on | 563–01 |

## MARK

| | |
|---|---|
| Mark the miracle of time | 097–03 |
| We mark your saints, how they became | 419–03 |

## MARKED

| | |
|---|---|
| God marked a line and told the sea | 283–01 |

## MARTYRS

| | |
|---|---|
| And the blessed martyrs follow | 460–03 |

## MARVEL

| | |
|---|---|
| Marvel now, O heaven and earth | 014–01 |

## MARVELED

| | |
|---|---|
| How they all marveled | 299–02 |

## MARVELS

| | |
|---|---|
| And God's marvels to all the people | 217–02 |

## MASTER

| | |
|---|---|
| Master who acts as a slave to them | 367–01 |
| Until it master find | 378–03 |

## MATCH

| | |
|---|---|
| Match these brilliant birds and lovely flowers | 352–04 |

## MAZE

| | |
|---|---|
| Inside the mind's dark maze | 349–05 |
| While life's dark maze I tread | 383–03 |

## MEADOW

| | |
|---|---|
| Flowery meadow, flashing sea | 464–02 |
| In the fresh green meadow | 173–01 |

## MEADOWS

| | |
|---|---|
| Fair are the meadows | 306–02 |

## MEAN

| | |
|---|---|
| And I mean, God helping, to be one too | 364–01 |
| And I mean to be one too | 364–03 |

## MEANING

| | |
|---|---|
| To know your meaning for our life | 515–02 |

## MEANS (N)

| | |
|---|---|
| All our means and all our living | 504–03 |
| By means of them, O Lord | 167–03 |
| Weakest means fulfill thy will | 163–02 |

## MEANS (V)

| | |
|---|---|
| All that it means to accept you as Lord | 516–03 |
| What it means in daily living | 461–03 |

## MEANT

| | |
|---|---|
| And meant to love and live | 358–01 |

## MEASURE

| | |
|---|---|
| Lord, you show us love's true measure | 429–04 |

**MEASURE** (cont.)

| | |
|---|---|
| May we find in fuller measure | 461–01 |
| Than the measure of the mind | 298–02 |
| With full measure meets their need | 244–03 |

**MEAT**

| | |
|---|---|
| Christ is our meat and drink indeed | 110–03 |

**MEDITATES**

| | |
|---|---|
| And meditates upon that law | 158–02 |

**MEEK**

| | |
|---|---|
| Like them, the meek and lowly | 442–05 |

**MEET**

| | |
|---|---|
| God be with you till we meet again | 540–04 |
| In Christ now meet both east and west | 439–04 |
| In Christ now meet both east and west | 440–04 |
| In him meet south and north | 439–04 |
| In him meet south and north | 440–04 |
| Meet to offer praise and prayer | 461–01 |
| O Lord, how shall I meet you | 011–01 |
| Our living Lord to meet | 552–02 |
| Till we meet again | 537–02 |
| Until we meet again | 536–01 |
| We meet before the throne at length | 444–04 |
| We meet you, O Christ, in many a guise | 311–01 |
| Where Moses and Elijah meet | 075–02 |
| You can meet them in school, or in lanes, or at sea | 364–03 |

**MEETS**

| | |
|---|---|
| Lo! Jesus meets us | 122–02 |

**MELODIES**

| | |
|---|---|
| In raptured melodies of prayer | 490–02 |

**MELODY**

| | |
|---|---|
| Make melody to him with the harp of ten strings | 185–02 |
| Our melody we raise | 088–03 |
| The melody on every tongue | 274–02 |
| To God make melody | 219–01 |

**MELT**

| | |
|---|---|
| Melt me, mold me | 322–00 |
| Melt the clouds of sin and sadness | 464–01 |

**MEMBER**

| | |
|---|---|
| As member of your cast | 522–02 |
| Gracious Lord, your member own | 493–04 |

**MEMBERS**

| | |
|---|---|
| As living members of a living Christ | 495–02 |
| Loud praying members | 458–04 |
| To the members of Christ's body | 314–02 |

**MEMORIAL**

| | |
|---|---|
| O blest memorial of our dying Lord | 519–02 |

**MEN**

| | |
|---|---|
| Men and women, richer, poorer | 343–02 |
| Men and women, young and old | 256–02 |
| Our men clear their eyes | 319–04 |

**MEND**

| | |
|---|---|
| God mend thine every flaw | 564–02 |

**MERCIES**

| | |
|---|---|
| All God's mercies to proclaim | 223–01 |
| All thy faithful mercies crown | 376–01 |
| Eternal are thy mercies, Lord | 229–03 |
| For God's mercies shall endure | 244–refrain |
| God's covenant mercies we review | 444–02 |
| Great are your mercies, O my Maker | 352–01 |
| On mercies multiplied | 165–01 |
| Praise God for those bountiful mercies | 258–03 |
| Praise the Lord, great mercies trace | 481–03 |
| The tender mercies of the Lord | 209–01 |
| Thy mercies how tender, how firm to the end | 476–05 |

**MERCY**

| | |
|---|---|
| And mercy, more than life | 564–03 |
| And mercy ne'er depart | 186–05 |
| Are big with mercy and shall break | 270–03 |
| Christ, have mercy | 565–00 |
| Christ, have mercy | 573–00 |
| Christ, have mercy upon us | 572–00 |
| Christ, have mercy upon us | 574–00 |
| God's boundless mercy will provide | 307–03 |
| God's gracious mercy keepeth | 483–02 |
| God's promised mercy is my fort | 240–03 |
| Great God, in mercy spare us | 291–03 |
| Great mercy shall surround | 184–05 |
| Have mercy, Lord, upon us | 133–02 |
| Have mercy on me, O God, in your kindness | 196–01 |
| Have mercy on me, O Lord | 182–01 |
| Have mercy on us | 566–00 |
| Have mercy on us | 575–05 |
| Have mercy on us, Jesus | 082–01 |
| Have mercy on us, living Lord | 195–01 |
| His mercy is forever sure | 220–04 |

**MINDS** (cont.)

| | |
|---|---|
| Into open minds and hearts | 461–01 |
| Take thou our minds, dear Lord, we humbly pray | 392–01 |
| We give our minds to understand your ways | 375–02 |

**MINERALS**

| | |
|---|---|
| Thank you, God, for minerals and ores | 266–02 |

**MINES**

| | |
|---|---|
| Deep in unfathomable mines | 270–02 |

**MINISTER**

| | |
|---|---|
| Lord, as we minister in different ways | 436–05 |

**MINISTRIES**

| | |
|---|---|
| Called to ministries of grace | 343–01 |
| Our ministries are different | 435–02 |
| That our ministries uniting | 523–04 |

**MINISTRY**

| | |
|---|---|
| In common ministry | 418–01 |
| Ministry in dedication | 132–03 |

**MIRACLE**

| | |
|---|---|
| But miracle of miracles | 034–03 |

**MISERY**

| | |
|---|---|
| And misery relieved | 386–02 |

**MISFORTUNES**

| | |
|---|---|
| Though misfortunes of the good abound | 187–06 |

**MISS**

| | |
|---|---|
| Lest we miss thy kingdom's goal | 420–03 |

**MISSION**

| | |
|---|---|
| As we in mission magnify the Crucified | 430–03 |
| Make your earthly mission known | 132–01 |
| Making strong our mission | 127–03 |
| We all are one in mission | 435–01 |
| We have no mission but to serve | 421–05 |

**MITE**

| | |
|---|---|
| Not a mite would I withhold | 391–04 |

**MOCKED**

| | |
|---|---|
| And mocked your saving kingship then | 007–01 |
| But I am mocked and put to scorn | 168–03 |

**MODEL**

| | |
|---|---|
| The working model for our faith | 330–04 |

**MOLD**

| | |
|---|---|
| Mold our actions to your will | 127–01 |
| Mold the mountains, fashion blossoms | 285–01 |

**MOMENT**

| | |
|---|---|
| This is the moment glorious | 443–04 |
| Though for a moment they appeal | 197–04 |
| Was this God's crowning moment | 071–02 |

**MOMENTS**

| | |
|---|---|
| In all life's brilliant, timeless moments | 550–03 |
| Make all our moments calm and bright | 510–05 |
| Make all our moments calm and bright | 511–05 |
| Take my moments and my days | 391–01 |

**MONARCH**

| | |
|---|---|
| Monarch of all things, fit us for thy mansions | 459–02 |
| Not as a monarch, but the child | 004–02 |

**MOON**

| | |
|---|---|
| And as long as the moon, throughout all generations | 204–05 |
| Moon and stars in shining height | 163–03 |
| The moon shines full at God's command | 288–01 |
| Thou silver moon with softer gleam | 455–01 |
| 'Twas in the moon of wintertime | 061–01 |
| Your glowing moon enhances night | 243–03 |

**MOONLIGHT**

| | |
|---|---|
| Fairer still the moonlight | 306–03 |
| Where spreading moonlight quivers | 278–03 |

**MOONS**

| | |
|---|---|
| Till moons shall wax and wane no more | 423–01 |

**MORN**

| | |
|---|---|
| And from morn to set of sun | 460–03 |
| Dark and cheerless is the morn | 462–02 |
| Dark and cheerless is the morn | 463–02 |
| Fragrant autumn morn | 480–01 |
| Hail that ever-blessed morn | 051–refrain |
| In Bethlehem, all on a Christmas morn | 016–04 |
| O Lord, with each returning morn | 474–04 |
| Shall be the morn of song | 442–03 |
| That blessed Christmas morn | 029–03 |

## MOVE

| | |
|---|---|
| And move and march wherever you have trod | 344–01 |
| It cannot freely move | 378–04 |
| Move within our fellowship | 127–01 |
| Move within our mortal frame | 131–03 |
| We move onward toward your goal | 285–02 |

## MOVED

| | |
|---|---|
| I never shall be moved | 197–01 |
| It shall not be moved | 193–05 |
| So that we may be moved | 358–03 |
| You moved on the waters | 319–01 |

## MULTITUDE

| | |
|---|---|
| A multitude keeping festival | 190–04 |

## MURDERER

| | |
|---|---|
| A murderer they save | 076–04 |

## MURMUR

| | |
|---|---|
| And every faithless murmur stilled | 483–01 |
| Like the murmur of the dove's song | 314–01 |

## MURMURS

| | |
|---|---|
| The murmurs of self-will | 388–03 |
| The murmurs of self-will | 389–03 |

## MUSIC

| | |
|---|---|
| All music but its own | 151–01 |
| And still their heavenly music floats | 038–02 |
| For music and a hope that lives | 328–01 |
| From whom comes the music in our voice | 484–01 |
| God gave us music, gave us voice | 328–refrain |
| How often, making music, we have found | 264–02 |
| Joyful music leads us sunward | 464–03 |
| Let music swell the breeze | 561–03 |
| Make music for thy Lord to hear | 455–03 |
| So let the music sound God's praise | 328–02 |
| The music for the singers' art | 328–03 |
| The music of the spheres | 293–01 |
| Their exultant music told | 486–01 |
| Through music blend the potencies | 490–03 |
| 'Tis music in the sinner's ears | 466–02 |
| When in our music God is glorified | 264–01 |

## MYRRH

| | |
|---|---|
| Bitter myrrh have I to give the infant Jesus | 064–04 |
| Bring we the myrrh of humility | 062–02 |
| Myrrh from the forest, or gold from the mine | 067–03 |
| Myrrh is mine; its bitter perfume | 066–04 |

## MYSTERIES

| | |
|---|---|
| At mysteries so bright | 151–02 |
| Earth's mysteries known or yet untold | 134–02 |

## MYSTERY

| | |
|---|---|
| By this great vision's mystery | 075–05 |
| Mystery shrouds our life and death | 406–04 |
| The mystery of Bethlehem | 034–03 |
| The mystery of your presence, Lord | 521–04 |
| Three in one: what mystery | 129–03 |
| We are one in the Spirit, in the great mystery | 273–03 |
| Your mystery to touch | 515–02 |

# N

## NAILED

| | |
|---|---|
| Christ who was nailed to the cross | 120–01 |
| They nailed him to a tree | 095–02 |
| Were you there when they nailed him to the tree | 102–02 |

## NAME (N)

| | |
|---|---|
| All those who know your name on earth | 212–05 |
| Almighty, victorious, thy great name we praise | 263–01 |
| And from your name shall never | 011–03 |
| And this one name confess | 255–06 |
| As your sacred name they hallow | 460–03 |
| At the name of Jesus every knee shall bow | 148–01 |
| At your great name, O Jesus, now | 004–03 |

Be its name "The Lord is there!"          413–04
Blessed be the name of the Lord           225–01
Blessed is the one who comes
    in the name of the Lord            232–26
Blest is your name, O living Lord         226–01
For when humbly in your name              504–01
Forever be your name adored               161–04
Forth in your dear name we go             427–04
God with an uncompleted name              330–02
Hallowed be your name                     571–00
Hallowed-a be thy name            589–response
His name is Jesus, God ever with us       055–02
His name, like sweet perfume, shall rise  423–02
His name shall be called Jesus            019–04
Holy God, we praise your name             460–01
How glorious is your name                 162–01
In the name of Christ to sup              504–02
In the name of Jesus, yes, we hear        348–01
In the name of Jesus, yes, we hold        348–03
In the name of Jesus, yes, we love        348–04
In the name of Jesus, yes, we see         348–02
In the name of the Lord                   568–00
In the name of the Lord                   581–00
In whate'er we do let your name
    receive the praise                 346–03
Jehovah is his name                       172–01
Jesus as the Son by name                  074–03
Jesus, the name that charms our fears     466–02
Just and holy is thy name                 303–03
Let the Redeemer's name be sung           229–01
Lord of light, your name outshining       425–01
Lord, our Lord, thy glorious name         163–01
Lord Sabaoth his name                     260–02
O blessed be thy name, Lord               395–03
O may your name be long adored            226–01
Of your esteemed and splendid name        548–02
One holy name she blesses                 442–02
One name we bear, one bread of life
    we break                           503–03
Praise his name in all the earth          027–03
Praise the name of the Lord               225–01
Savior, again to thy dear name we raise   539–01
The name all-victorious of Jesus extol    477–01
Their name an everlasting name            149–04
Thine the name of matchless worth         163–06
Thy name be ever praised! O Lord,
    make us free                       559–03
Thy name I love                           561–02
Thy name, O Jesus, be forever blest       526–01
Thy name we bless, O risen Lord           111–04
To glorify the Maker's name               287–03
To our Redeemer's name                    325–03

To praise your holy name, O Lord          500–03
To serve each other in your name          521–05
To witness in God's name                  435–02
We praise your holy name                  488–03
What name is given in Bethlehem           055–01
Where your name binds us together         136–02
Who in the Lord's name comest             088–01
Whose name forevermore be blest           601–05
Your changeless name of love              205–04
Your name shall stand forever             205–04

**NAME (V)**
Holy Spirit: Three we name you            460–04

**NAMES**
Some common names are these               255–05

**NATION**
God of every nation                       289–01
Jesus out of every nation                 144–01
Meant for every nation                    300–01
No nation is so blest                     255–06
Of every nation and race                  436–01
The nation rejoices                 177–refrain
Your own in every nation                  156–02

**NATIONS**
All nations give him service              204–11
All nations shall adore you               205–03
All the nations your own stay             159–03
And makes the nations prove               040–04
Before the nations God reveals            219–02
But nations fear and kingdoms shake       191–03
High above the nations is God             225–02
Joyful, all ye nations, rise              031–01
Let the nations be glad and sing for joy  202–04
Let the nations shout and sing            203–03
Lift the nations from the shadows         425–03
Nations conquer not their neighbor        401–01
Nations, cry aloud in wonder              074–03
Nations rage, wars to wage                192–02
O God, O God, let all the nations
    praise you                      202–refrain
Savior of the nations, come               014–01
The godless nations round                 237–02
The Lord alone let nations fear           216–02
The nations are in an uproar,
    the kingdoms totter                193–06
Though nations fail your power
    to own                             227–01
Though nations stand unsure               259–02
To bear before the nations                327–03

| | | |
|---|---|---|
| Night and stars, in God rejoice | 256–01 | **NOELS** |
| Night is drawing nigh | 541–01 | Noels ringing, tidings bringing 037–01 |
| No night, nor need, nor pain | 453–01 | |
| On a cold winter's night that was | | **NOISE** |
| so deep | 056–01 | Above the noise of selfish strife 408–01 |
| Poured out before you night and day | 168–01 | |
| Poured out before you night and day | 189–02 | **NOMADS** |
| Silent night, holy night | 060–01 | Some nomads traveled with their God 330–01 |
| That night the apostles met in fear | 116–04 | |
| That night the apostles met in fear | 117–02 | **NORTH** |
| The night draws nigh | 415–02 | From the north to southern pole 256–02 |
| The night is as the day, | | |
| the darkness light | 248–04 | **NOTES** |
| Through death's dark night | | And while the wave notes fall |
| to endless day | 374–05 | on my ear 324–02 |
| Till in the night of hate and war | 007–03 | In joyful notes resound 487–03 |
| To you this night is born a child | 054–02 | Like the notes that are woven into song 518–03 |
| Tossed on a cold, stormy night | 373–01 | Their notes of gladness blend 118–03 |
| We know that God is with us night | | |
| and morning | 342–01 | **NOURISHED** |
| When half spent was the night | 048–01 | That one is nourished like a tree 158–03 |
| When in the night I meditate | 165–01 | |
| When night is dim | 012–04 | **NUMBER** |
| Where all is night, may we sow light | 374–02 | In number shall abound 184–05 |

# O

| | | |
|---|---|---|
| **OATH** | | **OFFEND** |
| His oath, his covenant, his blood | 379–03 | Offend unknowingly 167–03 |
| | | |
| **OBEDIENCE** | | **OFFENDED** |
| In full obedience to our Lord | 421–05 | Ah, holy Jesus, how have you offended 093–01 |
| | | |
| **OBEY** | | **OFFENSES** |
| And we would obey it duly | 493–02 | All offenses purge away 551–03 |
| | | For our offenses given 110–01 |
| **OBEYED** | | My offenses, truly I know them 196–02 |
| You then obeyed God's call | 070–03 | |
| | | **OFFER** |
| **OBJECT** | | And offer all that faith can do 353–05 |
| An object of scorn to my neighbors | 182–03 | Offer praise and worship to God 160–05 |
| | | Singing, we offer prayer and meditation 459–01 |
| **OCEAN** | | That when you offer Jesus' prayer 349–06 |
| Ocean and mountain, stream, forest, | | To whom we offer praises 484–introduction |
| and flower | 147–02 | Vainly we offer each ample oblation 067–04 |
| That in thine ocean depths its flow | 384–01 | Yourself to scorn did offer 082–refrain |
| | | |
| **ODORS** | | **OFFERED** |
| Odors of Edom and offerings divine | 067–03 | And offered there in his presence 056–05 |

**OFFERED** (cont.)

| | |
|---|---|
| As they offered gifts most rare | 063–03 |
| Offered mercy's perfect deed | 427–01 |
| Then you will be offered young bulls on your altar | 196–10 |

**OFFERING**

| | |
|---|---|
| An offering to thee | 557–03 |
| Burnt offering from me you would refuse | 196–09 |
| Each a sacred offering brought | 486–03 |
| My heart's humble offering | 557–01 |
| Paschal Lamb, your offering, finished | 154–03 |
| What shall my offering be | 228–03 |

**OFFERINGS**

| | |
|---|---|
| Burnt offerings wholly consumed | 196–10 |

**OFFSPRING**

| | |
|---|---|
| God's offspring from on high | 019–04 |
| Offspring of the virgin's womb | 031–02 |

**OIL**

| | |
|---|---|
| Like precious oil upon the head | 241–02 |
| Your oil anoints my head | 172–02 |

**OLD**

| | |
|---|---|
| As of old on earth he stood | 005–02 |
| As those of old their firstfruits brought | 414–01 |
| Now as of old | 274–01 |
| Of old you gave your solemn oath | 601–03 |

**ONE**

| | |
|---|---|
| One in hope of heaven's blessing | 544–02 |
| One in love, your truth confessing | 544–02 |
| One in love's demands | 465–02 |
| One in might and one in glory | 416–04 |
| One in might and one in glory | 417–04 |
| One with each other, Lord, for one in thee | 503–04 |
| One with his rising, freed and forgiven | 492–02 |
| One with the Father, he is our Savior | 055–05 |
| We all are one in call | 435–01 |
| We all are one in mission | 435–03 |
| Yet all are one in thee, for all are thine | 526–04 |
| Yet one o'er all the earth | 442–02 |

**ONENESS**

| | |
|---|---|
| Our oneness in the Lord | 521–03 |

**ONES**

| | |
|---|---|
| None but his loved ones know | 310–04 |

**OPEN**

| | |
|---|---|
| O Lord, open my lips | 196–08 |
| Open my ears, that I may hear | 324–02 |
| Open my eyes, that I may see | 324–01 |
| Open my heart, and let me prepare | 324–03 |
| Open my mouth, and let me bear | 324–03 |
| Open now our ears and heart | 454–03 |
| Open now the crystal fountain | 281–02 |
| Open now thy gates of beauty | 489–01 |
| Open to me the gates of righteousness | 231–19 |
| Open to me the gates of righteousness | 232–19 |
| Open wide our hands, in sharing | 422–03 |
| Redeemer, come! I open wide | 008–03 |
| Then open thou our eyes that we may see | 503–04 |

**OPENED**

| | |
|---|---|
| And opened the life-gate that all may go in | 485–01 |
| Christ has opened paradise | 113–02 |
| He hath opened heaven's door | 028–02 |

**OPENS**

| | |
|---|---|
| That opens fisted minds | 471–02 |
| That opens us to unity | 386–03 |
| The Lord opens the eyes of the blind | 254–08 |

**OPPRESSED**

| | |
|---|---|
| The oppressed shall be the first to see | 332–01 |

**OPPRESSION**

| | |
|---|---|
| From oppression and violence he redeems their life | 204–14 |
| You come to break oppression | 205–01 |

**ORDAIN**

| | |
|---|---|
| O God, what you ordain is right | 284–01 |

**ORDAINED**

| | |
|---|---|
| Ordained our human race | 434–02 |

**ORDAINETH**

| | |
|---|---|
| Granted in what he ordaineth | 482–02 |

**ORDER (N)**

| | |
|---|---|
| By order from thy throne | 288–03 |
| The steadfast order sure | 278–01 |
| Your life-filled word brings order to | 255–04 |

**ORDER (V)**
Order our ways in your peace	120–06

**ORES**
In ores and atoms we unlock	287–01

**ORPHANS**
Alleluia! not as orphans	144–02

**OUTLIVE**
Outlive my love to thee	098–03

**OUTPASS**
Shall far outpass the power
   of human telling	313–03

**OVERFLOW**
Let it overflow with love	350–refrain

**OVERLOOK**
Yet not overlook her faults	523–03

**OVERSEE**
Oversee her life steadfastly	523–03

**OVERWHELMED**
Most surely then had overwhelmed
   our soul	236–02

**OWN**
So shalt thou, wondering,
   own God's way	286–03
Thee the Lord of lords we own	144–04
We own thy mercies, Lord,
   which never fail	275–01
While we own the mystery	460–04
You know that I own so little	377–02
You only Christ, as Lord we own	133–03

**OWNED**
By God alone are owned	214–03

**OX**
Ox and ass before him bow	028–01
Ox and ass beside him	046–02
Where ox and ass are feeding	053–02

**OXEN**
Oxen lowing, little knowing	037–01

# P

**PAGE**
Beyond the sacred page I seek thee,
   Lord	329–01
In the Bible's sacred page	331–01
That from the hallowed page	327–01

**PAIN**
All our pain and unbelief	406–02
But thine the deadly pain	098–02
From out their pain and strife	437–01
In all my pain and misery	301–02
O what needless pain we bear	403–01
Not yet was he to share our pain	035–02
Strong with you to suffer pain	077–02
To ease our cities' pain	437–03
Watching late in pain	541–03
Who pain didst undergo
   for my poor sake	457–01
Ye who long pain and sorrow bear	455–05

**PAINS**
But the pains which he endured	123–03
Untouched, unmoved by
   human pains	108–03
We come with self-inflicted pains	353–02

**PAINT**
You paint the wayside flower	560–02

**PALMS**
With palms and scattered garments
   strowed	090–01
With palms and scattered garments
   strowed	091–01
With palms before thee went	088–02

**PANGS**
Meanwhile the pangs of my sorrow	045–01
O the pangs his soul sustained	097–02

## PARDON (N)

| | |
|---|---|
| And pardon from your sin | 349–04 |
| He did not come for pardon | 072–01 |
| How can your pardon reach and bless | 347–02 |
| Pardon for sin and a peace that endureth | 276–03 |

## PARDON (V)

| | |
|---|---|
| Pardon and correct my sin | 178–02 |

## PARENT

| | |
|---|---|
| Like a loving parent caring | 479–03 |

## PARENTS

| | |
|---|---|
| Give to the parents love and patience | 497–03 |

## PART

| | |
|---|---|
| Born of the Spirit, do their part | 240–04 |
| But do thine own part faithfully | 282–03 |
| Forgiving others, take your part | 455–05 |
| Until this earthly part of me | 316–03 |
| Which part the seas and mold the land | 152–01 |

## PARTAKER

| | |
|---|---|
| Let me be a fit partaker | 506–02 |

## PARTAKES

| | |
|---|---|
| Partakes one holy food | 442–02 |

## PARTNER

| | |
|---|---|
| A partner in Christ's sacrifices | 421–03 |

## PARTNERS

| | |
|---|---|
| Called as partners in Christ's service | 343–01 |
| Equal partners in our caring | 343–01 |
| Make us partners in our living | 343–04 |

## PASS

| | |
|---|---|
| Mortal, we pass through beauty that decays | 528–01 |
| Pass the word around | 514–refrain |
| Swiftly pass the clouds of glory | 073–01 |

## PASSION

| | |
|---|---|
| One holy passion filling all my frame | 326–04 |
| To thee, before thy passion | 088–03 |

## PASSIONS

| | |
|---|---|
| From earth-born passions set me free | 301–01 |
| Till earthly passions turn | 313–02 |

## PAST

| | |
|---|---|
| A past that promised more | 330–02 |
| God of the past, our times are in thy hand | 275–02 |
| In all the past, through all our hopes and fears | 275–01 |
| Out from the gloomy past | 563–02 |
| That the dark past has taught us | 563–01 |
| While some remembering the past | 330–03 |

## PASTORS

| | |
|---|---|
| In your tending may all pastors | 523–02 |

## PASTURES

| | |
|---|---|
| And where the verdant pastures grow | 171–02 |
| Guiding me to greener pastures | 173–02 |
| He makes me down to lie in pastures green | 170–01 |
| In pastures fresh he makes me feed | 172–01 |
| In thy pleasant pastures feed us | 387–01 |

## PATH

| | |
|---|---|
| And bright is God's path on the wings of the storm | 476–02 |
| By this our path to trace | 327–03 |
| Christ is the path, and Christ the prize | 307–02 |
| Keep me from any path that gives you pain | 248–05 |
| Keep us forever in the path, we pray | 563–03 |
| The path of life thou showest me | 165–05 |
| Through each perplexing path of life | 269–03 |
| We have come, treading our path | 563–02 |
| Who from God's path have strayed | 188–01 |
| Yes, on through life's long path | 145–02 |
| Yes, on through life's long path | 146–02 |

## PATHS

| | |
|---|---|
| Along the paths of peace | 602–03 |
| From paths where hide the lures of greed | 408–02 |
| In lowly paths of service free | 357–01 |
| In paths of truth and grace | 172–01 |
| Within the paths of righteousness | 170–02 |

## PATHWAY

| | |
|---|---|
| A pathway through life's maze | 418–03 |
| For tomorrow's unknown pathway | 129–02 |
| Shall make life's pathway clear | 412–03 |
| Treading the pathway of death | 120–02 |

## PATHWAYS

| | |
|---|---|
| On pathways that are right | 175–02 |

**PEOPLE** (cont.)

| | |
|---|---|
| And empty people feel your grace | 226–02 |
| And people of all lands | 219–05 |
| And we who are God's people | 180–03 |
| And with God's people I will meet | 228–04 |
| And your people shall go forth in joy | 337–02 |
| Be to all people given | 133–01 |
| Born to set thy people free | 001–01 |
| Born to set thy people free | 002–01 |
| But God's people stand and in God's reign prevail | 169–04 |
| But people scorned and none | 076–02 |
| Calling people everywhere | 433–07 |
| Come, and thy people bless | 139–02 |
| Come, ye thankful people, come | 551–01 |
| Daily make us faithful people | 512–05 |
| For now in your people good pleasure you seek | 257–02 |
| Give to your people for the day's affliction | 529–04 |
| God is here! As we your people | 461–01 |
| God shall set the people free | 445–02 |
| Healed and strengthened as your people | 285–02 |
| Hear your people as they pray | 416–02 |
| Hear your people as they pray | 417–02 |
| Hungry people in need | 300–03 |
| I have heard my people cry | 525–01 |
| Let my people go | 334–01 |
| Let people see your works in me | 350–01 |
| Let the people praise you, Lord | 203–02 |
| Let the people rejoice | 485–refrain |
| Loud cheering people | 458–03 |
| No other people are so graced | 255–06 |
| On thy people pour thy power | 420–01 |
| On which your people stand | 443–01 |
| On your people, Lord, have mercy | 178–03 |
| One holy people gathered | 443–02 |
| One people in the name of Christ | 515–03 |
| Our people drift and die | 291–01 |
| People and realms of every tongue | 423–03 |
| People, look east | 012–01 |
| Praise Christ, all people here below | 591–00 |
| Preaching to the people | 299–03 |
| Teaching people to live to bless | 514–02 |
| The holy people said it was a shame | 302–03 |
| The people all around them | 128–02 |
| The people of the Hebrews | 088–02 |
| The people of the Lord unite | 235–02 |
| Thy people still are fed | 269–01 |
| To his people in distress | 478–02 |
| We are your people: Lord, by your grace | 436–01 |

| | |
|---|---|
| We, your people, make our prayer | 136–02 |
| When we your people pray, you hear us | 201–01 |
| When will people cease their fighting | 401–01 |
| While people say to me continually, "Where is your God?" | 190–03 |
| While thou dost thy people feed | 489–03 |
| Whose people know the joyful sound | 209–04 |
| Ye people of God's choice | 491–01 |
| Your people are your hands and feet | 437–03 |
| Your people arise | 319–04 |
| Your people despoil all the sweetness of earth | 337–02 |
| Your people long to greet you | 011–01 |

**PEOPLES**

| | |
|---|---|
| All peoples in one heart and mind | 009–03 |
| Peoples, clap your hands | 194–01 |
| Let the peoples praise you, O God | 202–03 |
| The peoples be led forth in peace | 337–01 |
| Till all the peoples of the earth | 252–03 |

**PERIL**

| | |
|---|---|
| For those in peril on the sea | 562–01 |
| In peril and temptation | 179–01 |
| O Lord, great is the peril | 373–01 |

**PERILS**

| | |
|---|---|
| When life's perils thick confound you | 540–03 |

**PERISH**

| | |
|---|---|
| Perish self in thy pure fire | 321–02 |
| We perish as we lose you | 007–03 |

**PERISHES**

| | |
|---|---|
| Who perishes will rise | 386–04 |

**PERMIT**

| | |
|---|---|
| Not lightly dost thou, Lord, permit | 228–05 |

**PERSON**

| | |
|---|---|
| Each person to embrace | 358–01 |

**PIERCE**

| | |
|---|---|
| Pierce the clouds of nature's night | 317–01 |
| Pierce the gloom of sin and grief | 462–03 |
| Pierce the gloom of sin and grief | 463–03 |

**PIERCED**

| | |
|---|---|
| Pierced and nailed you to the tree | 006–02 |
| They pierced him in the side | 095–03 |

Were you there when they pierced
   him in the side 102–03

**PILGRIM**
Pilgrim through this barren land 281–01

**PILGRIMAGE**
Who through this weary pilgrimage 269–01

**PILGRIMS**
The pilgrims find their home at last 145–03
The pilgrims find their home at last 146–03

**PILLAR**
A pillar of fire shining forth in the night 554–01

**PITCHED**
He pitched his tents on Canaan ground 153–02

**PITIED**
And pitied every groan 362–01

**PITY**
Amazing pity! Grace unknown 078–02
He has pity on the weak and the needy 204–13
Like the pity of a father 223–03
Take pity, Lord, I pray thee 395–01
Thy pity without end 098–03

**PLACE**
A place to build her nest 207–01
A place where all is joy and peace 527–03
A place where sin cannot molest 527–01
A place where we our Savior meet 527–02
And touching every place and time 108–02
Christ takes his place, the throne of God 141–01
Come to the place for which
   our fathers sighed 563–02
From its appointed place 166–03
How lovely is your dwelling place 208–01
I take my place with all the saints 522–02
Is your abiding place 207–01
Let it become your place 351–03
Lord, you have been our dwelling place 211–01
My dwelling place shall be 170–05
O how blessed is this place 489–01
O Savior, in this quiet place 390–01
Reigning omnipotent in every place 457–02
Right over the place where Jesus lay 056–04
The highest place that heaven affords 149–02
There is a place of comfort sweet 527–02
There is a place of full release 527–03
There is a place of quiet rest 527–01

There is no place where earth's failings 298–01
There is no place where earth's sorrows 298–01
There's a sweet, sweet Spirit
   in this place 398–01
They make it a place of springs 208–06
Till love creates a place 313–03
To the place where he is gone 049–04
When we shall leave this place 398–refrain
Within your holy place 198–02

**PLACES**
Make the rougher places plain 003–03

**PLAGUE**
Plague the world with awesome ill 401–02

**PLAIN**
Above the fruited plain 564–01
Born a king on Bethlehem's plain 066–02

**PLAINS**
Above its sad and lowly plains 038–02
All the plains were lit that night 027–02
Sweetly singing o'er the plains 023–01

**PLAINSONG**
Plainsong, tuneful hymns, and anthems 486–03

**PLAN (N)**
Joining all in heaven's plan 464–03
Thine is the mighty plan 278–01

**PLAN (V)**
As they plan to take my life 182–05
Those who plan some evil 541–03
To plan and work together 435–01

**PLANETS**
Loud rushing planets 458–01

**PLANT (N)**
There's not a plant or flower below 288–03

**PLANT (V)**
You plant your footsteps in the sea 270–01

**PLANTS**
Plants for us to cultivate 224–03

**PLAY**
Give, as I play the Christian's part 351–01
Play skillfully on the strings,
   with loud shouts 185–03

**PLEA**
Just as I am, without one plea — 370–01
This is my earnest plea — 359–01

**PLEAD**
Earth's Redeemer, plead for me — 144–03
We plead, O Lord, to see — 015–03

**PLEADING**
The silent word is pleading — 053–02
Will God your pleading hear — 405–02

**PLEADS**
Pleads for us and hears our cry — 112–03

**PLEAS**
Let my spoken, public pleas — 336–03

**PLEASE**
All that may please you best — 011–01

**PLEASED**
Then you will be pleased
with lawful sacrifice — 196–10
You are not pleased with sacrifice — 195–06

**PLEASES**
"To me be as it pleases God," she said — 016–03

**PLEASURE**
Still in thee lies purest pleasure — 365–03
'Tis the Father's pleasure we should
call him Lord — 148–01
To take whate'er thy Keeper's
pleasure — 282–02

**PLEASURES**
And pleasures evermore — 165–05

**PLEDGE (N)**
The pledge and seal of heaven — 517–03

**PLEDGE (V)**
I pledge to use in service and in love — 410–02

**PLOT**
As they plot together against me — 182–05

**PLOW**
We plow the fields and scatter — 560–01

**PLOWING**
For the plowing, sowing, reaping — 553–01

**PLOWSHARE**
Make plowshare out of sword — 434–01

**POET**
Poet and composer wrought — 486–03

**POINT**
Point thou the heavenly way — 301–03

**POINTS**
Yet, passing, points to that glad feast
above — 520–05

**POLE**
From pole to pole, that wars may cease — 151–03

**POLISH**
Polish us with loving care — 285–03

**POMP**
In lowly pomp ride on to die — 090–02
In lowly pomp ride on to die — 091–02

**PONDER**
And ponder all your ways — 198–04
Ponder nothing earthly minded — 005–01

**POOR**
And your poor with justice — 204–02
Raising up the poor from the dust — 225–03
The poor and those who have no helper — 204–12
The poor are rich, the weak are strong — 386–04
The poor cry out for strength and health — 431–02
To serve the poor and homeless first — 434–01
With the poor, oppressed, and lowly — 049–02

**POSSESS**
Shall possess the earth forever — 178–02
Shall soon possess the land — 188–05
Though I may give all I possess — 335–02

**POSSESSING**
May we see, in love's possessing — 544–02

**POSSESSIONS**
These possessions you shall rule — 159–03

**POUR**
And pour contempt on all my pride — 100–01
And pour contempt on all my pride — 101–01
I pour my soul out when I think — 189–03
Lord, pour your power upon us all — 206–02
O pour your sovereign Spirit out — 437–03

**PRAISE** (cont.)

**PRAISES**

**PRAY**

**PRAYER**

Our prayer attend 139–02
Prayer and praising we are raising 066–03
Take it to the Lord in prayer 403–02
The fervent prayer, with many a tear 079–01
Then let my prayer as incense rise 249–02
This all my prayer shall be 359–02
This all my prayer shall be 359–03
To him shall endless prayer be made 423–02
To you shall prayer unceasing 205–03
You kindly hear my prayer 212–04

## PRAYERS
By the prayers of faithful watchers 425–04
Dearer to God are the prayers
   of the poor 067–04
For her my prayers ascend 441–03
Hear, O Lord, our humble prayers 129–02
May the prayers in which we share 512–05
Of all my prayers, may this be chief 390–06
Our prayers we pledge, our love we tell 444–01

## PRAYING
Loving Spirit, praying in us 512–04
Someone's praying, Lord, kum ba yah 338–04

## PREACH
If you cannot preach like Peter 394–03
When I preach your loving ways 336–04

## PREACHING
With such preaching stark and bold 409–03

## PRECEPTS
God's precepts are direct and pure 167–01

## PREJUDICE
The prejudice that blinds 471–02

## PREPARE
Now prepare for God a way 003–02
Prepare the way, O Zion 013–01
You did for all prepare 605–02

## PRESENCE
And all knew your presence, Lord 486–02
And from your presence where, Lord,
   shall I fly 248–02
And I know they feel the presence
   of the Lord 398–01
And in his blissful presence eternally
   rejoice 089–03
And in thy presence rest 310–01

And still he is nigh—his presence
   we have 477–02
At the presence of God,
   who now comes 217–06
Before God's presence let us come 214–02
Christ's living presence greeting 470–03
His presence, always near 507–04
In presence of my foes 170–04
In presence of my foes you feed me 175–03
In thy presence to abide 551–04
In your presence I may rest 323–04
Into the presence of your
   own tomorrow 529–04
Let me thy inner presence feel 008–03
Still in presence move before us 129–02
Thine own dear presence to cheer
   and to guide 276–03
Through the moving of your presence 132–03
Waking or sleeping, thy presence
   my light 339–01
We know your presence here 437–02
Yet here thy presence we
   devoutly hail 519–01
Your presence is my stay 172–02

## PRESENT (N)
That the present has brought us 563–01
That were a present far too small 100–04

## PRESENT (V)
Be present, Lord, among us 358–01
Before thee we present 088–02
Reverently to him present 065–03

## PRESERVE
Preserve their days from inwardness
   of heart 532–03

## PRESS
Then if Satan on us press 077–03

## PRESSURES
If worldly pressures fray the mind 419–02

## PREY
Blest be the Lord, who made us not
   their prey 236–03

## PRIDE
And all a nation's pride, o'erthrown 007–02
But take away our pride 291–01
From pride of race and station 289–02

**PRIDE** (cont.)
Our pride is dust, our vaunt is stilled 007–04
Unconscious pride resists or shelves 380–03

**PRINCE**
The prince of darkness grim 260–03

**PRISONER**
And sets the prisoner free 466–03

**PRISONERS**
The Lord sets the prisoners free 254–08
The prisoners leap to lose their chains 423–04

**PRIVILEGE**
What a privilege to carry 403–01

**PRIZE (N)**
As thou our prize wilt be 310–05

**PRIZE (V)**
I prize her heavenly ways 441–04

**PROCEEDS**
Who from both fore'er proceeds 137–03

**PROCLAIM**
And there proclaim, my God,
    how great thou art 467–04
Now proclaim Messiah's birth 022–01
Proclaim God's salvation day by day 217–02
Proclaim in every place 013–03
Proclaim the captive's liberty 411–02
Proclaim the holy birth 043–02
Proclaim the holy birth 044–02
We'll proclaim Christ everywhere 285–03
Would then proclaim in grateful
    songs 475–01
You shall proclaim to Israel 601–04

**PROCLAIMED**
John proclaimed salvation near 409–03

**PROCLAIMS**
God now proclaims our full release 332–04
Proclaims his only Son aloud 075–03
Proclaims its Maker's glorious name 209–03

**PROCURED**
Procured my liberty 011–02

**PRODIGAL**
God of the prodigal 272–04

**PROFIT (N)**
The profit soon turns strangely thin 335–02
Their profit and their joy to know 149–05
What profit in defeat 181–03

**PROFIT (V)**
You're the one to profit when you say 398–02

**PROMISE**
A promise calling them ahead 330–01
Always your promise stands 279–05
And feel the promise is not vain 384–03
And none shall find God's promise vain 253–02
Because thy promise I believe 370–03
But his promise can be trusted 109–02
But in his promise we rejoice 399–02
By this promise that you love us 508–02
By this promise that you love us 509–02
In your promise is my comfort 323–04
The promise changed and grew 330–03

**PROMISED**
And, Jesus, I have promised 388–04
And, Jesus, I have promised 389–04
O Jesus, I have promised 388–01
O Jesus, I have promised 389–01
O Jesus, thou hast promised 388–04
O Jesus, thou hast promised 389–04
The Lord has promised good to me 280–04
Thou hast promised to receive us 387–02

**PROMISES**
Remembering past promises 600–05

**PROMOTES**
Promotes the insecure 600–04

**PRONOUNCED**
And then pronounced them good 288–02

**PROPHECY**
In prophecy and praise 330–03
Prophecy will fade away 318–03

**PROPHET**
Isaiah the prophet has written of old 337–01
The prophet of salvation 602–02
The prophet of the Lord 601–04

# Q

## QUEST
The quest for truth dispelling lies    152–04

## QUIET
The quiet of a steadfast faith    452–02

## QUIVER
As quiver full of arrows stored    238–03

# R

## RACE
Because our race, our skin is not
   the same    385–02
Encircling every race    471–03
For I don't want to run this race
   in vain    354–01
No alien race, no foreign shore    412–01
Of each succeeding race    269–02
Of every race and land    289–01
Our lost and fallen race    011–02
Rejoicing in the race    166–03
To save our sinful race    230–03
Whate'er your race may be    439–03
Whate'er your race may be    440–03

## RACES
Races joined, the church made one    422–02

## RADIANCE
We praise you for the radiance    327–01
With radiance brighter than the sun    550–01

## RAGE (N)
And calm amid its rage did sleep    562–02
His rage we can endure    260–03
Let neither rage nor anger gain    188–05

## RAGE (V)
Still rage the fires of hate today    035–03

## RAIMENT
And raiment fit provide    269–03

## RAIN
And soft, refreshing rain    560–01
And with the gentle rain    201–03
May he be like rain that falls
   on the mown grass    204–06
The early rain also covers it with pools    208–06

## RAINBOW
God of the rainbow    272–03
The rainbow of your peace
   will span creation    105–03

## RAISE
And we to you will ever raise    121–02
For Israel you now raise up    601–01
Here I raise my Ebenezer    356–02
Lord of all, to thee we raise    473–refrain
May raise the victor strain    118–02
Raise, renew the life we've lost    131–01
Raise the anthem manifold    256–02
Raise the fallen, cheer the faint    303–03
Raise the glad strain, Alleluia    451–01
Raise the glorious harvest home    551–04
Raise the song of harvest home    551–01
Raise us to thy glorious throne    001–04
Raise us to thy glorious throne    002–02
Raise your joys and triumphs high    113–01
To God our Creator triumphantly
   raise    554–01
We would raise our alleluias    129–02

## RAISED
Raised to an exalted height    163–04
Since we have been raised with you    346–02
We know that Christ is raised
   and dies no more    495–01

## RAMPARTS
And, all their ramparts breaking    443–03

**RANG**
Rang out the angel chorus     029–02

**RANK**
Rank on rank the host of heaven     005–03
To social rank or place     471–03

**RANKS**
Angel ranks in chorus sing     065–01
Through all ranks of creatures,
    to the central height     148–03

**RANSOM**
And ransom captive Israel     009–01

**RANSOMED**
As the ransomed return to God     018–05

**RANSOMS**
The Lord ransoms the souls
    of the servants     187–07

**RATE**
At this poor dying rate     126–03

**RAY**
Saw the strange star's shining ray     065–03
The Holy Spirit's cloudless ray     474–02

**RAYS**
The Lord in rays eternal     118–02

**REACH**
Cannot reach me here     365–02
If it would reach a monarch's throne     378–05
Shall reach the whole of humankind     380–05
We reach to take what is not ours     283–04

**REALITY**
In whom we find reality and dream     484–03

**REALM**
Were the whole realm of nature mine     100–04

**REALMS**
From the realms of endless day     005–03
In realms of clearer light     399–04
Through untraveled realms of space     268–02

**REAP**
May reap their sheaves with gladness     237–03
You'll reap good fruit
    from honest work     239–01

**REASON**
And there's not any reason, no,
    not the least     364–02

**REBUILD**
Rebuild the walls of Jerusalem     196–10
Rebuild your people with your love     195–07

**RECAPTURE**
Strongly recapture thoughts
    of resurrection     529–03

**RECAST**
And recast our life's intentions     073–03

**RECEIVE**
All we have to give, receive     461–04
And receive his servant care     547–02
And then receive us as your own     353–03
Just as I am, thou wilt receive     370–03
O receive my soul at last     303–01
Receive, I beseech thee     557–01
Receive our prayer     566–00
Receive our prayer     575–06
They shall receive forgiveness     177–03

**RECEIVED**
Received this gift divine     327–02

**RECOGNIZE**
We recognize the world's disease     380–04

**RECONCILIATION**
Christ brings reconciliation     296–02

**RECORD**
Record of the revelation     331–01

**RECORDED**
Recorded what they knew     330–03

**RECOUNT**
And recount all our frail human
    hopes     547–03
And recount the deeds of the Lord     231–17

**RECOVERED**
Recovered, held, and reexpressed     330–03

**RE-CREATION**
God's re-creation of the new day     469–03

## REDEEM

| | |
|---|---|
| God did indeed redeem my soul | 228–02 |
| Redeem me from distress | 250–04 |
| Redeem the time; its hours too swiftly fly | 415–02 |
| Redeem the whole creation | 289–01 |

## REDEEMED (N)

| | |
|---|---|
| Your own redeemed forever shield | 121–03 |

## REDEEMED (V)

| | |
|---|---|
| Hath redeemed us by his blood | 144–01 |
| We're so glad that you've redeemed us | 140–03 |

## REDEEMS

| | |
|---|---|
| God redeems you from destruction | 223–02 |
| Who redeems your life from the pit | 222–04 |

## REDEMPTION

| | |
|---|---|
| The day of the earth's redemption | 015–03 |

## REFINE

| | |
|---|---|
| Refine and test each passing aim | 349–03 |

## REFLECT

| | |
|---|---|
| Thus reflect your inward light | 336–04 |

## REFLECTION

| | |
|---|---|
| Would a true reflection be | 285–01 |

## REFRESH

| | |
|---|---|
| Fresh from God, refresh our spirits | 498–02 |
| O refresh us, O refresh us | 538–01 |
| Refresh thy people on their toilsome way | 262–04 |

## REFRESHMENT

| | |
|---|---|
| Find refreshment for my spirit | 173–01 |

## REFUGE

| | |
|---|---|
| A refuge where our feet have trod | 211–01 |
| For refuge from my cruel foe | 250–02 |
| God is our refuge and our strength | 191–01 |
| God is our refuge and strength | 193–01 |
| My refuge and my tower | 212–01 |
| My refuge most secure | 197–02 |
| Other refuge have I none | 303–02 |
| Our refuge, and our great reward | 010–03 |
| Our refuge be | 275–03 |
| Precious Savior, still our refuge | 403–03 |
| The God of Jacob is our refuge | 193–07 |
| To you who for refuge to Jesus have fled | 361–01 |
| We may a refuge find | 186–02 |

## REFUSE

| | |
|---|---|
| He'll not refuse to lend | 394–02 |
| Shall we again refuse you | 007–03 |

## REFUSED

| | |
|---|---|
| When I refused to listen to God's call | 410–01 |

## REIGN (N)

| | |
|---|---|
| As befits God's holy reign | 003–03 |
| Everlasting is your reign | 460–01 |
| God's glorious reign of peace | 386–05 |
| Has begun his reign | 594–05 |
| His reign shall know no end | 151–03 |
| Shall see Christ's promised reign of peace | 450–01 |
| The reign of death was ended | 110–02 |
| Your reign on earth begun | 205–01 |

## REIGN (V)

| | |
|---|---|
| And deathless it shall reign | 378–04 |
| And he shall reign forever | 019–04 |
| And reign without a rival there | 366–01 |
| Come, and reign over us | 139–01 |
| Evermore with you to reign | 416–03 |
| Evermore with you to reign | 417–03 |
| Jesus shall reign where-e'er the sun | 423–01 |
| Over us all to reign | 066–02 |
| Reign with thee in endless day | 538–03 |
| The Lord will reign forever | 254–10 |
| They reign with him above | 149–05 |
| Thou art our Lord! thou dost forever reign | 360–05 |
| When he comes to reign | 036–02 |
| Where Christ, the Lamb, does reign | 453–01 |
| Yet you still reign, and you alone | 227–01 |

## REIGNEST

| | |
|---|---|
| Thou reignest in glory, thou rulest in light | 263–04 |

## REIGNS

| | |
|---|---|
| And still God reigns supreme | 430–02 |
| God, who reigns on heaven's high steep | 213–03 |
| Our Savior in the Godhead reigns | 108–03 |
| Who exalted reigns: now with psalms rejoice | 194–02 |
| Who reigns enthroned above | 488–01 |
| Who reigns in highest heaven | 555–03 |

## REJOICE

| | |
|---|---|
| And now we rejoice, yes, now we rejoice in you | 157–01 |
| And rejoice with praise and singing | 018–01 |
| Come ye before him and rejoice | 220–01 |
| Good Christians all, rejoice and sing | 111–01 |
| Let all rejoice who have voice to raise | 264–04 |
| Let us rejoice and be glad in it | 231–24 |
| Let us rejoice and be glad in it | 232–24 |
| Lord, rejoice in all you make | 224–04 |
| Now rejoice, Jerusalem | 114–02 |
| Now rejoice, Jerusalem | 115–02 |
| Rejoice, again I say, rejoice | 155–refrain |
| Rejoice, give thanks, and sing | 145–01 |
| Rejoice, give thanks, and sing | 146–01 |
| Rejoice, give thanks, and sing | 155–01 |
| Rejoice in glorious hope | 155–03 |
| Rejoice, the Lord is King | 155–01 |
| Rejoice, ye pure in heart | 145–01 |
| Rejoice, ye pure in heart | 146–01 |

## REJOICING

| | |
|---|---|
| And great our rejoicing through Jesus the Son | 485–02 |
| Let our rejoicing rise high as the listening skies | 563–01 |
| Make me hear rejoicing and gladness | 196–05 |

## REKINDLE

| | |
|---|---|
| Rekindle faith among us | 128–04 |

## RELEASE (N)

| | |
|---|---|
| That all may find release | 289–03 |

## RELEASE (V)

| | |
|---|---|
| Release in us those healing truths | 380–03 |

## RELIANCE

| | |
|---|---|
| Place on the Lord reliance | 179–03 |

## RELIGION

| | |
|---|---|
| Thy true religion in our hearts increase | 262–03 |

## RELY

| | |
|---|---|
| On God the Lord rely | 286–04 |

## REMAIN

| | |
|---|---|
| How long will they all remain hard of heart | 160–02 |
| Secure, unmoved I shall remain | 165–02 |
| Shall forevermore remain | 154–03 |

## REMAINED

| | |
|---|---|
| If that the Lord had not with us remained | 236–01 |

## REMEMBER

| | |
|---|---|
| Jesus, remember me | 599–00 |
| Lord, do not remember sins | 178–01 |
| Lord, remember all your love | 178–01 |
| Remember, Lord, thy works of old | 295–02 |
| Remember not our sin | 195–01 |
| Remember not our sin's deep stain | 295–02 |
| Remember, the Lord does wonders for the godly | 160–03 |
| Therefore I remember you | 190–06 |
| Unto those who still remember | 223–05 |
| We remember, we remember, we remember Zion | 245–00 |
| We shall remember all the days we lived through | 342–04 |
| When I remember you at night | 198–04 |

## REMEMBERED

| | |
|---|---|
| They praised, remembered, handed on | 330–02 |

## REMEMBRANCE

| | |
|---|---|
| To wipe their remembrance from the earth | 187–04 |

## REMOVE

| | |
|---|---|
| Remove us from all tempting paths | 590–02 |

## REMOVES

| | |
|---|---|
| So far he removes our transgressions from us | 222–12 |

## RENDER

| | |
|---|---|
| O what shall I render | 557–01 |
| We render back the love thy mercy gave us | 360–04 |
| What shall I render to the Lord | 228–03 |

## RENEW

| | |
|---|---|
| Come and renew the face of the earth | 266–05 |
| Renew us every day | 195–07 |
| Renew us with your Spirit | 358–04 |
| Then renew tomorrow's song | 547–01 |

## RENEWED

| | |
|---|---|
| Renewed, and greatly comforted | 500–01 |

## REPAIR

| | |
|---|---|
| To Jesus I repair | 487–01 |

**REPAY**
I ne'er can repay thee 557–03
Nor repay us according to
  our iniquities 222–10

**REPEAT**
Repeat the sounding joy 040–02

**REPENT**
Now we repent and seek thy face 079–02

**REPENTANCE**
Bidding us to make repentance 003–02
He came to share repentance 072–02

**REPLENISH**
Replenish them with oil 015–02

**REPOSE**
Calm and sweet repose 541–02

**REPROACH**
And be without reproach
  when you judge 196–03
Through reproach and suffering won 425–02

**REQUEST**
Let my request accepted rise 249–03

**REQUIRE**
Did require of us a song 246–02
What does the Lord require 405–01

**RESCUE**
O rescue me, God, my helper 196–08
You rescue us from every foe 243–04

**RESCUED**
Rescued from sin's misery 137–02

**RESCUES**
Rescues us from all our foes 478–03

**RESENTMENT**
And bid resentment cease 347–04

**RESIDING**
God with us is now residing 022–02

**RESILIENCE**
And by testing faith's resilience 073–02

**RESIST**
Almighty Lord, what can resist
  your power 183–03

**RESOUND**
Let it resound loud as the rolling sea 563–01
Shall now resound with praise 230–04

**RESOUNDING**
Joyfully, heartily resounding 218–02

**RESOUNDS**
Resounds above the waters 180–01

**RESPECTS**
Respects each other's ways 386–01

**RESPOND**
May we respond with joyful praise 499–02
Respond, ye souls in endless rest 451–03
We respond in grateful worship 285–02
We respond with deep commitment 343–01

**RESPONDS**
Responds in every hour 128–03

**RESPONSE**
In response to your own saying 493–01

**REST (N)**
A rest upon the way 092–01
Let us find our rest in thee 001–01
Let us find our rest in thee 002–01
Let us find the promised rest 376–02
O Sabbath rest by Galilee 345–03
O'er Bethlehem it took its rest 056–04
There would I find a settled rest 172–03
Thy rest, thy joy, thy glory share 426–05
To thine untroubled rest 228–01
With those whose rest is won 442–05

**REST (V)**
And I am thine! I rest in thee 320–refrain
Do rest within your sheltering care 530–02
Great Spirit, come, and rest in me 320–refrain
Happy are they in God who rest 530–04
I rest in your own care 212–04
I rest me in the thought 293–01
I rest my weary soul in thee 384–01
I rest on his unchanging grace 379–02
O rest beside the weary road 038–03

## RIGHT

| | |
|---|---|
| Holy Spirit, right divine | 321–04 |
| If that the Lord had not our right maintained | 236–01 |
| Is his, is his by right | 149–02 |
| The right to have one's daily bread | 332–03 |
| The right to speak, the right to be | 332–03 |
| To you of right belongs | 549–03 |

## RIGHTEOUS

| | |
|---|---|
| Be glad in God, you righteous | 184–05 |
| Rejoice in the Lord, O you righteous | 185–01 |
| The righteous cry out and God hears | 187–05 |
| The righteous fear to speak | 443–03 |
| The righteous shall enter through it | 231–20 |
| The righteous shall enter through it | 232–20 |
| Where all the righteous go | 325–02 |

## RIGHTEOUSNESS

| | |
|---|---|
| And his righteousness | 333–01 |
| And righteousness in fountains | 205–02 |
| And your righteousness to a king's son | 204–01 |
| Dressed in his righteousness alone | 379–04 |
| For righteousness and bread | 358–04 |
| O God of righteousness and grace | 412–05 |
| Shall God's righteousness extend | 223–04 |
| With righteousness in field and town | 434–03 |
| With righteousness your rod | 437–04 |
| Your righteousness will then shine forth | 188–03 |

## RING

| | |
|---|---|
| And ring from all the trees | 561–03 |
| Ring with harmonies of liberty | 563–01 |

## RINGS

| | |
|---|---|
| Now through Christendom it rings | 112–02 |
| While rings the earth with Christ's glory and fame | 147–02 |

## RIPENS

| | |
|---|---|
| Ripens what we sow | 480–02 |

## RISE (N)

| | |
|---|---|
| Turning from the summit's rise | 073–01 |

## RISE (V)

| | |
|---|---|
| And rise on your wings | 319–01 |
| In vain you rise at morning break | 238–02 |
| Rise from the grave now, O Lord | 120–02 |
| Rise to all eternity | 303–04 |
| Rise up and follow thee | 345–02 |
| Rise up, and give us light | 017–01 |
| Rise up like eagles on the wing | 411–04 |
| Rise up, shepherd, and follow | 050–01 |
| Shall rise our song of grateful trust | 530–03 |
| They rise, and needs will have | 076–04 |
| Thus evermore shall rise to thee | 562–04 |
| Too soon we rise, the symbols disappear | 520–04 |

## RISEN

| | |
|---|---|
| Christ is risen | 569–00 |
| Christ is risen! Earth and heaven | 104–03 |
| Christ is risen! Get you gone | 104–03 |
| Christ is risen! He meets our eyes | 097–04 |
| Christ is risen! Hush in wonder | 104–01 |
| Christ is risen! Raise your spirits | 104–02 |
| Christ is risen! Shout Hosanna | 104–01 |
| Christ the Lord is risen again | 112–01 |
| Christ the Lord is risen today | 113–01 |
| For Christ the Lord is risen | 118–03 |
| If the Lord had never risen | 109–02 |
| Jesus Christ has risen to save us | 107–01 |
| Jesus Christ is risen today | 123–01 |
| That Christ, once dead, is risen | 128–02 |

## RISES

| | |
|---|---|
| Christ rises glorious from the dead | 119–03 |

## RISING

| | |
|---|---|
| And our rising by your will | 073–03 |

## RITE

| | |
|---|---|
| Let each cherished outward rite | 336–04 |

## RIVER

| | |
|---|---|
| And from the river to the ends of the earth | 204–08 |
| Holy river of God's city | 192–02 |
| Jordan river, chilly and cold | 315–02 |
| The river running by | 267–02 |
| There is a river whose streams make glad the city of God | 193–04 |

## RIVERS

| | |
|---|---|
| By the Babylonian rivers | 246–01 |
| From rivers of unfailing joy | 186–03 |
| Let rivers clap their hands | 219–05 |
| Rivers and seas and torrents roaring | 218–03 |
| The rivers and fountains | 554–02 |
| The rivers of sorrow shall not overflow | 361–03 |

## ROAD

| | |
|---|---|
| Steep though the road may be | 279–04 |

Stony the road we trod 563–02
Then we know that God still goes
 that road with us 407–refrain
You are my God; though dark my road 284–01

## ROBE

A ragged robe of rabbit skin 061–02
And robe of sorrow round you 007–01
Into a seamless robe, a fragile whole 266–04
Scourged, mocked, in purple robe
 arrayed 083–03
Take we the robe and the harp
 and the palm 147–04
Whose robe is the light,
 whose canopy space 476–02

## ROBED

You have robed yourself, and reigning 213–01

## ROBES

With robes of salvation you cover
 the meek 257–02

## ROCK

A rock and stronghold is my God 197–01
From rock and tempest, fire and foe 562–04
I say to God, my rock 190–09
Mountain rock and cave for beast 224–03
My rock of strength is found in God 197–02
On Christ, the solid Rock, I stand 379–refrain
On the rock of ages founded 446–01
On the rock there towers a cross 296–01
Our rock and cornerstone 471–04
Smitten rock with streaming side 154–04
Thou wast their rock, their fortress,
 and their might 526–02

## ROCKS

Amid the rocks and quicksands 327–02
Let rocks their silence break 561–03
Of rocks and trees, of skies and seas 293–01

## ROD

And thy rod and staff me comfort still 170–03
Bitter the chastening rod 563–02
The rod and staff my Shepherd holds 174–03
Thy rod and staff my comfort still 171–04
Your rod and staff, they comfort me 175–03
Your rod and staff will lead me 173–02

## RODE

Rode on in lowly state 089–02

## ROLL

Nor roll of stirring drums 447–02
Nor roll of stirring drums 448–02

## ROLLED

Rolled the stone away 122–01

## ROLLS

That rolls through arches dim 278–03

## ROOM

An upper room did our Lord prepare 094–01
Born in a borrowed room 030–01
In every room in our Father's house 094–04
Make room to breathe
 the living thought 349–01
We meet as in that upper room
 they met 503–02

## ROOT

Thou root of Jesse; David's Son,
 my Lord and Savior 069–01

## ROOTED

Rooted, grafted, built on thee 501–02

## ROSE (N)

Lo, how a rose e'er blooming 048–01
The rose I have in mind 048–02

## ROSE (V)

And he rose on Easter 299–06
Christ rose from depths of earth 470–02
For us he rose from death again 083–04

## ROUSES

That your blest Spirit rouses
 everywhere 424–01

## ROUTINES

In old routines or ventures new 419–04

## ROYALTY

Royalty and shepherds came 034–02

## RULE (N)

Christ brings God's rule, O Zion 013–02
For God's own rule for living life 255–05
His rule is peace and freedom 013–02
Rule and might o'er all possessing 069–01
Your rule is still increasing 205–03
Your rule is without end 205–03
Your Savior's rule embrace 013–03

## RULE (V)

| | |
|---|---|
| And Christ shall rule victorious | 289–04 |
| And rule in equity | 205–01 |
| And rule with equity | 219–06 |
| Let them not rule my soul | 167–04 |
| Now rule in every heart | 139–03 |
| Rule in all our hearts alone | 001–04 |
| Rule in all our hearts alone | 002–02 |

## RULER

| | |
|---|---|
| Be thou our ruler, guardian, guide, and stay | 262–02 |
| Ruler of all nature | 306–01 |
| The ruler of earth and the heavens | 120–03 |
| You, Lord, are ruler of all lands | 226–01 |

## RULERS

| | |
|---|---|
| All rulers bow before you | 205–03 |
| Our earthy rulers falter | 291–01 |
| Rulers of earth, give ear | 405–02 |
| Rulers of the world rise up | 159–01 |
| Rulers, peoples, now join to serve the Lord | 194–02 |

## RULES

| | |
|---|---|
| Christ rules o'er earth and heaven | 155–02 |
| He rules the world with truth and grace | 040–04 |

## RULEST

| | |
|---|---|
| Nor wanting, nor wasting, thou rulest in might | 263–02 |

## RULETH

| | |
|---|---|
| God ruleth on high, almighty to save | 477–02 |

## RUN

| | |
|---|---|
| Run the straight race through God's good grace | 307–02 |

## RUNS

| | |
|---|---|
| God's Word runs swiftly o'er the earth | 255–03 |
| It runs from east to farthest west | 166–04 |
| It runs to heaven and then right back | 315–02 |

## RUSH

| | |
|---|---|
| On the rush of the wind | 319–03 |
| When, in the rush of days, my will | 351–02 |
| With rush of wind and roar of flame | 124–01 |

# S

## SACRAMENT

| | |
|---|---|
| Here in this sacrament we see | 499–02 |
| In the sacrament of life | 305–02 |
| In thine own sacrament of bread and wine | 503–01 |

## SACRAMENTS

| | |
|---|---|
| Make as sacraments of you | 504–03 |

## SACRIFICE (N)

| | |
|---|---|
| Christ, by whose willing sacrifice we live | 375–03 |
| For in sacrifice you take not delight | 196–09 |
| God's own sacrifice complete | 097–03 |
| Her pure sacrifice of love | 473–05 |
| My sacrifice a contrite spirit | 196–09 |
| Sacrifice, love, peace and justice | 033–03 |
| Then as the evening sacrifice | 249–03 |
| To pay your morning sacrifice | 456–01 |
| To see the approaching sacrifice | 090–03 |
| To see the approaching sacrifice | 091–03 |

| | |
|---|---|
| What sacrifice desire | 405–01 |
| With every morning sacrifice | 423–02 |

## SACRIFICE (V)

| | |
|---|---|
| I sacrifice them to his blood | 100–02 |
| I sacrifice them to his blood | 101–02 |

## SADNESS

| | |
|---|---|
| And he feels for all our sadness | 049–03 |
| Does sadness fill my mind | 487–02 |
| Here in sadness eye and heart long for thy gladness | 069–02 |
| You gave us Jesus to defeat our sadness | 529–03 |

## SAGES

| | |
|---|---|
| And lo! the Eastern sages stand | 068–02 |
| Sages, leave your contemplations | 022–03 |

## SAID

| | |
|---|---|
| Be directly, simply said | 336–03 |

What more can be said than
   to you God hath said     361–01

## SAILOR
The sailor saw light from above     373–03
The sailor stood all alone     373–02

## SAINTS
All saints triumphant, raise the song     451–03
All the saints adore thee     138–02
Amid all the saints God's praises
   prolong     257–01
For all the saints who
   from their labors rest     526–01
For the saints of God are just folk
   like me     364–03
Let all the saints accord     228–06
Let saints and angels sing before you     017–03
Now praise the Lord, all living saints     255–01
O fearful saints, fresh courage take     270–03
Rejoice, O saints, rejoice     184–05
Saints within God's courts below     481–01
The saints have proved
   God's faithfulness     227–03
The saints shall not fail     257–04
The saints your grace receiving     207–03
They were all of them saints of God     364–01
Thousand, thousand saints attending     006–01
Thy chosen saints to die     228–05
To glorify the saints     155–03
Where saints and angels dwell above     295–04
Which all the saints with joy confess     218–01
With all thy saints on earth
   and saints at rest     503–03
With the saints who now adore you     508–03
With the saints who now adore you     509–03
Yet saints their watch are keeping     442–03
Your saints your mighty acts will show     252–03

## SAITH
Holy Scripture plainly saith     110–02
"Thus saith the Lord," bold Moses said     334–02

## SAKE
E'en for his own name's sake     170–02
For thy name's sake, O gracious Lord     250–04
O who am I that for my sake     076–01

## SALE
From sale and profanation     291–02

## SALVATION
And for us salvation won     137–02

And God sent us salvation     029–03
And have become my salvation     231–21
And have become my salvation     232–21
Ascribing salvation to Jesus our King     477–02
Bringing great salvation     300–01
Christ has brought us salvation     296–01
For my salvation     093–03
For us and our salvation     072–03
God does for our salvation     259–03
God has made known
   the great salvation     218–01
God is my strong salvation     179–01
He has become my salvation     231–14
Let us see thy great salvation     376–04
Look now for your salvation     015–02
Now is salvation ours     491–04
Our salvation has been purchased     107–03
Our salvation have procured     123–03
Salvation from the throne     230–02
Salvation to bestow     076–02
Salvation to God, who sits
   on the throne     477–03
The God of our salvation     483–01
The King of kings salvation brings     053–03
To preach your true salvation     443–01
Trinity blessed, send us thy salvation     459–03
Who came for our salvation     133–03
Your wonderful salvation     605–01

## SANCTIFY
And sanctify to thee thy deepest
   distress     361–03

## SANDS
Across the desert sands     330–01

## SANG
And sang the song of joy     237–01
And so they sang for joy     237–02
They sang their hymns of praise     088–03
Ye, who sang creation's story     022–01
You sang in a stable     319–03

## SAT
So we sat with staring vision     246–02
We sat down and wept, and wept
   for Zion     245–00
We sat down in grief and wept     246–01
Who sat and spoke unto the three     116–03

## SATISFIED
We shall be satisfied     186–03

**SATISFIES**
Who satisfies you with good as long
   as you live               222–05

**SATISFY**
You satisfy the hungry heart     521–refrain

**SAVE**
And save us with your might       206–02
Eternal Father, strong to save      562–01
How can he save us,
   how can he help us         055–03
Is mighty now to save          308–04
Jesus Christ, you save from sin    355–refrain
Please save my life from all danger   373–04
Save me from the soothing sin     336–02
Save me in your love           182–07
Save us from the time of trial      571–00
Save us from weak resignation     420–05
Save us, thy people,
   from consuming passion      360–01
Save us, we beseech you, O Lord    232–25
Still to save and make us whole     427–02
That you would save us from our foes   601–02
Thy holy one will save          165–04
You save me from all ill         184–03

**SAVED**
That saved a wretch like me      280–01
You saved them, rescued all your own   168–02

**SAVES**
And saves the crushed in spirit     187–05
And saves the lives of the needy     204–13
Hail him who saves you by his grace   142–02
Hail him who saves you by his grace   143–02
Saves us all from death's despair     290–04
Who saves the oppressed
   and feeds the poor           253–02

**SAVEST**
Thou savest those that on thee call    510–02
Thou savest those that on thee call    511–02

**SAW**
Alone and fasting, Moses saw      087–02

**SAY**
I say: you are my God         182–06
May all we say and do         437–02
While they say to me continually,
   "Where is your God?"        190–10

**SCAN**
And scan your work in vain      270–04

**SCATTER**
Scatter all my unbelief         462–03
Scatter all my unbelief         463–03

**SCATTERS**
Scatters fear and gloom        122–02

**SCENES**
In scenes exalted or depressed     265–03

**SCEPTER**
His the scepter, his the throne     144–01

**SCHEMES**
Delivered from our selfish schemes   450–01
Whose evil schemes succeed      188–04

**SCHISMS**
By schisms rent asunder        442–03

**SCIENCE**
What science cannot plumb or chart   287–03

**SCORN (N)**
And scorn of truth and right      289–02
But the Lord has scorn on them     159–02

**SCORN (V)**
Scorn thy Christ, assail thy ways    420–02

**SCORNS**
The Lord is high, yet scorns the proud   247–04

**SCRIPTURE**
Did scripture join with scripture     071–02

**SCRIPTURES**
According to the scriptures       598–00

**SEA**
And made the wide blue sea      294–01
Around the glassy sea         138–02
Beside the Syrian sea         345–02
Cruel the sea which seemed so wide   373–01
From sea to shining sea        564–01
I, the Lord of sea and sky       525–01
In the sea and air and field       163–05
Let the sea roar, and all its creatures   217–05
Of sea and fire and air         274–01

The sea, and all that is in them 254–06
The swelling sea obeys thy will 209–03
Threatening us on life's wild sea 373–05
To calm the stormy sea 201–02
To God the spacious sea belongs 214–04

**SEAL (N)**
Give it your seal of forgiveness
    and grace 516–02

**SEAL (V)**
Seal it for thy courts above 356–03

**SEARCH (N)**
From search for wealth and power 289–02

**SEARCH (V)**
And search for hope and faith 358–02
If they will search for God,
    their Savior confessing 177–03
Search me, O God, search me
    and know my heart 248–05
Search my heart while I run this race 354–05
To search for what is true 162–03
You search us still with eyes of flame 156–02

**SEAS**
And surging seas rampage 259–01
Dark seas of trouble roll 308–03
Deep seas obey thy voice 271–01
Is far deeper than the seas 381–01
Let seas in all their fullness roar 219–05
Through the seas there runs a road 494–02
Upon the seas of old 176–01

**SEASHORE**
See him at the seashore 299–03

**SEASON**
Humbled for a season,
    to receive a name 148–02

**SEASONS**
As seasons come and go 292–01
The seasons to command 255–03

**SEAT**
For there is judgment's royal seat 235–03

**SEATED**
You are seated at the right hand
    of the Father 566–00

You are seated at the right hand
    of the Father 575–06

**SECRET**
The secret of release 390–02
Then in the secret of my heart
    teach me wisdom 196–04

**SECRETS**
Nature's secrets open wide 465–03
To read the secrets of your work
    on high 297–01

**SECT**
Defying sect and faction 291–03

**SEE**
Now thee alone I see 359–02
O Jesus, nothing may I see 366–03
O may we ever clearly see 474–04
Shall their true Messiah see 006–02
That we may see aright 118–02
To see thee as thou art 278–04
Was blind, but now I see 280–01
We see and praise him here 507–04

**SEED**
One more seed is planted there 012–02
The good seed on the land 560–01
The seed by God provided 200–02
To plant the gospel seed 552–03
Whose seed a mighty race should be 601–03
Ye chosen seed of Israel's race 142–02
Ye chosen seed of Israel's race 143–02

**SEEDTIME**
The seedtime and the harvest 560–03

**SEEK**
And seek no bribe or gain 164–03
And seek where you are found 399–03
As we seek the realm of God 465–01
But seek to love unselfishly 374–04
Doth seek to work us woe 260–01
Early let us seek thy favor 387–03
Ever seek thy mercy seat 063–02
How good to those who seek 310–03
I seek you eagerly 198–01
In vain we seek for rest, for joy 437–01
Jesus, our Lord, may we not seek 374–03
Let all who seek you then rejoice 161–04
Now to seek and love and fear you 454–01

**SEEK** (cont.)

| | |
|---|---|
| Now with you I will seek other seas | 377–refrain |
| O let me seek thee, and O let me find | 326–02 |
| Seek and ye shall find | 333–02 |
| Seek out the lonely and God's mercy share | 424–02 |
| Seek out this soul of mine | 313–01 |
| Seek peace and pursue it | 187–03 |
| Seek the great desire of nations | 022–03 |
| Seek ye first the kingdom of God | 333–01 |
| Till we seek no other glory | 073–03 |
| To teach the ones who seek light | 552–02 |
| To them that seek thee thou art good | 510–02 |
| To them that seek thee thou art good | 511–02 |
| Who seek your house and on you call | 161–03 |

**SEEN**

| | |
|---|---|
| How blest are they who have not seen | 117–06 |
| How they had seen the risen Lord | 117–03 |
| Seen in the Christ, thy Son | 412–05 |
| The God of gods will be seen in Zion | 208–07 |
| Till all have seen and heard | 434–04 |

**SEERS**

| | |
|---|---|
| Your son shall be Emmanuel, by seers foretold | 016–02 |

**SEES**

| | |
|---|---|
| Our Maker sees and knows | 352–02 |

**SEIZED**

| | |
|---|---|
| Had seized their troubled mind | 058–02 |
| Had seized their troubled mind | 059–02 |
| Seized all the guilty world around | 312–00 |

**SELF**

| | |
|---|---|
| His own self for heavenly food | 005–02 |
| If self upon its sickness feeds | 390–03 |
| Who more than self their country loved | 564–03 |

**SELFISHNESS**

| | |
|---|---|
| Where no selfishness can sever | 136–02 |

**SELVES**

| | |
|---|---|
| Our true selves alone unmask | 512–02 |

**SEND**

| | |
|---|---|
| Send us from above | 465–04 |
| Whom shall I send | 525–01 |

**SENDS**

| | |
|---|---|
| All God sends us through the Son | 481–03 |

**SENSE**

| | |
|---|---|
| For sense of human worth | 437–01 |
| In a small or global sense | 343–03 |
| Let sense be dumb, let flesh retire | 345–05 |
| Linking sense to sound and sight | 473–03 |
| Send a sense of your presence as we seek leadership | 273–04 |

**SENT**

| | |
|---|---|
| For us he sent the Spirit here | 083–04 |
| Sent him to die, I scarce can take it in | 467–03 |
| Sent out to serve, as he was sent | 094–03 |
| 'Tis sent to announce a newborn King | 068–01 |

**SENTENCE**

| | |
|---|---|
| To speak the vital sentence | 072–02 |

**SEPARATION**

| | |
|---|---|
| One, though torn by separation | 135–03 |

**SERAPHIM**

| | |
|---|---|
| More glorious than the seraphim | 451–02 |

**SERAPHS**

| | |
|---|---|
| Bright seraphs, cherubim, and thrones | 451–01 |

**SERENITY**

| | |
|---|---|
| Bring us serenity | 279–04 |

**SERVANT**

| | |
|---|---|
| And servant of the Lord | 601–01 |
| And to each servant does the Master say | 415–01 |
| Each newborn servant of the Crucified | 371–02 |
| Lord, bid your servant go in peace | 603–01 |
| Lord God, you now have set your servant free | 604–00 |
| Not a servant, but a friend | 104–02 |
| Now may your servant, Lord | 605–01 |
| O Lord, you gave your servant John | 431–01 |
| The suffering servant true | 070–02 |
| There shall thy servant be | 388–04 |
| There shall thy servant be | 389–04 |
| Thy servant, Lord, am I | 228–05 |
| To be God's servant in this earthly life | 410–03 |
| Your servant finds enlightenment | 167–03 |

**SERVANTS**

| | |
|---|---|
| And as servants then employ us | 512–03 |
| As the servants of your grace | 425–01 |
| Come, all you servants of the Lord | 242–01 |
| Come, servants, now and offer laud | 226–01 |
| Hast all thy servants led | 269–01 |

Here, O Lord, your servants gather 465–01
Here the servants of the Servant 461–03
How satisfied your chosen servants 201–01
Lord, make us servants of your peace 374–01
Praise, you servants of the Lord 225–01
That your servants, Lord, in freedom 427–04
To your servants gathered here 524–01
We, your servants, bring the worship 427–01
Ye servants of God
    your Master proclaim 477–01
Your servants undergrid 289–03

**SERVE**
And serve you with their hands 233–02
Freely as Son of Man to serve 070–03
Him serve with mirth,
    his praise forthtell 220–01
May we serve as you intend 429–05
Serve thee as thy hosts above 376–03
Serve the Lord with holy fear 159–04
Serve you all my days 352–01
That we might serve you all our days 601–03
These are the ones we should serve 367–03
We will serve with faith anew 504–03
We would serve you, Lord, and give 486–04

**SERVED**
Such as served you faithfully 077–04

**SERVICE**
For service, too, is sacrament 094–03
Go forth in God's service and strong
    in God's might 257–03
His service is the golden cord 439–02
His service is the golden cord 440–02
In loving service all our days 499–02
In your service, Lord, defend us 508–04
In your service, Lord, defend us 509–04
May we in service to our God 434–04
Our service and our songs 558–03
That, likewise in God's service, we 070–04
You our service giving 127–01

**SERVING (N)**
Their serving to equip 552–04

**SERVING (V)**
Serving God above 348–04
Serving others, honoring you 268–03
Serving you by loving all 422–03

**SET**
Great God, in Christ you set us free 353–05
Thou, Lord, hast set me free 395–01

**SETTLE**
You settle ridges, soften furrows 201–03

**SEVER**
From you nothing ever can sever 157–02

**SHADES**
Removing shades of pride and fear 332–02
Though shades of death encompass me 174–03

**SHADOW**
And shadow of the grave 601–05
Beneath the shadow of thy wings 186–02
The shadow of a mighty rock 092–01
There is no shadow of turning
    with thee 276–01
With the shadow of thy wing 303–02

**SHADOWS**
And death's dark shadows put to flight 009–02
And earth's vain shadows flee 543–05
Deep in the shadows of the past 330–01
Shadows fall, but hope, prevailing 544–01
Shadows of the evening 541–01
Till shadows have vanished 554–01
Till the long shadows o'er
    our pathway lie 415–04

**SHAKE**
Shake off dull sloth, and joyful rise 456–01
What can shake thy sure repose 446–01

**SHALOM**
Forever God's shalom 239–04
In Christ's shalom 274–03
Shalom, shalom 537–02

**SHAME (N)**
For bearing shame and anguish 395–03
O shame to us who rest content 453–02

**SHAME (V)**
Shame our wanton, selfish gladness 420–03

**SHAPE**
To the shape of your designs 073–03

**SHARE**
All that see and share God's love 481–01
And share thy joy at last 301–04
As we share the death of Adam 109–02
Come, share with me
    my heart's devotion 475–04

**SHARE** (cont.)
O God, we share the image of your Son 385–03
Reborn we share with him an Easter life 495–02
Share in the Father's glory 133–03
Share inventive powers with you 268–01
Share your children's liberty 429–03
Singing, share our joy with all 432–00
We share by water in his saving death 495–02
We share our mutual woes 438–03
We share your pain and find your joy 035–05
What it is in Christ we share 461–01
When you come again, we will share
   your glory 346–02

**SHARED**
As he shared the loneliness 406–01

**SHARES**
And he shares in all our gladness 049–03
When a poor one who has nothing
   shares with strangers 407–01

**SHARING**
We are sharing the same communion
   meal 518–02

**SHEAVES**
Sheaves of summer turned golden
   by the sun 518–01

**SHED (N)**
Stood a lowly cattle shed 049–01

**SHED (V)**
Come, shed abroad a Savior's love 126–04
God shed his grace on thee 564–01
Shed o'er the world thy holy light 510–05
Shed o'er the world thy holy light 511–05
Shed within its walls alway 416–02
Shed within its walls alway 417–02

**SHEEP**
And for his sheep he doth us take 220–02
Sheep fast asleep, there on a hill 052–01
Why have you now left your sheep 051–02

**SHELTER (N)**
And his shelter was a stable 049–02
For shelter and for bread to eat 421–02
In shelter from the cold 274–01
O keep me in the shelter of
   your throne 199–03

Our shelter from the stormy blast 210–01
Within the shelter of thine arm 542–01
Within your shelter, loving God 212–01
Your shelter and your shade 234–03

**SHELTER (V)**
Lord, shelter us, our footsteps keep 215–03

**SHELTERS**
Shelters thee under his wings, yea,
   so gently sustaineth 482–02

**SHEPHERD**
As when the shepherd calls his sheep 521–01
If I were a shepherd, I would bring
   a lamb 036–04
My shepherd is the Lord 173–refrain
Savior, like a shepherd lead us 387–01
You are the shepherd, we the sheep 215–03

**SHEPHERDESS**
And one was a shepherdess
   on the green 364–01

**SHEPHERDS (N)**
Frightened shepherds hear them say 065–01
Of shepherds watching there 308–01
Say, you holy shepherds, say 051–02
Shepherds, in the fields abiding 022–02
Shepherds keep watch by their fire 052–01
Shepherds keeping vigil till
   the morning new 037–02
Shepherds quake at the sight 060–02
Shepherds saw the wondrous sight 027–02
Shepherds see a wondrous sight 065–01
Shepherds, why this jubilee 023–02
The shepherds feared and trembled 029–02
Was to certain poor shepherds
   in fields as they lay 056–01
While shepherds kept their watching 029–01
While shepherds watch are keeping 053–01
While shepherds watched their flocks
   by night 058–01
While shepherds watched their flocks
   by night 059–01
Whom shepherds guard
   and angels sing 053–refrain
You shepherds, shudder not
   with fright 026–00

**SHEPHERDS (V)**
Who shepherds us at every stage 402–01

## SHIELD (N)

| | |
|---|---|
| Behold our shield, O God | 208–09 |
| He will my shield and portion be | 280–04 |
| Nearer than ever, still our shield and sun | 520–04 |
| Our shield and defender, the Ancient of Days | 476–01 |

## SHIELD (V)

| | |
|---|---|
| And shield my soul from sin | 388–02 |
| And shield my soul from sin | 389–02 |

## SHINE

| | |
|---|---|
| And shine on you with radiant face | 242–02 |
| As shine the lights of eventide | 548–03 |
| Shine ever on my sight | 313–02 |
| Shine on us with the light of thy pure day | 457–02 |
| Shine through the gloom and point me to the skies | 543–05 |
| Shine upon us like the morning sun | 033–03 |
| Shine upon us, Savior, shine | 203–01 |
| You shine with holy light | 206–02 |

## SHINES

| | |
|---|---|
| Jesus shines brighter, Jesus shines purer | 306–03 |
| Shines on from age to age | 327–01 |
| Shines out the wonder of your cross | 035–04 |
| Shines through our night | 544–02 |
| Which shines on you today | 411–01 |
| Yonder shines the infant light | 022–02 |

## SHIP

| | |
|---|---|
| This single ship sailed the deep sea | 373–01 |

## SHOOTS

| | |
|---|---|
| Like olive shoots they shall surround | 239–02 |

## SHORE

| | |
|---|---|
| Offering up on every shore | 473–05 |
| On heaven's blissful shore | 150–03 |

## SHOULDER

| | |
|---|---|
| And on his shoulder gently laid | 171–03 |

## SHOUT (N)

| | |
|---|---|
| Reaching out with a shout of joy | 514–01 |
| The shout of rampart guards surrounds us | 017–01 |
| With shout of acclamation | 467–04 |

## SHOUT (V)

| | |
|---|---|
| Come shout the story | 177–04 |
| Shout for joy, all trees of the woods | 217–06 |
| Shout through them their joyful greeting | 074–02 |
| Shout to God with joy | 194–01 |
| You will hear the Christian shout | 449–03 |

## SHOUTS

| | |
|---|---|
| Let shouts of holy joy outburst | 119–02 |
| With glad shouts and songs of thanksgiving | 190–04 |

## SHOW

| | |
|---|---|
| Show us what we yet may do | 268–01 |

## SHOWER (N)

| | |
|---|---|
| As a gracious shower descend | 317–01 |

## SHOWER (V)

| | |
|---|---|
| Shower down thy radiance from above | 474–02 |
| You shower us with blessings | 207–03 |

## SHOWERS

| | |
|---|---|
| And then come gentle showers | 200–02 |
| Like showers that water the earth | 204–06 |
| You shall come down like showers | 205–02 |

## SHRINE

| | |
|---|---|
| Any shrine or sacred booth | 073–02 |

## SHUN

| | |
|---|---|
| Shun not suffering, shame, or loss | 097–02 |

## SHUNS

| | |
|---|---|
| And shuns the scorners' seat | 158–01 |

## SHUT

| | |
|---|---|
| And shut its glories in | 078–03 |

## SHUTS

| | |
|---|---|
| That shuts our hearts to thee | 412–04 |

## SICK

| | |
|---|---|
| God of the sick | 272–04 |

## SIDE

| | |
|---|---|
| Ever constant by your side | 077–05 |
| From your side this branch forever | 493–04 |
| If thou art by my side | 388–01 |
| If thou art by my side | 389–01 |
| My pierced side, O Thomas, see | 117–04 |

## SIDE (cont.)

| | |
|---|---|
| Set by the river's side | 158–03 |
| Side by side and friend with friend | 343–01 |
| Thou, Lord, wast at our side; all glory be thine | 559–02 |

## SIDETH

| | |
|---|---|
| Through him who with us sideth | 260–04 |

## SIFTED

| | |
|---|---|
| Who sifted, chose, and then preserved | 330–04 |

## SIGH (N)

| | |
|---|---|
| Are lighter than a sigh | 197–03 |
| O sovereign God, now hear our sigh | 161–01 |

## SIGH (V)

| | |
|---|---|
| Many sigh as they pray | 160–06 |

## SIGHS

| | |
|---|---|
| God hears thy sighs and counts thy tears | 286–01 |
| With sighs of deepest pain | 181–01 |

## SIGHT

| | |
|---|---|
| And evil in your sight | 195–02 |
| Before the sight of heaven | 184–01 |
| Is still with thee, nor leaves thy sight | 320–01 |
| O wondrous sight, O vision fair | 075–01 |
| Of sight regained, the end of greed | 332–01 |
| The Bridegroom is in sight | 017–01 |
| With full and endless sight | 399–04 |

## SIGHTS

| | |
|---|---|
| I see the sights that dazzle | 388–02 |
| I see the sights that dazzle | 389–02 |
| My sights set high on you | 522–04 |

## SIGN

| | |
|---|---|
| And this shall be the sign | 058–03 |
| And this shall be the sign | 059–03 |
| Baptized with the Spirit's sign | 498–01 |
| Is the sign of death and rising | 494–02 |
| Marked with the sign of Christ our King | 492–03 |
| Sign of blessing, power of love | 523–01 |
| The sign of second birth | 443–02 |
| Who by this sign didst conquer grief and pain | 360–05 |
| You have set your sign on me | 323–01 |

## SIGNS

| | |
|---|---|
| Living signs, Lord, of your care | 512–05 |
| Such awesome signs you do | 201–02 |
| What its signs of promise are | 020–01 |

## SILENCE

| | |
|---|---|
| Here in silence, as in speech | 461–02 |
| In silence reflect | 160–04 |
| The silence of eternity | 345–03 |
| While I kept guilty silence | 184–02 |

## SILVER

| | |
|---|---|
| Take my silver and my gold | 391–04 |

## SIN (N)

| | |
|---|---|
| All our sin, enslavement, and pain | 296–02 |
| And from all sin will set you free | 054–03 |
| And sin we shall be free | 438–04 |
| Born to save us from our sin | 065–02 |
| But all who would from sin be free | 103–02 |
| But each of us, though dead in sin | 103–03 |
| But they whom sin has wounded sore | 103–01 |
| False and full of sin I am | 303–03 |
| For human creature's sin | 078–03 |
| From their sin restrain | 541–03 |
| God has put away our sin | 223–03 |
| Have o'er sin the victory won | 014–03 |
| How blest are those whose great sin | 184–01 |
| In thee to conquer sin | 081–02 |
| Left alone with human sin | 099–02 |
| Let not sin o'ercloud this light | 014–04 |
| Lord, keep me from presumptuous sin | 167–04 |
| Mortals' sin to bear alone | 065–02 |
| My sin is always before me | 196–02 |
| Our sin and guilt are heavy, Lord | 195–02 |
| Sin and hell in conflict fell | 365–02 |
| Sin forgiving, fear dispelling | 544–03 |
| Take away my sin and sadness | 178–03 |
| Where sin is overthrown | 274–03 |
| You take away the sin of the world | 566–00 |
| You take away the sin of the world | 575–05 |

## SIN (V)

| | |
|---|---|
| Do not sin but tremble | 160–04 |

## SINFUL

| | |
|---|---|
| Alleluia! here the sinful | 144–03 |

## SING

| | |
|---|---|
| Alleluia! sing to Jesus | 144–01 |
| And sing the song of joy | 237–03 |
| And sing today with one accord | 111–04 |
| And sing to God right thankfully | 110–01 |
| And sing to you with joyful voice | 161–04 |
| And sing with hearts uplifted high | 111–03 |

| | | | |
|---|---|---|---|
| And they will sing of all your ways | 247–03 | Sing praise, field and flower | 480–02 |
| Christ is alive! Let Christians sing | 108–01 | Sing praise in this and every hour | 226–01 |
| Come, sing a song of harvest | 558–01 | Sing praise to God, who reigns above | 483–01 |
| Come sing, O church, in joy | 430–01 | Sing praise unto the name of God | 226–01 |
| Come sing to God, O living saints | 181–01 | Sing praises that endure | 255–01 |
| Come, sing with joy to God | 215–01 | Sing praises to God's name | 181–01 |
| Eternal One, to you we sing | 226–02 | Sing praises to his name, | |
| Good Shepherd, may I sing thy praise | 171–06 | he forgets not his own | 559–01 |
| Great God, we sing that mighty hand | 265–01 | Sing praises to our heavenly Lord | 056–06 |
| How shall we sing the Lord's song | 246–03 | Sing, pray, and swerve not | |
| I sing a song of the saints of God | 364–01 | from God's ways | 282–03 |
| I sing aloud thy praises | 483–04 | Sing through all Jerusalem | 051–refrain |
| I sing of mercies that endure | 209–01 | Sing to God and praise the Name | 217–01 |
| I sing the goodness of the Lord | 288–02 | Sing to him a new song | 185–03 |
| I sing the mighty power of God | 288–01 | Sing to the glory of God | 120–01 |
| I sing the wisdom that ordained | 288–01 | Sing to the Lord, all the earth | 217–01 |
| I'm gonna sing so | 369–04 | Sing to the Lord a new song | 458–01 |
| Joyfully sing to our Savior | 106–04 | Sing to the Lord with cheerful voice | 220–01 |
| Let us sing psalms to God with grace | 214–02 | Sing together, celebrate | 039–02 |
| Let us sing, sing, sing | 300–refrain | Sing we the song of the Lamb | |
| May we sing for joy when we see | | that was slain | 147–04 |
| the battle won | 169–02 | Sing we to our God above | 123–04 |
| O come and sing unto the Lord | 214–01 | Sing with all the people of God | 594–03 |
| O gratefully sing God's power | | Sing with hearts, sing with souls | 484–refrain |
| and God's love | 476–01 | Sing you "Noel!" Day is nigh | 052–03 |
| O Lord, we sing with joyful hearts | 484–refrain | Sing your praise to God, | |
| O sing a new song to the Lord | 216–01 | sing with joyful voice | 194–02 |
| O sing a new song to the Lord | 217–01 | Sing your praise with joy and love | 203–03 |
| O sing a song of Bethlehem | 308–01 | Then do we sing with deepest joy | 233–04 |
| O sing a song of Calvary | 308–04 | Therefore we sing to greet our King | 017–03 |
| O sing a song of Galilee | 308–03 | To thee we sing | 561–04 |
| O sing a song of Nazareth | 308–02 | To whom we sing with gladness | 484–refrain |
| O sing of fragrant flowers' breath | 308–02 | We sing and let the truth resound | 328–01 |
| O sing this Easter Day | 105–refrain | We sing and praise your fame | 162–05 |
| O sing to our God, O sing to our God | 472–01 | We sing the glories of your word | 243–04 |
| O sing to the Lord, O sing God | | We sing to you our praises | 470–04 |
| a new song | 472–01 | We will sing praises | |
| O sing ye! Alleluia | 455–02 | with a new song | 458–refrain |
| Sing a song full of the faith | 563–01 | We would sing our loud hosannas | 129–03 |
| Sing a song full of the hope | 563–01 | When I sing a psalm or hymn | 336–04 |
| Sing, all the earth and bless that Name | 216–01 | Who, like me, should sing | |
| Sing, all ye citizens of heaven above | 041–03 | God's praise | 479–01 |
| Sing, all ye citizens of heaven above | 042–03 | Yet sing to God our hope, our love, | |
| Sing alleluia and rejoice | 328–refrain | our praise | 528–01 |
| Sing, choirs of angels, sing | | | |
| in exultation | 041–03 | **SINGERS** | |
| Sing, choirs of angels, sing | | When the singers and cymbals | 486–02 |
| in exultation | 042–03 | | |
| Sing "Holy, holy, holy" | 470–01 | **SINGING (N)** | |
| Sing Hosanna, everyone | 104–03 | Praise for the singing | 469–01 |
| Sing, O heavens, and earth reply | 113–01 | | |
| Sing our harvest song | 480–02 | **SINGING (V)** | |
| Sing our Maker's faithfulness | 479–02 | Singing forevermore | 150–03 |

**SINGING (V)** (cont.)

Singing to the Father, Son,
and Holy Ghost                        526–06

Someone's singing, Lord, kum ba yah    338–03

**SINGS**

Sings your praise as Lord and King     127–03

Then sings my soul, my Savior God,
to thee                         467–refrain

**SINK**

I sink in life's alarms               378–02

**SINNED**

Against you only have we sinned        195–02

Against you, you alone, have I sinned  196–02

**SINNER**

A sinner was I conceived              196–03

O Lord, even a sinner like me         373–04

O sinner, why don't you answer   382–refrain

To the sinner, to us all              296–03

You will hear the sinner cry          449–02

**SINNERS**

And sinners may return to you         196–07

For sinners such as I                 078–01

For sinners such as I                 395–03

For sinners to die                    557–01

God and sinners reconciled            031–01

O Lamb for sinners wounded            395–02

See the Lamb for sinners slain        006–01

Sinners to redeem and save            123–02

**SINS**

All our sins and griefs to bear       403–01

All the sins I have committed         355–02

And how great your sins may be        381–01

And took our sins away                308–04

Bearing all my sins in bitter agony   299–05

From my sins turn away your face      196–05

My sins and my wrongdoing             395–01

No more let sins and sorrows grow     040–03

Our sins and all our wickedness       079–03

Our sins by you were taken       082–refrain

Quitting all the sins you prized      409–01

There are no sins that Christ
our Savior                      381–01

Was it for sins that I have done      078–02

**SIT**

And as you sit at God's right hand    133–02

On those who sit in darkness          602–03

To all who sit in darkest night       601–05

**SITUATIONS**

In living situations                  358–03

**SKEIN**

Its tangled skein of care             419–02

**SKIES**

O beautiful for spacious skies        564–01

Shining in the Spirit's skies         545–04

Still through the cloven skies
they come                       038–02

Through open skies to sing the praise 418–01

To God enthroned above the skies      249–02

**SKILL**

And too impressed by our own skill    287–01

Of never-failing skill                270–02

Then with skill and consecration      486–04

**SKILLS**

All our varied skills and arts        461–01

Blending human skills together        343–02

Skills and time are ours for pressing 422–02

**SKY**

God made the sky where airplanes fly  294–01

Now above the sky he's king           123–03

On Israel's God, who made the sky     253–02

**SLAIN**

And one was slain by
a fierce wild beast             364–02

Once for all when you were slain      154–03

**SLANDER**

I have heard the slander of the crowd 182–05

**SLAVES**

Serving as though we are slaves       367–04

**SLEEP (N)**

Above thy deep and dreamless sleep    043–01

Above thy deep and dreamless sleep    044–01

And from three days' sleep in death   114–02

And from three days' sleep in death   115–02

And with sweet sleep
mine eyelids close              542–03

From sleep and from damnation         291–02

Sleep that shall me
more vigorous make              542–03

## SLEEP (V)

| | |
|---|---|
| O sleep, dear holy Baby | 045–01 |
| Sleep in heavenly peace | 060–01 |
| Sleep, sleep, sleep | 047–02 |
| That I, before I sleep, may be | 542–02 |

## SLEEPERS

| | |
|---|---|
| "Sleepers, wake!" A voice astounds us | 017–01 |

## SLEEPS

| | |
|---|---|
| He sleeps this night so chill | 047–01 |
| Your Guardian never sleeps | 234–02 |

## SLUMBER

| | |
|---|---|
| Bethlehem in slumber lies | 065–01 |
| He lies in slumber deep | 047–02 |
| Midnight slumber lies o'er all | 065–02 |

## SLUMBERED

| | |
|---|---|
| He who slumbered in the grave | 112–02 |

## SMILE (N)

| | |
|---|---|
| Glad when thy gracious smile we see | 510–04 |
| Glad when thy gracious smile we see | 511–04 |

## SMILE (V)

| | |
|---|---|
| Thou may'st smile at all thy foes | 446–01 |

## SMITE

| | |
|---|---|
| If not, I'll smite your firstborn dead | 334–02 |
| Smite death's threatening wave before you | 540–04 |

## SNARE

| | |
|---|---|
| As from the snare a bird escapeth free | 236–03 |
| From the snare you will deliver | 178–02 |

## SNOW

| | |
|---|---|
| God sends the snow in winter | 560–01 |
| I, the Lord of snow and rain | 525–02 |
| See amid the winter's snow | 051–01 |
| Snow had fallen, snow on snow | 036–01 |
| The snow lay on the ground, the stars shone bright | 057–01 |

## SNOWSTORM

| | |
|---|---|
| Loud blowing snowstorm | 458–01 |

## SOCIETY

| | |
|---|---|
| To a just society | 429–04 |

## SOLACE

| | |
|---|---|
| A solace here I find | 487–02 |
| Filled with solace, light, and grace | 489–01 |
| Thou wilt find a solace there | 403–03 |

## SOLDIER

| | |
|---|---|
| And one was a soldier, and one was a priest | 364–02 |

## SOLDIERS

| | |
|---|---|
| O may thy soldiers, faithful, true, and bold | 526–03 |
| The soldiers sought the child in vain | 035–02 |

## SOLITARY

| | |
|---|---|
| Where the solitary labor | 305–02 |

## SOLITUDE

| | |
|---|---|
| All is solitude and gloom | 097–04 |

## SON

| | |
|---|---|
| Son of God and Mary's son | 137–02 |

## SONG

| | |
|---|---|
| A joyful song of praise | 200–04 |
| A song of thanksgiving | 554–01 |
| A song to your maker and ruler now raise | 257–01 |
| All praise to God for song God gives | 328–01 |
| Alleluia be our song | 107–01 |
| An endless song of thankful praise | 068–04 |
| And let our song be heard | 435–03 |
| As song God places in the heart | 328–03 |
| Be this the eternal song | 487–04 |
| Ever ascending the song and the prayer | 147–03 |
| High the song of triumph swell | 014–02 |
| In song let God be glorified | 328–03 |
| In song lift up your voice | 184–05 |
| In the triumph song of life | 464–03 |
| My song is love unknown | 076–01 |
| So shall our song of triumph ever be | 371–04 |
| Sweet freedom's song | 561–03 |
| Thankful song shall rise forever | 422–01 |
| That all may hear the grateful song | 483–04 |
| That ancient song we sing | 089–03 |
| That glorious song of old | 038–01 |
| The song of triumph has begun | 119–01 |
| This may be our endless song | 125–03 |
| With song in the night high praises accord | 257–03 |
| With the song children sing | 046–01 |

Lord, enthroned in heavenly splendor 154–01
O Light whose splendor thrills
  and gladdens 550–01
O splendor of God's glory bright 474–01
O the splendor and majesty
  of God's presence 217–04
Pavilioned in splendor and girded
  with praise 476–01
The eternal splendor wearing 549–01
The Father's splendor clothes
  the Son with life 495–03
'Tis only the splendor of light
  hideth thee 263–04
Was there a sudden splendor 071–01
You came, but not in splendor bright 004–02

**SPLENDORS**
Its ancient splendors fling 038–04
The solemn splendors of the night 292–02

**SPLINTERED**
Are splintered by God's glance 259–03

**SPOIL**
Let them come out with Egypt's spoil 334–03

**SPOKE**
For he spoke, and it came to be 185–09
From Christ, who spoke as none
  e'er spoke 399–01
My God spoke and the chariot
  did stop 445–01
Then you spoke through your prophets 319–02
Thus spoke the seraph, and forthwith 058–05
Thus spoke the seraph, and forthwith 059–05

**SPOKEN**
Christ is spoken and seen and heard 514–01
For truly God has spoken once 197–05
God has spoken 331–01

**SPOUSE**
With fruitful spouse you'll parent now 239–02

**SPREAD**
And over me you have spread
  out your hand 248–01
And spread Christ's liberating word 421–05
O spread thy covering wings around 269–04
Spread good news,
  proclaim Christ's name 107–01
Spread the good news o'er all the earth 106–02

That spread the flowing seas abroad 288–01
You spread a table before me,
  before all my foes 173–03

**SPREADEST**
Thou spreadest a table in my sight 171–05

**SPREADS**
My Shepherd even spreads a feast 174–04
Now spreads the fame of his dear name 308–02
Spreads its vanguard on the way 005–03

**SPRING (N)**
It has no spring of action sure 378–03
Spring, summer, winter, autumn, all 255–03
The spring of joy that shall incline 500–02
'Tis the spring of souls today 114–02
'Tis the spring of souls today 115–02

**SPRING (V)**
Spring in your path to birth 205–02
Spring thou up within my heart 303–04

**SPRINGS**
Springs gush forth at your
  own bidding 224–02

**SQUADRONS**
The winged squadrons of the sky 090–03
The winged squadrons of the sky 091–03

**STABLE**
Jesus in a stable 300–03

**STABLE-PLACE**
In the bleak midwinter a stable-place
  sufficed 036–02

**STAFF**
Protecting us with staff and rod 259–01

**STAGE**
From stage to stage on life's
  unfolding way 532–04
Your daily stage of duty run 456–01

**STAIN**
Cleansing us from every stain 154–03
To wash away the crimson stain 240–02

**STALL**
She laid him in a stall at Bethlehem 057–02

Whose stars serenely burn    278–01

**STATION**
In its everlasting station    213–02

**STATUTES**
For when your statutes we obey    233–04
The statutes of the Lord are just    167–01

**STAY**
And close by thee to stay    081–01
And stay by my side until morning
   is nigh    024–02
And stay by my side until morning
   is nigh    025–02
Here might I stay and sing    076–05
O Jesus, ever with us stay    510–05
O Jesus, ever with us stay    511–05
Stay right here with us    398–refrain
Stay with me through each dark night    350–02
Stay with us, our hearts indwelling    544–03

**STEAL**
Steal across the sky    541–01

**STEALS**
Steals on the ear the distant triumph
   song    526–05

**STEEDS**
The steeds and chariots of flame    087–02

**STEEL**
Steel and machines    458–02

**STEEP**
On the lonely mountain steep    051–02

**STEM**
From tender stem hath sprung    048–01

**STEPS**
As with joyful steps they sped    063–02
With painful steps and slow    038–03

**STEWARDS**
As stewards of the earth may we    434–04
As stewards true receive    428–02
To live as stewards of the earth    434–02

**STILLED**
Stilled our rude hearts with thy word
   of consoling    261–02

**STING**
From death's dread sting
   your servants free    119–04
Its sting is lost forever    110–02
Where is death's sting? Where, grave,
   thy victory    543–04

**STIR**
Stir me from placidness    319–refrain

**STONE**
The stone has rolled away    105–refrain
The stone that the builders rejected    231–22
The stone that the builders rejected    232–22
Till not a stone was left on stone    007–02

**STOOP**
Stoop to my weakness, mighty as
   thou art    326–01

**STOOPS**
Stoops to you in likeness lowly    506–01

**STOP**
And there it did both stop and stay    056–04

**STORE**
From heaven's abundant store    200–01
From your rich and endless store    422–01

**STORM**
God of the storm    272–02
No storm or flood shall reach them    184–03
Through the storm, through
   the night    404–01
Till the storm of life is past    303–01

**STORMS**
Above the storms of passion    388–03
Above the storms of passion    389–03
Ere the winter storms begin    551–01
Storms in our lives, cruel and cold    373–05
Though the storms may gather    365–03
Through storms and times of calm    490–05
With their heaviest storms assail us    365–02

**STORY**
Beautiful the story    027–03
Foretold in sacred story    013–01
Fulfilling prophets' story    605–02
Heard the story, tidings of a
   gospel true    037–02

My strength was spent with grief 184–02
New strength and hope are given
    from above 410–02
New strength to sight 544–02
O give us strength in thee to fight 081–02
Our strength is in your might,
    your might alone 520–02
Put forth the strength
    that God has granted 475–02
Strength for today and bright hope
    for tomorrow 276–03
Strength to my fainting heart 383–02
Strong in your strength to venture
    and to dare 424–02
That in thy strength we evermore endure 457–05
That strength and power belong to God 197–05
The Lord is my strength and my might 231–14
The strength to finish what I start 351–01
They go from strength to strength 208–07
We have strength to hold 348–03
While strength and beauty fill
    the courts 216–03
You are my strength, my shield,
    my rock 183–03
You have the strength to make
    the mountains 201–02
Yours is the strength that sustains
    dedication 516–01

## STRENGTHEN
Come strengthen us to live in love 431–03
I'll strengthen thee, help thee 361–02
Lord, strengthen those who labor 289–03
May the God of Jacob strengthen you 169–01

## STRENGTHENED
Strengthened by Christ who is my all
    in all 410–03

## STRESS
Whose stern, impassioned stress 564–02

## STRETCH
Stretch wide our sights to global view 499–04

## STRETCHED
God, who stretched
    the spangled heavens 268–01
Who stretched a living fabric
    on our frame 385–01

## STREW
Sometimes they strew his way 076–03

## STRIFE
Amid the battle's strife 301–02
Amid the clashing strife 378–06
And when the strife is fierce,
    the warfare long 526–05
Dwelling in the daily strife 305–02
In liberating strife 564–03
It was a strange and dreadful strife 110–02
Needed in our strife 465–04
The strife is o'er, the battle done 119–01
Torn by endless strife 465–03
Where there is strife, may we make one 374–01

## STRINGS
Praise God with strings and with pipes 258–02
With strings, yes, with the lyre 219–04

## STRIVE
As we strive for peace with vigor 401–03
In vain we strive to rise 126–02
Lest we strive for self alone 422–02

## STRIVING
Our striving would be losing 260–02
Stirring us to tireless striving 427–03

## STRIVINGS
Till all our strivings cease 345–04

## STRONG
Where strong devour the weak 443–03

## STRONGHOLD
The God of Jacob is our stronghold 193–refrain

## STRUGGLE
And struggle with each choice 386–03
We feebly struggle, they in glory shine 526–04
We struggle to be human 358–02

## STUNG
You stung with the sand 319–02

## SUBJECTION
All to us subjection yield 163–05

## SUBMISSION
Perfect submission, all is at rest 341–03
Perfect submission, perfect delight 341–02

## SUBSTANCE
And all our substance and our
    strength receive 457–03

**SUCCEED**

Not succeed to harm or curse me | 178–03

**SUCCESS**

For you must give success | 277–02
In my success I felt secure | 181–02
Till all success be nobleness | 564–03
Where there is small success | 279–03

**SUFFER**

And all who suffer want are blest | 423–04
As I suffer all alone | 178–03
For all thou didst suffer | 557–03
I will suffer nought to hide thee | 365–01
Suffer and serve till all are fed | 353–04
Suffer to redeem our loss | 123–01
They suffer with their Lord below | 149–05
When at last all those who suffer
find their comfort | 407–02
Whether we suffer or sing rejoicing | 400–03

**SUFFERED**

He suffered on the tree | 078–02
He suffered shame and scorn | 103–02
What thou, my Lord, hast suffered | 098–02
Who suffered there for me | 092–02

**SUFFERING**

Of suffering overpast | 081–04
With bitter suffering,
hard to understand | 342–03
Yet steadfast he to suffering goes | 076–04

**SUFFERS**

Christ suffers still, yet loves the more | 108–04

**SUMMER**

Summer and winter, and springtime
and harvest | 276–02

**SUMMONS (N)**

Glad thy summons to obey | 538–03
Their urgent summons clearly spoken | 017–01

**SUMMONS (V)**

And summons us to life | 274–04

**SUN**

A sun and shield forever | 207–03
A sun resplendent in its might | 156–01
And where the sun that shines
becomes | 453–03

As a sun hath risen | 114–02
As a sun hath risen | 115–02
As clear as noonday sun | 188–03
Before the rising sun | 210–03
Bright as sun and moon together | 012–04
Bright shining as the sun | 280–05
Enduring as the sun | 167–02
Facing the rising sun of our new day
begun | 563–01
For the Lord God is a sun and shield | 208–11
Hail the sun of righteousness | 031–03
Hail the sun of righteousness | 032–03
Let sun and moon and stars and light | 134–01
'Neath sun or moon, by day or night | 234–03
Opening to the sun above | 464–01
Suń and moon and all creation | 479–04
Sun and moon, and stars of light | 473–02
Sun and moon both mark the seasons | 224–03
Sun and moon, bow down before him | 478–04
Sun and moon, uplift your voice | 256–01
Sun, moon, and stars in their courses
above | 276–02
Sun, who all my life does brighten | 506–02
The pleasant summer sun | 267–03
The rising sun shall shine on us | 601–05
The sun begins to rise | 602–03
The sun in its orbit obediently shine | 554–02
The sun shone out with fairer light | 121–01
The sun that bids us rest is waking | 546–04
The sun to rule the day | 288–01
Thou burning sun with golden beam | 455–01
Well might the sun in darkness hide | 078–03
When the sun of bliss is beaming | 084–03
Where brighter than the sun
he glows | 075–01
Your sun brings forth
each morning's light | 243–03

**SUNLIGHT**

Mine is the sunlight | 469–03

**SUNS**

Suns around which planets turn | 131–02
Till suns shall rise and set no more | 229–03

**SUNSET**

The sunset, and the morning | 267–02

**SUNSHINE**

Fair is the sunshine | 306–03
In sunshine and storm here you stay | 157–02
Spreading sunshine in the land | 350–01

**SUP**
There sup with us in love divine     505–02

**SUPPER**
And after supper he washed their feet     094–03

**SUPPLICATION**
And hear my supplication     240–01
Hear, O hear our supplication     317–02

**SUPPLIED**
Will surely be supplied     175–01

**SUPPLY**
My Shepherd will supply my need     172–01
Well supply thy sons and daughters     446–02

**SUPPORT**
And support you for the glory
    of God's name     169–01
Still support and comfort me     303–02
Support me in the whelming flood     379–03

**SUPPORTS**
The Lord supports the fainting mind     253–03
Supports those in distress     600–05

**SURPASSING**
Surpassing all but you     162–03

**SURROUND**
All surround the small town Bethlehem     033–01
That surround each person's sorrows     343–04

**SURROUNDED**
Now scornfully surrounded     098–01

**SURVEY**
If I survey the ground I tread     288–02
When I survey the wondrous cross     100–01
When I survey the wondrous cross     101–01

**SUSTAIN**
Sustain me, lead me out     522–03

Sustain us by thy faith
    and by thy power     457–03
Sustain us in our mission, Lord     418–02

**SUSTAINS**
Christ sustains us as of old     461–03

**SWALLOW**
And the swallow a nest for herself     208–03

**SWALLOWED**
We surely had been swallowed up alive     236–01

**SWAY**
Leave to God's sovereign sway     286–03

**SWEEP**
Sweep across the crystal sea     144–03

**SWEETNESS**
Praise for the sweetness     469–02

**SWEPT**
Are swept from off the land     158–04
You swept through the desert     319–02

**SWERVE**
And swerve from life's intended course     283–04

**SWORDS**
May swords of hate fall
    from our hands     450–01
The swords of scorn divide     291–01
Then will all our swords be plowshares     401–03

**SYMBOLS**
Here are symbols to remind us     461–02

**SYNAGOGUE**
When in the synagogue and temple     486–02

**SYSTEMS**
Imprisoned in systems, you long
    to be free     311–02
Oppressive systems snare us     291–03

# T

## TABLE

| | |
|---|---|
| And spread thy table in our heart | 505–01 |
| At God's table together we shall sit | 518–04 |
| At the table he sets the tone | 514–02 |
| At your table, confirm our intention | 516–02 |
| At your table, each time of returning | 516–03 |
| Does still my table spread | 172–02 |
| Here are table, font, and pulpit | 461–02 |
| My table thou hast furnished | 170–04 |
| Now to your table spread | 515–01 |
| The table of forgiveness | 358–03 |
| This is the heavenly table for us spread | 520–03 |
| Thou at the table, blessing, yet dost stand | 503–02 |

## TAKE

| | |
|---|---|
| And take, content what you have sent | 284–02 |
| Freely let me take of thee | 303–04 |
| Take myself, and I will be | 391–06 |
| That God, the Son of God, should take | 083–01 |
| We take it thankfully and without trembling | 342–03 |

## TAKEN

| | |
|---|---|
| Who has taken him away | 097–04 |

## TALENT

| | |
|---|---|
| Whatever talent God has given me | 410–02 |

## TALENTS

| | |
|---|---|
| Born with talents, make us servants | 422–02 |
| Let us talents and tongues employ | 514–01 |
| To use the talents given | 552–03 |

## TASK

| | |
|---|---|
| In our worldwide task of caring | 553–02 |
| No matter if the task is great or small | 410–03 |

## TASTE (N)

| | |
|---|---|
| Bring a taste of love unknown | 104–01 |

## TASTE (V)

| | |
|---|---|
| Taste and see | 187–refrain |
| Taste and see the goodness of the Lord | 187–refrain |
| We taste thee, O thou living bread | 510–03 |
| We taste thee, O thou living bread | 511–03 |

## TAUGHT

| | |
|---|---|
| For which, O Lord, you taught us to prepare | 342–02 |
| You taught us, Lord, to pray | 347–01 |

## TEACH

| | |
|---|---|
| And as you teach the world your name | 351–03 |
| And teach us how to share our bread | 421–04 |
| As we teach and testify | 107–02 |
| I graciously will teach you | 184–04 |
| I will teach you the fear of the Lord | 187–02 |
| Lord, teach us all an attitude | 556–refrain |
| Lord, teach us wisdom in our hearts | 195–03 |
| O teach me, Lord, that I may teach | 426–03 |
| O teach your wandering pilgrims | 327–03 |
| Savior, teach us so to rise | 097–04 |
| So teach us how to count our days | 211–04 |
| Teach me by that bitter cry | 099–04 |
| Teach me some melodious sonnet | 356–01 |
| Teach me the discerning eye | 323–03 |
| Teach me the patience of unanswered prayer | 326–03 |
| Teach me the struggles of the soul to bear | 326–03 |
| Teach me the way that I should go | 250–02 |
| Teach me the wayward feet to stay | 357–02 |
| Teach me thy patience; still with thee | 357–03 |
| Teach me thy will to heed | 250–03 |
| Teach me to feel that thou art always nigh | 326–03 |
| Teach me to love thee as thine angels love | 326–04 |
| Teach our minds and train our senses | 486–04 |
| Teach us as sister, brother | 358–01 |
| Teach us, O Lord, to trust in you | 590–01 |
| Teach us, O Lord, your lessons | 358–02 |
| Teach us to care for people | 358–02 |
| Teach us to know the Father, Son | 125–03 |
| Teach us to know the truth that sets us free | 392–01 |
| Teach us to serve without pride or pretension | 516–02 |
| Teach us to turn from sinfulness | 412–04 |
| Teach us, to whom you give such rich resources | 297–02 |
| Teach us with thee to mourn our sins | 081–01 |
| That I may teach transgressors your ways | 196–07 |
| That we may teach your ways | 195–05 |

## TEACHER

| | |
|---|---|
| Jesus, teacher, dwell with us | 465–02 |
| Teacher, healer, suffering Servant | 523–02 |

## TEACHINGS

| | |
|---|---|
| By your teachings true and holy | 454–01 |

## TEAR (N)

| | |
|---|---|
| The sympathizing tear | 438–03 |

## TEAR (V)

| | |
|---|---|
| Let us tear their bonds from us | 159–01 |

## TEARS

| | |
|---|---|
| And where the tears are wiped from eyes | 453–01 |
| For her my tears shall fall | 441–03 |
| God of our silent tears | 563–03 |
| My tears have been my constant food | 189–02 |
| My tears have been my food [both] day and night | 190–03 |
| Our tears have been both food and drink | 206–03 |
| Tears and smiles like us he knew | 049–03 |
| Tears have wasted my eyes, my throat, and my heart | 182–01 |
| That with tears has been watered | 563–02 |
| Though tears may tarry for the night | 181–01 |
| Undimmed by human tears | 564–04 |
| Where all is tears, may we sow joy | 374–02 |
| Wipe sorrow's tears away | 383–03 |
| With loud and bitter tears | 181–02 |

## TELL

| | |
|---|---|
| And tell how great your glory is | 247–03 |
| But simply tell you all | 390–03 |
| But who can tell how often they | 167–03 |
| Go, tell it on the mountain | 029–refrain |
| Nightly tell their maker's might | 163–03 |
| None can tell what pangs unknown | 099–01 |
| O tell of God's might, O sing of God's grace | 476–02 |
| Tell all the world God's wondrous ways | 216–02 |
| Tell all who mourn; outcasts belong | 386–04 |
| Tell heathen nations far and near | 216–02 |
| Tell its grim, demonic chorus | 104–03 |
| Tell me thy secret; help me bear | 357–01 |
| Tell of God's glory among the nations | 217–02 |
| Tell of peace, thus says our God | 003–01 |
| Tell old Pharaoh, Let my people go | 334–refrain |
| Tell the good news: Christ is born now | 033–02 |

| | |
|---|---|
| Tell the wonders, sing God's worth | 481–02 |
| Tell the world that Christ is risen | 109–01 |
| Tell the world what God has done | 433–02 |
| Tell them that their sins I cover | 003–01 |
| Tell your joyful news today | 051–02 |
| You can tell the love of Jesus | 394–03 |
| You tell us God is good | 030–03 |

## TELLING

| | |
|---|---|
| Telling Christians everywhere | 433–01 |

## TELLS

| | |
|---|---|
| For the Bible tells me so | 304–01 |
| Tells God's anguish and delight | 135–01 |
| Tells us what the Lord did say | 159–03 |

## TEMPEST

| | |
|---|---|
| While the tempest still is high | 303–01 |

## TEMPLE

| | |
|---|---|
| A living temple built on Christ | 471–04 |
| And so your temple calls us | 207–01 |
| Come, let us in God's temple meet | 235–01 |
| Come to God's own temple, come | 551–01 |
| Let it be thy temple now | 489–02 |
| Make it a temple, set apart | 008–02 |
| Now to his temple draw near | 482–01 |
| Praise God in the holy temple | 258–03 |
| See him in the temple | 299–02 |
| To this temple, where we call you | 416–02 |
| To this temple, where we call you | 417–02 |

## TEMPLES

| | |
|---|---|
| Nevermore thy temples leave | 376–03 |

## TEMPTATION

| | |
|---|---|
| He came to share temptation | 072–03 |

## TEMPTATIONS

| | |
|---|---|
| For us temptations sharp he knew | 083–02 |

## TEMPTED

| | |
|---|---|
| Tempted, and yet undefiled | 077–01 |
| When we are tempted to betray your Son | 086–02 |
| When we are tempted to deny your Son | 086–01 |

## TEMPTER

| | |
|---|---|
| For us the tempter overthrew | 083–02 |

## TEND

| | |
|---|---|
| I will tend the poor and lame | 525–03 |

Let all things living join the song 251–04
Let all things now living 554–01
Let all things seen and unseen 118–03
Makes all green things grow 480–02
Many and great, O God, are thy things 271–01
My God has done great things for me 600–02
Of all things near and far 560–02
Of the things that are, that have been 309–01
Pure and set on things 346–02
Rich in things and poor in soul 420–03
Since former things have passed away 431–01
The precious things thou dost impart 426–03
These things I remember
as I pour out my soul 190–04
Till all things now living unite
in thanksgiving 554–02
To all things and people with God 296–02
To think the One who made all things 162–02
What great things God has done
for me 475–01
Who has made all things well 267–04
Who o'er all things so wondrously
reigneth 482–02
Who wondrous things hath done 555–01
You in all things are supreme 346–01

**THINK**
And think my work's in vain 394–01
And when I think that God,
his Son not sparing 467–03
Lord Jesus, think on me 301–01
Think on your pity and your love
unswerving 093–04

**THIRST (N)**
And thirst our souls from thee to fill 510–03
And thirst our souls from thee to fill 511–03
Our thirst shall be supplied 186–03
Your thirst for my salvation 011–02

**THIRST (V)**
For you I thirst like deserts parched
and dried 199–01
May what we thirst for soon
our portion be 519–04

**THIRSTING**
Thirsting after thee 365–01

**THIRSTY**
When the thirsty water give unto
us all 407–01

**THORNS**
By thorns with which they crowned you 007–01
New thorns to pierce that steady brow 007–01
Nor thorns infest the ground 040–03
Or thorns compose so rich a crown 100–03
Or thorns compose so rich a crown 101–03
With thorns, thine only crown 098–01

**THOROUGHFARE**
A thoroughfare for freedom beat 564–02

**THOUGHT (N)**
Forever in my thought the Lord 165–02
How passing thought and fantasy 083–01
In kindling thought and glowing word 426–04
Jesus, the very thought of thee 310–01
No thought can reach,
no tongue declare 366–01
Thou my best thought, by day
or by night 339–01
Thought, speech, sight are ours by grace 136–01

**THOUGHT (V)**
They thought that they were dreaming 237–01

**THOUGHTS**
All our thoughts inspire 127–02
For all gentle thoughts and mild 473–04
Guarding our thoughts and our passions
controlling 261–02
Hence all thoughts of sadness 365–03
With thoughts as clear as morning's ray 474–03

**THOUSAND**
Is better than a thousand 207–02
Than a thousand elsewhere 208–10

**THREATEN**
Should threaten to undo us 260–03

**THREATENS**
That threatens all of life 434–02

**THREATS**
And bitter threats are hurled 289–01

**THREE**
But the greatest of the three 318–04

**THRESHOLDS**
On shadowed thresholds fraught
with fears 408–02

## THRONE

| | |
|---|---|
| Almighty God, thy lofty throne | 209–02 |
| Before his throne rejoice | 150–01 |
| Before our Father's throne | 438–02 |
| Before thy throne of grace | 269–02 |
| Christ came from heaven's throne | 076–02 |
| Faultless to stand before the throne | 379–04 |
| Fit to answer at your throne | 422–02 |
| High on your central throne | 006–03 |
| Is to the throne ascended | 180–03 |
| It shall be thy royal throne | 391–05 |
| Messiah's sure and lasting throne | 235–03 |
| Prince of Peace, make here your throne | 493–04 |
| So be it, Lord; thy throne shall never | 546–05 |
| The Lamb upon his throne | 151–01 |
| To sit upon the throne | 176–04 |
| To the throne of Godhead, to the Father's breast | 148–03 |
| To the throne of the Son of God | 062–02 |
| Trembling come before the throne | 159–04 |
| You gave up your throne in God's glory | 157–01 |
| You on your throne shall rest | 205–04 |

## THRONED

| | |
|---|---|
| Not throned afar, remotely high | 108–03 |

## THRONG (N)

| | |
|---|---|
| How I went with the throng | 190–04 |
| O that with yonder sacred throng | 142–04 |
| O that with yonder sacred throng | 143–04 |

## THRONG (V)

| | |
|---|---|
| Come, throng the courts, and offerings bring | 216–04 |
| That throng the earth, the sea, the sky | 475–04 |

## THRONGS

| | |
|---|---|
| Among these restless throngs abide | 408–05 |

## THUNDER

| | |
|---|---|
| God proclaiming, in its thunder | 074–03 |
| Take not your thunder from us | 291–01 |
| Thunder like a mighty flood | 144–01 |

## THWART

| | |
|---|---|
| That thwart awhile divine intent | 152–02 |

## TIDE

| | |
|---|---|
| O praise the tide of grace | 471–05 |
| The swelling tide had o'er us spread its wave | 236–02 |
| The tide of time shall never | 205–04 |

## TIDES

| | |
|---|---|
| Its surging tides and waves were free | 283–01 |

## TIDINGS

| | |
|---|---|
| And tidings of salvation | 013–03 |
| Glad tidings of great joy I bring | 054–01 |
| Glad tidings of great joy I bring | 058–02 |
| Glad tidings of great joy I bring | 059–02 |
| Glad tidings of our God to bring | 068–01 |
| Glad tidings of the King of kings | 010–01 |
| Good tidings to the poor | 411–02 |
| The great glad tidings tell | 043–04 |
| The great glad tidings tell | 044–04 |
| What the gladsome tidings be | 023–02 |
| What tidings brings it Israel | 052–02 |
| When Thomas first the tidings heard | 117–03 |

## TIE

| | |
|---|---|
| Blest be the tie that binds | 438–01 |
| Keep love's tie unbroken, Lord | 508–03 |
| Keep love's tie unbroken, Lord | 509–03 |

## TIMBREL

| | |
|---|---|
| Praise God with timbrel and dancing | 258–01 |
| With timbrel and harp | 257–02 |

## TIME

| | |
|---|---|
| All hail, in time appointed | 205–01 |
| And when time lays its hand | 534–03 |
| Every time I feel the Spirit | 315–refrain |
| Every time I think about Jesus | 096–01 |
| From all time where thought can soar | 213–02 |
| From this time forth and evermore | 226–01 |
| From this time forth and forevermore | 225–01 |
| God for fledging time has chosen | 012–03 |
| Infinite in time and space | 268–01 |
| Late in time behold him come | 031–02 |
| No time for rest, till glows the western sky | 415–04 |
| No time, no near nor far | 412–01 |
| Sovereign Lord of time and space | 136–01 |
| The time has come, O maidens wise | 017–01 |
| The time is near | 012–01 |
| Till the appointed time is nigh | 099–02 |
| Time, like an ever rolling stream | 210–04 |
| Where time and tears will be no more | 386–05 |

## TIMES

| | |
|---|---|
| In times of calm and strife | 373–04 |
| In times of trouble and distress | 212–04 |

**TOUCH** (cont.)

| | |
|---|---|
| Touch we now your garment's hem | 504–01 |
| We may not touch his hands and side | 399–02 |

**TOUCHED**

| | |
|---|---|
| Who touched the truth, who burned for what is right | 528–02 |

**TOWEL**

| | |
|---|---|
| Then take the towel, and break the bread | 353–04 |

**TOWER**

| | |
|---|---|
| Salvation's tower on high | 601–01 |

**TOWERS**

| | |
|---|---|
| Beneath our gleaming towers of wealth | 431–02 |

**TOWN**

| | |
|---|---|
| O little town of Bethlehem | 043–01 |
| O little town of Bethlehem | 044–01 |
| To you, in David's town this day | 058–03 |
| To you, in David's town this day | 059–03 |

**TRACE**

| | |
|---|---|
| I trace the rainbow through the rain | 384–03 |

**TRADITION**

| | |
|---|---|
| Glad of tradition, help us to see | 436–03 |

**TRAIN (N)**

| | |
|---|---|
| There is but one train upon this track | 315–02 |

**TRAIN (V)**

| | |
|---|---|
| Train us for our common task | 512–02 |

**TRAINED**

| | |
|---|---|
| So Daniel trained his mystic sight | 087–03 |

**TRANSCEND**

| | |
|---|---|
| Transcend the lofty sky | 186–01 |

**TRANSFIGURE**

| | |
|---|---|
| Lord, transfigure our perception | 073–03 |

**TRANSFORM**

| | |
|---|---|
| Transform now our living | 127–01 |

**TRANSGRESSION**

| | |
|---|---|
| Mine, mine was the transgression | 098–02 |
| To take away transgression | 205–01 |

**TRANSGRESSIONS**

| | |
|---|---|
| From all of my transgressions | 395–01 |
| When our transgressions overwhelm us | 201–01 |

**TRANSPORT**

| | |
|---|---|
| And O what transport of delight | 171–05 |

**TRAVEL**

| | |
|---|---|
| As forward we travel from light into light | 554–01 |

**TRAVELER**

| | |
|---|---|
| Traveler, ages are its own | 020–02 |
| Traveler, blessedness and light | 020–02 |
| Traveler, darkness takes its flight | 020–03 |
| Traveler, lo, the Prince of Peace | 020–03 |
| Traveler, o'er yon mountain's height | 020–01 |
| Traveler, yes; it brings the day | 020–01 |

**TRAVELERS**

| | |
|---|---|
| All travelers guard in danger's hour | 562–04 |

**TREAD**

| | |
|---|---|
| O tread the city's streets again | 408–05 |
| When I tread the verge of Jordan | 281–03 |

**TREASON**

| | |
|---|---|
| It is my treason, Lord, that has undone you | 093–02 |

**TREASURE (N)**

| | |
|---|---|
| A treasure safe on high | 011–03 |
| Bringing down the richest treasure | 317–01 |
| Great God of heaven, my treasure thou art | 339–02 |
| Jesus, priceless treasure | 365–01 |
| Lord, how vast and deep its treasure | 506–03 |
| Treasure too you have entrusted | 422–03 |

**TREASURE (V)**

| | |
|---|---|
| You treasure up your bright designs | 270–02 |

**TREASURES**

| | |
|---|---|
| All our costliest treasures bring | 063–03 |

**TREE**

| | |
|---|---|
| Instead of the thorn tree the fir tree shall grow | 337–01 |
| O Lord, once lifted on the glorious tree | 371–03 |
| See, a spreading tree has grown | 104–01 |
| The tree must be planted by human decree | 311–03 |

The tree springs to life and our hope
   is restored 311–04
Throned upon the awful tree 099–01
Upon the cruel tree 395–01
We see you, Lord Jesus,
   still bearing your tree 311–02

**TREES**
Trees you give the birds for shelter 224–03

**TREMBLE**
We tremble not for him 260–03

**TRIALS**
Have we trials and temptations 403–02
In all trials, fears, and needs 137–03
In my trials, Lord, walk with me 363–02
When through fiery trials thy pathway
   shall lie 361–04
When trials, troubles, hurts arise 233–03

**TRIBES**
Hark! all the tribes hosanna cry 090–01
Hark! all the tribes hosanna cry 091–01

**TRIBUTE**
Or tribute bid you bring 405–01
The tribute of our grateful praise 121–02

**TRIED**
Have tried, with thoughts uncouth 278–02

**TRIM**
Trim the hearth and set the table 012–01

**TRIUMPH (N)**
Alleluia! His the triumph 144–01
Now is the triumph of our King 111–01

**TRIUMPH (V)**
And triumph evermore 155–01
I triumph still, if thou abide with me 543–04
Triumph in redeeming grace 538–01
Triumph o'er the shades of night 462–01
Triumph o'er the shades of night 463–01

**TRIUMPHED**
For Christ the Lord has triumphed 430–04

**TRIUMPHS**
O Christ, thy triumphs now begin 090–02
O Christ, thy triumphs now begin 091–02
The triumphs of God's grace 466–01

**TROD**
Let us go where Christ has trod 132–04

**TROOPS**
King Herod's troops would soon appear 035–01

**TROUBLE**
All the trouble I have known 178–03
Is there trouble anywhere 403–02
Trouble is near me, none can help 168–04
When I'm in trouble, Lord,
   walk with me 363–03
When trouble is at hand 191–04

**TROUBLES**
For I will be near thee, thy troubles
   to bless 361–03

**TRUMPET**
With the trumpet make accord 486–02

**TRUMPETS**
Trumpets and organs, set in motion 218–02

**TRUST (N)**
A trust, O Lord, from thee 428–01
All my trust on thee is stayed 303–02
As we place our trust in you 185–refrain
Because on God my trust is stayed 165–03
From trust in bombs that shower 289–02
In simple trust like theirs who heard 345–02
In trust that triumphs over wrong 357–03
In you, Lord, I have put my trust 183–01
My only trust and Savior of my heart 457–01
O put your trust in God, my help 189–04
Of broken trust and chosen wrong 353–02
Put your trust in the Lord 160–05
Therefore my trust is in the Lord 240–03
They are not worth your trust 197–04
With childlike trust that fears nor pain
   nor death 533–02

**TRUST (V)**
All those who trust the Lord for strength 255–02
And trust my Maker unto death 226–02
Because I trust in you alone 212–02
Blest are those who trust in God 159–04
But as for me, I trust in you, Lord 182–06
But those who trust our own God 184–05
If thou but trust in God to guide thee 282–01
In thee do we trust, nor find thee to fail 476–05
Let Israel trust in God alone 227–03

**TRUST (V)** (cont.)

| | |
|---|---|
| O I trust in the Savior; now in my life abide | 373–03 |
| O Lord, you are my God, I trust in you | 182–refrain |
| That I trust in you to keep me | 178–01 |
| Trust and love God more than all | 498–04 |
| Trust, and thy trusting soul shall prove | 307–03 |
| Trust God, do good, dwell in the land | 188–02 |
| Trust God, it will be done | 188–03 |
| Trust no other claim than those | 409–02 |
| Trust the acts, believe the word | 107–03 |
| Trust the love which conquers fear | 406–03 |
| Trust the rich promises of grace | 282–03 |
| We trust in thee | 275–01 |
| We would gladly trust God's Word | 298–02 |
| Who trust in God's unchanging love | 282–01 |
| Whom shall we trust but thee, O Lord | 295–03 |
| With all who trust our Savior | 552–04 |
| You trust in God, so let us see | 168–03 |

**TRUSTS**

| | |
|---|---|
| O Lord of hosts, happy is everyone who trusts in you | 208–12 |

**TRUTH**

| | |
|---|---|
| And the truth that makes us free | 285–01 |
| Are truth and love and boundless grace | 209–02 |
| Be our truth, our life | 465–04 |
| Eternal truth attends thy word | 229–03 |
| For you are the Truth | 465–02 |
| Gladly the warm truth everywhere | 324–03 |
| God's truth abideth still | 260–04 |
| God's truth be thine affiance | 179–03 |
| His truth at all times firmly stood | 220–04 |
| His truth to triumph through us | 260–03 |
| Holy Spirit, truth divine | 321–01 |
| In longing to believe a truth beyond our reach | 515–02 |
| In truth and charity | 521–05 |
| Just is our God, whose truth victorious | 218–03 |
| Now Israel may say, and that in truth | 236–01 |
| O God of truth, whom science seeks | 412–03 |
| O praise persistent truth | 471–02 |
| O truth unchanged, unchanging | 327–01 |
| Shining truth to guide our souls | 131–02 |
| Sure as thy truth shall last | 441–05 |
| Thy truth unchanged hath ever stood | 510–02 |
| Thy truth unchanged hath ever stood | 511–02 |
| The truth we dimly knew | 347–03 |
| Thou art full of truth and grace | 303–03 |
| Thou art thyself the truth | 278–02 |

| | |
|---|---|
| Till truth from falsehood part | 278–02 |
| To do the truth in love | 358–03 |
| To the truth may we be found | 538–02 |
| To you, O God of truth and law | 233–05 |
| Truth and courage, faith and power | 465–04 |
| Truth and unending righteousness | 218–01 |
| Truth beyond all thought's recall | 523–03 |
| Truth of our life, Mary's Child | 030–03 |
| Where truth is spoken, children spared | 386–02 |
| Whose truth forever stands secure | 253–02 |
| With truth your royal diadem | 437–04 |

**TRUTHS**

| | |
|---|---|
| For the truths that still confound us | 553–03 |

**TRY**

| | |
|---|---|
| Try me, O God, my mind and spirit try | 248–05 |
| We try in vain to save our world | 431–03 |

**TUBES**

| | |
|---|---|
| Loud boiling test tubes | 458–03 |

**TUMBLES**

| | |
|---|---|
| That tumbles walls of fear | 471–01 |

**TUMULT**

| | |
|---|---|
| And bade its angry tumult cease | 562–03 |
| And tumult of her war | 442–04 |
| Through all tumult you endure | 192–01 |

**TUNE**

| | |
|---|---|
| In vain we tune our formal songs | 126–02 |
| Tune my heart to sing thy grace | 356–01 |
| Tune our ears to hear your call | 132–03 |

**TURN**

| | |
|---|---|
| And turn away from strife | 164–02 |
| And turn sad hearts to you | 437–02 |
| Early let us turn to thee | 387–02 |
| Gifted by you, we turn to you | 422–01 |
| Our God, to whom we turn | 278–01 |
| They turn away | 525–02 |
| Turn from evil, practice good | 187–03 |
| Turn from sin and be baptized | 409–01 |
| Turn not from his griefs away | 097–01 |
| We turn, unfilled, to heed thy call | 510–01 |
| We turn, unfilled, to heed thy call | 511–01 |

**TURNED**

| | |
|---|---|
| But soon they turned to laughing | 237–01 |
| But when you turned aside your face | 181–02 |

**TURNS**
And turns my life to gall    390–03

**TWELVE**
Then to the Twelve and to many
    faithful witnesses    598–00
Ye holy twelve, ye martyrs
    strong    451–03

**TWILIGHT**
As twilight hovers near at sunset    550–02
When twilight comes and the sun sets    547–01

**TWO**
Be with these two who now
    before you wait    532–01
Two or three are met together    504–01

# U

**UNBELIEF**
Our unbelief is sure to err    270–04

**UNCLASP**
That shall unclasp and set me free    324–01

**UNCTION**
Thy blessed unction from above    125–02

**UNDEFILED**
There he lay, the undefiled    027–01

**UNDERSTAND**
Or slow to understand    184–04

**UNDERSTANDING**
Give them the understanding
    that is kind    532–02

**UNFAITH**
From old unfaith our souls release    007–03

**UNFOLDEST**
Unfoldest blessings on your way    455–04

**UNION**
May through their union other lives
    be blessed    532–02

**UNITE**
All wondrously unite to sing    152–01
Unite around the sacred board    500–03
We unite to pray    465–01

**UNITED**
Now let us be united    435–03

**UNITY**
In holy unity    241–01

**UNIVERSE**
The universe, restored and whole,
    will sing    495–04

**UNRIGHTEOUSNESS**
I am all unrighteousness    303–03

**UNWORTHINESS**
And my unworthiness    092–02

**UPBUILD**
Upbuild your servants as we work    418–01

**UPHOLDS**
He upholds the widow and the orphan    254–09
Who upholds and comforts us    137–03

**UPRIGHT**
Praise befits the upright    185–01

**URGE**
Urge us from fledgling faith    418–01
Urge us to strong faith and action    132–02

**USE (N)**
For our use thy folds prepare    387–01
From earthly use for heaven's employ    008–02

**USE (V)**
God can use me anywhere    369–01
In all we use, to serve your holy will    297–02
O use me, Lord, use even me    426–05
Or the Lord will use the rod    159–04

**USE (V)** (cont.)

| | |
|---|---|
| Use our talents in your kingdom | 425–01 |
| Use the love your Spirit kindles | 427–02 |
| Use them your holy purpose to fulfill | 375–01 |
| Use us to fulfill your purpose | 425–01 |
| Use us to make the earth like heaven above | 392–02 |
| We use the flame that we acquire | 287–01 |

**USHER**

| | |
|---|---|
| And usher in the morning | 026–00 |

**UTTERANCE**

| | |
|---|---|
| There is no utterance or speech | 166–02 |

**UTTERS**

| | |
|---|---|
| He utters his voice, the earth melts | 193–06 |

# V

**VALE**

| | |
|---|---|
| In death's dark vale I fear no ill | 171–04 |

**VALLEY**

| | |
|---|---|
| As they go through the valley of Baca | 208–06 |
| Downward toward the shadowed valley | 073–01 |
| Through the valley to the cross | 073–02 |

**VALLEYS**

| | |
|---|---|
| And her valleys are green and where the waters flow | 273–02 |
| From the valleys of sleep | 319–01 |
| Let the valleys rise in meeting | 003–02 |
| Praise God down in the low valleys | 258–04 |

**VANISH**

| | |
|---|---|
| Moses and Elijah vanish | 073–01 |

**VARIES**

| | |
|---|---|
| It varies with the wind | 378–03 |

**VEIL (N)**

| | |
|---|---|
| O Christ, whom now beneath a veil we see | 519–04 |
| Thou within the veil hast entered | 144–04 |

**VEIL (V)**

| | |
|---|---|
| Veil their faces to the presence | 005–04 |

**VEINS**

| | |
|---|---|
| From veins of stone we lift up fire | 287–01 |

**VENTURE**

| | |
|---|---|
| And venture into space | 162–04 |
| To venture and to soar | 418–01 |

**VENTURED**

| | |
|---|---|
| We have ventured worlds undreamed of | 268–02 |

**VESSEL**

| | |
|---|---|
| Now let us be a vessel | 435–03 |

**VESTURE**

| | |
|---|---|
| Lord of lords, in human vesture | 005–02 |

**VICTIMS**

| | |
|---|---|
| And victims made because we own our name | 385–02 |
| The victims of injustice cry | 421–02 |

**VICTOR**

| | |
|---|---|
| Victor in the wilderness | 077–03 |

**VICTORIES**

| | |
|---|---|
| By the victories of meekness | 425–02 |

**VICTORS**

| | |
|---|---|
| Victors in the midst of strife | 464–03 |

**VICTORY**

| | |
|---|---|
| And didst the victory win | 081–02 |
| And eternal victory | 309–03 |
| Endless is the victory | 122–01 |
| His the victory alone | 144–01 |
| Praise to the Crucified for victory | 371–04 |
| The victory of life is won | 119–01 |
| The victory remained with life | 110–02 |
| Till victory is won | 563–01 |
| Where your victory, O grave | 113–03 |
| With you the victory win | 443–03 |

## VIEW (N)

| | |
|---|---|
| To human view displayed | 058–04 |
| To human view displayed | 059–04 |

## VIEW (V)

| | |
|---|---|
| View science as our savior | 558–02 |
| View the Lord of life arraigned | 097–02 |

## VIGILS

| | |
|---|---|
| And late your nightly vigils keep | 238–02 |

## VIGOR

| | |
|---|---|
| Like the vigor of the wind's rush | 314–01 |

## VINE

| | |
|---|---|
| From you, one holy vine | 418–02 |
| One single fruitful vine | 517–03 |
| Precious vine, let nothing sever | 493–04 |
| Vine of heaven, thy love supplies | 501–02 |

## VINEYARD

| | |
|---|---|
| Of vineyard, flock, and field | 414–01 |

## VIRGIN

| | |
|---|---|
| Of Mary, chosen virgin mild | 054–02 |

## VIRTUES

| | |
|---|---|
| Virtues, archangels, angels' choirs | 451–01 |
| Whose joyful virtues put to shame | 419–03 |

## VISION

| | |
|---|---|
| A vision of our God brought near | 332–02 |
| A vision of the world to come | 431–01 |
| And faith's fair vision changes into sight | 275–02 |
| And gives our vision voice | 386–03 |
| Be thou my vision, O Lord of my heart | 339–01 |
| Come, Lord, make real John's vision fair | 431–03 |
| Empowering us to catch the vision | 430–02 |
| Keep bright in us the vision | 289–04 |
| May your vision be our own | 132–02 |
| Still be my vision, O Ruler of all | 339–03 |
| The vision of thy glory and thy grace | 519–04 |
| Thyself the vision passing by | 292–03 |
| Till with the vision glorious | 442–04 |
| With a mighty vision | 127–03 |

## VISIONS

| | |
|---|---|
| Brighter visions beam afar | 022–03 |

| | |
|---|---|
| Visions of rapture now burst on my sight | 341–02 |
| With visions of a world at peace | 471–05 |

## VISIT

| | |
|---|---|
| And visit it with your own ardor glowing | 313–01 |
| Visit then this soul of mine | 462–03 |
| Visit then this soul of mine | 463–03 |
| Visit us with thy salvation | 376–01 |

## VISITS

| | |
|---|---|
| Who visits and redeems us | 602–01 |

## VISTAS

| | |
|---|---|
| And vistas newly seen from space | 152–01 |

## VOCATION

| | |
|---|---|
| How clear is our vocation, Lord | 419–01 |

## VOICE

| | |
|---|---|
| And find a voice to praise God's name | 218–03 |
| And when my voice is lost in death | 253–01 |
| As with ceaseless voice they cry | 005–04 |
| At this voice the world takes heed | 192–03 |
| Before God's thundering voice | 191–03 |
| By the Spirit's voice within | 331–04 |
| Every voice in concert ring | 309–02 |
| For the herald's voice is calling | 003–02 |
| Giving voice to all our sighs | 512–04 |
| Hark! A voice from yonder manger | 021–02 |
| Hear his voice, Oh! sheer delight | 547–02 |
| Heaven's voice, the dazzling light | 073–01 |
| My voice unwearied raises | 483–04 |
| My voice your goodness raise | 181–04 |
| No voice has ever heard | 166–02 |
| Nor voice can sing, nor heart can frame | 310–02 |
| Not of voice alone, but heart | 427–01 |
| O still, small voice of calm | 345–04 |
| Take my voice, and let me sing | 391–03 |
| The Father's voice from out the cloud | 075–03 |
| The voice of lamentation | 240–01 |
| The voice of prayer is never silent | 546–03 |
| The voice of prayer, the hymn of praise | 075–05 |
| Then, when thy voice shall bid our conflict cease | 539–04 |
| Voice and instrument in union | 486–03 |
| We hear thy voice, O Son of Man | 408–01 |
| Whose voice in cadent echoes | 180–01 |
| Wild and lone the prophet's voice | 409–01 |
| With everlasting voice you sound | 156–02 |

**VOICE** (cont.)

| | |
|---|---|
| With faith's bright songful voice | 471–07 |
| With the ceaseless voice of prayer | 314–03 |
| With voice of prayer and thankful song | 189–03 |
| Your still small voice be heard | 289–03 |

**VOICES**

| | |
|---|---|
| And infant voices shall proclaim | 423–03 |
| Can our voices veil the sorrow | 246–03 |
| Evermore your voices raising | 022–04 |
| Let faithful voices sing your praise | 550–03 |
| O that I had a thousand voices | 475–01 |
| Sweetest angel voices | 021–01 |
| To God our voices raise | 214–01 |
| Voices of truth thou sendest clear | 324–02 |
| Voices raised the psalmists' songs | 486–02 |
| With voices praise the sovereign God | 219–04 |
| Your voices raise | 215–01 |

**VOICING**

| | |
|---|---|
| We, too, should be voicing | 554–02 |

**VOUCHSAFE**

| | |
|---|---|
| Vouchsafe to me thy grace | 098–02 |

**VOW**

| | |
|---|---|
| Now we our vow of faith renew | 499–04 |
| What was your vow and vision | 071–01 |
| When the sacred vow is made | 524–02 |

**VOWED**

| | |
|---|---|
| You vowed to set your people free | 601–03 |

**VOWS**

| | |
|---|---|
| And daily vows ascend | 205–03 |
| Lord, I my vows to you renew | 456–02 |
| May keep the vows that we have made | 497–01 |
| My thankful vows to pay | 228–04 |
| Our vows, our prayers, we now present | 269–02 |
| To pay their vows, God's grace to own | 235–03 |
| Vows are renewed and our courage restored | 516–03 |

**VOYAGE**

| | |
|---|---|
| That, all life's voyage through | 327–02 |

# W

**WAIT**

| | |
|---|---|
| And, now departing, wait thy word of peace | 539–01 |
| And patiently I wait your day | 284–02 |
| And wait till God appeareth | 240–04 |
| Be still before the Lord and wait | 188–04 |
| For those who wait upon the Lord | 188–05 |
| I wait for it with patience | 240–03 |
| Only be still, and wait God's leisure | 282–02 |
| Silently now I wait for thee | 324–refrain |
| Though I seem to wait in vain | 178–01 |
| Wait patiently; so shall this night | 286–02 |
| Wait the coming of the Spirit | 461–01 |
| We wait the mighty Lord, our God celebrating | 177–05 |
| We wait your revelation | 007–04 |
| What though I wait the livelong night | 240–04 |

**WAITING**

| | |
|---|---|
| And confidently waiting, come what may | 342–01 |

| | |
|---|---|
| And the Lord is waiting still | 413–03 |
| Our Savior is waiting | 381–02 |
| Who is this glorious one, for whom we are waiting | 177–05 |

**WAITS**

| | |
|---|---|
| As one who waits throughout the night | 381–02 |
| Behold, the King of glory waits | 008–01 |
| She waits the consummation | 442–04 |
| The King of glory waits | 176–03 |
| Waits for God who answers prayer | 489–01 |

**WAKE**

| | |
|---|---|
| Wake my spirit, clear my sight | 321–01 |

**WAKES**

| | |
|---|---|
| She wakes and hurries through the night | 071–02 |

**WALK (N)**

| | |
|---|---|
| O for a closer walk with God | 396–01 |

O for a closer walk with God ... 397–01
So shall my walk be close with God ... 396–04
So shall my walk be close with God ... 397–04

**WALK (V)**

Although I walk in trouble, Lord ... 247–04
And me to walk doth make ... 170–02
And to always walk upright ... 350–02
And walk the road the saints
  have trod ... 434–04
From those who walk uprightly ... 208–11
He had to walk it by himself ... 080–01
I safely walk by day and night ... 212–01
I walk through darkest night ... 175–02
O Master, let me walk with thee ... 357–01
O, nobody else can walk it for us ... 080–02
O, nobody else could walk it for him ... 080–01
Though I walk through the darkest
  of shadows ... 173–02
Walk humbly with your God ... 405–01
Walk in our streets again ... 030–04
Walk thou beside us lest
  the tempting byways ... 360–03
Walk together in beauty as we dwell
  in harmony ... 273–03
Walk with gladness in the morning ... 104–02
We have to walk it by ourselves ... 080–02
We must walk this lonesome valley ... 080–02
We walk by faith and not by sight ... 399–01
We walk the pilgrim way ... 470–04
We who walk forth in thy greatness
  confiding ... 261–03
We'll humbly walk with God ... 405–03
When I walk through the shades
  of death ... 172–02
Why must I walk about mournfully ... 190–09
Yea, though I walk in death's dark vale ... 170–03
Yet still you walk our streets, O Christ ... 437–02
You patiently walk close beside us ... 157–02

**WALKED**

Jesus walked this lonesome valley ... 080–01
Of him who walked upon the sea ... 308–03
Who walked upon the foaming deep ... 562–02

**WALKS**

Israel walks a journey ... 296–03
Walks not where sinners meet ... 158–01
Who walks within God's ways ... 239–01

**WALL**

Breaking down each wall or fence ... 343–03

**WALLS**

God's going to build up
  Zion's walls ... 445–refrain
Her walls before thee stand ... 441–02
The city walls shall stand ... 191–04
The walls of gold entomb us ... 291–01
With salvation's walls surrounded ... 446–01
Within its walls to rest ... 207–01
Within these walls cry,
  "Glory, glory, glory!" ... 180–03
Within thy walls let peace abide ... 235–04
Within whose foursquare walls
  shall come ... 453–01

**WANDER**

Nor wander from the pathway ... 388–01
Nor wander from the pathway ... 389–01
Prone to wander, Lord, I feel it ... 356–03
Wherever I may wander ... 294–01

**WANDERINGS**

Till all our wanderings cease ... 269–04

**WANT**

I want Jesus to walk with me ... 363–01
Lord, I want to be a Christian ... 372–01
Lord, I want to be like Jesus ... 372–04
Lord, I want to be more holy ... 372–03
Lord, I want to be more loving ... 372–02
The Lord's my Shepherd, I'll not want ... 170–01
The Lord's my Shepherd. I'll not want ... 174–01
Thou, O Christ, art all I want ... 303–03

**WANTED**

You only wanted that I should follow ... 377–01

**WANTS**

All our wants and woes ... 352–02
By you their wants are all supplied ... 251–02
For our wants to be supplied ... 551–01
No doubt our inmost wants are clear ... 282–02
Now, our wants and burdens leaving ... 545–03

**WAR**

No longer bled by war ... 471–05
That war may haunt the earth
  no more ... 452–04
Till sin's fierce war shall cease ... 447–02
Till sin's fierce war shall cease ... 448–02

**WARFARE**

And their warfare now is over ... 003–01

## WARMTH

That givest us both warmth and light 455–03
The warmth to swell the grain 560–01

## WARNING

But hear the angel's warning 026–00
Then warning came of danger near 035–01

## WARNINGS

And his timeless warnings hold 409–03

## WARS

God knows our wars
and make them cease 259–03
He makes wars cease to the end
of the earth 193–09
Make wars throughout the world
to cease 295–01
Wars are ended, spears are broken 192–03

## WASH

O wash me, I shall be whiter
than snow 196–04
O wash me more and more
from my guilt 196–01

## WASHES

Silently washes their feet 367–01

## WATCH (N)

For God keeps watch within that place 238–04
Short as the watch that ends the night 210–03
Their watch of wondering love 043–02
Their watch of wondering love 044–02

## WATCH (V)

Up, watch with expectation 015–01
Watch by our side 544–03
Watch our sleeping, guard our waking 544–01
Watch with him one bitter hour 097–01

## WATCHED

As we watched at dead of night 051–03

## WATCHERS

Ye watchers and ye holy ones 451–01

## WATCHES

The Lord watches over the strangers 254–09

## WATCHING

Watching and waiting, looking above 341–03

## WATCHMAN

Watchman, does its beauteous ray 020–01
Watchman, let your wanderings cease 020–03
Watchman, tell us of the night 020–01
Watchman, will its beams alone 020–02

## WATCHMEN

Zion hears the watchmen singing 017–02

## WATER

And to the still water will guide me 173–01
Baptized in water, sealed by the Spirit 492–01
Born of water and the Spirit 493–02
By water and the word 442–01
Out of deep, unordered water 494–01
Thank you, God, for water, soil, and air 266–01
There is water in the font 494–refrain
There is water in the river 494–refrain
Thou flowing water pure and clear 455–03
Water on the human forehead 494–02
With this water God has sealed you 498–01

## WATERS

As the waters cover the seas 337–01
By the waters, the waters of Babylon 245–00
From living waters raise new saints 124–02
Of quiet waters I drink deep 174–02
The flowing waters sealed 292–01
The waters of God's goodness flow 259–02
The waters of the springtime 200–01
The waters spread below 556–02
Though foaming waters roar 191–02
Though its waters roar and foam 193–03
Through the Red Sea waters 114–01
Through the Red Sea waters 115–01
When through the deep waters
I call thee to go 361–03
While the nearer waters roll 303–01

## WAVES (N)

All your waves and billows
have gone over me 190–07
And bade its waves be still 308–03
For amber waves of grain 564–01
God made its waves and tides 214–04
Its angry waves thy voice can still 209–03
Through waves and clouds and storms 286–02
Waves billowing high 373–02
With waves so high 373–01

## WAVES (V)

While all around us waves
the golden grain 415–01

## WAY

| | |
|---|---|
| A level way appear | 013–01 |
| A long way from your home | 030–01 |
| And are steadfast in God's way | 223–05 |
| And in the right and perfect way | 250–03 |
| And make it their life's way | 552–01 |
| But the way of the wicked he brings to ruin | 254–09 |
| By a new way none ever trod | 141–01 |
| Christ of the upward way, my guide divine | 344–01 |
| Far down the future's broadening way | 357–04 |
| For you are the Way | 465–01 |
| Give way to love and peace | 289–04 |
| God has been this way before | 494–03 |
| Hoping to be shown the way | 401–03 |
| I am going to walk with Jesus all the way | 398–02 |
| In you my way is sure | 212–03 |
| Is not your way for me | 390–05 |
| Jesus, Savior, be our way | 465–04 |
| Keep us in the narrow way | 063–04 |
| Let your way and will be shown | 132–01 |
| Make straight the way for God within | 010–02 |
| O God, in a mysterious way | 270–01 |
| O Love, how gracious is thy way | 366–03 |
| Resounding all the way | 076–03 |
| Show me your way of righting wrong | 351–04 |
| So keep us in your way | 206–01 |
| That your way may be known upon the earth | 202–02 |
| The casual way we wear your name | 419–03 |
| The way of God you will prepare | 601–04 |
| The way of sinners, far from God | 158–05 |
| The way that you should go | 184–04 |
| Their way to God is known | 158–05 |
| This is the way we should live with you | 367–04 |
| Thou who hast brought us thus far on the way | 563–03 |
| Thus all my gladsome way along | 483–04 |
| To help them find your way | 437–03 |
| To teach the way of life and peace | 428–04 |
| We have come over a way | 563–02 |
| When my way grows drear | 404–02 |

## WAYS

| | |
|---|---|
| And sinful in our ways | 195–03 |
| But wisdom's ways are never found | 287–02 |
| For you are good in all your ways | 252–02 |
| He made known his ways to Moses | 222–07 |
| In many marvelous ways | 600–01 |
| Lord, you are just in all your ways | 251–03 |
| The ways of sin afford | 207–02 |
| To walk the ways of peace | 601–05 |
| Ways to order human life | 343–04 |
| We'll go our different ways | 507–05 |
| Whose ways are right and true | 233–01 |
| Whose ways are servanthood | 453–03 |

## WEAKNESS

| | |
|---|---|
| Dying in weakness but rising to reign | 147–04 |
| Jesus knows our every weakness | 403–02 |

## WEALTH

| | |
|---|---|
| And let your wealth increase | 188–02 |
| Here is our common wealth | 515–03 |
| The wealth of this good land | 414–01 |
| To claim as if their wealth were ours | 287–01 |
| With all its wealth untold | 176–01 |

## WEAN

| | |
|---|---|
| Wean it from earth, through all its pulses move | 326–01 |

## WEAPON

| | |
|---|---|
| From every weapon death can wield | 121–03 |

## WEAPONS

| | |
|---|---|
| Weapons idle, used no more | 401–01 |

## WEARINESS

| | |
|---|---|
| And all our weariness upon you lean | 520–01 |

## WEARY

| | |
|---|---|
| Jesus, give the weary | 541–02 |
| The weary find eternal rest | 423–04 |

## WEATHER

| | |
|---|---|
| Shining beyond the frosty weather | 012–04 |

## WEBS

| | |
|---|---|
| Weaving webs of death and pain | 159–01 |

## WEEP

| | |
|---|---|
| That shall not weep again | 453–01 |

## WELCOME

| | |
|---|---|
| And what you most would welcome | 560–03 |
| How welcome you aright | 011–01 |
| We welcome now into Christ's fold | 499–03 |
| We welcome one world family | 386–03 |
| Welcome God to come into our hearts as our guest | 273–04 |
| Welcome in unwearied strains | 114–02 |

**WELCOME** (cont.)

| | |
|---|---|
| Welcome in unwearied strains | 115–02 |
| Wilt welcome, pardon, cleanse, relieve | 370–03 |

**WELCOMED**

| | |
|---|---|
| Who welcomed here the Christ-child with a song | 057–02 |

**WEPT**

| | |
|---|---|
| As you once wept above Jerusalem | 424–03 |
| I have wept for love of them | 525–02 |
| Jesus wept with open grief | 406–02 |
| When Jesus wept, the falling tear | 312–00 |

**WHALE**

| | |
|---|---|
| God of the whale | 272–01 |

**WHEAT**

| | |
|---|---|
| We are wheat by the same great Sower sown | 518–02 |
| Wheat alone shall fill God's store | 409–02 |
| Wheat and tares together sown | 551–02 |

**WHEELS**

| | |
|---|---|
| That wheels in splendor through the midnight sky | 297–01 |

**WHIPPED**

| | |
|---|---|
| They whipped and they stripped and they hung me high | 302–03 |

**WHISPER**

| | |
|---|---|
| Whisper thy praise | 359–03 |

**WHISPERED**

| | |
|---|---|
| Then you whispered in silence | 319–03 |

**WHOLE**

| | |
|---|---|
| And bids us seize the whole of life | 453–04 |
| The whole of their good lives long | 364–02 |

**WHOLENESS**

| | |
|---|---|
| That wholeness is our deepest need | 380–02 |
| The wholeness that, enriching us | 380–05 |

**WICKED**

| | |
|---|---|
| Before you, Lord, the wicked fall | 161–02 |
| The wicked, like the driven chaff | 158–04 |
| The wicked oppressing now cease from distressing | 559–01 |

**WIDENESS**

| | |
|---|---|
| Like the wideness of the sea | 298–01 |
| Show the wideness of your mercy | 512–04 |
| There's a wideness in God's mercy | 298–01 |

**WIDOWED**

| | |
|---|---|
| The widowed and the parentless | 253–03 |

**WIFE**

| | |
|---|---|
| I am not yet a wife | 019–05 |

**WILDERNESS**

| | |
|---|---|
| Across the wilderness | 564–02 |
| The wilderness is fruitful | 200–03 |
| Traveling through this wilderness | 538–01 |

**WILL**

| | |
|---|---|
| A just and righteous will | 219–02 |
| And God's good will unfailingly | 133–01 |
| And has God's will been done | 349–03 |
| And your holy will obey | 203–02 |
| Bidding us to do God's will | 409–01 |
| By whom thy will was done | 412–05 |
| Caused by human, stubborn will | 401–02 |
| Early let us do thy will | 387–03 |
| God's holy will to do | 070–02 |
| God's righteous will | 415–03 |
| God's will be done | 553–02 |
| Good will to all on earth | 292–02 |
| In your holy will instruct me | 178–01 |
| It is my own holy will | 159–02 |
| Let thy will be done indeed | 489–03 |
| My will is not my own | 378–05 |
| Not thinking of the Maker's will | 287–01 |
| O God, your will be done | 291–03 |
| O God, your will disclose | 277–03 |
| Ready, my God, thy will to see | 324–refrain |
| Take my will, and make it thine | 391–05 |
| They come to learn the will of God | 235–03 |
| Thy will be done | 589–01 |
| Until with thee I will one will | 316–02 |
| Your holy will abiding | 284–01 |
| Your will be done | 571–00 |
| Your will be done | 590–01 |
| Your will, O God, be done | 086–refrain |

**WILLS**

| | |
|---|---|
| Take thou our wills, Most High | 392–03 |

**WIN**

| | |
|---|---|
| And he must win the battle | 260–02 |

## WITHER

| | |
|---|---|
| For they shall wither like the grass | 188–01 |
| Then wither and perish; but naught changeth thee | 263–03 |

## WITNESS

| | |
|---|---|
| Thy sacred witness bear | 139–03 |

## WITNESSES

| | |
|---|---|
| Two chosen witnesses of grace | 075–03 |

## WOE

| | |
|---|---|
| Our utmost woe and loss | 072–03 |

## WOES

| | |
|---|---|
| For woes and fear surround me here | 183–02 |
| When the woes of life o'ertake me | 084–02 |

## WOLF

| | |
|---|---|
| The wolf shall lie down with the lamb | 337–01 |
| Then shall the wolf dwell with the lamb | 450–02 |

## WOMEN

| | |
|---|---|
| Christian women, Christian men | 348–01 |
| On women, men, and children | 128–03 |
| Our women see visions | 319–04 |
| The faithful women went their way | 116–02 |

## WON

| | |
|---|---|
| Thou hast won my heart to serve thee solely | 069–01 |

## WONDER

| | |
|---|---|
| For the wonder of each hour | 473–02 |
| Lost in wonder, love, and praise | 376–04 |
| Nature's wonder, Jesus' wisdom | 422–01 |
| O Lord my God! when I in awesome wonder | 467–01 |
| Our wonder, our transport, when Jesus we see | 485–02 |
| The wonder of his love | 149–05 |
| The wonder of thy name | 292–03 |
| Though with a scornful wonder | 442–03 |
| With wonder and thanksgiving | 517–02 |
| Wonder of wonder, here revealed | 499–01 |

## WONDERS

| | |
|---|---|
| And wonders of his love | 040–04 |
| For the wonders that astound us | 553–03 |
| Great wonders you perform | 270–01 |
| Lord, how thy wonders are displayed | 288–02 |
| The mighty wonders you have wrought | 252–01 |
| The wonders that thy people told | 295–02 |
| To God who has great wonders done | 218–01 |
| Two wonders I confess | 092–02 |
| What wonders bless the land | 556–01 |

## WOODLANDS

| | |
|---|---|
| Fairer still the woodlands | 306–02 |

## WOODS

| | |
|---|---|
| Thy woods and templed hills | 561–02 |
| When through the woods and forest glades I wander | 467–02 |

## WORD

| | |
|---|---|
| According to your Word | 019–06 |
| According to your word | 605–01 |
| All praise to God, whose sacred word | 328–04 |
| And give thy word success | 139–02 |
| And he never said a mumbalin' word | 095–01 |
| And to spread the gospel Word | 422–03 |
| As those who know God's living Word | 255–06 |
| Blessed Jesus, at your word | 454–01 |
| Blest are all those who keep your word | 233–02 |
| By some clear, winning word of love | 357–02 |
| By the word of the Lord the heavens were made | 185–06 |
| By the word of your commanding | 224–02 |
| For God's redeeming word | 435–03 |
| For the word of the Lord is upright | 185–04 |
| For this is God's word | 257–04 |
| Fresh from the Word | 469–01 |
| God, whose word cannot be broken | 446–01 |
| God, your word is still creating | 285–03 |
| God's sacred word is so profound | 328–01 |
| God's word upholds my fainting spirit | 240–03 |
| His word my hope secures | 280–04 |
| In prophet's word you spoke of old | 488–02 |
| Invited by your holy word | 340–03 |
| Let in your Word | 183–01 |
| Let us, like them, without a word | 345–02 |
| Let your word dwell richly in us as we teach and sing | 346–03 |
| Lo, at thy word the waters were formed | 271–01 |
| Lord, we would hear your word | 215–04 |
| Lord, your word is ever true | 213–04 |
| May your Word among us spoken | 512–05 |
| Not a word shall fail of the promises once made | 169–03 |
| O praise the word of faith | 471–04 |
| O Savior, whose almighty word | 562–02 |
| One little word shall fell him | 260–03 |
| One word of your supporting breath | 172–02 |

| | |
|---|---|
| Shown through word and deed | |
| and prayer | 523–02 |
| So with us now you keep your word | 601–02 |
| Thanks to God whose Word Incarnate | 331–03 |
| Thanks to God whose Word | |
| is answered | 331–04 |
| Thanks to God whose Word | |
| is published | 331–02 |
| Thanks to God whose word was written | 331–01 |
| That God's word is never broken | 003–03 |
| That word above all earthly powers | 260–04 |
| The sacred word through | |
| sacred song | 328–refrain |
| The word gives both the life and light | 328–02 |
| The Word of grace hath purged away | 110–03 |
| Thy word our law, thy paths | |
| our chosen way | 262–02 |
| To every place their word | 166–02 |
| To hear God's word and thus be fed | 332–03 |
| To hear the angel's word | 019–03 |
| To live according to your word | 419–01 |
| To you, O living Word | 233–05 |
| What other word can please | 255–05 |
| With the word, the Lord is coming | 012–05 |
| Word made flesh, our lives to win | 065–02 |
| You are true to your word | 173–02 |
| Your sovereign word of peace | 452–04 |
| Your word commands response | 274–04 |
| Your word in days of old | 601–02 |
| Your word is now fulfilled | 603–01 |
| Your word is true, your ways are just | 530–03 |

**WORDS**

| | |
|---|---|
| And with these words rejoice | 471–07 |
| Bare words cannot enfold | 490–02 |
| By whom the words of life were spoken | 502–00 |
| For the words which you have spoken | 508–01 |
| For the words which you have spoken | 509–01 |
| Free of tangled words that mask | 336–03 |
| Give us words of fire and flame | 129–03 |
| In all your words, your gracious deeds | 251–01 |
| In ever-changing words of light | 292–03 |
| In feeble words to bind thee | 278–02 |
| In words of sharp surprise | 071–02 |
| Let all my words and all my thought | 167–04 |
| Lord, the words your lips are telling | 213–04 |
| May these words and thoughts | |
| be pleasing | 224–04 |
| No gracious words we hear | 399–01 |
| Nor the words of God's victorious | |
| right hand | 169–03 |
| She wondered at his words | 019–06 |

| | |
|---|---|
| The words God spoke of old | 167–02 |
| Those well-worn words impart | 349–01 |
| To live the words we say | 347–01 |
| With burning words of victory won | 124–03 |
| With words and actions kind | 277–03 |
| Words of challenge, said with care | 343–03 |
| Words of comfort, words of vision | 343–03 |
| Words of hope to all who hear | 409–03 |
| Your words can turn us back to dust | 211–02 |

**WORK (N)**

| | |
|---|---|
| A work to do, a place to fill | 402–03 |
| Alike at work and prayer | 487–01 |
| And all his work is done in faithfulness | 185–04 |
| And all my work be praise | 172–03 |
| Are but the work of human hands | 227–02 |
| For the work of ministry | 429–refrain |
| For you according to our work | 197–06 |
| "God's work," replied the people | 237–02 |
| I said that this is my own work | 181–02 |
| In work that keeps faith sweet | 357–03 |
| Is angels' work below | 428–03 |
| Love's redeeming work is done | 113–02 |
| So shall thy work be done | 286–04 |
| The work God's hands have made | 166–01 |
| Though our work is hard | 480–01 |
| Until life's work is done | 414–03 |
| Wasted work and wasted play | 413–02 |
| Where there's work to dare and do | 285–03 |
| Your noblest work is to adore | 475–02 |

**WORK (V)**

| | |
|---|---|
| And work your sovereign will | 270–02 |
| Go work today | 415–01 |
| Humbly let us work and trust | 352–02 |
| I'm gonna work so | 369–02 |
| May work our profit and thy praise | 079–05 |
| Praying, let us work for peace | 432–00 |
| Who work and pray by night, by day | 242–01 |
| You must work all good within us | 454–02 |
| You must work while it is day | 413–02 |

**WORKERS**

| | |
|---|---|
| For workers of our day | 552–01 |
| Loud building workers | 458–02 |
| Unwilling, workers idled stand | 431–02 |
| You have come to join the workers | 305–01 |

**WORKS (N)**

| | |
|---|---|
| All thy wondrous works proclaim | 163–01 |
| All thy works shall praise thy name | 138–04 |
| All thy works with joy surround thee | 464–02 |

## WORKS (N) (cont.)

| | |
|---|---|
| Come, behold the works of the Lord | 193–08 |
| God's matchless works expand | 556–01 |
| Good works of service are for offering | 400–02 |
| Our works, alas! are all in vain | 240–02 |
| The works of states are in your hands | 226–01 |
| The works of such abide | 158–03 |
| To all your works your love extends | 252–02 |
| To praise thy wondrous works, O Lord | 209–02 |
| To which your mighty works unfold | 486–01 |
| Your works will give you thanks, O Lord | 252–03 |

## WORKS (V)

| | |
|---|---|
| No one works like him | 153–refrain |
| The Lord works vindication | 222–06 |

## WORLD

| | |
|---|---|
| A world in need now summons us | 414–02 |
| A world redeemed by Christlike love | 414–02 |
| A world that was created for | 434–03 |
| Across the world, across the street | 421–02 |
| Across this wide world, we shall always find | 400–04 |
| All the world is God's own field | 551–02 |
| And all the world sings, "Glory, glory, glory!" | 180–01 |
| And lest the world go hungry | 558–04 |
| And nothing in the world beneath | 166–04 |
| And the whole world give back the song | 038–04 |
| And though this world, with devils filled | 260–03 |
| Asking that the world around us | 429–03 |
| Baby Jesus came into this world on Christmas day | 039–01 |
| Bring to our world of strife | 452–04 |
| But in this world of sin | 043–03 |
| But in this world of sin | 044–03 |
| Calling the whole world to rejoice | 218–02 |
| Come, come, world forlorn | 034–refrain |
| Drawing near a world that spurns him | 413–03 |
| Ever shall be, world without end | 578–00 |
| For the world new life has won | 107–03 |
| From this world to the sky | 118–01 |
| God made the world and at its birth | 434–02 |
| God made the world, and me | 294–01 |
| Here, as in the world around us | 461–01 |
| In the world to which you send us | 508–04 |
| In the world to which you send us | 509–04 |
| In this world and the next | 555–02 |
| In which the world began | 278–01 |
| In whom this world rejoices | 555–01 |
| Kind Maker of the world, O hear | 079–01 |

| | |
|---|---|
| Let all the world in every corner sing | 468–refrain |
| Let me see the world from high | 323–03 |
| Let the round world keep triumph | 118–03 |
| Let the world rejoice and shout | 109–03 |
| Living, working in our world | 433–01 |
| Make a lost world your home | 325–05 |
| O for a world preparing for | 386–05 |
| O for a world where everyone | 386–01 |
| O for a world where goods are shared | 386–02 |
| O'er all the weary world | 038–02 |
| O'er all the world from shore to shore | 226–01 |
| Prepared by you for all the world to see | 604–00 |
| Savior, from the world away | 538–03 |
| That show a world awesome and grand | 152–01 |
| That the world may trust your promise | 429–02 |
| The Savior of the world is here | 008–01 |
| The world abounds with God's free grace | 556–01 |
| The world and all therein are thine | 209–03 |
| The world does glorify | 549–03 |
| The world in solemn stillness lay | 038–01 |
| The world is bright with the joyous saints | 364–03 |
| The world is ever near | 388–02 |
| The world is ever near | 389–02 |
| This is my Father's world | 293–01 |
| This is the Savior of the world | 603–02 |
| This world is made for your home | 352–04 |
| This world sees her oppressed | 442–03 |
| Through all the world a watch is keeping | 546–02 |
| Throughout the world complete your reign | 590–01 |
| Till all the world adore his sacred name | 371–refrain |
| Till all the world shall learn thy love | 408–06 |
| Till this hungry world is fed | 512–03 |
| To all the world, and gladly sing | 054–01 |
| To all the world glad news we bring | 111–01 |
| To serve your world today | 437–03 |
| When all the world seems ours | 279–02 |
| When the whole world was still | 319–03 |
| When this old world drew on toward night | 004–02 |
| Where the world is still in pain | 104–03 |
| Who for the world was sacrificed | 133–02 |
| Whom all the world cannot contain | 521–04 |
| Whose brave new world lies torn and rent | 152–02 |
| Working for a world that's new | 432–00 |
| World of bird and beast and, later | 494–01 |
| World without end | 577–00 |

## WORLDS

| | |
|---|---|
| World without end | 578–00 |
| World without end | 579–00 |
| Yet when again in this same world you give us | 342–04 |

## WORLDS

| | |
|---|---|
| As long as worlds endure | 443–01 |
| Enthroned above all worlds | 206–02 |
| Ere the worlds began to be | 309–01 |
| Of shining worlds in splendor through the skies | 262–01 |
| There are new worlds to explore | 296–03 |
| To fill all worlds, to crown all things | 353–04 |

## WORMWOOD

| | |
|---|---|
| O the wormwood and the gall | 097–02 |

## WORSHIP (N)

| | |
|---|---|
| As worship moved us to a more profound | 264–02 |
| Called from worship to your service | 427–04 |
| Our worship let us bring | 214–05 |
| Seek in worship to explore | 461–03 |
| Through songful worship, know that truth | 490–02 |

## WORSHIP (V)

| | |
|---|---|
| And worship God in humbleness | 455–06 |
| And worship only thee | 396–03 |
| And worship only thee | 397–03 |
| As we worship, grant us vision | 427–03 |
| By this we worship and are freed | 335–03 |
| Come, worship God, come, kneel and bow | 215–02 |
| O worship the King, all glorious above | 476–01 |
| They who worship you and fear you | 178–02 |
| To worship from afar | 034–02 |
| To worship, sing, and pray | 128–01 |
| We bless, we worship you, we raise | 133–01 |
| We worship God and sing with joy | 328–04 |
| We worship you | 575–03 |
| We worship you, we give you thanks | 566–00 |
| Worship Christ, the newborn King | 022–refrain |
| Worship God through length of days | 256–02 |
| Worship now with shouts of gladness | 107–03 |
| Worship would be joy for aye | 065–03 |
| Worship you, the Lamb who died | 154–04 |

## WORSHIPED

| | |
|---|---|
| Worshiped the beloved with a kiss | 036–03 |

## WORSHIPING

| | |
|---|---|
| Worshiping God Most High | 066–03 |

## WOUND

| | |
|---|---|
| As with a deadly wound in my body | 190–10 |

## WOUNDED

| | |
|---|---|
| To make the wounded whole | 394–refrain |

## WOUNDS

| | |
|---|---|
| Deep were his wounds and red | 103–01 |
| Lord, by your wounds on Calvary | 119–04 |
| Rich wounds, yet visible above | 151–02 |
| 'Tis thy wounds our healing give | 501–02 |
| To heal earth's wounds and end our bitter strife | 360–02 |

## WRAP

| | |
|---|---|
| Wrap now thy peace, like a mantle, around us | 261–02 |

## WRAPS

| | |
|---|---|
| Wraps us country folk | 480–02 |

## WRATH

| | |
|---|---|
| God brings wrath upon their work | 159–02 |
| The wrath of nations now restrain | 295–01 |
| Wrath and vengeance to restrain | 163–02 |
| Yea, when their wrath against us fiercely rose | 236–02 |
| You keep me safe from my foe's wrath | 247–04 |

## WREATHS

| | |
|---|---|
| For all wreaths of empire meet upon his brow | 148–04 |

## WRECKS

| | |
|---|---|
| Towering o'er the wrecks of time | 084–01 |

## WRING

| | |
|---|---|
| Wring gold from human pain | 453–02 |

## WRIT

| | |
|---|---|
| Deep writ upon the human heart | 488–02 |

## WRITINGS

| | |
|---|---|
| For all the writings that survived | 330–04 |

## WRONG

| | |
|---|---|
| Seeing wrong and setting right | 433–04 |
| That though the wrong seems oft so strong | 293–02 |
| The wrong that I have done this day | 542–02 |
| Who do no wrong, but keep their word | 164–03 |

## WRONGS

And still our wrongs
   may weave you now    007–01

## WROUGHT

All is made and wrought and done    137–01
Till thou hast wrought its chain    378–04

# Y

## YEAR

A glad new year to all the earth    054–04
The opening year your mercy shows    265–01
The year in beauty flows    292–03
The year of God's own jubilee    332–01

## YEARNING

And so the yearning strong    313–03

## YEARS

And my years with sighs    182–02
And that future years shall see    309–01
God of our weary years    563–03
God of the coming years, through paths
   unknown    275–03
Long years have come and gone    430–02
Lord of our closing years    279–05
Lord of our growing years    279–01
Lord of our middle years    279–03
Lord of our older years    279–04
Lord of our strongest years    279–02
Of those younger years behind me    178–01
Our years are but threescore and ten    211–03
Promised from eternal years    051–01
Still to countless years the same    479–03
That sees beyond the years    564–04
The hidden years had ended    072–04
Through all the years the same    215–03
To distant years in Palestine    108–02
To endless years the same    210–02
When we've been there
   ten thousand years    280–05
When with the ever-circling years    038–04

## YIELD

I yield my flickering torch to thee    384–02
Shall we then yield him,
   in costly devotion    067–03
We yield ourselves to thee—time,
   talents, all    392–04
Yield your life to God's control    409–01

## YIELDED

Who yielded his life an atonement
   for sin    485–01

## YOKE

Loosed from Pharaoh's bitter yoke    114–01
Loosed from Pharaoh's bitter yoke    115–01
Your yoke is hard to bear    419–02

## YOUNG

So the young can find repose    547–01
The young a faith for life may find    497–04
The young and old to
   Christ belong    497–02
To young and old the gospel
   gladness bear    415–02
Where she may lay her young    208–03

## YOUTH

From youth to age, by night and day    145–02
From youth to age, by night and day    146–02
So that your youth is renewed
   like the eagle's    222–05
Through youth, maturity, and age    402–01

# Z

## ZEAL

My zeal inspire    383–02
With zeal and joyfulness    277–02

## ZEST

Who bids us never lose
   our zest    402–03

# II. Topical Index

# A

# B

45 O Sleep, Dear Holy Baby
47 Still, Still, Still
48 Lo, How a Rose E'er Blooming
49 Once in Royal David's City
53 What Child Is This
54 From Heaven Above
55 That Boy-Child of Mary
57 The Snow Lay on the Ground
144 Alleluia! Sing to Jesus!
600 Song of Mary

**Massah**
215 Come, Sing with Joy to God

**Moses**
73 Swiftly Pass the Clouds of Glory
74 Jesus on the Mountain Peak
75 O Wondrous Sight, O Vision Fair
87 The Glory of These Forty Days
222 Psalm 103
334 When Israel Was in Egypt's Land

**Mount Mizar**
190 Psalm 42

**Nazareth**
305 Jesus, Our Divine Companion
308 O Sing a Song of Bethlehem
330 Deep in the Shadows of the Past

**Olivet**
89 Hosanna, Loud Hosanna

**Palestine**
108 Christ Is Alive!

**Paul**
394 There Is a Balm in Gilead

**Peter**
73 Swiftly Pass the Clouds of Glory
394 There Is a Balm in Gilead
598 This Is the Good News

**Pharaoh**
114 Come, Ye Faithful, Raise the Strain
115 Come, Ye Faithful, Raise the Strain
334 When Israel Was in Egypt's Land

**Red Sea**
114 Come, Ye Faithful, Raise the Strain
115 Come, Ye Faithful, Raise the Strain

**Satan**
26 Break Forth, O Beauteous Heavenly Light
77 Forty Days and Forty Nights
81 Lord, Who Throughout These Forty
    Days
97 Go to Dark Gethsemane
348 Christian Women, Christian Men

**Seba**
204 Psalm 72
**Sheba**
204 Psalm 72
**Simeon**
603 Song of Simeon
604 Song of Simeon
605 Song of Simeon
**Tarshish**
204 Psalm 72
**Thomas**
117 O Sons and Daughters, Let Us Sing!
**Twelve**
547 When Twilight Comes
598 This Is the Good News
**Zechariah**
601 Song of Zechariah
602 Song of Zechariah
**Zion**
13 Prepare the Way
17 "Sleepers, Wake!" A Voice Astounds Us
18 The Desert Shall Rejoice
144 Alleluia! Sing to Jesus!
159 Why Are Nations Raging
176 The Earth and All That Dwell Therein
201 Praise Is Your Right, O God, in Zion
208 Psalm 84
235 With Joy I Heard My Friends Exclaim
245 By the Waters of Babylon
241 Behold the Goodness of Our Lord
246 By the Babylonian Rivers
254 Psalm 146
257 Give Praise to the Lord
416 Christ Is Made the Sure Foundation
417 Christ Is Made the Sure Foundation
441 I Love Thy Kingdom, Lord
445 Great Day!
446 Glorious Things of Thee Are Spoken
489 Open Now Thy Gates of Beauty

**BLESSING/BLESSINGS**
161 As Morning Dawns
200 To Bless the Earth
201 Praise Is Your Right, O God, in Zion
242 Come, All You Servants of the Lord
270 O God, in a Mysterious Way
276 Great Is Thy Faithfulness
398 There's a Sweet, Sweet Spirit
418 God, Bless Your Church with Strength!
423 Jesus Shall Reign Where'er the Sun
542 All Praise to Thee, My God, This Night
555 Now Thank We All Our God

**BODY OF CHRIST**
*See* CHURCH

**BROTHERHOOD AND SISTERHOOD OF HUMANKIND**
*See also* SOCIAL CONCERN
134 Creating God, Your Fingers Trace
358 Help Us Accept Each Other

367 Jesu, Jesu, Fill Us with Your Love
385 O God, We Bear the Imprint of Your Face
386 O for a World
422 God, Whose Giving Knows No Ending
436 We Are Your People
457 I Greet Thee, Who My Sure Redeemer Art
564 O Beautiful for Spacious Skies

# C

**CALLS TO WORSHIP**
*See* WORSHIP

**CALMNESS**
*See* PEACE, PERSONAL (SPIRITUAL)

**CHALLENGE**
132 Come, Great God of All the Ages
179 God Is My Strong Salvation
268 God, Who Stretched the Spangled
307 Fight the Good Fight
415 Come, Labor On
418 God, Bless Your Church with Strength!
420 God of Grace and God of Glory
447 Lead On, O King Eternal
448 Lead On, O King Eternal

**CHARITY**
*See* LOVE FOR OTHERS

**CHILDREN**
49 Once in Royal David's City
88 All Glory, Laud, and Honor
89 Hosanna, Loud Hosanna
163 Lord, Our Lord, Thy Glorious Name
238 Unless the Lord the House Shall Build
279 Lord of Our Growing Years
304 Jesus Loves Me!
450 O Day of Peace
461 God Is Here!
496 Lord Jesus Christ, Our Lord Most Dear
497 With Grateful Hearts Our Faith Professing
498 Child of Blessing, Child of Promise

**CHILDREN'S HYMNS**
*See* Appendix, page 337

**CHRIST THE KING/ASCENSION, 141–157**

**CHRISTIAN LIFE**
*See* LIFE IN CHRIST

**CHRISTIAN NURTURE**
*See* LIFE IN CHRIST

**CHRISTIAN SERVICE**
*See* SERVICE

**CHRISTIAN WARFARE**
179 God Is My Strong Salvation
260 A Mighty Fortress Is Our God
301 Lord Jesus, Think on Me
307 Fight the Good Fight
388 O Jesus, I Have Promised
389 O Jesus, I Have Promised
447 Lead On, O King Eternal
448 Lead On, O King Eternal
526 For All the Saints
559 We Gather Together

**CHRISTIANS**
53 What Child Is This
108 Christ Is Alive!
111 Good Christians All, Rejoice and Sing!
130 Let Every Christian Pray
148 At the Name of Jesus
150 Come, Christians, Join to Sing
348 Christian Women, Christian Men
371 Lift High the Cross
372 Lord, I Want to Be a Christian
433 There's a Spirit in the Air
437 Our Cities Cry to You, O God
500 Become to Us the Living Bread
507 I Come with Joy
552 Give Thanks, O Christian People

# D

# E

# F

# G

## By an Individual
276   Great Is Thy Faithfulness
281   Guide Me, O Thou Great Jehovah
288   I Sing the Mighty Power of God
467   How Great Thou Art
475   O That I Had a Thousand Voices
478   Praise, My Soul, the King of Heaven
479   Praise, My Soul, the God of Heaven
482   Praise Ye the Lord, the Almighty
483   Sing Praise to God, Who Reigns Above
542   All Praise to Thee, My God, This Night

## By Creation
267   All Things Bright and Beautiful
272   God of the Sparrow
455   All Creatures of Our God and King
458   Earth and All Stars
464   Joyful, Joyful, We Adore Thee
469   Morning Has Broken
473   For the Beauty of the Earth
475   O That I Had a Thousand Voices
487   When Morning Gilds the Skies

## By the Community
106   Alleluia, Alleluia! Give Thanks
133   All Glory Be to God on High
138   Holy, Holy, Holy! Lord God Almighty!
139   Come, Thou Almighty King
140   Holy, Holy
220   All People That on Earth Do Dwell
260   A Mighty Fortress Is Our God
262   God of the Ages, Whose Almighty Hand
263   Immortal, Invisible, God Only Wise
451   Ye Watchers and Ye Holy Ones
458   Earth and All Stars
459   Father, We Praise Thee
460   Holy God, We Praise Your Name
461   God Is Here!
468   Let All the World in Every Corner Sing
469   Morning Has Broken
470   O Day of Radiant Gladness
472   O Sing to the Lord
473   For the Beauty of the Earth
476   O Worship the King, All Glorious Above!
477   Ye Servants of God, Your Master
480   Praise Our God Above
481   Praise the Lord, God's Glories Show
484   Sing with Hearts
485   To God Be the Glory
486   When the Morning Stars Together
487   When Morning Gilds the Skies
488   The God of Abraham Praise
491   Stand Up and Bless the Lord
546   The Day Thou Gavest, Lord, Is Ended
555   Now Thank We All Our God

559   We Gather Together
580   Holy, Holy, Holy

## GOD
### Call of
409   Wild and Lone the Prophet's Voice
410   When I Had Not Yet Learned of Jesus
410   Yee Jun Ae Joo Nim Eul Nae Ka Mol La

### Creator
*See also* GOD: MAKER
  4   Creator of the Stars of Night
134   Creating God, Your Fingers Trace
135   God Is One, Unique and Holy
136   Sovereign Lord of All Creation
137   We All Believe in One True God
151   Crown Him with Many Crowns
162   O Lord, Our God, How Excellent
166   The Heavens Above Declare God's Praise
176   The Earth and All That Dwell Therein
200   To Bless the Earth
220   All People That on Earth Do Dwell
221   Psalm 103
224   Bless the Lord, My Soul and Being
229   From All That Dwell Below the Skies
243   We Thank You, Lord, for You Are Good
254   Psalm 146
267   All Things Bright and Beautiful
268   God, Who Stretched the Spangled
        Heavens
272   God of the Sparrow
273   O God the Creator
274   O God of Earth and Space
285   God, You Spin the Whirling Planets
288   I Sing the Mighty Power of God
290   God Created Heaven and Earth
291   O God of Earth and Altar
292   All Beautiful the March of Days
293   This Is My Father's World
297   O Lord of Every Shining Constellation
319   Spirit
455   All Creatures of Our God and King
467   How Great Thou Art
469   Morning Has Broken
486   When the Morning Stars Together
523   God the Spirit, Guide and Guardian
544   Day Is Done
554   Let All Things Now Living
558   Come, Sing a Song of Harvest
560   We Plow the Fields and Scatter
562   Eternal Father, Strong to Save

### Deliverance
237   When God Delivered Israel
338   When Israel Was in Egypt's Land

## Eternity and Power

62 Bring We the Frankincense of Our Love
64 From a Distant Home
133 All Glory Be to God on High
138 Holy, Holy, Holy! Lord God Almighty!
139 Come, Thou Almighty King
147 Blessing and Honor
162 O Lord, Our God, How Excellent
163 Lord, Our Lord, Thy Glorious Name
169 In the Day of Need
180 The God of Heaven
201 Praise Is Your Right, O God, in Zion
202 Psalm 67
210 Our God, Our Help in Ages Past
211 Lord, You Have Been Our Dwelling Place
213 God, Our Lord, a King Remaining
215 Come, Sing with Joy to God
226 Sing Praise Unto the Name of God
229 From All That Dwell Below the Skies
259 A Mighty Fortress Is Our God
260 A Mighty Fortress Is Our God
263 Immortal, Invisible, God Only Wise
288 I Sing the Mighty Power of God
309 Of the Father's Love Begotten
411 Arise, Your Light Is Come!
412 Eternal God, Whose Power Upholds
472 O Sing to the Lord
476 O Worship the King, All Glorious Above!
478 Praise, My Soul, the King of Heaven
483 Sing Praise to God, Who Reigns Above
488 The God of Abraham Praise
555 Now Thank We All Our God

## Faithfulness

129 Come, O Spirit, Dwell Among Us
209 My Song Forever Shall Record
244 Let Us with a Gladsome Mind
251 Your Faithfulness, O Lord, Is Sure
275 God of Our Life
276 Great Is Thy Faithfulness
277 O God, Our Faithful God
403 What a Friend We Have in Jesus
461 God Is Here!
478 Praise, My Soul, the King of Heaven
479 Praise, My Soul, the God of Heaven
536 Lord, Make Us More Holy
538 Lord, Dismiss Us with Thy Blessing

## Fatherhood

140 Holy, Holy
276 Great Is Thy Faithfulness
293 This Is My Father's World
309 Of the Father's Love Begotten
345 Dear Lord and Father of Mankind

459 Father, We Praise Thee
485 To God Be the Glory
562 Eternal Father, Strong to Save
566 Glory to God in the Highest
575 Glory to God in the Highest

## Goodness

241 Behold the Goodness of Our Lord
187 Psalm 187
243 We Thank You, Lord, for You Are Good

## Guidance

161 As Morning Dawns
170 The Lord's My Shepherd, I'll Not Want
171 The King of Love My Shepherd Is
172 My Shepherd Will Supply My Need
173 Psalm 23
174 The Lord's My Shepherd
175 The Lord's My Shepherd, All My Need
206 O Hear Our Cry, O Lord
234 I to the Hills Will Lift My Eyes
248 You Are Before Me, Lord
250 When Morning Lights the Eastern Skies
261 God of Compassion, in Mercy Befriend Us
262 God of the Ages, Whose Almighty Hand
268 God, Who Stretched the Spangled Heavens
269 O God of Bethel, by Whose Hand
275 God of Our Life
281 Guide me, O Thou Great Jehovah
282 If Thou but Trust in God to Guide Thee
284 O God, What You Ordain Is Right
339 Be Thou My Vision
354 Guide My Feet
404 Precious Lord, Take My Hand
444 We Gather Here to Bid Farewell
540 God Be with You Till We Meet Again
554 Let All Things Now Living
555 Now Thank We All Our God
559 We Gather Together

## Help

*See also* GOD: PROTECTION
169 In the Day of Need
179 God Is My Strong Salvation
253 I'll Praise My Maker

## Holiness

138 Holy, Holy, Holy! Lord God Almighty!
222 Psalm 103
580 Holy, Holy, Holy
581 Holy, Holy, Holy Lord

## Holy Name

263 Immortal, Invisible, God Only Wise
292 All Beautiful the March of Days
303 Jesus, Lover of My Soul
460 Holy God, We Praise Your Name

559  We Gather Together
597  Bless the Lord, O My Soul

**Image of**

285  God, You Spin the Whirling Planets
297  O Lord of Every Shining Constellation
311  We Meet You, O Christ
385  O God, We Bear the Imprint
        of Your Face
474  O Splendor of God's Glory Bright
494  Out of Deep, Unordered Water

**Kingdom**

*See also* CHURCH TRIUMPHANT

    1  Come, Thou Long-Expected Jesus
    2  Come, Thou Long-Expected Jesus
    3  Comfort, Comfort You My People
    6  Jesus Comes with Clouds Descending
    7  Lord Christ, When First You Came
        to Earth
  13  Prepare the Way
  14  Savior of the Nations, Come
  18  The Desert Shall Rejoice
  38  It Came Upon the Midnight Clear
  40  Joy to the World!
145  Rejoice, Ye Pure in Heart!
146  Rejoice, Ye Pure in Heart!
155  Rejoice, the Lord Is King
205  All Hail to God's Anointed
230  This Is the Day the Lord Hath Made
252  O Lord, You Are My God and King
259  A Mighty Fortress Is Our God
260  A Mighty Fortress Is Our God
289  O God of Every Nation
332  Live Into Hope
333  Seek Ye First
337  Isaiah the Prophet Has Written of Old
351  Give to Me, Lord, a Thankful Heart
386  O for a World
408  Where Cross the Crowded Ways of Life
423  Jesus Shall Reign Where'er the Sun
437  Our Cities Cry to You, O God
441  I Love Thy Kingdom, Lord
443  O Christ, the Great Foundation
447  Lead On, O King Eternal
448  Lead On, O King Eternal
460  Holy God, We Praise Your Name
477  Ye Servants of God, Your Master
        Proclaim
508  For the Bread Which You Have Broken
509  For the Bread Which You Have Broken
546  The Day Thou Gavest, Lord, Is Ended
589  Our Father, Which Art in Heaven
599  Jesus, Remember Me

**Law of**

158  The One Is Blest
167  God's Law Is Perfect and Gives Life
223  O My Soul, Bless Your Redeemer
233  Blest Are the Uncorrupt in Heart
255  Now Praise the Lord
283  God Marked a Line and Told the Sea
319  Spirit
405  What Does the Lord Require
488  The God of Abraham Praise
554  Let All Things Now Living

**Love for**

  62  Bring We the Frankincense of Our Love
126  Come, Holy Spirit, Heavenly Dove
140  Holy, Holy
298  There's a Wideness in God's Mercy
326  Spirit of God, Descend Upon My Heart
359  More Love to Thee, O Christ
362  I Love the Lord, Who Heard My Cry

**Love of**

    7  Lord Christ, When First You Came to
        Earth
  48  Lo, How a Rose E'er Blooming
107  Celebrate with Joy and Singing
126  Come, Holy Spirit, Heavenly Dove
157  Our King and Our Sovereign, Lord Jesus
161  As Morning Dawns
171  The King of Love My Shepherd Is
181  Come Sing to God
185  Psalm 33
186  Thy Mercy and Thy Truth, O Lord
198  O God, You Are My God
199  O Lord, You Are My God
212  Within Your Shelter, Loving God
222  Psalm 103
232  Psalm 118:19–20
243  We Thank You, Lord, for You Are Good
276  Great Is Thy Faithfulness
282  If Thou but Trust in God to Guide Thee
295  O God of Love, O God of Peace
298  There's a Wideness in God's Mercy
341  Blessed Assurance, Jesus Is Mine!
353  Great God, Your Love Has Called Us Here
370  Just as I Am, Without One Plea
376  Love Divine, All Loves Excelling
402  Now Praise the Hidden God of Love
406  Why Has God Forsaken Me?
408  Where Cross the Crowded Ways of Life
412  Eternal God, Whose Power Upholds
425  Lord of Light, Your Name Outshining
471  O Praise the Gracious Power
473  For the Beauty of the Earth

## GOSPEL

## GRACE

## GRATITUDE

*See also* THANKSGIVING HYMNS

## GREAT COMMISSION

## GRIEF

## GROWTH

## GUIDANCE

*See* GOD: GUIDANCE; JESUS CHRIST:
  GUIDANCE

## GUILT

*See* SIN

# H

544  Day Is Done
555  Now Thank We All Our God

**HERITAGE**
210  Our God, Our Help in Ages Past
260  A Mighty Fortress Is Our God
364  I Sing a Song of the Saints of God
420  God of Grace and God of Glory
421  The Church of Christ in Every Age
460  Holy God, We Praise Your Name
555  Now Thank We All Our God

**HOLINESS**
162  O Lord, Our God, How Excellent
164  Lord, Who May Dwell Within
         Your House
187  Psalm 34:9–22
231  Psalm 118:14–24
232  Psalm 118:19–29
316  Breathe on Me, Breath of God
376  Love Divine, All Loves Excelling
392  Take Thou Our Minds, Dear Lord
412  Eternal God, Whose Power Upholds
429  Lord, You Give the Great Commission
508  For the Bread Which You Have Broken
509  For the Bread Which You Have Broken
536  Lord, Make Us More Holy

**HOLY INNOCENTS**
 35  In Bethlehem a Newborn Boy
 45  O Sleep, Dear Holy Baby
 45  A La Ru

**HOLY SCRIPTURE, 327–331**
 71  Lord, When You Came to Jordan
110  Christ Jesus Lay in Death's Strong Bands
158  The One Is Blest
167  God's Law Is Perfect and Gives Life
183  In You, Lord, I Have Put My Trust
233  Blest Are the Uncorrupt in Heart
243  We Thank You, Lord, for You Are Good
247  I Will Give Thanks with My Whole Heart
255  Now Praise the Lord
304  Jesus Loves Me!
321  Holy Spirit, Truth Divine
332  Live Into Hope
336  As a Chalice Cast of Gold
346  Christ, You Are the Fullness
361  How Firm a Foundation
454  Blessed Jesus, at Your Word
469  Morning Has Broken

530  O Lord of Life, Where'er They Be
598  This Is the Good News

**HOLY SPIRIT, 313–326**
*See also* DAY OF PENTECOST
**As Breath**
316  Breathe on Me, Breath of God
523  God the Spirit, Guide and Guardian
**As Comforter**
139  Come, Thou Almighty King
313  Come Down, O Love Divine
**As Dove**
 70  Christ, When for Us You Were
         Baptized
 72  When Jesus Came to Jordan
105  Because You Live, O Christ
126  Come, Holy Spirit, Heavenly Dove
300  Down to Earth, as a Dove
314  Like the Murmur of the Dove's Song
320  The Lone, Wild Bird
325  Spirit Divine, Attend Our Prayers
396  O for a Closer Walk with God
397  O for a Closer Walk with God
398  There's a Sweet, Sweet Spirit
523  God the Spirit, Guide and Guardian
**As Flame**
125  Come, Holy Spirit, Our Souls Inspire
131  Wind Who Makes All Winds That Blow
136  Sovereign Lord of All Creation
523  God the Spirit, Guide and Guardian
**Gifts**
125  Come, Holy, Spirit, Our Souls Inspire
318  Gracious Spirit, Holy Ghost
524  Holy Spirit, Lord of Love
**Guidance**
325  Spirit Divine, Attend Our Prayers
433  There's a Spirit in the Air
**Illumination**
324  Open My Eyes That I May See
**Indwelling**
326  Spirit of God, Descend Upon My Heart
**Nature**
321  Holy Spirit, Truth Divine
323  Loving Spirit
**Presence**
120  Hail Thee, Festival Day!
139  Come, Thou Almighty King
195  Have Mercy on Us, Living Lord
313  Come Down, O Love Divine
314  Like the Murmur of the Dove's Song
315  Every Time I Feel the Spirit

# I

# J

**Lamb of God**
*See* JESUS CHRIST: LAMB OF GOD
**Life**
465   Here, O Lord, Your Servants Gather
**Light of the World**
*See* JESUS CHRIST: LIGHT OF THE WORLD
**Lord of Hosts**
176   The Earth and All That Dwell Therein
192   God, Our Help and Constant Refuge
206   O Hear Our Cry, O Lord
259   A Mighty Fortress Is Our God
416   Christ Is Made the Sure Foundation
417   Christ Is Made the Sure Foundation
**Lord of Lords**
144   Alleluia! Sing to Jesus!
149   The Head That Once Was Crowned
153   He Is King of Kings
**Lord of the Dance**
302   I Danced in the Morning
**Love**
 12   People, Look East
108   Christ Is Alive!
313   Come Down, O Love Divine
366   Jesus, They Boundless Love to Me
376   Love Divine, All Loves Excelling
464   Joyful, Joyful, We Adore Thee
523   God the Spirit, Guide and Guardian
544   Day Is Done
**Lover of Concord**
120   Hail Thee, Festival Day!
**Master**
308   O Sing a Song of Bethlehem
357   O Master, Let Me Walk with Thee
388   O Jesus, I Have Promised
389   O Jesus, I Have Promised
408   Where Cross the Crowded Ways
        of Life
415   Come, Labor On
466   O for a Thousand Tongues to Sing
477   Ye Servants of God, Your Master
        Proclaim
**Messiah**
  6   Jesus Comes with Clouds Descending
 22   Angels, from the Realms of Glory
 71   Lord, When You Came to Jordan
 87   The Glory of These Forty Days
235   With Joy I Heard My Friends Exclaim
**Monarch**
 67   Brightest and Best of the Stars of the
        Morning
**Morning Star**
 69   O Morning Star, How Fair and Bright

**Prince of Glory**
100   When I Survey the Wondrous Cross
101   When I Survey the Wondrous Cross
**Prince of Life**
 76   My Song Is Love Unknown
122   Thine Is the Glory
**Prince of Peace**
 20   Watchman, Tell Us of the Night
 31   Hark! The Herald Angels Sing
 32   Hark! The Herald Angels Sing
437   Our Cities Cry to You, O God
493   Dearest Jesus, We Are Here
**Redeemer**
  4   Creator of the Stars of Night
  8   Lift Up Your Heads, Ye Mighty
        Gates
 67   Brightest and Best of the Stars of the
        Morning
 78   Alas! And Did My Savior Bleed
 89   Hosanna, Loud Hosanna
 97   Go to Dark Gethsemane
120   Hail Thee, Festival Day!
144   Alleluia! Sing to Jesus!
151   Crown Him with Many Crowns
153   He Is King of Kings
167   God's Law Is Perfect and Gives Life
223   O My Soul, Bless Your Redeemer
229   From All That Dwell Below the Skies
325   Spirit Divine, Attend Our Prayers
395   Have Mercy, Lord, on Me
441   I Love Thy Kingdom, Lord
457   I Greet Thee, Who My Sure
        Redeemer Art
466   O for a Thousand Tongues to Sing
527   Near to the Heart of God
**Rock**
379   My Hope Is Built on Nothing Less
**Ruler**
339   Be Thou My Vision
**Ruler of Nature**
120   Hail Thee, Festival Day!
**Savior**
  8   Lift Up Your Heads, Ye Mighty
        Gates
 10   On Jordan's Bank the Baptist's Cry
 14   Savior of the Nations, Come
 27   Gentle Mary Laid Her Child
 29   Go, Tell It on the Mountain
 40   Joy to the World!
 48   Lo, How a Rose E'er Blooming
 49   Once in Royal David's City
 51   See Amid the Winter's Snow

## K—L

# M

# N

# O

# R

## RECONCILIATION

## REDEMPTION

*See also* ATONEMENT

## REFORMATION DAY

## REFUGE

## RENEWAL AND REVIVAL

## REPENTANCE

*See also* PENITENCE AND CONFESSION

# S

# T

# U

## UNBELIEF

270 O God, in a Mysterious Way
399 We Walk by Faith and Not by Sight
410 When I Had Not Yet Learned of Jesus
462 Christ, Whose Glory Fills the Skies
463 Christ, Whose Glory Fills the Skies
522 Lord, When I Came Into This Life

## UNION WITH CHRIST

*See also* JESUS CHRIST: PRESENCE
 69 O Morning Star, How Fair and Bright
271 Many and Great, O God, Are Thy
      Things
302 I Danced in the Morning
346 Christ, You Are the Fullness
357 O Master, Let Me Walk with Thee
365 Jesus, Priceless Treasure
366 Jesus, Thy Boundless Love to Me
370 Just as I Am, Without One Plea
375 Lord of All Good
376 Love Divine, All Loves Excelling
378 Make Me a Captive, Lord
391 Take My Life
392 Take Thou Our Minds, Dear Lord
400 When We Are Living

## UNITY

*See also* COMMUNITY; JESUS CHRIST:
      UNITY
  9 O Come, O Come, Emmanuel
136 Sovereign Lord of All Creation
241 Behold the Goodness of Our Lord
273 O God the Creator
343 Called as Partners in Christ's Service
416 Christ Is Made the Sure Foundation
417 Christ Is Made the Sure Foundation
422 God, Whose Giving Knows No
      Ending
425 Lord of Light, Your Name Outshining
435 We All Are One in Mission
438 Blest Be the Tie That Binds
439 In Christ There Is No East or West
440 In Christ There Is No East or West
442 The Church's One Foundation
443 O Christ, the Great Foundation
465 Here, O Lord, Your Servants Gather
499 Wonder of Wonders, Here Revealed
517 We Come as Guests Invited
526 For All the Saints
546 The Day Thou Gavest, Lord,
      Is Ended

# V—Z

## VISION

 71 Lord, When You Came to Jordan
 75 O Wondrous Sight, O Vision Fair
127 Come, O Spirit
129 Come, O Spirit, Dwell Among Us
132 Come, Great God of All the Ages
273 O God the Creator
275 God of Our Life
289 O God of Every Nation
332 Live Into Hope
339 Be Thou My Vision
351 Give to Me, Lord, a Thankful Heart
427 Lord, Whose Love Through Humble Service
430 Come Sing, O Church, in Joy!
431 O Lord, You Gave Your Servant John
442 The Church's One Foundation
453 O Holy City, Seen of John

## VOCATION

*See* CONFIRMATION; ORDINATION
285 God, You Spin the Whirling Planets
419 How Clear Is Our Vocation, Lord

## WAR

159 Why Are Nations Raging
169 In the Day of Need
193 Psalm 46
236 Now Israel May Say
259 A Mighty Fortress Is Our God
262 God of the Ages, Whose Almighty Hand
289 O God of Every Nation
295 O God of Love, O God of Peace
360 Hope of the World
401 When Will People Cease Their Fighting?
420 God of Grace and God of Glory

# III.
# Index of Scriptural Allusions
# (Scripture to Hymn)

**DEUTERONOMY** (cont.)

| | | |
|---|---|---|
| **5:22–23** | 138 | Holy, Holy, Holy! Lord God Almighty! |
| **5:33** | 167 | God's Law Is Perfect and Gives Life |
| **6:4** | 566 | Glory to God in the Highest |
| | 575 | Glory to God in the Highest |
| **6:4–7** | 497 | With Grateful Hearts Our Faith Professing |
| **6:5** | 326 | Spirit of God, Descend Upon My Heart |
| | 392 | Take Thou Our Minds, Dear Lord |
| **7:6** | 142 | All Hail the Power of Jesus' Name |
| | 143 | All Hail the Power of Jesus' Name |
| **7:9** | 276 | Great Is Thy Faithfulness |
| **8:3** | 329 | Break Thou the Bread of Life |
| | 540 | God Be with You Till We Meet Again |
| **8:15–16** | 269 | O God of Bethel, by Whose Hand |
| **8:16** | 446 | Glorious Things of Thee are Spoken |
| **16:16** | 235 | With Joy I Heard My Friends Exclaim |
| **26:1–3** | 414 | As Those of Old Their Firstfruits Brought |
| **26:1–11** | 558 | Come, Sing a Song of Harvest |
| **26:2–3** | 553 | For the Fruit of All Creation |
| **28:1–14** | 238 | Unless the Lord the House Shall Build |
| **28:6** | 234 | I to the Hills Will Lift My Eyes |
| **31:6** | 361 | How Firm a Foundation |
| | 420 | God of Grace and God of Glory |
| | 476 | O Worship the King, All Glorious Above! |
| **31:8** | 476 | O Worship the King, All Glorious Above! |
| | 559 | We Gather Together |
| **32:3** | 477 | Ye Servants of God, Your Master Proclaim |
| | 483 | Sing Praise to God, Who Reigns Above |
| **32:4** | 284 | O God, What You Ordain Is Right |
| **32:10** | 441 | I Love Thy Kingdom, Lord |
| **33:25** | 276 | Great Is Thy Faithfulness |
| **33:27** | 259 | A Mighty Fortress Is Our God |
| | 260 | A Mighty Fortress Is Our God |
| | 340 | Eternal Light, Shine in My Heart |
| | 365 | Jesus, Priceless Treasure |
| | 530 | O Lord of Life, Where'er They Be |
| | 540 | God Be with You Till We Meet Again |
| | 542 | All Praise to Thee, My God, This Night |

**JOSHUA**

| | | |
|---|---|---|
| **1:5** | 476 | O Worship the King, All Glorious Above! |
| **1:9** | 361 | How Firm a Foundation |
| **3:1–17** | 281 | Guide Me, O Thou Great Jehovah |
| **24:15** | 239 | How Happy Is Each Child of God |
| | 533 | O Perfect Love |

**RUTH**

| | | |
|---|---|---|
| **2:12** | 269 | O God of Bethel, by Whose Hand |
| | 303 | Jesus, Lover of My Soul |
| | 482 | Praise Ye the Lord, the Almighty |

**1 CHRONICLES** (cont.)

|  |  |
|---|---|
| | 258 . . . . . . . . . . . . . Praise Ye the Lord |
| **15:16** | 257 . . . . . . . . . . . . . Give Praise to the Lord |
| | 258 . . . . . . . . . . . . . Praise Ye the Lord |
| **16:4–13** | 264 . . . . . . . . . . . . . When in Our Music God Is Glorified |
| **16:8** | 555 . . . . . . . . . . . . . Now Thank We All Our God |
| **16:10** | 446 . . . . . . . . . . . . . Glorious Things of Thee Are Spoken |
| **16:23–33** | 216 . . . . . . . . . . . . . O Sing a New Song to the Lord |
| | 217 . . . . . . . . . . . . . O Sing a New Song |
| **16:25–36** | 483 . . . . . . . . . . . . . Sing Praise to God, Who Reigns Above |
| **16:28** | 180 . . . . . . . . . . . . . The God of Heaven |
| **16:29** | 8 . . . . . . . . . . . . . . Lift Up Your Heads, Ye Mighty Gates |
| | 476 . . . . . . . . . . . . . O Worship the King, All Glorious Above! |
| **16:31** | 230 . . . . . . . . . . . . . This Is the Day the Lord Hath Made |
| **16:31–34** | 554 . . . . . . . . . . . . . Let All Things Now Living |
| **16:34–36** | 555 . . . . . . . . . . . . . Now Thank We All Our God |
| **16:36** | 491 . . . . . . . . . . . . . Stand Up and Bless the Lord |
| **17:16–17** | 280 . . . . . . . . . . . . . Amazing Grace, How Sweet the Sound |
| **17:20** | 138 . . . . . . . . . . . . . Holy, Holy, Holy! Lord God Almighty! |
| **21:1–22:6** | 181 . . . . . . . . . . . . . Come Sing to God |
| **23:30** | 487 . . . . . . . . . . . . . When Morning Gilds the Skies |
| | 491 . . . . . . . . . . . . . Stand Up and Bless the Lord |
| **29:5** | 391 . . . . . . . . . . . . . Take My Life |
| **29:10–13** | 478 . . . . . . . . . . . . . Praise, My Soul, the King of Heaven |
| | 479 . . . . . . . . . . . . . Praise, My Soul, the God of Heaven |
| **29:11** | 209 . . . . . . . . . . . . . My Song Forever Shall Record |
| **29:11–12** | 139 . . . . . . . . . . . . . Come, Thou Almighty King |
| **29:11–13** | 476 . . . . . . . . . . . . . O Worship the King, All Glorious Above! |
| **29:13** | 555 . . . . . . . . . . . . . Now Thank We All Our God |
| **29:14** | 428 . . . . . . . . . . . . . We Give Thee but Thine Own |

**2 CHRONICLES**

|  |  |
|---|---|
| **5:13–14** | 486 . . . . . . . . . . . . . When the Morning Stars Together |
| **20:1–30** | 169 . . . . . . . . . . . . . In the Day of Need |
| **20:21** | 180 . . . . . . . . . . . . . The God of Heaven |
| **29:30** | 63 . . . . . . . . . . . . . . As with Gladness Men of Old |

**EZRA**

|  |  |
|---|---|
| **3:11** | 298 . . . . . . . . . . . . . There's a Wideness in God's Mercy |
| **6:16** | 227 . . . . . . . . . . . . . Now Unto Us, O Lord of Heaven |

**NEHEMIAH**

|  |  |
|---|---|
| **2–7** | 445 . . . . . . . . . . . . . Great Day! |
| **9:5** | 491 . . . . . . . . . . . . . Stand Up and Bless the Lord |
| **9:6** | 267 . . . . . . . . . . . . . All Things Bright and Beautiful |
| **9:17** | 478 . . . . . . . . . . . . . Praise, My Soul, the King of Heaven |
| | 479 . . . . . . . . . . . . . Praise, My Soul, the God of Heaven |

PSALMS (cont.)

**PSALMS** (cont.)

ISAIAH (cont.)

**ISAIAH** (cont.)

|  |  |
|---|---|
| | 2 . . . . . . . . . . . . . . . Come, Thou Long-Expected Jesus |
| | 29 . . . . . . . . . . . . . Go, Tell It on the Mountain |
| | 391 . . . . . . . . . . . . Take My Life |
| **52:8** | 17 . . . . . . . . . . . . . "Sleepers, Wake!" A Voice Astounds Us |
| | 20 . . . . . . . . . . . . . Watchman, Tell Us of the Night |
| | 155 . . . . . . . . . . . . Rejoice, the Lord Is King |
| **52:10** | 218 . . . . . . . . . . . . New Songs of Celebration Render |
| | 219 . . . . . . . . . . . . To God Compose a Song of Joy |
| **52:13** | 477 . . . . . . . . . . . . Ye Servants of God, Your Master Proclaim |
| **53** | 78 . . . . . . . . . . . . . Alas! And Did My Savior Bleed |
| **53:2** | 48 . . . . . . . . . . . . . Lo, How a Rose E'er Blooming |
| **53:3** | 102 . . . . . . . . . . . . Were You There? |
| **53:3–5** | 93 . . . . . . . . . . . . . He Never Said a Mumbalin' Word |
| | 98 . . . . . . . . . . . . . O Sacred Head, Now Wounded |
| **53:4–5** | 151 . . . . . . . . . . . . Crown Him with Many Crowns |
| **53:5** | 103 . . . . . . . . . . . . Deep Were His Wounds, and Red |
| | 119 . . . . . . . . . . . . The Strife Is O'er |
| **53:5–12** | 355 . . . . . . . . . . . . Hear the Good News of Salvation |
| **53:6** | 85 . . . . . . . . . . . . . What Wondrous Love Is This |
| | 171 . . . . . . . . . . . . The King of Love My Shepherd Is |
| **53:7** | 82 . . . . . . . . . . . . . O Lamb of God Most Holy! |
| | 95 . . . . . . . . . . . . . He Never Said a Mumbalin' Word |
| **55:6** | 399 . . . . . . . . . . . . We Walk by Faith and Not by Sight |
| **55:6–7** | 381 . . . . . . . . . . . . O Come Unto the Lord |
| | 396 . . . . . . . . . . . . O for a Closer Walk with God |
| | 397 . . . . . . . . . . . . O for a Closer Walk with God |
| **55:7** | 298 . . . . . . . . . . . . There's a Wideness in God's Mercy |
| **55:10** | 560 . . . . . . . . . . . . We Plow the Fields and Scatter |
| **55:12** | 200 . . . . . . . . . . . . To Bless the Earth |
| | 201 . . . . . . . . . . . . Praise Is Your Right, O God, in Zion |
| **55:12–13** | 40 . . . . . . . . . . . . . Joy to the World! |
| **57:2** | 539 . . . . . . . . . . . . Savior, Again to Thy Dear Name We Raise |
| **57:15** | 233 . . . . . . . . . . . . Blest Are the Uncorrupt in Heart |
| | 310 . . . . . . . . . . . . Jesus, the Very Thought of Thee |
| | 376 . . . . . . . . . . . . Love Divine, All Loves Excelling |
| | 460 . . . . . . . . . . . . Holy God, We Praise Your Name |
| **58** | 79 . . . . . . . . . . . . . Kind Maker of the World |
| **58:6–7** | 407 . . . . . . . . . . . . When a Poor One |
| **58:10** | 383 . . . . . . . . . . . . My Faith Looks Up to Thee |
| | 510 . . . . . . . . . . . . Jesus, Thou Joy of Loving Hearts |
| | 511 . . . . . . . . . . . . Jesus, Thou Joy of Loving Hearts |
| **59:7–15** | 337 . . . . . . . . . . . . Isaiah the Prophet Has Written of Old |
| **59:20** | 9 . . . . . . . . . . . . . . O Come, O Come, Emmanuel |
| **60** | 337 . . . . . . . . . . . . Isaiah the Prophet Has Written of Old |
| **60:1–3** | 20 . . . . . . . . . . . . . Watchman, Tell Us of the Night |
| | 411 . . . . . . . . . . . . Arise, Your Light Is Come! |
| **60:18** | 446 . . . . . . . . . . . . Glorious Things of Thee Are Spoken |
| **60:19** | 384 . . . . . . . . . . . . O Love That Wilt Not Let Me Go |
| **61:1** | 9 . . . . . . . . . . . . . . O Come, O Come, Emmanuel |
| | 253 . . . . . . . . . . . . I'll Praise My Maker |

**DANIEL** (cont.)
|       |     |                  |
| ----- | --- | ---------------- |
| **7:14** | 289 . . . . . . . . . . . . . O God of Every Nation |
| **7:22** | 139 . . . . . . . . . . . . . Come, Thou Almighty King |

**HOSEA**
| **13:14** | 110 . . . . . . . . . . . . . Christ Jesus Lay in Death's Strong Bands |
| **14:9** | 351 . . . . . . . . . . . . . Give to Me, Lord, a Thankful Heart |

**JOEL**
| **2:13** | 478 . . . . . . . . . . . . . Praise, My Soul, the King of Heaven |
|          | 479 . . . . . . . . . . . . . Praise, My Soul, the God of Heaven |

**AMOS**
| **5:24** | 434 . . . . . . . . . . . . . Today We All Are Called to Be Disciples |
| **6:1–7** | 380 . . . . . . . . . . . . . O Christ, the Healer |

**JONAH**
| **4:2** | 478 . . . . . . . . . . . . . Praise, My Soul, the King of Heaven |
|         | 479 . . . . . . . . . . . . . Praise, My Soul, the God of Heaven |

**MICAH**
| **4:1–3** | 401 . . . . . . . . . . . . . When Will People Cease Their Fighting? |
|           | 434 . . . . . . . . . . . . . Today We All Are Called to Be Disciples |
|           | 442 . . . . . . . . . . . . . The Church's One Foundation |
|           | 450 . . . . . . . . . . . . . O Day of Peace |
|           | 452 . . . . . . . . . . . . . O Day of God, Draw Nigh |
| **4:1–4** | 289 . . . . . . . . . . . . . O God of Every Nation |
| **4:3** | 151 . . . . . . . . . . . . . Crown Him with Many Crowns |
| **4:3–5** | 295 . . . . . . . . . . . . . O God of Love, O God of Peace |
| **5:2** | 31 . . . . . . . . . . . . . Hark! The Herald Angels Sing |
|         | 32 . . . . . . . . . . . . . Hark! The Herald Angels Sing |
|         | 43 . . . . . . . . . . . . . O Little Town of Bethlehem |
|         | 44 . . . . . . . . . . . . . O Little Town of Bethlehem |
| **6:6–8** | 405 . . . . . . . . . . . . . What Does the Lord Require |
|           | 560 . . . . . . . . . . . . . We Plow the Fields and Scatter |
| **6:8** | 396 . . . . . . . . . . . . . O for a Closer Walk with God |
|         | 397 . . . . . . . . . . . . . O for a Closer Walk with God |
| **6:9** | 408 . . . . . . . . . . . . . Where Cross the Crowded Ways of Life |
| **7:7** | 387 . . . . . . . . . . . . . Savior, Like a Shepherd Lead Us |
| **7:8** | 179 . . . . . . . . . . . . . God is My Strong Salvation |
| **7:18** | 376 . . . . . . . . . . . . . Love Divine, All Loves Excelling |

**NAHUM**
| **1:3** | 478 . . . . . . . . . . . . . Praise, My Soul, the King of Heaven |
|         | 479 . . . . . . . . . . . . . Praise, My Soul, the God of Heaven |
| **1:7** | 540 . . . . . . . . . . . . . God Be with You Till We Meet Again |
| **1:15** | 391 . . . . . . . . . . . . . Take My Life |

**HABAKKUK**
| **1:12** | 31 . . . . . . . . . . . . . Hark! The Herald Angels Sing |
|          | 32 . . . . . . . . . . . . . Hark! The Herald Angels Sing |
| **2:3–4** | 240 . . . . . . . . . . . . . Out of the Depths |

**MATTHEW** (cont.)

| Scripture | Hymn |
|-----------|------|
| 8:17 | 103 . . . . . . . . . . . . Deep Were His Wounds and Red |
| 8:23–27 | 373 . . . . . . . . . . . . Lonely the Boat |
|  | 562 . . . . . . . . . . . . Eternal Father, Strong to Save |
| 8:26 | 201 . . . . . . . . . . . . Praise Is Your Right, O God, in Zion |
|  | 308 . . . . . . . . . . . . O Sing a Song of Bethlehem |
|  | 560 . . . . . . . . . . . . We Plow the Fields and Scatter |
| 9:21–22 | 301 . . . . . . . . . . . . Lord Jesus, Think on Me |
| 9:27–30 | 254 . . . . . . . . . . . . Psalm 146 |
| 9:36 | 360 . . . . . . . . . . . . Hope of the World |
|  | 408 . . . . . . . . . . . . Where Cross the Crowded Ways of Life |
| 9:37–38 | 415 . . . . . . . . . . . . Come, Labor On |
|  | 551 . . . . . . . . . . . . Come, Ye Thankful People, Come |
| 10:26–33 | 342 . . . . . . . . . . . . By Gracious Powers |
| 10:32 | 364 . . . . . . . . . . . . I Sing a Song of the Saints of God |
|  | 526 . . . . . . . . . . . . For All the Saints |
| 10:38 | 97 . . . . . . . . . . . . . Go to Dark Gethsemane |
|  | 393 . . . . . . . . . . . . Take Up Your Cross, the Savior Said |
| 10:39 | 357 . . . . . . . . . . . . O Master, Let Me Walk with Thee |
|  | 378 . . . . . . . . . . . . Make Me a Captive, Lord |
| 10:40–42 | 311 . . . . . . . . . . . . We Meet You, O Christ |
|  | 433 . . . . . . . . . . . . There's a Spirit in the Air |
| 10:42 | 408 . . . . . . . . . . . . Where Cross the Crowded Ways of Life |
| 11:2–5 | 466 . . . . . . . . . . . . O for a Thousand Tongues to Sing |
| 11:15 | 324 . . . . . . . . . . . . Open My Eyes That I May See |
| 11:17 | 302 . . . . . . . . . . . . I Danced in the Morning |
| 11:25–26 | 270 . . . . . . . . . . . . O God, in a Mysterious Way |
| 11:28 | 403 . . . . . . . . . . . . What a Friend We Have in Jesus |
| 11:28–29 | 376 . . . . . . . . . . . . Love Divine, All Loves Excelling |
| 11:28–30 | 381 . . . . . . . . . . . . O Come Unto the Lord |
|  | 408 . . . . . . . . . . . . Where Cross the Crowded Ways of Life |
|  | 419 . . . . . . . . . . . . How Clear Is Our Vocation, Lord |
|  | 527 . . . . . . . . . . . . Near to the Heart of God |
| 12:8 | 230 . . . . . . . . . . . . This Is the Day the Lord Hath Made |
| 12:20–21 | 260 . . . . . . . . . . . . A Mighty Fortress Is Our God |
|  | 293 . . . . . . . . . . . . This Is My Father's World |
| 12:21 | 360 . . . . . . . . . . . . Hope of the World |
| 13:11 | 454 . . . . . . . . . . . . Blessed Jesus, at Your Word |
| 13:16 | 324 . . . . . . . . . . . . Open My Eyes That I May See |
| 13:18–43 | 551 . . . . . . . . . . . . Come, Ye Thankful People, Come |
| 13:37–38 | 560 . . . . . . . . . . . . We Plow the Fields and Scatter |
| 13:44 | 339 . . . . . . . . . . . . Be Thou My Vision |
| 13:44–46 | 365 . . . . . . . . . . . . Jesus, Priceless Treasure |
| 13:55 | 305 . . . . . . . . . . . . Jesus, Our Divine Companion |
| 14:13–21 | 329 . . . . . . . . . . . . Break Thou the Bread of Life |
| 14:14 | 376 . . . . . . . . . . . . Love Divine, All Loves Excelling |
|  | 408 . . . . . . . . . . . . Where Cross the Crowded Ways of Life |
| 14:22–23 | 361 . . . . . . . . . . . . How Firm a Foundation |
| 14:24–33 | 562 . . . . . . . . . . . . Eternal Father, Strong to Save |
| 14:25 | 308 . . . . . . . . . . . . O Sing a Song of Bethlehem |
| 15:31 | 466 . . . . . . . . . . . . O for a Thousand Tongues to Sing |
| 15:32 | 408 . . . . . . . . . . . . Where Cross the Crowded Ways of Life |

**MATTHEW** (cont.)

| | | |
|---|---|---|
| **15:32–38** | 421 | . . . . . . . . . . . The Church of Christ in Every Age |
| **16:15–18** | 441 | . . . . . . . . . . . I Love Thy Kingdom, Lord |
| | 442 | . . . . . . . . . . . The Church's One Foundation |
| **16:16** | 598 | . . . . . . . . . . . This Is the Good News |
| **16:18** | 446 | . . . . . . . . . . . Glorious Things of Thee Are Spoken |
| | 546 | . . . . . . . . . . . The Day Thou Gavest, Lord, Is Ended |
| **16:24** | 97 | . . . . . . . . . . . Go to Dark Gethsemane |
| | 384 | . . . . . . . . . . . O Love That Wilt Not Let Me Go |
| **16:24–25** | 277 | . . . . . . . . . . . O God, Our Faithful God |
| **16:24–27** | 393 | . . . . . . . . . . . Take Up Your Cross, the Savior Said |
| **16:27–28** | 6 | . . . . . . . . . . . Jesus Comes with Clouds Descending |
| **17:1–8** | 73 | . . . . . . . . . . . Swiftly Pass the Clouds of Glory |
| | 74 | . . . . . . . . . . . Jesus on the Mountain Peak |
| | 75 | . . . . . . . . . . . O Wondrous Sight, O Vision Fair |
| **17:1–9** | 87 | . . . . . . . . . . . The Glory of These Forty Days |
| **17:20–21** | 531 | . . . . . . . . . . . Not for Tongues of Heaven's Angels |
| **18:3** | 493 | . . . . . . . . . . . Dearest Jesus, We Are Here |
| **18:10** | 478 | . . . . . . . . . . . Praise, My Soul, the King of Heaven |
| | 479 | . . . . . . . . . . . Praise, My Soul, the God of Heaven |
| **18:10–14** | 170 | . . . . . . . . . . . The Lord's My Shepherd, I'll Not Want |
| | 171 | . . . . . . . . . . . The King of Love My Shepherd Is |
| | 172 | . . . . . . . . . . . My Shepherd Will Supply My Need |
| | 173 | . . . . . . . . . . . Psalm 23 |
| | 175 | . . . . . . . . . . . The Lord's My Shepherd, All My Need |
| | 272 | . . . . . . . . . . . God of the Sparrow |
| **18:12–14** | 426 | . . . . . . . . . . . Lord, Speak to Me, That I May Speak |
| **18:20** | 136 | . . . . . . . . . . . Sovereign Lord of All Creation |
| | 338 | . . . . . . . . . . . Kum ba Yah |
| | 438 | . . . . . . . . . . . Blest Be the Tie That Binds |
| | 504 | . . . . . . . . . . . Draw Us in the Spirit's Tether |
| **18:21** | 358 | . . . . . . . . . . . Help Us Accept Each Other |
| **18:21–35** | 347 | . . . . . . . . . . . Forgive Our Sins as We Forgive |
| **19:4–6** | 532 | . . . . . . . . . . . O God, You Give Humanity Its Name |
| | 533 | . . . . . . . . . . . O Perfect Love |
| | 534 | . . . . . . . . . . . The Grace of Life Is Theirs |
| **19:13–15** | 89 | . . . . . . . . . . . Hosanna, Loud Hosanna |
| | 304 | . . . . . . . . . . . Jesus Loves Me! |
| | 408 | . . . . . . . . . . . Where Cross the Crowded Ways of Life |
| | 496 | . . . . . . . . . . . Lord Jesus Christ, Our Lord Most Dear |
| **19:21** | 339 | . . . . . . . . . . . Be Thou My Vision |
| **20:1–16** | 553 | . . . . . . . . . . . For the Fruit of All Creation |
| **20:22** | 342 | . . . . . . . . . . . By Gracious Powers |
| **21:1–11** | 90 | . . . . . . . . . . . Ride On! Ride On in Majesty! |
| | 91 | . . . . . . . . . . . Ride On! Ride On in Majesty! |
| **21:1–16** | 89 | . . . . . . . . . . . Hosanna, Loud Hosanna |
| **21:1–17** | 88 | . . . . . . . . . . . All Glory, Laud, and Honor |
| **21:5** | 230 | . . . . . . . . . . . This Is the Day the Lord Hath Made |
| **21:9** | 76 | . . . . . . . . . . . My Song Is Love Unknown |
| | 230 | . . . . . . . . . . . This Is the Day the Lord Hath Made |
| | 568 | . . . . . . . . . . . Holy, Holy, Holy Lord |
| | 580 | . . . . . . . . . . . Holy, Holy, Holy |

**MATTHEW** (cont.)

|  |  |
|---|---|
|  | 581 . . . . . . . . . . . . Holy, Holy, Holy Lord |
| **21:16** | 162 . . . . . . . . . . . . O Lord, Our God, How Excellent |
|  | 163 . . . . . . . . . . . . Lord, Our Lord, Thy Glorious Name |
|  | 423 . . . . . . . . . . . . Jesus Shall Reign Where'er the Sun |
| **21:21** | 531 . . . . . . . . . . . . Not for Tongues of Heaven's Angels |
| **21:42** | 231 . . . . . . . . . . . . Psalm 118:14–24 |
|  | 232 . . . . . . . . . . . . Psalm 118:19–29 |
|  | 416 . . . . . . . . . . . . Christ Is Made the Sure Foundation |
|  | 417 . . . . . . . . . . . . Christ Is Made the Sure Foundation |
| **22:9** | 408 . . . . . . . . . . . . Where Cross the Crowded Ways of Life |
| **22:34–40** | 348 . . . . . . . . . . . . Christian Women, Christian Men |
|  | 367 . . . . . . . . . . . . Jesu, Jesu, Fill Us with Your Love |
|  | 436 . . . . . . . . . . . . We Are Your People |
| **22:37** | 391 . . . . . . . . . . . . Take My Life |
|  | 392 . . . . . . . . . . . . Take Thou Our Minds, Dear Lord |
| **23:23** | 405 . . . . . . . . . . . . What Does the Lord Require |
| **23:37** | 303 . . . . . . . . . . . . Jesus, Lover of My Soul |
|  | 424 . . . . . . . . . . . . May Grateful Hymns Be Rising |
|  | 482 . . . . . . . . . . . . Praise Ye the Lord, the Almighty |
|  | 547 . . . . . . . . . . . . When Twilight Comes |
| **24:12** | 126 . . . . . . . . . . . . Come, Holy Spirit, Heavenly Dove |
| **24:29–30** | 449 . . . . . . . . . . . . My Lord! What a Morning |
| **24:30** | 6 . . . . . . . . . . . . Jesus Comes with Clouds Descending |
| **24:31** | 379 . . . . . . . . . . . . My Hope Is Built on Nothing Less |
|  | 442 . . . . . . . . . . . . The Church's One Foundation |
| **25:1–13** | 15 . . . . . . . . . . . . Rejoice! Rejoice, Believers |
|  | 17 . . . . . . . . . . . . "Sleepers, Wake!" A Voice Astounds Us |
| **25:14–30** | 410 . . . . . . . . . . . . When I Had Not Yet Learned of Jesus |
|  | 422 . . . . . . . . . . . . God, Whose Giving Knows No Ending |
|  | 425 . . . . . . . . . . . . Lord of Light, Your Name Outshining |
| **25:21–23** | 415 . . . . . . . . . . . . Come, Labor On |
| **25:31** | 38 . . . . . . . . . . . . It Came Upon the Midnight Clear |
|  | 151 . . . . . . . . . . . . Crown Him with Many Crowns |
| **25:31–40** | 431 . . . . . . . . . . . . O Lord, You Gave Your Servant John |
| **25:31–46** | 6 . . . . . . . . . . . . Jesus Comes with Clouds Descending |
| **25:34–40** | 407 . . . . . . . . . . . . When a Poor One |
|  | 421 . . . . . . . . . . . . The Church of Christ in Every Age |
|  | 428 . . . . . . . . . . . . We Give Thee but Thine Own |
|  | 433 . . . . . . . . . . . . There's a Spirit in the Air |
|  | 434 . . . . . . . . . . . . Today We All Are Called to Be Disciples |
|  | 558 . . . . . . . . . . . . Come, Sing a Song of Harvest |
| **25:37–45** | 553 . . . . . . . . . . . . For the Fruit of All Creation |
| **25:40** | 408 . . . . . . . . . . . . Where Cross the Crowded Ways of Life |
| **26:17–29** | 547 . . . . . . . . . . . . When Twilight Comes |
| **26:26–28** | 94 . . . . . . . . . . . . An Upper Room Did Our Lord Prepare |
|  | 429 . . . . . . . . . . . . Lord, You Give the Great Commission |
|  | 512 . . . . . . . . . . . . Living Word of God Eternal |
|  | 514 . . . . . . . . . . . . Let Us Talents and Tongues Employ |
|  | 515 . . . . . . . . . . . . Now to Your Table Spread |
| **26:26–29** | 502 . . . . . . . . . . . . Bread of the World in Mercy Broken |
|  | 503 . . . . . . . . . . . . Come, Risen Lord |

**MATTHEW** (cont.)

**MATTHEW** (cont.)

| | | |
|---|---|---|
| | 422 . . . . . . . . . . . . | God, Whose Giving Knows No Ending |
| | 426 . . . . . . . . . . . . | Lord, Speak to Me, That I May Speak |
| | 429 . . . . . . . . . . . . | Lord, You Give the Great Commission |
| | 434 . . . . . . . . . . . . | Today We All Are Called to Be Disciples |
| | 435 . . . . . . . . . . . . | We All Are One in Mission |
| | 466 . . . . . . . . . . . . | O for a Thousand Tongues to Sing |
| | 514 . . . . . . . . . . . . | Let Us Talents and Tongues Employ |
| **28:20** | 543 . . . . . . . . . . . . | Abide with Me |

**MARK**

| | | |
|---|---|---|
| **1:1–4** | 87 . . . . . . . . . . . . . | The Glory of These Forty Days |
| **1:1–8** | 3 . . . . . . . . . . . . . . | Comfort, Comfort You My People |
| **1:2–8** | 409 . . . . . . . . . . . . | Wild and Lone the Prophet's Voice |
| **1:9–11** | 71 . . . . . . . . . . . . . | Lord, When You Came to Jordan |
| | 72 . . . . . . . . . . . . . | When Jesus Came to Jordan |
| **1:9–13** | 83 . . . . . . . . . . . . . | O Love, How Deep, How Broad, How High |
| **1:10** | 126 . . . . . . . . . . . . | Come, Holy Spirit, Heavenly Dove |
| | 326 . . . . . . . . . . . . | Spirit of God, Descend Upon My Heart |
| | 398 . . . . . . . . . . . . | There's a Sweet, Sweet Spirit |
| **1:12–13** | 79 . . . . . . . . . . . . . | Kind Maker of the World |
| | 80 . . . . . . . . . . . . . | Jesus Walked This Lonesome Valley |
| | 81 . . . . . . . . . . . . . | Lord, Who Throughout These Forty Days |
| **1:14–20** | 302 . . . . . . . . . . . . | I Danced in the Morning |
| **1:16–20** | 345 . . . . . . . . . . . . | Dear Lord and Father of Mankind |
| | 377 . . . . . . . . . . . . | Lord, You Have Come to the Lakeshore |
| **1:30–34** | 380 . . . . . . . . . . . . | O Christ, the Healer |
| **2:1–12** | 302 . . . . . . . . . . . . | I Danced in the Morning |
| **2:14** | 345 . . . . . . . . . . . . | Dear Lord and Father of Mankind |
| **3:1–6** | 302 . . . . . . . . . . . . | I Danced in the Morning |
| **4:14** | 374 . . . . . . . . . . . . | Lord, Make Us Servants of Your Peace |
| **4:26–29** | 553 . . . . . . . . . . . . | For the Fruit of All Creation |
| **4:35–41** | 361 . . . . . . . . . . . . | How Firm a Foundation |
| **4:36–41** | 373 . . . . . . . . . . . . | Lonely the Boat |
| | 562 . . . . . . . . . . . . | Eternal Father, Strong to Save |
| **4:39** | 308 . . . . . . . . . . . . | O Sing a Song of Bethlehem |
| | 560 . . . . . . . . . . . . | We Plow the Fields and Scatter |
| **5:15** | 380 . . . . . . . . . . . . | O Christ, the Healer |
| | 345 . . . . . . . . . . . . | Dear Lord and Father of Mankind |
| **5:24–43** | 424 . . . . . . . . . . . . | O Jesus Christ, May Grateful Hymns Be Rising |
| **5:36** | 307 . . . . . . . . . . . . | Fight the Good Fight |
| **6:3** | 305 . . . . . . . . . . . . | Jesus, Our Divine Companion |
| **6:30–44** | 329 . . . . . . . . . . . . | Break Thou the Bread of Life |
| **6:34** | 408 . . . . . . . . . . . . | Where Cross the Crowded Ways of Life |
| | 421 . . . . . . . . . . . . | The Church of Christ in Every Age |
| **6:47–52** | 562 . . . . . . . . . . . . | Eternal Father, Strong to Save |
| **6:48** | 308 . . . . . . . . . . . . | O Sing a Song of Bethlehem |
| **7:1–8** | 336 . . . . . . . . . . . . | As a Chalice Cast of Gold |
| **7:14–15** | 336 . . . . . . . . . . . . | As a Chalice Cast of Gold |
| **7:21–23** | 336 . . . . . . . . . . . . | As a Chalice Cast of Gold |
| **7:37** | 466 . . . . . . . . . . . . | O for a Thousand Tongues to Sing |
| **8:1–9** | 421 . . . . . . . . . . . . | The Church of Christ in Every Age |

**MARK** (cont.)

| | | |
|---|---|---|
| **14:26** | 264 . . . . . . . . . . . . | When in Our Music God Is Glorified |
| **14:32–42** | 97 . . . . . . . . . . . . | Go to Dark Gethsemane |
| **14:62** | 6 . . . . . . . . . . . . | Jesus Comes with Clouds Descending |
| **15:1** | 97 . . . . . . . . . . . . | Go to Dark Gethsemane |
| **15:17–18** | 98 . . . . . . . . . . . . | O Sacred Head, Now Wounded |
| **15:17–20** | 7 . . . . . . . . . . . . | Lord Christ, When First You Came to Earth |
| | 83 . . . . . . . . . . . . | O Love, How Deep, How Broad, How High |
| **15:24–25** | 102 . . . . . . . . . . . . | Were You There? |
| **15:34** | 96 . . . . . . . . . . . . | Calvary |
| **15:37** | 83 . . . . . . . . . . . . | O Love, How Deep, How Broad, How High |
| **15:46** | 102 . . . . . . . . . . . . | Were You There? |
| **16:1–6** | 116 . . . . . . . . . . . . | O Sons and Daughters, Let Us Sing! |
| **16:1–8** | 107 . . . . . . . . . . . . | Celebrate with Joy and Singing |
| **16:6** | 113 . . . . . . . . . . . . | Christ the Lord Is Risen Today! |
| | 123 . . . . . . . . . . . . | Jesus Christ Is Risen Today |

**LUKE**

| | | |
|---|---|---|
| **1:14** | 21 . . . . . . . . . . . . | All My Heart Today Rejoices |
| **1:26–38** | 16 . . . . . . . . . . . . | The Angel Gabriel from Heaven Came |
| | 19 . . . . . . . . . . . . | To a Maid Engaged to Joseph |
| **1:31–33** | 55 . . . . . . . . . . . . | That Boy-Child of Mary |
| **1:32–33** | 155 . . . . . . . . . . . . | Rejoice, the Lord Is King |
| | 423 . . . . . . . . . . . . | Jesus Shall Reign Where'er the Sun |
| **1:32–35** | 1 . . . . . . . . . . . . | Come, Thou Long-Expected Jesus |
| | 2 . . . . . . . . . . . . | Come, Thou Long-Expected Jesus |
| **1:33** | 66 . . . . . . . . . . . . | We Three Kings of Orient Are |
| | 259 . . . . . . . . . . . . | A Mighty Fortress Is Our God |
| | 260 . . . . . . . . . . . . | A Mighty Fortress Is Our God |
| | 546 . . . . . . . . . . . . | The Day Thou Gavest, Lord, Is Ended |
| **1:33–35** | 31 . . . . . . . . . . . . | Hark! The Herald Angels Sing |
| | 32 . . . . . . . . . . . . | Hark! The Herald Angels Sing |
| **1:46–55** | 225 . . . . . . . . . . . . | Praise the Lord! |
| | 226 . . . . . . . . . . . . | Sing Praise Unto the Name of God |
| | 600 . . . . . . . . . . . . | Song of Mary |
| **1:50** | 222 . . . . . . . . . . . . | Psalm 103 |
| | 223 . . . . . . . . . . . . | O My Soul, Bless Your Redeemer |
| **1:66** | 53 . . . . . . . . . . . . | What Child Is This |
| **1:68–79** | 601 . . . . . . . . . . . . | Song of Zechariah |
| | 602 . . . . . . . . . . . . | Song of Zechariah |
| **1:77–79** | 5 . . . . . . . . . . . . | Let All Mortal Flesh Keep Silence |
| | 28 . . . . . . . . . . . . | Good Christian Friends, Rejoice |
| | 60 . . . . . . . . . . . . | Silent Night, Holy Night |
| | 67 . . . . . . . . . . . . | Brightest and Best of the Stars of the Morning |
| **1:78** | 462 . . . . . . . . . . . . | Christ, Whose Glory Fills the Skies |
| | 463 . . . . . . . . . . . . | Christ, Whose Glory Fills the Skies |
| | 476 . . . . . . . . . . . . | O Worship the King, All Glorious Above! |
| **1:78–79** | 9 . . . . . . . . . . . . | O Come, O Come, Emmanuel |
| **1:79** | 539 . . . . . . . . . . . . | Savior, Again to Thy Dear Name We Raise |
| **2:1–7** | 1 . . . . . . . . . . . . | Come, Thou Long-Expected Jesus |
| | 2 . . . . . . . . . . . . | Come, Thou Long-Expected Jesus |
| | 43 . . . . . . . . . . . . | O Little Town of Bethlehem |

**JOHN** (cont.)

**JOHN** (cont.)

| | | |
|---|---|---|
| **10:10** | 31 . . . . . . . . . . . . . | Hark! The Herald Angels Sing |
| | 32 . . . . . . . . . . . . . | Hark! The Herald Angels Sing |
| | 296 . . . . . . . . . . . . | Walk On, O People of God |
| | 427 . . . . . . . . . . . . | Lord, Whose Love Through Humble Service |
| **10:14–15** | 171 . . . . . . . . . . . . | The King of Love My Shepherd Is |
| **10:14–16** | 387 . . . . . . . . . . . . | Savior, Like a Shepherd Lead Us |
| **10:17** | 111 . . . . . . . . . . . . | Good Christians All, Rejoice and Sing! |
| **10:27** | 171 . . . . . . . . . . . . | The King of Love My Shepherd Is |
| | 387 . . . . . . . . . . . . | Savior, Like a Shepherd Lead Us |
| **10:28** | 527 . . . . . . . . . . . . | Near to the Heart of God |
| **10:30** | 135 . . . . . . . . . . . . | God Is One, Unique and Holy |
| **11:1–44** | 406 . . . . . . . . . . . . | Why Has God Forsaken Me? |
| **11:25** | 529 . . . . . . . . . . . . | Lord of the Living |
| **11:26** | 316 . . . . . . . . . . . . | Breathe on Me, Breath of God |
| **11:35** | 312 . . . . . . . . . . . . | When Jesus Wept |
| **12:12–13** | 89 . . . . . . . . . . . . . | Hosanna, Loud Hosanna |
| **12:12–15** | 90 . . . . . . . . . . . . . | Ride On! Ride On in Majesty! |
| | 91 . . . . . . . . . . . . . | Ride On! Ride On in Majesty |
| **12:12–16** | 88 . . . . . . . . . . . . . | All Glory, Laud, and Honor |
| **12:13** | 232 . . . . . . . . . . . . | Psalm 118:19–29 |
| | 568 . . . . . . . . . . . . | Holy, Holy, Holy Lord |
| | 581 . . . . . . . . . . . . | Holy, Holy, Holy Lord |
| **12:26** | 357 . . . . . . . . . . . . | O Master, Let Me Walk with Thee |
| | 388 . . . . . . . . . . . . | O Jesus, I Have Promised |
| | 389 . . . . . . . . . . . . | O Jesus, I Have Promised |
| | 393 . . . . . . . . . . . . | Take Up Your Cross, the Savior Said |
| **12:32** | 371 . . . . . . . . . . . . | Lift High the Cross |
| **12:35–36** | 411 . . . . . . . . . . . . | Arise, Your Light Is Come! |
| **12:46** | 462 . . . . . . . . . . . . | Christ, Whose Glory Fills the Skies |
| | 463 . . . . . . . . . . . . | Christ, Whose Glory Fills the Skies |
| **13:1** | 387 . . . . . . . . . . . . | Savior, Like a Shepherd Lead Us |
| **13:1–17** | 367 . . . . . . . . . . . . | Jesu, Jesu, Fill Us with Your Love |
| **13:3–5** | 94 . . . . . . . . . . . . . | An Upper Room Did Our Lord Prepare |
| | 427 . . . . . . . . . . . . | Lord, Whose Love Through Humble Service |
| **13:4–5** | 353 . . . . . . . . . . . . | Great God, Your Love Has Called Us Here |
| **13:7** | 270 . . . . . . . . . . . . | O God, in a Mysterious Way |
| **13:12–15** | 427 . . . . . . . . . . . . | Lord, Whose Love Through Humble Service |
| **13:13–14** | 357 . . . . . . . . . . . . | O Master, Let Me Walk with Thee |
| **13:13–15** | 516 . . . . . . . . . . . . | Lord, We Have Come at Your Own Invitation |
| **13:14–15** | 94 . . . . . . . . . . . . . | An Upper Room Did Our Lord Prepare |
| **13:15** | 372 . . . . . . . . . . . . | Lord, I Want to Be a Christian |
| | 426 . . . . . . . . . . . . | Lord, Speak to Me, That I May Speak |
| **13:34–35** | 358 . . . . . . . . . . . . | Help Us Accept Each Other |
| | 408 . . . . . . . . . . . . | Where Cross the Crowded Ways of Life |
| | 433 . . . . . . . . . . . . | There's a Spirit in the Air |
| | 434 . . . . . . . . . . . . | Today We All Are Called to Be Disciples |
| | 438 . . . . . . . . . . . . | Blest Be the Tie That Binds |
| | 491 . . . . . . . . . . . . | Stand Up and Bless the Lord |
| | 504 . . . . . . . . . . . . | Draw Us in the Spirit's Tether |
| **13:35** | 357 . . . . . . . . . . . . | O Master, Let Me Walk with Thee |
| **14:1** | 510 . . . . . . . . . . . . | Jesus, Thou Joy of Loving Hearts |

**JOHN** (cont.)

|  |  |
|---|---|
|  | 511 . . . . . . . . . . . . . Jesus, Thou Joy of Loving Hearts |
| **14:1–3** | 459 . . . . . . . . . . . . . Father, We Praise Thee |
| **14:2–3** | 49 . . . . . . . . . . . . . Once in Royal David's City |
| **14:3** | 388 . . . . . . . . . . . . . O Jesus, I Have Promised |
|  | 389 . . . . . . . . . . . . . O Jesus, I Have Promised |
|  | 467 . . . . . . . . . . . . . How Great Thou Art |
| **14:6** | 457 . . . . . . . . . . . . . I Greet Thee, Who My Sure Redeemer Art |
|  | 465 . . . . . . . . . . . . . Here, O Lord, Your Servants Gather |
|  | 485 . . . . . . . . . . . . . To God Be the Glory |
|  | 493 . . . . . . . . . . . . . Dearest Jesus, We Are Here |
|  | 515 . . . . . . . . . . . . . Now to Your Table Spread |
| **14:15–21** | 313 . . . . . . . . . . . . . Come Down, O Love Divine |
| **14:16** | 125 . . . . . . . . . . . . . Come, Holy Spirit, Our Souls Inspire |
|  | 433 . . . . . . . . . . . . . There's a Spirit in the Air |
| **14:16–17** | 139 . . . . . . . . . . . . . Come, Thou Almighty King |
|  | 325 . . . . . . . . . . . . . Spirit Divine, Attend Our Prayers |
|  | 376 . . . . . . . . . . . . . Love Divine, All Loves Excelling |
| **14:17** | 321 . . . . . . . . . . . . . Holy Spirit, Truth Divine |
| **14:20** | 339 . . . . . . . . . . . . . Be Thou My Vision |
| **14:21** | 376 . . . . . . . . . . . . . Love Divine, All Loves Excelling |
| **14:26** | 454 . . . . . . . . . . . . . Blessed Jesus, at Your Word |
| **14:27** | 120 . . . . . . . . . . . . . Hail Thee, Festival Day! |
|  | 286 . . . . . . . . . . . . . Give to the Winds Thy Fears |
|  | 373 . . . . . . . . . . . . . Lonely the Boat |
|  | 413 . . . . . . . . . . . . . All Who Love and Serve Your City |
|  | 539 . . . . . . . . . . . . . Savior, Again to Thy Dear Name We Raise |
| **15:1** | 493 . . . . . . . . . . . . . Dearest Jesus, We Are Here |
|  | 501 . . . . . . . . . . . . . Bread of Heaven, on Thee We Feed |
| **15:1–5** | 418 . . . . . . . . . . . . . God, Bless Your Church with Strength! |
| **15:3** | 166 . . . . . . . . . . . . . The Heavens Above Declare God's Praise |
| **15:4** | 302 . . . . . . . . . . . . . I Danced in the Morning |
| **15:4–5** | 339 . . . . . . . . . . . . . Be Thou My Vision |
| **15:5** | 314 . . . . . . . . . . . . . Like the Murmur of the Dove's Song |
|  | 501 . . . . . . . . . . . . . Bread of Heaven, on Thee We Feed |
|  | 517 . . . . . . . . . . . . . We Come As Guests Invited |
| **15:8** | 504 . . . . . . . . . . . . . Draw Us in the Spirit's Tether |
| **15:9** | 310 . . . . . . . . . . . . . Jesus, the Very Thought of Thee |
| **15:9–10** | 366 . . . . . . . . . . . . . Jesus, Thy Boundless Love to Me |
| **15:9–11** | 384 . . . . . . . . . . . . . O Love That Wilt Not Let Me Go |
| **15:9–17** | 157 . . . . . . . . . . . . . Our King and Our Sovereign, Lord Jesus |
| **15:10–11** | 510 . . . . . . . . . . . . . Jesus, Thou Joy of Loving Hearts |
|  | 511 . . . . . . . . . . . . . Jesus, Thou Joy of Loving Hearts |
| **15:12** | 358 . . . . . . . . . . . . . Help Us Accept Each Other |
| **15:12–17** | 343 . . . . . . . . . . . . . Called as Partners in Christ's Service |
| **15:13** | 85 . . . . . . . . . . . . . What Wondrous Love Is This |
| **15:13–16** | 403 . . . . . . . . . . . . . What a Friend We Have in Jesus |
| **15:14** | 388 . . . . . . . . . . . . . O Jesus, I Have Promised |
|  | 389 . . . . . . . . . . . . . O Jesus, I Have Promised |
| **16:5–16** | 317 . . . . . . . . . . . . . Holy Ghost, Dispel Our Sadness |
| **16:13** | 282 . . . . . . . . . . . . . If Thou but Trust in God to Guide Thee |
| **16:19–24** | 149 . . . . . . . . . . . . . The Head That Once Was Crowned |
| **16:33** | 84 . . . . . . . . . . . . . In the Cross of Christ I Glory |

**JOHN** (cont.)

|  |  |  |
|---|---|---|
|  | 155 | Rejoice, the Lord Is King |
|  | 293 | This Is My Father's World |
|  | 373 | Lonely the Boat |
|  | 559 | We Gather Together |
| **17:17** | 329 | Break Thou the Bread of Life |
| **17:21** | 339 | Be Thou My Vision |
| **17:24** | 443 | O Christ, the Great Foundation |
|  | 488 | The God of Abraham Praise |
| **17:26** | 316 | Breathe on Me, Breath of God |
| **18:1–40** | 97 | Go to Dark Gethsemane |
| **18:11** | 342 | By Gracious Powers |
| **18:36** | 447 | Lead On, O King Eternal |
|  | 448 | Lead On, O King Eternal |
| **19** | 97 | Go to Dark Gethsemane |
|  | 99 | Throned Upon the Awful Tree |
| **19:2** | 7 | Lord Christ, When First You Came to Earth |
|  | 100 | When I Survey the Wondrous Cross |
|  | 101 | When I Survey the Wondrous Cross |
| **19:2–3** | 98 | O Sacred Head, Now Wounded |
| **19:16–18** | 102 | Were You There? |
| **19:16–34** | 103 | Deep Were His Wounds, and Red |
| **19:17–18** | 78 | Alas! And Did My Savior Bleed |
|  | 84 | In the Cross of Christ I Glory |
|  | 95 | He Never Said a Mumbalin' Word |
|  | 100 | When I Survey the Wondrous Cross |
|  | 101 | When I Survey the Wondrous Cross |
| **19:17–30** | 93 | Ah, Holy Jesus |
| **19:25** | 92 | Beneath the Cross of Jesus |
| **19:30** | 95 | He Never Said a Mumbalin' Word |
|  | 96 | Calvary |
| **19:32–34** | 100 | When I Survey the Wondrous Cross |
|  | 101 | When I Survey the Wondrous Cross |
| **19:34** | 95 | He Never Said a Mumbalin' Word |
|  | 102 | Were You There? |
| **20** | 121 | That Easter Day with Joy Was Bright |
| **19:36** | 187 | Psalm 34:9–22 |
| **19:41–42** | 102 | Were You There? |
| **20** | 121 | That Easter Day with Joy Was Bright |
| **20:1** | 105 | Because You Live, O Christ |
| **20:1–18** | 97 | Go to Dark Gethsemane |
| **20:6–7** | 122 | Thine Is the Glory |
| **20:11–18** | 113 | Christ the Lord Is Risen Today! |
| **20:19–23** | 116 | O Sons and Daughters, Let Us Sing! |
| **20:19–29** | 117 | O Sons and Daughters, Let Us Sing! |
| **20:19–31** | 399 | We Walk by Faith and Not by Sight |
| **20:20** | 151 | Crown Him with Many Crowns |
| **20:22** | 316 | Breathe on Me, Breath of God |
|  | 376 | Love Divine, All Loves Excelling |
| **20:27–28** | 122 | Thine Is the Glory |
| **20:31** | 466 | O for a Thousand Tongues to Sing |
| **21:15** | 359 | More Love to Thee, O Christ |
|  | 493 | Dearest Jesus, We Are Here |

**ACTS** (cont.)
| 4:23–31 | 159 . . . . . . . . . . . Why Are Nations Raging |
|---|---|
| 4:24 | 274 . . . . . . . . . . . O God of Earth and Space |
| | 467 . . . . . . . . . . . How Great Thou Art |
| 4:31 | 325 . . . . . . . . . . . Spirit Divine, Attend Our Prayers |
| 4:32–35 | 515 . . . . . . . . . . . Now to Your Table Spread |
| 4:33 | 111 . . . . . . . . . . . Good Christians All, Rejoice and Sing |
| 5:30 | 308 . . . . . . . . . . . O Sing a Song of Bethlehem |
| 5:30–31 | 149 . . . . . . . . . . . The Head That Once Was Crowned |
| 5:31 | 155 . . . . . . . . . . . Rejoice, the Lord Is King |
| 7:2–53 | 330 . . . . . . . . . . . Deep in the Shadows of the Past |
| 9:3–5 | 462 . . . . . . . . . . . Christ, Whose Glory Fills the Skies |
| | 463 . . . . . . . . . . . Christ, Whose Glory Fills the Skies |
| 9:31 | 325 . . . . . . . . . . . Spirit Divine, Attend Our Prayers |
| 10:35 | 439 . . . . . . . . . . . In Christ There Is No East or West |
| | 440 . . . . . . . . . . . In Christ There Is No East or West |
| 10:37 | 10 . . . . . . . . . . . On Jordan's Bank the Baptist's Cry |
| 10:39–40 | 308 . . . . . . . . . . . O Sing a Song of Bethlehem |
| 10:44 | 322 . . . . . . . . . . . Spirit of the Living God |
| 11:15 | 322 . . . . . . . . . . . Spirit of the Living God |
| 13:29–30 | 308 . . . . . . . . . . . O Sing a Song of Bethlehem |
| 13:32–33 | 111 . . . . . . . . . . . Good Christians All, Rejoice and Sing! |
| 14:17 | 160 . . . . . . . . . . . Psalm 4 |
| | 480 . . . . . . . . . . . Praise Our God Above |
| | 560 . . . . . . . . . . . We Plow the Fields and Scatter |
| 14:22 | 559 . . . . . . . . . . . We Gather Together |
| 17:25 | 263 . . . . . . . . . . . Immortal, Invisible, God Only Wise |
| 17:26 | 439 . . . . . . . . . . . In Christ There Is No East or West |
| | 440 . . . . . . . . . . . In Christ There Is No East or West |
| 17:26–28 | 275 . . . . . . . . . . . God of Our Life |
| 17:27 | 483 . . . . . . . . . . . Sing Praise to God, Who Reigns Above |
| | 527 . . . . . . . . . . . Near to the Heart of God |
| 17:27–30 | 396 . . . . . . . . . . . O for a Closer Walk with God |
| 17:28 | 457 . . . . . . . . . . . I Greet Thee, Who My Sure Redeemer Art |
| 17:31 | 341 . . . . . . . . . . . Blessed Assurance, Jesus Is Mine! |
| 18:10 | 437 . . . . . . . . . . . Our Cities Cry to You, O God |
| 20:7 | 470 . . . . . . . . . . . O Day of Radiant Gladness |
| 20:28 | 341 . . . . . . . . . . . Blessed Assurance, Jesus Is Mine! |
| | 442 . . . . . . . . . . . The Church's One Foundation |
| | 519 . . . . . . . . . . . Thee We Adore, O Hidden Savior, Thee |
| | 523 . . . . . . . . . . . God the Spirit, Guide and Guardian |
| 20:32 | 526 . . . . . . . . . . . For All the Saints |
| | 364 . . . . . . . . . . . I Sing a Song of the Saints of God |
| | 540 . . . . . . . . . . . God Be with You Till We Meet Again |
| 26:18 | 383 . . . . . . . . . . . My Faith Looks Up to Thee |
| 26:18 | 510 . . . . . . . . . . . Jesus, Thou Joy of Loving Hearts |
| | 511 . . . . . . . . . . . Jesus, Thou Joy of Loving Hearts |
| 26:22 | 265 . . . . . . . . . . . Great God, We Sing That Mighty Hand |

**ROMANS**
| 1:3 | 58 . . . . . . . . . . . While Shepherds Watched Their Flocks |

**ROMANS** (cont.)

|  |  |
|---|---|
|  | 59 . . . . . . . . . . . . . While Shepherds Watched Their Flocks |
| **1:17** | 383 . . . . . . . . . . . . . My Faith Looks Up to Thee |
| **1:20** | 467 . . . . . . . . . . . . . How Great Thou Art |
|  | 480 . . . . . . . . . . . . . Praise Our God Above |
| **1:28–32** | 380 . . . . . . . . . . . . . O Christ, the Healer |
| **3:4** | 195 . . . . . . . . . . . . . Have Mercy on Us, Living Lord |
|  | 196 . . . . . . . . . . . . . Psalm 51 |
| **3:21–26** | 296 . . . . . . . . . . . . . Walk On, O People of God |
| **3:24–25** | 466 . . . . . . . . . . . . . O for a Thousand Tongues to Sing |
| **4:6–8** | 184 . . . . . . . . . . . . . How Blest Are Those |
| **4:20–21** | 488 . . . . . . . . . . . . . The God of Abraham Praise |
| **4:24–25** | 106 . . . . . . . . . . . . . Alleluia, Alleluia! Give Thanks |
| **5:1–2** | 383 . . . . . . . . . . . . . My Faith Looks Up to Thee |
| **5:1–5** | 379 . . . . . . . . . . . . . My Hope Is Built on Nothing Less |
|  | 531 . . . . . . . . . . . . . Not for Tongues of Heaven's Angels |
| **5:2** | 356 . . . . . . . . . . . . . Come, Thou Fount of Every Blessing |
| **5:5** | 125 . . . . . . . . . . . . . Come, Holy Spirit, Our Souls Inspire |
|  | 126 . . . . . . . . . . . . . Come, Holy Spirit, Heavenly Dove |
|  | 321 . . . . . . . . . . . . . Holy Spirit, Truth Divine |
|  | 323 . . . . . . . . . . . . . Loving Spirit |
|  | 324 . . . . . . . . . . . . . Open My Eyes That I May See |
|  | 326 . . . . . . . . . . . . . Spirit of God, Descend Upon My Heart |
|  | 392 . . . . . . . . . . . . . Take Thou Our Minds, Dear Lord |
| **5:6** | 467 . . . . . . . . . . . . . How Great Thou Art |
| **5:6–8** | 98 . . . . . . . . . . . . . O Sacred Head, Now Wounded |
| **5:6–11** | 78 . . . . . . . . . . . . . Alas! And Did My Savior Bleed |
|  | 93 . . . . . . . . . . . . . Ah, Holy Jesus |
|  | 100 . . . . . . . . . . . . . When I Survey the Wondrous Cross |
|  | 101 . . . . . . . . . . . . . When I Survey the Wondrous Cross |
| **5:8** | 85 . . . . . . . . . . . . . What Wondrous Love Is This |
| **5:12–21** | 260 . . . . . . . . . . . . . A Mighty Fortress Is Our God |
| **5:13** | 432 . . . . . . . . . . . . . Song of Hope |
|  | 444 . . . . . . . . . . . . . We Gather Here to Bid Farewell |
| **5:15–21** | 290 . . . . . . . . . . . . . God Created Heaven and Earth |
| **5:20** | 40 . . . . . . . . . . . . . Joy to the World! |
| **5:20–21** | 280 . . . . . . . . . . . . . Amazing Grace, How Sweet the Sound |
|  | 303 . . . . . . . . . . . . . Jesus, Lover of My Soul |
| **6:1–4** | 492 . . . . . . . . . . . . . Baptized in Water |
| **6:1–11** | 502 . . . . . . . . . . . . . Bread of the World in Mercy Broken |
| **6:4** | 495 . . . . . . . . . . . . . We Know that Christ Is Raised |
|  | 499 . . . . . . . . . . . . . Wonder of Wonders, Here Revealed |
| **6:5–11** | 108 . . . . . . . . . . . . . Christ Is Alive! |
| **6:9** | 113 . . . . . . . . . . . . . Christ the Lord Is Risen Today! |
|  | 495 . . . . . . . . . . . . . We Know That Christ Is Raised |
| **6:9–10** | 114 . . . . . . . . . . . . . Come, Ye Faithful, Raise the Strain |
|  | 115 . . . . . . . . . . . . . Come, Ye Faithful, Raise the Strain |
|  | 119 . . . . . . . . . . . . . The Strife Is O'er |
|  | 123 . . . . . . . . . . . . . Jesus Christ Is Risen Today |
|  | 155 . . . . . . . . . . . . . Rejoice, the Lord Is King |
| **6:11** | 103 . . . . . . . . . . . . . Deep Were His Wounds, and Red |
| **6:13** | 350 . . . . . . . . . . . . . Fill My Cup |

**ROMANS** (cont.)

**1 CORINTHIANS** (cont.)

**1 CORINTHIANS** (cont.)

## 2 TIMOTHY

## TITUS

**HEBREWS** (cont.)

| | | |
|---|---|---|
| **13:2** | 407 | When a Poor One |
| **13:5** | 521 | You Satisfy the Hungry Heart |
| **13:5–6** | 361 | How Firm a Foundation |
| **13:6** | 172 | My Shepherd Will Supply My Need |
| **13:7** | 523 | God the Spirit, Guide and Guardian |
| **13:8** | 260 | A Mighty Fortress Is Our God |
| | 309 | Of the Father's Love Begotten |
| | 488 | The God of Abraham Praise |
| | 543 | Abide with Me |
| | 555 | Now Thank We All Our God |
| **13:15** | 150 | Come, Christians, Join to Sing |
| | 473 | For the Beauty of the Earth |
| | 483 | Sing Praise to God, Who Reigns Above |
| | 551 | Come, Ye Thankful People, Come |
| | 555 | Now Thank We All Our God |
| | 560 | We Plow the Fields and Scatter |
| **13:20–21** | 174 | The Lord's My Shepherd |
| | 387 | Savior, Like a Shepherd Lead Us |
| | 402 | Now Praise the Hidden God of Love |
| | 444 | We Gather Here to Bid Farewell |
| | 539 | Savior, Again to Thy Dear Name We Raise |

**JAMES**

| | | |
|---|---|---|
| **1:5** | 420 | God of Grace and God of Glory |
| | 430 | Some Sing, O Church, in Joy! |
| **1:10–11** | 188 | Fret Not for Those Who Do Wrong Things |
| **1:10–17** | 263 | Immortal, Invisible, God Only Wise |
| **1:12** | 307 | Fight the Good Fight |
| | 364 | I Sing a Song of the Saints of God |
| | 526 | For All the Saints |
| **1:17** | 244 | Let Us with a Gladsome Mind |
| | 276 | Great Is Thy Faithfulness |
| | 288 | I Sing the Mighty Power of God |
| | 473 | For the Beauty of the Earth |
| | 560 | We Plow the Fields and Scatter |
| | 564 | O Beautiful for Spacious Skies |
| **2:1** | 439 | In Christ There Is No East or West |
| | 440 | In Christ There Is No East or West |
| **2:14–17** | 427 | Lord, Whose Love Through Humble Service |
| **2:15–17** | 407 | When a Poor One |
| **3:13–17** | 412 | Eternal God, Whose Power Upholds |
| **3:17–18** | 434 | Today We All Are Called to Be Disciples |
| **4:7–10** | 301 | Lord Jesus, Think on Me |
| **4:8** | 527 | Near to the Heart of God |
| **5:8** | 8 | Lift Up Your Heads, Ye Mighty Gates |
| **5:13–16** | 380 | O Christ, the Healer |
| | 390 | O Savior, in This Quiet Place |

**1 PETER**

| | | |
|---|---|---|
| **1:2–3** | 485 | To God Be the Glory |
| **1:3** | 123 | Jesus Christ Is Risen Today |
| | 360 | Hope of the World |

**REVELATION** (cont.)

# IV.
# Index of Scriptural Allusions
# (Hymn to Scripture)

1. **Come, Thou Long-Expected Jesus**
Psalm 34:17–19
Isaiah *9:6–7; 52:7; 61:1–2*
Daniel 7:13–14
Haggai *2:7*
Matthew 1:21–23; *2:2*
Luke 1:32–35; 2:1–7, 32; 4:18

2. *See* no. 1

3. **Comfort, Comfort You My People**
Isaiah *40:1–8*
Matthew *4:16*
Mark 1:1–8

4. **Creator of the Stars of Night**
Isaiah 45:23
Romans 14:9
Philippians *2:10–11*

5. **Let All Mortal Flesh Keep Silence**
Psalms 2:11; 89:5–7
Isaiah *6:1–3*
Habakkuk *2:20*
Zechariah 2:13
Matthew 2:11
Luke 1:77–79
John 1:4–5, 14; *6:35–58*
Philippians 2:6–7, 12
Revelation *4:8–11;* 19:11–16

6. **Jesus Comes with Clouds Descending**
Daniel 7:13–14
Zechariah 12:10; 14:9
Matthew 16:27–28; 24:30; 25:31–46
Mark 13:26–27; 14:62
Luke *21:27–28, 31*
Acts *1:9–11*
1 Thessalonians *4:16–17*
2 Thessalonians 1:7–10
Titus 2:13
Hebrews 9:28
Revelation *1:7–8*

7. **Lord Christ, When First You Came to Earth**
Matthew 27:28–29
Mark 13:2; *15:17–20*
John 19:2
2 Corinthians 5:17

8. **Lift Up Your Heads, Ye Mighty Gates**
1 Chronicles 16:29
Psalm *24:7–10*
Luke 21:28
2 Corinthians 4:6
James 5:8
Revelation 3:20

9. **O Come, O Come Emmanuel**
Exodus 3:15
Psalm 137:1–5
Isaiah *7:14; 11:1,* 10; *22:22;* 25:8; 35:10; 59:20; 61:1
Haggai *2:7*
Malachi 4:2
Matthew *1:23*
Luke *1:78–79*
Revelation *3:7–8;* 22:20

10. **On Jordan's Bank the Baptist's Cry**
Numbers 6:25
Psalm 62:2
Isaiah 40:3–5; 61:1–3
Malachi 3:1
Matthew 3:3
Luke *3:2–20*
John *1:15–30*
Acts *10:37*

11. **O Lord, How Shall I Meet You?**
Luke 12:23
John 3:16
Colossians 3:1–2
2 Timothy 4:8
1 Peter 5:4

12. **People, Look East**
Isaiah 40:4

13. **Prepare the Way**
Isaiah 40:3–5
Luke 3:4–6

14. **Savior of the Nations, Come**
Psalm 68:18
Proverbs 8:24
Luke 2:6–7
John 1:14
Ephesians 4:8

15. **Rejoice! Rejoice, Believers**
Matthew *25:1–13*
Revelation 20 and 21

16. **The Angel Gabriel from Heaven Came**
Luke 1:26–38

17. **"Sleepers, Wake!" A Voice Astounds Us**
Isaiah 52:8
Matthew *25:1–13*
1 Corinthians 2:9
Revelation *19:6–9;* 21:21

18. **The Desert Shall Rejoice**
Isaiah 35

19. **To a Maid Engaged to Joseph**
Luke 1:26–38

20. **Watchman, Tell Us of the Night**
Isaiah *21:11–12;* 40:9; 52:8; 60:1–3
Romans 13:12

21. **All My Heart Today Rejoices**
Matthew 2:9–14
Luke 1:14; *2:8–20*

22. **Angels, from the Realms of Glory**
Job *38:7*
Haggai *2:7*
Malachi *3:1*
Matthew *2:1–12*
Luke *2:6–20*
John 1:9
Hebrews 1:6

23. **Angels We Have Heard on High**
Luke *2:8–14*

24. **Away in a Manger**
Matthew 2:9
Mark 10:13–16
Luke 2:7, 12, 16

25. *See* no. 24

26. **Break Forth, O Beauteous Heavenly Light**
Isaiah *9:2–7*
Luke *2:8–14*
John 1:14; 8:12
Ephesians 2:14

27. **Gentle Mary Laid Her Child**
Matthew 2:1–12
Luke *2:7–20*
Galatians 4:4–5

28. **Good Christian Friends, Rejoice**
Luke 1:77–79; *2:7, 10–20*
Ephesians 1:3–12
1 Timothy 1:15

29. **Go, Tell It on the Mountain**
Isaiah 40:9; *52:7*
Matthew 1:21
Luke *2:6–20*

30. **Born in the Night, Mary's Child**
Isaiah 9:2
Matthew 4:16
Luke 2:4–7
John 1:11–12

31. **Hark! The Herald Angels Sing**
Psalm 67:4
Isaiah *7:14; 9:6–7*
Micah 5:2
Habakkuk 1:12
Malachi *4:2*
Matthew *1:22–23*
Luke 1:33–35; *2:11, 13–14*
John 1:4–5, 14; 3:3–17; *8:12;* 10:10
2 Corinthians 5:19
Galatians 4:4–6
Philippians 2:8
Hebrews 1:6

32. *See* no. 31

33. **Holy Night, Blessed Night**
Luke 2:8–20

34. **In Bethlehem a Babe Was Born**
Matthew 2:1–12
Luke 2:6–16

35. **In Bethlehem a Newborn Boy**
Matthew *2:13–16*

36. **In the Bleak Midwinter**
1 Kings 8:27
Proverbs 23:26
Matthew 2:11
Luke 2:8–14

**37. Infant Holy, Infant Lowly**
Luke *2:6–20*
Revelation 17:14

**38. It Came Upon the Midnight Clear**
Genesis 11:6–7
Isaiah *9:6*
Matthew 25:31
Luke *2:9–14*
Hebrews 1:6

**39. Joyful Christmas Day Is Here**
Luke 2:6–20

**40. Joy to the World!**
Genesis *3:17–18*
Psalm *98*
Isaiah 55:12–13
Luke *2:10–11*
Romans 5:20
Galatians 3:13
Revelation 11:15; 22:3

**41. O Come, All Ye Faithful**
Psalm 95:6
Matthew 2:1–11
Luke *2:9–15*
John *1*:1–5, *14*

**42.** *See* no. 41

**43. O Little Town of Bethlehem**
Job *38:7*
Isaiah *7:14;* 9:2
Micah *5:2*
Matthew *1:23; 2:1–12*
Luke 2:1–7, 11, 14
John 1:9; 3:16

**44.** *See* no. 43

**45. O Sleep, Dear Holy Baby**
Matthew 2:13–15

**46. On This Day Earth Shall Ring**
Matthew 2:1–11
Luke 2:6–14

**47. Still, Still, Still**
Luke 2:6–7, 13–14

**48. Lo, How a Rose E'er Blooming**
Song of Solomon 2:1
Isaiah *11:1,* 10; *35:1–2;* 53:2
Luke 2:7

**49. Once in Royal David's City**
Luke *2:4–7,* 11–12, 40, 52
John 14:2–3
Philippians 2:5–11
Hebrews 2:18

**50. Rise Up, Shepherd, and Follow**
Luke 2:8–16

**51. See Amid the Winter's Snow**
Luke 2:8–20

**52. Sheep Fast Asleep**
Matthew 2:10–11
Luke 2:8–16

**53. What Child Is This**
Matthew *2:1–12*
Luke 1:66; *2:6–20*
Revelation 19:16

**54. From Heaven Above**
Exodus 3:7
Psalms 40:9; 48:2; 145:19
Luke *2:1–18,* 32

**55. That Boy-Child of Mary**
Psalm 51:15
Luke 1:31–33; 2:7
John 3:16

**56. The First Nowell**
Matthew *2:1–12*
Luke *2:8–20*
Galatians 4:4–5
Ephesians 1:7–8

**57. The Snow Lay on the Ground**
Luke 2:4–7, 13–14

**58. While Shepherds Watched Their Flocks**
Luke *2:8–14*
Romans 1:3

**59.** *See* no. 58

**60. Silent Night, Holy Night**
Matthew 1:23; 2:9–10
Luke 1:77–79; *2:6–20*

61. 'Twas in the Moon of Wintertime
Matthew 2:9–11
Luke 2:6–18

62. Bring We the Frankincense of Our Love
Matthew 2:1–12

63. As with Gladness Men of Old
Exodus 25:17, 22
2 Chronicles 29:30
Matthew 2:1–12
Ephesians 1:3–4

64. From a Distant Home
Matthew 2:1–12

65. Midnight Stars Make Bright the Sky
Matthew 2:1–12
Luke 2:8–14

66. We Three Kings of Orient Are
Isaiah 9:7
Matthew 2:1–12
Luke 1:33

67. Brightest and Best of the Stars of the Morning
Isaiah 14:12
Matthew 2:1–12
Luke 1:77–79; 2:7, 11–12

68. What Star Is This, with Beams So Bright
Numbers 24:17
Matthew 2:1–12

69. O Morning Star, How Fair and Bright
Psalm 45
Isaiah 11:1
Luke 2:11
2 Peter 1:19
Jude 21
Revelation 22:16

70. Christ, When for Us You Were Baptized
Psalm 40:8
Isaiah 42:1
Matthew 3:16–17

71. Lord, When You Came to Jordan
Matthew 3:13–17

Mark 1:9–11
Luke 3:21–22

72. When Jesus Came to Jordan
Matthew 3:13–17
Mark 1:9–11
Luke 3:21–22

73. Swiftly Pass the Clouds of Glory
Matthew 17:1–8
Mark 9:2–8
Luke 9:28–36

74. Jesus on the Mountain Peak
Matthew 17:1–8
Mark 9:2–8
Luke 9:28–36

75. O Wondrous Sight, O Vision Fair
Matthew 17:1–8
Mark 9:2–8
Luke 9:28–36

76. My Song Is Love Unknown
Lamentations 1:12
Matthew 21:9
Luke 23:18–25
John 3:14–21
Acts 3:14–15

77. Forty Days and Forty Nights
Matthew 4:1–11
Luke 4:1–13
Hebrews 2:17–18; 4:15–16

78. Alas! And Did My Savior Bleed
Isaiah 53
Matthew 27:45
John 19:17–18
Romans 5:6–11; 12:1
2 Corinthians 5:14
Ephesians 1:7; 2:13
Colossians 1:11–23
1 Timothy 1:15
Titus 2:14
Hebrews 9:12–26
1 John 1:7; 4:19

79. Kind Maker of the World
Isaiah 58
Matthew 4:1–2
Mark 1:12–13

Luke 4:1–2
1 John 1:9

80. **Jesus Walked This Lonesome Valley**
Matthew 4:1–11
Mark 1:12–13
Luke 4:1–13
Hebrews 4:15

81. **Lord, Who Throughout These Forty Days**
Matthew *4:1–11*
Mark 1:12–13
Luke 4:1–13

82. **O Lamb of God Most Holy!**
Isaiah 53:7
John 1:29
1 Peter 1:19–21
1 John 3:5
Revelation 5:6

83. **O Love, How Deep, How Broad, How High**
Matthew 3:13; 4:1–11; 27:27–31
Mark 1:9–13; 15:17–20, 37
Luke 4:1–13
Ephesians *3:18*–19
Philippians 2:7

84. **In the Cross of Christ I Glory**
Isaiah 35:10
Luke 14:27
John 16:33; 19:17–18
1 Corinthians 1:17–19, 31
Galatians *6:14*
Colossians 1:20
Hebrews 1:3
1 Peter 2:24

85. **What Wondrous Love Is This**
Exodus 3:14
Isaiah 53:6
John 3:16; 8:58; 15:13
Romans 5:8
Galatians *3:13*
Ephesians 3:17–19
Philippians 2:6–11
1 John 3:1, 16; 4:9–10
Revelation *5:12–13; 7:9–10*

86. **When We Are Tempted to Deny Your Son**
Matthew 26:69–75

87. **The Glory of These Forty Days**
Exodus 19:20
2 Kings 2:11
Daniel 6–7
Matthew 3:1–3; 17:1–9
Mark 1:1–4; 9:2–10
Luke 9:28–36

88. **All Glory, Laud, and Honor**
Psalms *24:7–10;* 29:1; *118:25–27*
Zechariah 9:9
Matthew *21:1–17*
Mark *11:1–11*
Luke *19:29–38*
John *12:12–16*
Jude 25
Revelation 5:12–13; 7:9–12

89. **Hosanna, Loud Hosanna**
Matthew 19:13–15; *21:1–16*
Mark 10:13–16; *11:8–11*
Luke 18:15–17; 19:29–38
John *12:12–13*

90. **Ride On! Ride On in Majesty!**
Zechariah *9:9*
Matthew *21:1–11*
Mark 11:7–11
John *12:12–15*
Hebrews 1:3
Revelation 1:5–6; 11:15

91. *See* no. 90

92. **Beneath the Cross of Jesus**
Isaiah 4:6; 25:4–5; *32:2*
Luke 9:23
John 19:25
1 Corinthians 1:17–18
Galatians *6:14*

93. **Ah, Holy Jesus**
Isaiah *53*:3–5
John 19:17–30
Romans 5:6–11
Galatians 3:13
1 Peter 3:18

**94. An Upper Room Did Our Lord Prepare**
Matthew 26:26–28; 27:35
Mark 14:15, 22–24
John 13:3–5, 14–15

**95. He Never Said a Mumbalin' Word**
Isaiah 53:7
John 19:17–18, 30, 34
Acts 2:23

**96. Calvary**
Matthew 27:46
Mark 15:34
Luke 23:46
John 19:30

**97. Go to Dark Gethsemane**
Matthew 10:38; 16:24; 26:36–45
Mark 8:34; *14:32–42; 15:1*
Luke 9:23; 14:27; 22:44; *23:33;* 24:1
John *18:1–40; 19;* 20:1–18
1 Corinthians 15:22
Philippians *2:7–11*
Colossians 4:2
Hebrews 2:18; 4:15; 12:2
1 Peter 2:21; 4:12–13

**98. O Sacred Head, Now Wounded**
Isaiah *53:3–5;* 63:9
Zechariah 12:10
Matthew *27:26–50*
Mark 15:17–18
Luke 24:26
John *19:2–3*
Romans 5:6–8
2 Corinthians 5:14–15
Philippians 2:8
Hebrews 2:9
1 Peter 2:24; 3:18
1 John 4:19

**99. Throned Upon the Awful Tree**
Psalm 22:1
Matthew 27:46
John 19

**100. When I Survey the Wondrous Cross**
Matthew 26:28
John 19:2, 17–18, 32–34
Romans 5:6–11; 12:1
1 Corinthians *1:17–18,* 31; 2:2

Galatians 2:20; *6:14*
Philippians *3:3–11*
Hebrews 9:12–26
1 Peter 2:24
1 John 2:15–16

**101.** *See* no. 100

**102. Were You There?**
Isaiah 53:3
Matthew *27:35–60*
Mark *15:24–25,* 46
Luke 23:33, 50–53
John 19:16–18, 34, 41–42
Philippians 2:8

**103. Deep Were His Wounds, and Red**
Isaiah 53:5
Matthew 8:17
John 19:16–34
Romans 6:11
1 Peter 2:22–25

**104. Christ Is Risen! Shout Hosanna!**
Isaiah 35:1–2
Matthew 28:1–7
Luke 24:1–7

**105. Because You Live, O Christ**
Isaiah 35:1–2
Matthew 28:1–7
Luke 24:1–2
John 20:1

**106. Alleluia, Alleluia! Give Thanks**
Psalm 67:4
Zephaniah 3:14
Luke 24:7
Romans 4:24–25
1 Corinthians 15
Galatians 2:20

**107. Celebrate with Joy and Singing**
Matthew 28:1–10
Mark 16:1–8
Luke 24:1–9

**108. Christ Is Alive!**
Romans 6:5–11

**109. Christ Is Risen**
Isaiah 25:8

Matthew 28:1–10
1 Corinthians *15*:12–23

**110. Christ Jesus Lay in Death's Strong Bands**
Isaiah *25:8*
Hosea 13:14
Matthew *28:6–9*
John 6:55
1 Corinthians *5:7–8;* 15:26–28, 54–57

**111. Good Christians All, Rejoice and Sing!**
Matthew 28:1–7
John 10:17
Acts 4:33; 13:32–33

**112. Christ the Lord Is Risen Again**
Matthew 28:1–7
1 Timothy 6:15–16
Revelation 7:9–12; 19:16

**113. Christ the Lord Is Risen Today!**
Psalms 8:1; 22:29; 150:6
Isaiah 25:7–8; *44:23;* 49:13
Matthew *28:1–9*
Mark 16:6
Luke 24:6
John 20:11–18
Acts 2:24–28
Romans 6:9
1 Corinthians *15:*4, *54–57*

**114. Come, Ye Faithful, Raise the Strain**
Exodus 13:3; 14:15–22, 29; *15:1–21*
Isaiah 9:2; 61:3
John 6:40
Acts 2:24–28
Romans 6:9–10
1 Corinthians 15:54–57
Colossians 1:11–14

**115.** *See* no. 114

**116. O Sons and Daughters, Let Us Sing!**
Matthew 28:1–9
Mark 16:1–6
Luke *24:1–12*
John *20:19–23*
2 Corinthians 6:18

**117. O Sons and Daughters, Let Us Sing!**
John 20:19–29
2 Corinthians 6:18

**118. The Day of Resurrection!**
Exodus 12:11–14; 14:22
Psalm 148:4–5
Isaiah 9:2
Matthew 28:1–9
Luke 24:1–7
Acts 2:24–28
1 Corinthians 15:57
2 Corinthians 4:6

**119. The Strife Is O'er**
Psalms 45:3–4; 96:1–2; 145:13
Isaiah 25:7–9; 53:5
Mark 10:34
Luke 24:6
Romans 6:9–10
1 Corinthians 15:51–57
1 Peter 2:24
Revelation 1:18; 19:1–2

**120. Hail Thee, Festival Day!**
Psalm 150:6
Isaiah 11:2
John 1:3–5; 3:16; 14:27
Acts 2:1–4
1 John 1:9

**121. That Easter Day with Joy Was Bright**
Matthew 28:9
Luke 24:34
John *20*

**122. Thine Is the Glory**
Isaiah 25:8
Matthew 28:2, 9, 16–17
John 20:6–7, 27–28
Romans *8:37*
1 Corinthians *15:54–57*

**123. Jesus Christ Is Risen Today**
Psalm 149:1
Matthew *28:1–9*
Mark 16:6
Luke *24:6–7*
Romans 6:9–10
1 Corinthians 15:3–4, 54–57
Hebrews *12:2*
1 Peter 1:3, 18–20
Revelation 1:5–6

**124. Spirit of God, Unleashed on Earth**
Acts 2:1–13

**125. Come, Holy Spirit, Our Souls Inspire**
Psalm 45:7
Isaiah 11:2
Ezekiel 36:27
Matthew 3:11
Luke 11:13
John 14:16
Acts 2:3–4, 38
Romans *5:5;* 8:11–16, 26–27
1 Corinthians 6:19; 12:4–11
Ephesians 3:16

**126. Come, Holy Spirit, Heavenly Dove**
Matthew *3:16;* 24:12
Mark 1:10
Luke 3:22
John 1:32; *6:36*
Romans *5:5*
Galatians 5:22

**127. Come, O Spirit**
Acts 2:1–4

**128. On Pentecost They Gathered**
Acts 2:1–11

**129. Come, O Spirit, Dwell Among Us**
Psalm 118:22
Acts 2:1–11; 4:11
1 Peter 2:6–7

**130. Let Every Christian Pray**
Acts 2:1–11

**131. Wind Who Makes All Winds That Blow**
Acts 2:1–13

**132. Come, Great God of All the Ages**
Ephesians 2:20
Colossians 1:15–20

**133. All Glory Be to God on High**
Psalm 46
Luke 2:13–14
John 1:29

**134. Creating God, Your Fingers Trace**
Genesis 1:1
Isaiah 45:7

**135. God Is One, Unique and Holy**
John 1:1–3; 10:30
Ephesians 4:4–6

**136. Sovereign Lord of All Creation**
Genesis 1
Psalm 148
Matthew 18:20
Galatians 6:2
Ephesians 4:2–3

**137. We All Believe in One True God**
Psalm 104
2 Corinthians 1:4
Ephesians 4:4–6
Philippians 2:5–8
Colossians 1:20
Hebrews 2:9; 5:9

**138. Holy, Holy, Holy! Lord God Almighty!**
Exodus 33:17–23
Deuteronomy 5:22–23
2 Samuel 7:22
1 Chronicles 17:20
Psalms 5:3; 59:16; 97:2; 145:10
Isaiah 6:2–3, 5; 45:6
Revelation 1:4, *8; 4:6, 8–11;* 15:4

**139. Come, Thou Almighty King**
Exodus 15:18
1 Chronicles 29:11–12
Psalms 29:2; *45:3–4;* 47:7–8; 83:18; 103:19
Daniel *7:9, 13, 22*
John *1:14; 14:16–17*
Romans *8:16*
Ephesians 6:17
Revelation 19:11–16

**140. Holy, Holy**
Psalms 63:4; 134:2
Isaiah 40:9
1 Timothy 2:8
Revelation 4:8

**141. A Hymn of Glory Let Us Sing**
Genesis 15:1
Acts 1:9–11

**142. All Hail the Power of Jesus' Name**
Deuteronomy 7:6
Job 36:3
Psalms 66:1; 68:34; 145:21; 148:2
Isaiah *11:1; 62:3*
Romans 8:29–30
Ephesians 1:4–6

Philippians *2:9–11*
Hebrews 2:7–8, 12
2 Peter 1:16
Revelation 5:9–14; 7:9–11; 11:15

**143.** *See* no. 142

**144. Alleluia! Sing to Jesus!**
Psalm 78:25
Proverbs 23:11
Isaiah 66:1
Matthew 28:18
Luke 24:50–53
John 6:32
Acts 1:9
Hebrews 9:11–14
Revelation 5; 19:1

**145. Rejoice, Ye Pure in Heart!**
Psalms *20:4–5;* 24:3–6; 32:11; *33:1;* 60:4;
    105:1–3; *147:1,* 7; 148:12–13
Matthew 5:8
Philippians *4:4*
Colossians 3:16
1 Timothy 6:12

**146.** *See* no. 145

**147. Blessing and Honor**
Isaiah 6:3
Revelation *5:12–13;* 7:12–14

**148. At the Name of Jesus**
Psalms 8; 72:19
Isaiah 11:10; 45:23
Matthew 1:21
John *1:1–3;* 3:16–17
Acts *4:12*
Romans 8:3
Philippians *2:5–12*
Hebrews 1:4; 2:10

**149. The Head That Once Was Crowned**
Psalm 103:19
John 16:19–24
Acts 2:36; 5:30–31
Ephesians 2:4–6
Philippians 2:5–11
2 Timothy 2:12
Hebrews 2:9–10; 12:2–4
Revelation 1:18

**150. Come, Christians, Join to Sing**
Psalms 30:4; 67:3; *95:1–2;* 145:2; 150:6

Colossians 3:16
Hebrews 13:15
Revelation 5:11–13

**151. Crown Him with Many Crowns**
Psalms 22:16; 45:6; 46:9; 72:5–17
Isaiah 2:4; *9:6–7;* 53:4–5
Micah 4:3
Matthew 25:31
John 20:20
Romans 8:34; 14:9
2 Corinthians 5:15
Hebrews 2:7–10; 12:2
1 John 2:25
Revelation 1:5–6; 5; 7:9–12; *19:1, 12*

**152. Earth's Scattered Isles and Contoured Hills**
Psalms 33; 72:1–4; 104:5–9

**153. He Is King of Kings**
1 Timothy 6:15–16
Revelation 19:16

**154. Lord, Enthroned in Heavenly Splendor**
Exodus 16:15; 17:6
John 6:51
1 Corinthians 15:23
Hebrews 9:11–12

**155. Rejoice, the Lord Is King**
Psalms 35:18; 95; 106:47; 145:1–2, *13*
Isaiah 45:23; 52:8
Zechariah 14:9
Matthew 28:18
Luke 1:32–33
John 16:33
Acts 5:31
Romans 6:9–10; 14:8–9
Ephesians 1:20–21
Philippians 2:9–11; *4:4–5*
1 Thessalonians 4:17
Hebrews *1:3*
Revelation *1:18*

**156. You, Living Christ, Our Eyes Behold**
Daniel 7:9–13
Revelation 1:13–18; 5:9; 7:9–10

**157. Our King and Our Sovereign, Lord Jesus**
John 15:9–17

**158. The One Is Blest**
Psalms 1; 15; 24
Matthew 5:3–12

**159. Why Are Nations Raging**
Psalm 2
Acts 4:23–31

**160. Psalm 4**
Numbers 6:25
Psalms 3:5; 4; 11:5; 88:13
Acts 14:17
Ephesians 4:26

**161. As Morning Dawns**
Psalm 5
Revelation 21:8

**162. O Lord, Our God, How Excellent**
Genesis 1:26–27
Psalm 8
Matthew 21:16
Hebrews 2:6–8

**163. Lord, Our Lord, Thy Glorious Name**
Genesis 1:26–27
Psalm 8
Matthew 21:16
Hebrews 2:6–8

**164. Lord, Who May Dwell Within Your House**
Exodus 20:1–17
Psalms 15; 24:3–6
Isaiah 1:10–17; 33:14–16

**165. When in the Night I Meditate**
Psalm 16
Acts 2:25–28

**166. The Heavens Above Declare God's Praise**
Psalms *19:1–6;* 119:89; 138:2
Malachi *4:2*
John 15:3
1 Peter 1:24–25

**167. God's Law Is Perfect and Gives Life**
Deuteronomy 5:33
Psalm 19:7–14; 104:34

**168. Lord, Why Have You Forsaken Me**
Psalms 22; 69:1–21
Matthew 27:39–40, 46

**169. In the Day of Need**
2 Chronicles 20:1–30
Psalm 20

**170. The Lord's My Shepherd, I'll Not Want**
Psalm 23
Isaiah 40:11
Matthew 18:10–14
Luke 15:3–7
John 10:1–30

**171. The King of Love My Shepherd Is**
Psalms 23; 79:13; 95:7
Isaiah 53:6
Ezekiel 34:11–13
Matthew 18:10–14
Luke *15:3–7*
John *10:9, 14–15,* 27
1 Peter 2:25

**172. My Shepherd Will Supply My Need**
Psalm *23*
Isaiah 40:11
Matthew 18:10–14
Luke 15:3–7
John 10:1–30
Hebrews *13:6*

**173. Psalm 23**
*See* no. 170

**174. The Lord's My Shepherd**
Psalms 23; 78:52
Isaiah 40:11
John 10:1–6
Hebrews 13:20–21
1 Peter 5:7

**175. The Lord's My Shepherd, All My Need**
*See* no. 170

**176. The Earth and All That Dwell Therein**
Genesis 1:1–10
2 Samuel 6
Psalm 24
1 Corinthians 10:25–26

**177. Psalm 24**
Genesis 1:1–10
2 Samuel 6
Psalm 24
1 Corinthians 10:25–26

**178. Lord, to You My Soul Is Lifted**
Deuteronomy 4:31
Nehemiah 9:31
Psalm 25

**179. God Is My Strong Salvation**
Exodus 15:2
2 Samuel 22:29
Psalms 27; 29:11
Isaiah 26:3
Micah 7:8
Romans 8:31
Ephesians 6:10
2 Thessalonians 3:3

**180. The God of Heaven**
1 Chronicles 16:28
2 Chronicles 20:21
Psalm 29

**181. Come Sing to God**
1 Chronicles 21:1–22:6
Psalm 30

**182. Psalm 31:9–16**
Psalms 22:14–16; 31:9–16

**183. In You, Lord, I Have Put My Trust**
Psalm 31
Luke 23:46

**184. How Blest Are Those**
Psalm 32
Romans 4:6–8

**185. Psalm 33**
Psalm 33
Isaiah 42:10
Ephesians 5:19
Revelation 5:9

**186. Thy Mercy and Thy Truth, O Lord**
Psalms 33:4–5; 36

**187. Psalm 34:9–22**
Psalm 34:9–22
John 19:36
1 Peter 3:8–12

**188. Fret Not for Those Who Do Wrong Things**
Psalm 37
James 1:10–11
1 Peter 5:7

**189. As Deer Long for the Streams**
Psalms 42:1–7; 63:1; 143:6
John 4:14

**190. Psalm 42**
Psalms 42; 63:6

**191. God Is Our Refuge and Our Strength**
Deuteronomy 4:7
Psalms 46; 48:8; 93:3–4

**192. God, Our Help and Constant Refuge**
Deuteronomy 4:7
Psalms 46; 48:8; 93:3–4
Isaiah 2:4

**193. Psalm 46**
Deuteronomy 4:7
Psalms 46; 48:8; 93:3–4
Isaiah 2:4

**194. People, Clap Your Hands!**
Genesis 12:2–3
Psalm 47
Revelation 4:9–10

**195. Have Mercy on Us, Living Lord**
Psalm 51
Romans 3:4

**196. Psalm 51**
Psalm 51
Romans 3:4

**197. My Soul in Silence Waits for God**
Psalm 62
Jeremiah 17:10
1 Timothy 6:6–10
Revelation 2:23; 22:12

**198. O God, You Are My God**
Psalms 18:35; 27:4; 42:8; 63

**199. O Lord, You Are My God**
Psalms 18:35; 27:4; 42:8; 63

**200. To Bless the Earth**
Psalm 65
Isaiah 55:12

**201. Praise Is Your Right, O God, in Zion**
Psalm 65
Isaiah 55:12
Matthew 8:26
Hebrews 9:14

**202. Psalm 67**
Numbers 6:24–26
Psalm 67

**203. God of Mercy, God of Grace**
Numbers 6:24–26
Psalm 67

**204. Psalm 72**
1 Kings 3:9
Psalm 72

**205. All Hail to God's Anointed**
1 Kings 3:9
Psalm 72

**206. O Hear Our Cry, O Lord**
Numbers 6:25
2 Kings 17:1–6
Psalm 80

**207. How Lovely, Lord**
2 Kings 18:13–16
Psalm 84

**208. Psalm 84**
2 Kings 18:13–16
Psalm 84

**209. My Song Forever Shall Record**
Genesis 1:1
1 Chronicles 29:11
Psalms 36:5; 40:10; 89

**210. Our God, Our Help in Ages Past**
Genesis 1:2, 9–10

Psalms 33:20; *90:1–5; 91:1*
Isaiah 25:4
Revelation 4:8

**211. Lord, You Have Been Our Dwelling Place**
Genesis 3:19
Psalm 90

**212. Within Your Shelter, Loving God**
Psalm 91
Matthew 4:6
Luke 4:10–11

**213. God, Our Lord, a King Remaining**
Genesis 1:6–10
Psalm 93

**214. O Come and Sing Unto the Lord**
Psalm 95
Hebrews 3:7–4:13

**215. Come, Sing with Joy to God**
Psalm 95
Hebrews 3:7–4:13

**216. O Sing a New Song to the Lord**
1 Chronicles 16:23–33
Psalm 96

**217. O Sing a New Song**
1 Chronicles 16:23–33
Psalm 96

**218. New Songs of Celebration Render**
Psalms 96:1; 98
Isaiah 44:23; 52:10

**219. To God Compose a Song of Joy**
Psalms 96:1; 98
Isaiah 44:23; 52:10

**220. All People That on Earth Do Dwell**
Psalms 67:3; 79:13; 98:3–4; *100;* 118:19;
    148:11–13; *150*:6

**221.** *See* no. 220

**222. Psalm 103**
Exodus 33:12–13
Psalm 103
Luke 1:50

**223. O My Soul, Bless Your Redeemer**
Exodus 33:12–13
Psalm 103
Luke 1:50

**224. Bless the Lord, My Soul and Being**
Genesis 1
Psalm 104

**225. Praise the Lord!**
1 Samuel 2:3–8
Psalm 113
Luke 1:46–55

**226. Sing Praise Unto the Name of God**
1 Samuel 2:3–8
Psalm 113
Luke 1:46–55

**227. Not Unto Us, O Lord of Heaven**
Ezra 6:16
Psalm 115
Isaiah 44:9–20

**228. O Thou, My Soul, Return in Peace**
Psalm 116
Isaiah 38:10–20
Matthew 26:27

**229. From All That Dwell Below the Skies**
Psalms 66:1; 67:3; 72:5–17; 113:1–2; 117;
    145:21; 150:6
1 Peter 2:9
Revelation 7:9–12; 15:4

**230. This Is the Day the Lord Hath Made**
Genesis 1:3–5
Exodus 20:8–11
Leviticus 23:1–3
1 Chronicles 16:31
Psalms 38:22; 96:11; *118*
Zechariah 9:9
Matthew 12:8; 21:5, 9
Mark 11:9
Ephesians 2:4–6
2 Timothy 2:8

**231. Psalm 118:14–24**
Psalm 118:14–24
Isaiah 12:2
Matthew 21:42
Mark 12:10–11

Luke 20:17
Acts 4:11
Ephesians 2:20
1 Peter 2:7

**232. Psalm 118:19–29**
Numbers 6:25
Psalm 118:19–29
Matthew 21:42
Mark 12:10–11
Luke 20:17
John 12:13
Acts 4:11
Ephesians 2:20
1 Peter 2:7

**233. Blest Are the Uncorrupt in Heart**
Psalm 119:1–16
Proverbs 22:11
Isaiah 57:15
Matthew 5:1–12

**234. I to the Hills Will Lift My Eyes**
Deuteronomy 28:6
Psalm 121

**235. With Joy I Heard My Friends Exclaim**
Deuteronomy 16:16
Psalm 122

**236. Now Israel May Say**
Psalm 124
Romans 8:31

**237. When God Delivered Israel**
Psalm 126
Isaiah 35

**238. Unless the Lord the House Shall Build**
Deuteronomy 28:1–14
Psalm 127

**239. How Happy Is Each Child of God**
Numbers 6:24
Joshua 24:15
Psalms 1:1–3; 127:3–5; 128

**240. Out of the Depths**
Psalms 40:1–4, 11–12; 71:2; 120:1; *130*
Habakkuk 2:3–4
Galatians 2:16
Ephesians 2:8–9

241. **Behold the Goodness of Our Lord**
Exodus 29:7
Leviticus 9:22–24; 21:10
Numbers 6:24–26
Psalm 133

242. **Come, All You Servants of the Lord**
1 Chronicles 9:33
Psalms 63:4; 134

243. **We Thank You, Lord, for You Are Good**
Genesis 1:16
Psalm 136

244. **Let Us with a Gladsome Mind**
Genesis 1:3
Psalms 63:3; 100:5; 106:1; 107:8–9; *136;* 145:9
James 1:17

245. **By the Waters of Babylon**
Psalm 137
Lamentations 2:8

246. **By the Babylonian Rivers**
Psalm 137
Isaiah 24:8

247. **I Will Give Thanks with My Whole Heart**
2 Samuel 6:17
Psalm 138

248. **You Are Before Me, Lord**
Psalm 139
Jeremiah 23:23–24

249. **O Lord, Make Haste to Hear My Cry**
Psalm 141
Revelation 5:8; 8:3–4

250. **When Morning Lights the Eastern Skies**
Psalms 1:2; 143
Matthew 6:10

251. **Your Faithfulness, O Lord, Is Sure**
Psalms 104:5–30; 145:13–21
Lamentations 3:22–23

252. **O Lord, You Are My God and King**
Exodus 34:6
Numbers 14:18

Psalm 145:1–13
Isaiah 38:19

253. **I'll Praise My Maker**
Psalm 146
Proverbs 16:20
Isaiah 61:1

254. **Psalm 146**
Psalm 146
Matthew 9:27–30
Revelation 14:7

255. **Now Praise the Lord**
Nehemiah 12:27–43
Psalm 147

256. **Let the Whole Creation Cry**
Genesis 1
Psalm 148

257. **Give Praise to the Lord**
Exodus 15:20
1 Chronicles 13:8; 15:16
Psalms 149; 150
Isaiah 38:20

258. **Praise Ye the Lord**
Exodus 15:20
1 Chronicles 13:8; 15:16
Psalm 150
Isaiah 38:20

259. **A Mighty Fortress Is Our God**
Deuteronomy 33:27
2 Samuel *22:2*
Psalms *18:2;* 31:3; *46:1;* 71:3; 91:2; 144:2
Isaiah 26:4; 40:28
Jeremiah 16:19
Daniel 4:3
Luke 1:33
Colossians 2:15

260. **A Mighty Fortress Is Our God**
Deuteronomy 33:27
2 Samuel *22:2*
Psalms *18:2;* 31:3; *46:1;* 71:3; 91:2; 144:2
Isaiah 7:7; 26:4; 40:28
Jeremiah 16:19
Daniel 4:3
Matthew 12:20–21
Luke 1:33
Romans 5:12–21
Galatians 5:22–23
Ephesians 6:10–12

Philippians 2:9
Colossians 2:15
Hebrews 2:14–18; 13:8

**261. God of Compassion, in Mercy Befriend Us**
Psalm 51:1
Isaiah 63:7–9

**262. God of the Ages, Whose Almighty Hand**
Exodus 3:15
Psalms 22:4; 29:11; 33:12; 44:1–4; 77:14;
　　90:1–2; 147:12–15
Proverbs 14:34
Isaiah *40:25–26*
1 Timothy 2:1–2

**263. Immortal, Invisible, God Only Wise**
Exodus 33:20
Job 37:21–24
Psalms 27:1; *36:6; 90:5–6;* 104:1–5;
　　121:3–4; 147:8
Isaiah *6:2*–3
Daniel *7:9*
Luke 10:21–22
John 1:1–14; 8:12
Acts 17:25
Romans 16:27
1 Corinthians 8:6
2 Corinthians 4:6
1 Timothy *1:17; 6:15–16*
James 1:10–17
1 John 1:5
Jude 25
Revelation 21:23

**264. When in Our Music God Is Glorified**
1 Chronicles 16:4–13
Psalms 33:1–9; 92:1–4; 98; *150*
Matthew 26:30
Mark *14:26*
Colossians 3:16

**265. Great God, We Sing That Mighty Hand**
Psalms 65:11; *89:13*
Lamentations 3:22–24
Acts *26:22*
1 Peter 5:6

**266. Thank You, God, for Water, Soil, and Air**
Genesis 1:1
Luke 15:13

**267. All Things Bright and Beautiful**
Genesis *1:31*
Nehemiah 9:6
Psalms 19:1–6; *104*:24; 116:7; 136:3–9
Ecclesiastes 3:11
Matthew 6:28–29
John 1:3
Hebrews 11:3
Revelation 4:11

**268. God, Who Stretched the Spangled Heavens**
Genesis 1:1, 16
Psalm 136:3–9
Isaiah 44:24

**269. O God of Bethel, by Whose Hand**
Genesis 28:19–22
Deuteronomy 8:15–16
Ruth 2:12
Psalm 57:1

**270. O God, in a Mysterious Way**
2 Samuel *22:7–20*
Job 28; 36:27–29
Psalms *77:19; 104:3*
Ecclesiastes 3:11
Isaiah 40:28
Daniel *2:22;* 4:35
Matthew 11:25–26
John *13:7*
Romans *8:28; 11:33–35*

**271. Many and Great, O God, Are Thy Things**
Genesis 1:6–10, 14–18
Psalms 95:4–5; 104:1–9, 24
Jeremiah 10:12–13
Romans 6:23

**272. God of the Sparrow**
Genesis 1; 2
Matthew 18:10–14

**273. O God the Creator**
Genesis 1
Romans 15:5

**274. O God of Earth and Space**
Genesis 1
Psalms 34:14; 46:1; 104:14, 27–28; 111;
　　145:9, 16
Acts 4:24
1 Peter 3:8–12

**275. God of Our Life**
Psalms 13:5–6; 28:7; *31:15;* 102:5–27;
    139:1
Isaiah 40:21–31
Acts 17:26–28

**276. Great Is Thy Faithfulness**
Genesis *8:22*
Deuteronomy 4:31; 7:9; 33:25
Psalms 9:10; 19:1–4; 23:4; 36:5–7; 57:10;
    89:1–2
Lamentations *3:22–23*
Malachi *3:6*
1 Corinthians 1:4–9
Philippians 4:19
2 Timothy 2:13
Hebrews 10:23
James *1:17*

**277. O God, Our Faithful God**
Matthew 16:24–25
2 Thessalonians 3:3
2 Timothy 2:13

**278. O God, to Whom We Turn**
Psalms 25:5; 33; 40:1–3
Ephesians 1:18–19
Philippians 4:6–8
Colossians 1:10–11

**279. Lord of Our Growing Years**
Psalm 39:4–5
Colossians 1:10–12
2 Peter 1:3–11

**280. Amazing Grace, How Sweet the Sound**
2 Samuel 7:28
1 Chronicles *17:16–17*
Psalms 73:26 *142:5;* 145:1–2
John 1:16–17; 9:25
Romans 5:20–21
1 Corinthians *15:10*
2 Corinthians 9:8
Ephesians 1:6–7; *2:8*
Titus 2:11

**281. Guide Me, O Thou Great Jehovah**
Exodus *13:21–22;* 14:26–31; 16:4–18;
    17:6; 40:38
Numbers 20:8–11
Deuteronomy 1:33
Joshua *3:1–17*
Nehemiah *9:19–20*
Psalms 18:2; *28:7; 34:1–4; 48:14;*
    *78:*15–16, 52; *139:10*

Zechariah 13:1
John 4:14; 6:35–38, 48–51
1 Corinthians 10:1–4
Hebrews *11:13–14*
1 Peter 2:11
Revelation 7:9–17; 22:1–2

**282. If Thou but Trust in God to Guide Thee**
Psalms 27:14; 42:5; 46:1, 10; *55:22–23;*
    62:1, 2
Isaiah 40:29
Matthew 7:24
Luke 6:48
John 16:13

**283. God Marked a Line and Told the Sea**
Genesis 2:4–9, 15–17
Exodus 20:1–17
Job 38:8–11
Proverbs 8:23–31

**284. O God, What You Ordain Is Right**
Deuteronomy 32:4
Psalm 23

**285. God, You Spin the Whirling Planets**
Genesis 1; 2
2 Corinthians 5:17–20

**286. Give to the Winds Thy Fears**
Psalms *37:5;* 56; 65:5–13
Isaiah 41:10
John 14:27
Romans 8:28
Hebrews 4:16
1 Peter 5:7

**287. God Folds the Mountains Out of Rock**
Job *28*
Proverbs 8

**288. I Sing the Mighty Power of God**
Genesis 1:12, *16,* 21, 24, *31*
Psalms *33:5–9*; 59:16; 65:5–13; *95:3–6*
James *1:17*
Revelation 4:11

**289. O God of Every Nation**
Isaiah 2:2–4
Daniel 7:14
Micah 4:1–4
1 John 2:2; 4:9–10
Revelation 11:15

**290. God Created Heaven and Earth**
Genesis 1:1–3, 31
Psalms 96:3–9; 148
Isaiah 40:18–20
Romans 5:15–21

**291. O God of Earth and Altar**
Job 26:14
Romans 16:17
2 Timothy 4:3–4

**292. All Beautiful the March of Days**
Psalm 19:1–4
Luke 2:14

**293. This Is My Father's World**
Psalms *19:1; 24:1;* 50:10–12; 103:19;
104:24; *145:10–13*
Matthew 12:20–21
John 16:33
Romans 16:20
1 Corinthians 15:24–25
2 Peter 3:13
Revelation 12:10

**294. Wherever I May Wander**
Psalms 65:6–7; 121

**295. O God of Love, O God of Peace**
Psalms 25:7; *29:10–11;* 40:1; *46:9*
Micah *4:3–5*

**296. Walk On, O People of God**
John 10:10
Romans 3:21–26
2 Corinthians 5:17–20

**297. O Lord of Every Shining
Constellation**
Genesis *1:16, 27*
Job 38:31–33
Psalms 8:5–6; 19

**298. There's a Wideness in God's Mercy**
Ezra 3:11
Psalms *33*:4; 36:5; *86:5, 15;* 98:9;
*103:8–13*
Isaiah 55:7
Lamentations 3:22–23
Romans 8:18–39; *11:33–35*
Ephesians 2:4–6
1 John 4:16–18

**299. Amen, Amen**
Luke 2:7, 46–47; 5:1; 22:39–44; 23:33;
24:1–8
John 1:14

**300. Down to Earth, as a Dove**
Matthew 3:16–17; 5:6
John 6:33–34

**301. Lord Jesus, Think on Me**
Psalms 25:7; 40:17; 106:4
Matthew 9:21–22
Luke 22:40; 23:42–43
Hebrews 4:9
James 4:7–10

**302. I Danced in the Morning**
Matthew 11:17
Mark *1:14–20;* 2:1–12; *3:1–6*
John 15:4

**303. Jesus, Lover of My Soul**
Ruth 2:12
Psalms 32:7; 36:7, 9; *57:1;* 61:3–4; *91:4;*
107:30; 111:9; 147:3
Isaiah *25:4; 32:2;* 42:16
Zechariah 13:1
Matthew 23:37
Luke 7:21–22; 13:34
John 1:14; 4:10–14
Romans 5:20–21
Ephesians 3:16–19
1 John 1:8–9
Revelation 7:17

**304. Jesus Loves Me!**
Proverbs 8:17
Matthew 19:13–15
Mark 10:13–16
Luke 18:15–17

**305. Jesus, Our Divine Companion**
Matthew 13:55
Mark 6:3
John 6:32–33
1 Corinthians 15:58

**306. Fairest Lord Jesus**
Psalm *45:2*
John 5:23; 8:12
1 Corinthians 1:31
Philippians 2:9–11
1 Thessalonians 2:19–20

**306. Fairest Lord Jesus** (cont.)
1 Timothy 6:16
Hebrews 1:3
1 John 3:3
Revelation 22:16

**307. Fight the Good Fight**
Psalms 25:15; 27:8; 55:22
Malachi 3:6
Mark 5:36
Romans 8:37
1 Corinthians 9:24–26; 15:57–58
Ephesians 6:10–20
Philippians 1:27–30; 3:14
1 Timothy *6:12*
2 Timothy 2:3–5; *4:7*
Hebrews 10:23; 12:1
James 1:12
1 Peter 5:7–9
Revelation 2:10

**308. O Sing a Song of Bethlehem**
Matthew 8:26; 14:25
Mark 4:39; 6:48
Luke 2:8–14; 8:24
John 6:19
Acts 5:30; 10:39–40; 13:29–30

**309. Of the Father's Love Begotten**
Psalms 113:2; 145:1; 150:6
Matthew 1:20
John *1:1, 14*
Philippians 2:7–11
Colossians 1:15–20
Hebrews 13:8
Revelation *1:8;* 4:8; 21:6; 22:13

**310. Jesus, the Very Thought of Thee**
1 Samuel 2:8
Psalms 34:18; *51:17;* 66:2; 104:34
Isaiah 57:15
Matthew 7:7–8
Luke 11:9–10
John 15:9
Acts 2:28; 4:12
Romans 15:13
1 Corinthians 2:9; 13:12
Ephesians 3:17, 19
Philippians 1:21
1 Thessalonians 2:19–20
1 Peter 1:8–9, 21

**311. We Meet You, O Christ**
Matthew 10:40–42
Hebrews 13:1–3

**312. When Jesus Wept**
Luke 19:41
John 11:35

**313. Come Down, O Love Divine**
Psalms 27:1; 119:105
Isaiah 6:7
John 14:15–21
Acts *1:8*

**314. Like the Murmur of the Dove's Song**
Ezekiel 37:5–6
John 3:8; 15:5
Acts 2:1–11

**315. Every Time I Feel the Spirit**
Exodus 19:16–18
Luke 11:13

**316. Breathe on Me, Breath of God**
Genesis 2:7
Job 33:4
Ezekiel 36:27; 37:9
John 3:5–7; 11:26; 17:26; *20:22*
Romans 8:9–11
2 Corinthians 3:18
Galatians 5:22–25
1 John 4:11–13

**317. Holy Ghost, Dispel Our Sadness**
John 16:5–16
Acts 1:8
Ephesians 3:14–19

**318. Gracious Spirit, Holy Ghost**
1 Corinthians 13

**319. Spirit**
Genesis 1:6–9
Exodus 20:1–21
Psalm 104:5–9
Luke 2:7; 23:46
Acts 2:1–4, 17

**320. The Lone, Wild Bird**
Psalm 139:7–10
Matthew 3:16

**321. Holy Spirit, Truth Divine**
Psalm 119:105

Luke 24:49
John 1:1, 4–5; 14:17
Acts 1:8
Romans 5:5; 8:1–4
1 Corinthians 6:19
2 Corinthians 3:17
Galatians 5:17–18
Ephesians *3:16*
2 Timothy 1:7
1 John 5:7

### 322. Spirit of the Living God
Ezekiel 36:27
Acts 2:4; 10:44; *11:15*
Romans 8:11

### 323. Loving Spirit
Ezekiel 36:27
Romans 5:5
Ephesians 1:11–14
Colossians 1:9–10
2 Thessalonians 2:13–15

### 324. Open My Eyes That I May See
Exodus 4:12
Psalms 40:6, 8; 51:15; *119:18*
Proverbs 15:31
Matthew 11:15; 13:16
Mark 8:18
Luke 10:23–24
John 8:32
Romans 5:5
Ephesians 1:18–19; 4:15
Colossians 1:9

### 325. Spirit Divine, Attend Our Prayers
Genesis 1:2–4
Psalm 23:3
Isaiah 11:2
Ezekiel 36:27
Matthew 3:11, 16
John 14:16–17
Acts *1:8;* 2:1–4; 4:31; 9:31
Romans 8:9
Galatians 5:25

### 326. Spirit of God, Descend Upon My Heart
Deuteronomy 6:5
Job 32:8
Psalms 51:10–12; 145:18
Matthew *3:16;* 7:7–8
Mark 1:10; 12:30
Luke 3:22; 10:27; 11:9–10

John 1:32–33
Romans *5:5*
Galatians *5:25–26*
Ephesians 3:16

### 327. O Word of God Incarnate
Psalm 119:*105,* 130, 160
Isaiah 40:8
Matthew 5:16
Mark 13:31
John *1:1–5, 14;* 5:39
1 Corinthians 13:12
2 Peter 1:19
Revelation 1:3

### 328. All Praise to God for Song God Gives
Psalms 98; 119:105
2 Timothy 3:15–17

### 329. Break Thou the Bread of Life
Deuteronomy 8:3
Psalms 42:1; 119:45
Jeremiah 15:16
Matthew 4:4; 14:13–21
Mark 6:30–44
John 5:39; *6:35;* 8:32; 17:17
2 Timothy 3:15–16

### 330. Deep in the Shadows of the Past
Exodus 3:13–14
Acts 7:2–53
2 Timothy 3:15–17

### 331. Thanks to God Whose Word Was Written
John 1:14
1 Corinthians 2:10–16
2 Timothy 3:15–17
2 Peter 1:20–21

### 332. Live Into Hope
Isaiah 61:1–3
Luke 4:16–20

### 333. Seek Ye first
Matthew *6:33;* 7:7
Luke 11:1–13

### 334. When Israel Was in Egypt's Land
Exodus 3:7–12; 5:1; 8:1; 11:4–5;
    12:35–36

**335. Though I May Speak**
1 Corinthians 13

**336. As a Chalice Cast of Gold**
Mark 7:1–8, 14–15, 21–23

**337. Isaiah the Prophet Has Written of Old**
Isaiah 11; 59:7–15; 60; 61:1–4
Habakkuk 2:14

**338. Kum ba Yah**
Psalm 145:18–19
Matthew 18:20
Philippians 4:4–6

**339. Be Thou My Vision**
Psalms 17:15; 73:25; 139:17–18
Matthew 13:44; 19:21
John 14:20; 15:4–5; 17:21
1 Corinthians 8:6
Philippians 3:7
Hebrews 7:26
1 John 4:13

**340. Eternal Light, Shine in My Heart**
Deuteronomy 33:27
John 1:1–5; 3:15–16; 6:54; 8:12

**341. Blessed Assurance, Jesus Is Mine!**
Genesis 28:12
Psalm 146:2
Isaiah 12:2
Acts 17:31; 20:28
Romans 8:16
1 Corinthians 7:23
Galatians 4:7
Titus 2:13; 3:5–7
Revelation *1:5–6;* 7:14

**342. By Gracious Powers**
Psalm 116:13
Matthew 10:26–33; 20:22
Mark 10:38
John 18:11

**343. Called as Partners in Christ's Service**
John 15:12–17
2 Corinthians 1:3–6
Galatians 6:2
Ephesians 2:15–22
Philippians 1:3–11
Colossians 4:6

**344. Christ of the Upward Way**
Psalms 24:3–4; 48:14; 73:23–24
Isaiah 6:8
Ephesians 5:17
Philippians 2:12–13; 3:14

**345. Dear Lord and Father of Mankind**
1 Kings *9:1–13; 19:11–12*
Isaiah 26:3; 30:15
Matthew *4:18–22*
Mark *1:16–20;* 2:14; *5:15*
Luke 5:11; 6:12
Ephesians 4:6
2 Timothy 1:9
1 Peter 2:9
1 John 1:9

**346. Christ, You Are the Fullness**
John 1:1–3
Colossians 1:15–18; 3:1–4, 15–18

**347. Forgive Our Sins as We Forgive**
Matthew 5:21–24; *6:9–15;* 18:21–35
Mark 11:24–25
Colossians 3:13–14

**348. Christian Women, Christian Men**
Leviticus 19:18
Matthew 22:34–40
Mark 12:28–34
Luke 10:25–37

**349. Let All Who Pray the Prayer Christ Taught**
Matthew 6:6–14
Luke 11:2–4

**350. Fill My Cup**
Psalm 116:13
John 4:5–15; 6:35
Romans 6:13
2 Timothy 2:21

**351. Give to Me, Lord, a Thankful Heart**
1 Kings 3:9
Isaiah 61:3
Hosea 14:9
Matthew 6:10
Colossians 1:9–14

**352. Great Are Your Mercies, O My Maker**
Matthew 6:25–34
Luke 12:22–31

Philippians 4:6
1 Peter 5:7

### 353. Great God, Your Love Has Called Us Here
John 13:4–5
Romans 6:22; 8:22–25
Galatians 5:13–14
Ephesians 2:8–10
1 Peter 2:9–10
1 John 3:11–18

### 354. Guide My Feet
1 Corinthians 9:24–27
2 Timothy 2:5
Hebrews 12:1–3

### 355. Hear the Good News of Salvation
Isaiah 53:5–12
1 Corinthians 15:3
1 Peter 2:24
1 John 1:9

### 356. Come, Thou Fount of Every Blessing
1 Samuel *7:12*
Psalms 36:9; 68:19; 119:10
Zechariah *13:1*
Romans 5:2; 8:12–14
2 Corinthians 1:22
Ephesians 1:3, 13–14; 2:7–8

### 357. O Master, Let Me Walk with Thee
Genesis 5:22, 24
Matthew 4:19; 10:39
Mark 9:35
Luke 6:40; 21:19
John 12:26; 13:13–14, 35
Galatians *5:13*
Colossians 1:10
1 John 2:6
Revelation 14:12

### 358. Help Us Accept Each Other
Leviticus 19:18
Matthew 18:21
John 3:21; 13:34–35; *15:12*
Romans 15:7
Ephesians 4:15
1 John 3:23

### 359. More Love to Thee, O Christ
Psalm 116:1
John 21:15

Philippians *1:9*, 20–24
2 Thessalonians 3:5
1 John 4:19

### 360. Hope of the World
Matthew 9:36; 12:21
John 6:35–51
Romans 8:24; 15:13
1 Corinthians 15:57
Galatians 4:6
Colossians 1:27
1 Timothy *1:1*
1 Peter 1:3

### 361. How Firm a Foundation
Deuteronomy 31:6
Joshua 1:9
Psalms 28:16; *46:1*; 62:7
Isaiah 28:16; *41:10; 43:1–7*
Matthew 14:22–23
Mark 4:35–41
Luke 8:22–25; *21:33*
Acts 2:27
1 Corinthians 3:11
2 Corinthians *12:9*
2 Timothy 2:19
Hebrews 6:18; *13:5–6*
1 Peter 1:7; 2:6; 4:12
2 Peter *1:4*

### 362. I Love the Lord, Who Heard My Cry
Psalm *116:1–9*
Hebrews 4:16

### 363. I Want Jesus to Walk with Me
Genesis 28:15
Psalm 23:4
Isaiah 43:2

### 364. I Sing a Song of the Saints of God
Psalm 22:4–5
Matthew 10:32
Luke 12:8
Acts 20:32
1 Timothy 6:12
Hebrews 11:4–12, 17–38; 12:1
James 1:12
Revelation 2:10; 14:13

### 365. Jesus, Priceless Treasure
Deuteronomy 33:27
Psalms *42:1–2*; 46:2–3; *84:2*
Isaiah 35:10

365. **Jesus, Priceless Treasure** (cont.)
Matthew *13:44–46*
Hebrews 9:14
1 Peter 1:19

366. **Jesus, Thy Boundless Love to Me**
Psalm 86:11
John 15:9–10
Romans 8:35–39
Galatians 2:20
Ephesians 2:4–5; *3:17–19*
1 John 3:1, 16

367. **Jesu, Jesu, Fill Us with Your Love**
Leviticus 19:18
Matthew 22:34–40
Mark 12:28–34
John 13:1–17
Romans 13:9

368. **I've Got Peace Like a River**
Romans 14:17; 15:13
Galatians 5:22

369. **I'm Gonna Live So God Can Use Me**
Ephesians 2:10
Colossians 1:10
2 Timothy 2:20–21

370. **Just as I Am, Without One Plea**
Psalm 51:1–2
Isaiah 1:18
Matthew 26:28
Mark 14:24
John 1:29; 6:37
1 Corinthians 1:9
Colossians 1:13–14
Titus 3:5
1 John *1:7–9*
Revelation 22:17

371. **Lift High the Cross**
John *12:32*
1 Corinthians 1:18
2 Corinthians 1:21–22
Galatians 6:14
Philippians 2:8–11
Colossians 2:13–15

372. **Lord, I Want to Be a Christian**
John 13:15
Ephesians 4:23–24
1 Peter 2:21
1 John 3:2

373. **Lonely the Boat**
Matthew 8:23–27
Mark 4:36–41
Luke 8:22–25
John 14:27; 16:33

374. **Lord, Make Us Servants of Your Peace**
Mark 4:14
Galatians 6:7–10

375. **Lord of All Good**
Romans 12:1
2 Corinthians 9:6–8
Ephesians 1:11–12

376. **Love Divine, All Loves Excelling**
Psalms *34:1;* 51:12; *106:4*
Isaiah 57:15
Micah 7:18
Malachi *3:1*
Matthew 11:28–29; *14:14*
Luke 24:51–53
John 14:16–17, 21; 20:22
Romans 7:24–25; 8:1–5
2 Corinthians *3:18; 5:17*
Galatians 5:1
Ephesians 5:27
Philippians 1:6
Hebrews 4:3–11
2 Peter 3:13–14
1 John *4:7–21*
Jude 24–25
Revelation *1:8; 4:10;* 7:15; *21:3–6;* 22:13

377. **Lord, You Have Come to the Lakeshore**
Matthew 4:18–22
Mark 1:16–20
Luke 5:1–11
John 1:35–42

378. **Make Me a Captive, Lord**
Matthew 10:39
Romans 12:1–2
2 Corinthians 5:14–15
Galatians 2:20
Ephesians 3:1

379. **My Hope Is Built on Nothing Less**
Psalms 40:2; 125:1
Isaiah 61:10
Matthew 7:24–28; 24:31
Luke 6:46–49
Acts 4:12

Romans 5:1–5
1 Corinthians *3:11*
1 Thessalonians 4:16–17
1 Timothy 2:5
Hebrews 6:17–*19*
1 Peter 3:15
Jude 24
Revelation 19:8

### 380. O Christ, the Healer
Psalm 102:1–7
Amos 6:1–7
Mark 1:30–34; 5:15
Romans 1:28–32
Ephesians 4
James 5:13–16

### 381. O Come Unto the Lord
Isaiah 55:6–7
Matthew 11:28–30
Luke 15:11–32
Ephesians 2:1

### 382. Somebody's Knocking at Your Door
Matthew 7:7–8
Luke 11:9–11
Revelation *3:20*

### 383. My Faith Looks Up to Thee
Psalms 73:24; 112:4; 118:8
Isaiah 25:8; 35:10; 42:16; 51:11; *58:10*
John 1:29
Acts 26:18
Romans 1:17; 5:1–2
2 Corinthians 12:9
Ephesians 3:12
Hebrews *12:2*
1 Peter 2:9
Revelation *7:17;* 21:4

### 384. O Love That Wilt Not Let Me Go
Genesis *9:13*–15
2 Samuel 22:29
Psalms 30:5; 36:9
Isaiah 60:19
Jeremiah *31:3*
Matthew 16:24
John 8:12; 15:9–11
Romans 8:35–39
Galatians 6:14
Ephesians 3:17–19
Revelation 21:4

### 385. O God, We Bear the Imprint of Your Face
Genesis 1:27
Colossians 3:10–11

### 386. O for a World
Romans 12:16; 15:5–6
1 Corinthians 1:27–29
Philippians 2:1–4

### 387. Savior, Like a Shepherd Lead Us
Psalms *23:1–3;* 103:10–12
Proverbs 8:17
Isaiah 40:11
Ezekiel 34:14–15, 23
Micah 7:7
John 6:37; *10:*4, *14–16,* 27; 13:1
1 Corinthians 6:19–20; *7:23*
Ephesians 2:4–5
Titus 3:5
Hebrews 4:16; 13:20–21

### 388. O Jesus, I Have Promised
1 Samuel 3:10
Psalms 48:14; 119:151
Luke 9:23–24, *57–62*
John *12:26;* 14:3; 15:14
Romans 12:11
2 Corinthians 5:15
Colossians 3:24
1 Peter 2:25
Revelation 14:13

### 389. *See* no. 388

### 390. O Savior, in This Quiet Place
Luke 18:9–14
1 Timothy 2:1–2
James 5:13–16

### 391. Take My Life
Numbers 6:1–12
1 Chronicles 29:5
Isaiah *52:7*
Nahum 1:15
Matthew 22:37
Romans 6:13; 10:15; *12:1–2*
1 Corinthians *6:19–20*
2 Timothy 2:20–21

### 392. Take Thou Our Minds, Dear Lord
Deuteronomy 6:5

**392. Take Thou Our Minds,**
**Dear Lord** (cont.)
Matthew 22:37
Luke 10:27
John 8:32
Romans 5:5
2 Corinthians 10:5
Philippians *2:15*

**393. Take Up Your Cross, the Savior Said**
Psalm 23:4
Matthew 10:38; *16:24*–27
Mark *8:34*–38
Luke 9:18–24, 57–62; 14:25–33
John 12:26
2 Corinthians 12:9–10
Hebrews 12:1–3
1 Peter 2:21

**394. There Is a Balm in Gilead**
Jeremiah *8:22;* 46:11
2 Corinthians 5:14

**395. Have Mercy, Lord, on Me**
Psalms 25:6–7, 57:1
Isaiah 63:8–9
Ephesians 2:4–6
1 Peter 1:3–4
1 John 1:9

**396. O for a Closer Walk with God**
Genesis 5:24
Psalms 34:18; 51:12; 57:13; 139:23–24
Proverbs 4:18
Isaiah 55:6–7
Micah *6:8*
Acts 17:27–30
Galatians 5:16
Ephesians 5:8

**397.** *See* no. 396

**398. There's a Sweet, Sweet Spirit**
Psalm 133:1
Matthew 3:16
Mark 1:10
Luke 3:22
John 1:32–33
Ephesians 3:16–19

**399. We Walk by Faith and Not by Sight**
Isaiah 55:6
John 20:19–31

2 Corinthians 5:7
1 Peter 1:8–9

**400. When We Are Living**
Romans 14:8
Galatians 2:20
Philippians 1:20–21

**401. When Will People Cease Their Fighting?**
Psalms 2; 120:6–7; 140:1–2
Isaiah 2:2–4
Micah 4:1–3
Matthew 5:9

**402. Now Praise the Hidden God of Love**
Psalms 23; 37:23–25
Proverbs 16:9
Jeremiah 10:23
Hebrews 13:20–21

**403. What a Friend We Have in Jesus**
Psalms 6:9; 27:10; 55:22
Proverbs 18:24
Matthew 11:28
Mark 11:24
John *15:13–16*
Romans 12:12
Ephesians 3:12
Philippians *4:6*
1 Thessalonians 5:17
Hebrews 4:15
1 Peter 5:7
1 John 5:14–15

**404. Precious Lord, Take My Hand**
Psalm 139:10
Isaiah 41:13

**405. What Does the Lord Require**
Isaiah 1:10–17
Micah *6:6–8*
Zechariah 7:9–10
Matthew 23:23
Luke 12:42

**406. Why Has God Forsaken Me?**
Psalm 22:1
Matthew 27:46
Luke 23:46
John 11:1–44

**407. When a Poor One**
Isaiah 58:6–7

Matthew 25:34–40
Hebrews 13:2
James 2:15–17

**408. Where Cross the Crowded Ways of Life**
Micah 6:9
Matthew 4:23–24; *9:36; 10:42; 11:18–20;*
        14:14; 15:32; 19:13–15; 22:9;
        25:40
Mark 6:34; 8:2; *9:41*
Luke 7:13; 10:27
John 13:34–35
1 John 3:17–18

**409. Wild and Lone the Prophet's Voice**
Matthew 3:1–12
Mark 1:2–8
Luke 3:2–17
John 1:29

**410. When I Had Not Yet Learned of Jesus**
Matthew 25:14–30
Ephesians 2:1–10
Colossians 1:13
Titus 2:11–14

**411. Arise, Your Light Is Come!**
Isaiah 40:31; 60:1–3; 61:1–2
John 8:12; 12:35–36
Ephesians 5:14

**412. Eternal God, Whose Power Upholds**
Psalms 54:4; 72:18–19; 90:2
Isaiah 11:9
Matthew 28:19–20
Galatians 5:22–24
James 3:13–17
1 John 4:7–12

**413. All Who Love and Serve Your City**
Psalm 90:12
Proverbs 21:13
Ezekiel *48:35*
Luke 19:41
John 9:4; 14:27
Ephesians 2:13–22

**414. As Those of Old Their Firstfruits Brought**
Exodus 23:16
Deuteronomy 26:1–3
Malachi 3:10
Romans 12:1–2

**415. Come, Labor On**
Matthew 9:37–38; *25:21–23*
John *4:34–35;* 9:4
2 Corinthians 4:7
Ephesians 5:16

**416. Christ Is Made the Sure Foundation**
1 Kings 8:27–30
Psalm 18:6
Matthew 21:42
Mark *12:10*
Luke 20:17
John 2:13–16
Acts 4:11
1 Corinthians *3:11*
Ephesians 1:22–23; *2:20–22*
Colossians 1:18
2 Timothy 2:12; 2:19
1 Peter 2:4–7
Revelation 21

**417.** *See* no. 416

**418. God, Bless Your Church with Strength**
Psalm 80:8–11
John 15:1–5
Colossians 1:9–14

**419. How Clear Is Our Vocation, Lord**
Isaiah 6:8
Matthew 11:28–30
2 Timothy 3:16–17
Hebrews 11; 12:2
1 John 5:3

**420. God of Grace and God of Glory**
Deuteronomy 31:6
Esther 4:14
Psalm 84:11–12
2 Corinthians 10:4
Ephesians *6:10–17*
Colossians 1:9–12
2 Timothy 1:7
Hebrews 4:16
James 1:5

**421. The Church of Christ in Every Age**
Psalm 72:12–13
Isaiah 42:1–4
Matthew 15:32–38; 25:34–40; 28:19–20
Mark 6:34; 8:1–9; 9:30–37; 10:43–45
Romans 12:1

**422. God, Whose Giving Knows No Ending**
Matthew 25:14–30; 28:19–20
Luke 12:21
John 3:27
Romans 12:1–8
1 Peter 4:10–11

**423. Jesus Shall Reign Where'er the Sun**
Job 3:17–18
Psalms *19:4–6;* 67; *72:*5, *8–19*
Isaiah 9:7; 61:1
Daniel 4:3
Matthew 21:16
Luke 1:32–33
1 Corinthians 15:27
Philippians 2:9–11
Colossians 3:16
Hebrews 1:8
Revelation 5:12–13; 7:9–10; *11:15*

**424. O Jesus Christ, May Grateful Hymns Be Rising**
Matthew 23:37
Mark 5:24–43
Luke 13:34–35
Romans 15:1
Philippians 4:13
2 Timothy 1:7

**425. Lord of Light, Your Name Outshining**
Isaiah 42:1–9
Matthew *6:10;* 25:14–30
Luke 18:1
Ephesians 3:19

**426. Lord, Speak to Me, That I May Speak**
Exodus 16:4–5, 31
1 Samuel 3:10
Psalm 119:12–13
Isaiah 50:4
Matthew 18:12–14; 28:19–20
Luke 15:4–6
John 6:48–51; *13:15*
Romans 6:13; 12:1–2; 14:7
2 Timothy *2:2*
Revelation 22:4

**427. Lord, Whose Love Through Humble Service**
Isaiah 61:1–2
John 10:10; 13:3–5, 12–15
Romans 12
Ephesians 3:14–19
Colossians 3:16–17

James 2:14–17
1 John 3:6–18

**428. We Give Thee but Thine Own**
Genesis 28:22
Leviticus 27:30–33
1 Chronicles *29:14*
Haggai 2:8
Malachi 3:8–10
Matthew 6:1–4; 25:34–40
1 Corinthians 16:2
2 Corinthians 9:6–8
1 Peter 4:10

**429. Lord, You Give the Great Commission**
Matthew 26:26–28; *28:19–20*
Luke 9:2; 10:9; 23:34
1 Corinthians 11:23–25

**430. Come Sing, O Church, in Joy!**
Psalms 33:10–11; 90:1–2
Isaiah 40:21–24; 63:16
Colossians 1:10–13
James 1:5
Revelation 5:5; 17:14

**431. O Lord, You Gave Your Servant John**
Matthew 25:31–40
Revelation 21; 22

**432. Song of Hope**
Isaiah 9:2; 42:1–7, 16; 51:4
John 8:12
Romans 15:13
1 John 3:14–18

**433. There's a Spirit in the Air**
Matthew 10:40–42; 25:34–40
Mark 9:40–41
John 13:34–35; 14:16
1 Corinthians 11:23–26
2 Corinthians 5:17–21
1 Peter 1:9
1 John 4:19–21

**434. Today We All Are Called to Be Disciples**
Genesis 1:1, 27–30; 2:15
Psalm 8:6–8
Amos 5:24
Proverbs 22:8
Isaiah 2:4; 42:7
Micah 4:1–3
Matthew 25:34–40; 28:19–20

John 13:34–35
Colossians 3:17
James 3:17–18
1 John 3:16–18

**435. We All Are One in Mission**
Matthew 28:19–20
Romans 12:4–8
1 Corinthians 12
Ephesians 4:11–13

**436. We Are Your People**
Leviticus 19:18
Matthew 22:34–40
Mark 12:28–31
Luke 10:27–28
Romans 12:4–8
1 Corinthians 11:23–25; 12
Ephesians 4:11–13

**437. Our Cities Cry to You, O God**
Isaiah 9:6–7
Matthew 5:14–16
John 1:14
Acts 18:10
Galatians 5:16–17
Ephesians 2:1–5; 5:8–18
Colossians 3:17
2 Timothy 2:20–21
1 John 2:15–17

**438. Blest Be the Tie That Binds**
Psalm 133:1
Matthew 18:20
John 13:34–35
Romans 12:5; 15:1–2
1 Corinthians 12:27
Galatians *3:28;* 6:2
Colossians *2:2*
Hebrews 4:16; 13:1
1 Peter 3:8
1 John 1:7

**439. In Christ There Is No East or West**
Psalms 33:13; 133:1
Luke 13:29
Acts 10:35; 17:26
Romans *8:14–17;* 12:5
1 Corinthians *12*:13
Galatians *3:26–28*
Ephesians 4:1–6
Colossians *3:11*

James *2:1*
1 Peter 2:17

**440.** *See* no. 439

**441. I Love Thy Kingdom, Lord**
Deuteronomy 32:10
Psalms *26:8;* 137
Zechariah *2:8*
Matthew 16:15–18
Romans 14:17
Ephesians *5:*23, *25*–27

**442. The Church's One Foundation**
Isaiah 2:4
Micah 4:1–3
Matthew *16:15–18;* 24:31
Mark 13:27
John 3:5
Acts 2:42, 47; 20:28
1 Corinthians *3:11;* 10:17
Ephesians 1:22–23; *2:19–22; 4:4–6; 5:23,*
*25–27*
Colossians 1:18
Hebrews 3:1–6; 9:28; 12:1
Revelation 5:9; 7:14; 21:2, 9

**443. O Christ, the Great Foundation**
Psalm 118:22
John 17:24
2 Corinthians 5:17
Ephesians 2:19–23; 4:5–7; 5:25–27;
6:10–18
1 Peter 2:4–6

**444. We Gather Here to Bid Farewell**
Numbers 6:24–26
Romans 5:13
Hebrews 13:20–21
3 John 5–8

**445. Great Day!**
Leviticus 25:8
Nehemiah 2–7
Psalm 102:16
Isaiah 14:32
Revelation 21:15

**446. Glorious Things of Thee Are Spoken**
Exodus *13:21–22;* 16:4, 31; 17:1–6; 33:14
Leviticus 26:12
Numbers 9:15–16

**446. Glorious Things of Thee
Are Spoken** (cont.)
Deuteronomy 1:33; 8:16
1 Chronicles 16:10
Nehemiah 9:19
Psalms 9:11; 46:4–5; 48:1–2; *87:1–3*
Isaiah 4:5; 26:1; *33:20–21;* 60:18
Matthew *7:24–25; 16:18*
John 4:10–14; 7:38
Revelation 7:17; 21:2–3; 22:1, 17

**447. Lead On, O King Eternal**
Isaiah 48:17
John 18:36
1 Corinthians 15:56–58
Galatians 6:14
Ephesians 6:10–20
Philippians 1:27–30
1 Timothy 6:12
2 Timothy 2:3–4; *4:7–8*

**448.** *See* no. 447

**449. My Lord! What a Morning**
Matthew 24:29–30
1 Corinthians 15:51–52
Revelation *6:12–17*

**450. O Day of Peace**
Isaiah 2:2–4; 11:6–9; 65:17–25
Micah 4:1–3

**451. Ye Watchers and Ye Holy Ones**
Psalm 148:1–2, 11–13
Colossians *1:16*
Hebrews 12:1
Revelation 4:8–11

**452. O Day of God, Draw Nigh**
Genesis 1:3
Psalms 94:2–3; 96:13; 105:7
Isaiah 2:2–4, 12; 3:13; 66:16
Jeremiah 25:31
Micah 4:1–3
1 Corinthians 3:13
2 Timothy 4:7–8
2 Peter 3:4–7, 11–13
1 John 4:16–17
Revelation 20:11–12

**453. O Holy City, Seen of John**
Isaiah 25:8
Revelation 3:12; 21:1–22:5

**454. Blessed Jesus, at Your Word**
2 Samuel 22:29
Psalm 34:15
Matthew 13:11
Luke 11:28
John 14:26
1 Corinthians 2:10
Ephesians 2:18; 3:3–5

**455. All Creatures of Our God and King**
Psalms 65:8; 96:1–6; 97:6; 136:1–9;
*145:10*–13; *148; 150:6*
Jeremiah 32:17–20
Romans 11:36
1 Corinthians 8:6
Revelation 4:11; 14:7

**456. Awake, My Soul, and with the Sun**
Psalms 5:3; 50:14; 61:8; 92:2; *108:2–3;*
139:2
Lamentations 3:22–23
Malachi 1:11
Matthew 5:16
John *9:4*
Romans 13:12

**457. I Greet Thee, Who My Sure Redeemer
Art**
Psalms 78:7; 133:1
John 14:6
*Acts 4:12;* 17:28
Romans 15:13
2 Corinthians 4:6
Ephesians 2:4–5
Colossians 1:10–12
Hebrews 12:2
1 Peter 5:7
1 John 4:13–14

**458. Earth and All Stars**
Psalms 96:1; *98:*1, 7–8; *148*

**459. Father, We Praise Thee**
Psalm 104:33–34
John 14:1–3

**460. Holy God, We Praise Your Name**
Psalms 30:4; 90:2; 145:21

Isaiah *6:2–3;* 57:15
Ephesians *1:19–23*
Hebrews 1:8; *12:1–3*
1 Peter 2:9
Revelation 4:8–11; 6:9–11; 15:4

### 461. God Is Here!
Isaiah 42:1
1 Corinthians 11:2; 12:27–31
2 Corinthians 4:5
2 Thessalonians 2:15
Titus 2:11–14
1 Peter 2:9–10

### 462. Christ, Whose Glory Fills the Skies
Proverbs *4:18*
Lamentations 3:22–23
Malachi *4:2*
Luke 1:78
John 1:4–9; 8:12; 12:46
Acts 9:3–5
2 Corinthians 4:6
Hebrews 1:3
2 Peter 1:19
Revelation 21:23

### 463. *See* no. 462

### 464. Joyful, Joyful, We Adore Thee
Job 38:7
Psalms 32:11; 98; 103:22; 104; 145:10
Habakkuk 3:18
Malachi 4:2
Luke 19:38
1 John 1:7

### 465. Here, O Lord, Your Servants Gather
John 10:9; 14:6
Romans 10:12–13
Ephesians 2:13–19

### 466. O for a Thousand Tongues to Sing
Psalms *35:28;* 66:2; 71:23; 96:1–4;
103:1–4; 119:172
Isaiah *1:18;* 12:4–5; *35:5–6;* 61:1–3
Matthew *11:2–5;* 15:31; 28:19–20
Mark 7:37
Luke *4:18;* 7:22
John 8:34–36; 20:31
Romans 3:24–25

2 Corinthians 1:3–7
Ephesians 1:7
Philippians 2:9–11
1 Peter 5:7
Revelation 5:12

### 467. How Great Thou Art
Deuteronomy 3:24
Psalms 8:3; *19:1; 48:1;* 145:3
John *14:3*
Acts 4:24
Romans 1:20; 5:6; 8:32
1 Thessalonians *4:16–17*

### 468. Let All the World in Every Corner Sing
Psalms 44:4; 48:10; 95:2–3; *96:1; 100:4;*
148:11–13; 150:6
Ephesians 5:19
Colossians 3:16

### 469. Morning Has Broken
Genesis *1:3–5*
Exodus *16:7*
Psalms *5:3;* 59:16

### 470. O Day of Radiant Gladness
Genesis 1:3; 2:2, 3
Psalm 118:24
Matthew 28:1
Acts 2:1–4; 20:7
Hebrews 4:9–10

### 471. O Praise the Gracious Power
Ephesians 2:11–22

### 472. O Sing to the Lord
Psalms 149:1; 150

### 473. For the Beauty of the Earth
Genesis 1:11–18
Psalms 19:1–6; 104:24; 107:21–22; 148
Ecclesiastes *3:11*
Romans 12:9–10
Colossians 3:14
Hebrews *13:15*
James *1:17*
Revelation 14:7

### 474. O Splendor of God's Glory Bright
Genesis 1:1–3

**474. O Splendor of God's Glory Bright** (cont.)
Malachi 4:2
John *1:1–9; 8:12*
2 Corinthians 4:6
Hebrews 1:3

**475. O That I Had a Thousand Voices**
Psalms 13:6; 35:28; 104; 126:2–3; 145:10–13; 148

**476. O Worship the King, All Glorious Above!**
Deuteronomy 31:6, 8
Joshua 1:5
2 Samuel 22:11–22
1 Chronicles 16:29; 29:11–13
Psalms 18:10–11; 21:13; 46:1; 47:6–7; 84:11; 91:4 *103:14; 104:1–28;* 145:1–13
Daniel *7:9*
Luke 1:78
John 4:23
1 Timothy 6:15–16

**477. Ye Servants of God, Your Master Proclaim**
Deuteronomy *32:3*
Psalms 35:18; 85:9; 96:1–10; *103:19–22;* 113:1–5; 145:12
Isaiah 52:13
Philippians 2:9–11
1 Timothy 6:16
Jude 24–25
Revelation 1:5–6; *5:9–14; 7:9–12;* 19:1; 22:3

**478. Praise, My Soul, the King of Heaven**
1 Chronicles 29:10–13
Nehemiah 9:17
Psalms 36:5; 47:6; 91:12; *103:1–22;* 145:8; 148:2
Lamentations 5:19
Daniel 4:37
Joel 2:13
Jonah 4:2
Nahum 1:3
Matthew 18:10
1 Timothy 1:17
Revelation 5:9; 7:9

**479. Praise, My Soul, the God of Heaven**
*See* no. 478

**480. Praise Our God Above**
Psalm 65:9–13
Acts 14:17
Romans 1:20

**481. Praise the Lord, God's Glories Show**
Psalms 103:21; 105:1; 145:3; *148; 150*

**482. Praise Ye the Lord, the Almighty**
Ruth 2:12
Job *22:26*
Psalms *42:11;* 43:5; 57:1; 61:4; *91:4; 100:2; 103:*1–6; 118:14; 145:21; *150:6*
Matthew 23:37
Luke 13:34

**483. Sing Praise to God, Who Reigns Above**
Deuteronomy *32:3*
1 Kings 18:39
1 Chronicles 16:25–36
Psalms 18:18; 34:18; *46:1;* 47:6–7; 68:19; *121:4;* 139:7
Isaiah 12:2–5; 66:13
Jeremiah 51:8
Acts 17:27
Hebrews 13:15
1 Peter 2:9

**484. Sing with Hearts**
Psalms 100; 150
Ephesians 5:19–20
Colossians 3:16–17

**485. To God Be the Glory**
Psalms *29:2;* 71:19; 72:18–19; 96:8; 118:19; *126:2–3;* 138:5
John 1:14; *3:16–17;* 10:9; 14:6
1 Corinthians 10:31; 15:3
Galatians 1:5
Colossians 1:14
1 Timothy 1:15–17
1 Peter 1:2–3
1 John 3:2

**486. When the Morning Stars Together**
2 Corinthians *5:13–14*
Job *38:7*
Psalm 150:3–5
Ephesians 5:19–20
Colossians 3:16–17

**487. When Morning Gilds the Skies**
1 Chronicles 23:30
Psalms *5:3;* 30:4–5; 57:8; *59:16–17;*
    112:4; 148
Matthew 28:9
Philippians 4:4–7
1 Thessalonians 5:16–18
2 Peter 1:19; 2:9
Revelation 5:12

**488. The God of Abraham Praise**
Genesis 15:1
Exodus *3:6, 14;* 15:2
Psalms 16:11; 22:23; 106:48; 145:
    1–3
Isaiah *6:3*
Jeremiah 23:36
Lamentations 5:19
Daniel *7:9*
Malachi 3:6
John 8:58; 17:24
Romans 4:20–21
2 Corinthians 3:3
Galatians 3:7–9
Philippians 2:9–10
Hebrews 1:1; 13:8
Revelation 1:4, 8; *4:8;* 5:13; 11:17

**489. Open Now Thy Gates of Beauty**
Genesis 28:16–17
Psalms 50:2; 118:19–21
1 Corinthians 3:16
Ephesians 5:19–20
Colossians 3:16–17
Revelation 22:1–5

**490. With Glad, Exuberant Carolings**
Psalm 95:2
Ephesians 5:15–20
Colossians 3:16–17

**491. Stand Up and Bless the Lord**
1 Chronicles 16:36; 23:30
Nehemiah *9:5*
Psalms 2:11; 17:1; 22:23; *34:3;* 51:15;
    63:4; 103:21; 118:14; 134;
    145:1–2
Isaiah *6:6–7*
John 13:34–35
Hebrews 12:28
1 Peter 2:9

**492. Baptized in Water**
Romans 6:1–4
Galatians 3:27–29
Ephesians 1:13
Colossians 2:12

**493. Dearest Jesus, We Are Here**
Matthew 18:3
John 3:5; 14:6; 15:1; 21:15

**494. Out of Deep, Unordered Water**
Genesis 1:1–7, 21, 25–27
Exodus 14:22
1 Corinthians 10:1–2
Ephesians 1:13

**495. We Know That Christ Is Raised**
Acts 2:24
Romans 6:4, 9
2 Corinthians 5:17
Colossians 2:12
Revelation 1:18; 22:17

**496. Lord Jesus Christ, Our Lord Most Dear**
Matthew 19:13–15
Mark 10:13–16
Luke 18:15–17

**497. With Grateful Hearts Our Faith Professing**
Deuteronomy 6:4–7
Proverbs 22:6
Ephesians 6:1–4
Titus 2:7

**498. Child of Blessing, Child of Promise**
1 Samuel 1:27–28
Proverbs 22:6
Mark 10:13–16
John 3:3–5
Ephesians 1:13

**499. Wonder of Wonders, Here Revealed**
Romans 6:4
Galatians 3:26–29
Ephesians 1:13

**500. Become to Us the Living Bread**
John 4:14; 6:35–58
1 Corinthians 10:16; 11:23–26

**501. Bread of Heaven, on Thee We Feed**
John 6:32–35, 41–48, 51–54; 15:1, 5

**501. Bread of Heaven,
on Thee We Feed** (cont.)
Romans 11:17–20
1 Corinthians 10:16

**502. Bread of the World in Mercy Broken**
Psalm 51:17
Matthew 26:26–29
Luke 22:17–20; 24:30
John 6:51, 58
Romans 6:1–11
1 Corinthians 11:23–28

**503. Come, Risen Lord**
Psalm 119:18
Matthew 26:26–29
Luke 22:19; 24:28–43
1 Corinthians 11:23–26
Ephesians 4:3–6

**504. Draw Us in the Spirit's Tether**
Matthew 18:20
John 13:34–35; 15:8
1 Corinthians 11:23–26

**505. Be Known to Us in Breaking Bread**
Luke 24:30–35
1 Corinthians 11:23–26
Ephesians 3:17–19

**506. Deck Yourself, My Soul, with
Gladness**
Psalms 95:6; 118:27
Matthew 26:26–29
John 6:35–58
1 Corinthians 11:23–28
Ephesians 3:14–20

**507. I Come with Joy**
Matthew 8:11;
1 Corinthians 10:16–17; 11:23–26
Colossians 3:14–15

**508. For the Bread Which You Have
Broken**
Mark 14:22–25
Luke 11:2–4; 22:15–20
1 Corinthians 11:23–26
Hebrews 12:2

**509.** *See* no. 508

**510. Jesus, Thou Joy of Loving Hearts**
Psalms 100:5; 107:9
Isaiah 58:10
Jeremiah 29:13
Luke 11:9–10
John 1:4–5; 4:10–14; 6:35–58; 14:1;
    15:10–11
Acts 2:21; 26:18
1 Corinthians 1:9
Ephesians 3:17
Philippians 4:19
Colossians 1:13
Hebrews 11:6
1 Peter 1:8–9; 2:9
2 Peter 1:3
Revelation 7:17

**511.** *See* no. 510

**512. Living Word of God Eternal**
Exodus 4:12
Matthew 26:26–28
Luke 22:17–20
John 1:1–5; 3:16–17; 6:35
Acts 2:42
Romans 8:26–27; 14:11
1 Corinthians 2:13; 11:23–29
2 Corinthians 5:20
2 Timothy 3:16–17

**513. Let Us Break Bread Together**
Psalm 51:1
Matthew 26:26–30
Luke 22:17–20; 24:30
John 6:53–58
Acts 2:42
1 Corinthians 11:23–28; 13:12

**514. Let Us Talents and Tongues Employ**
Matthew 26:26–28; 28:19–20
Luke 22:17–20
Romans 7:4
1 Corinthians 11:23–26
Colossians 1:10; 3:17

**515. Now to Your Table Spread**
Matthew 26:26–28
Luke 22:17–20
John 1:4; 14:6
Acts 2:44–46; 4:32–35
1 Corinthians 11:23–26
Colossians 2:2–3

**516. Lord, We Have Come at Your Own Invitation**
Psalm 143:10
Matthew 26:26–30
Luke 22:17–20
1 Corinthians 11:23–26
2 Corinthians 5:20
Ephesians 1:4; 3:16
2 Thessalonians 2:13
1 Peter 4:10–11

**517. We Come as Guests Invited**
Matthew 26:26–30
Luke 22:17–20
John 6:35–58; 15:5
1 Corinthians 11:23–26

**518. Sheaves of Summer**
Matthew 26:26–30
Luke 22:19–20
1 Corinthians 11:23–26
Ephesians 4:1–6
Titus 3:3–7

**519. Thee We Adore, O Hidden Savior, Thee**
Matthew 26:26–30
Luke 22:17–20
John 6:53–58
Acts 20:28
1 Corinthians 11:23–26
2 Corinthians 3:12–18

**520. Here, O Our Lord, We See You Face to Face**
Psalms 27:8; 46:1; 84:11
Matthew 26:26–30
Luke 22:17–20
John 6:48
1 Corinthians 11:23–26
Ephesians 3:16
1 Peter 5:7
Revelation *19:9;* 21:1–5

**521. You Satisfy the Hungry Heart**
Matthew 26:26–30
Luke 22:17–20
John 6:33–34; 10:1–6
1 Corinthians *10:16–17;* 11:23–26
Ephesians 3:17
Colossians 3:16–17
Hebrews 13:5

**522. Lord, When I Came Into This Life**
Isaiah 49:1
Jeremiah 1:5
Galatians 1:15
2 Thessalonians 1:11–12
2 Peter 1:3–11

**523. God the Spirit, Guide and Guardian**
Isaiah 61:1
Acts 20:28
1 Corinthians 12:27–28
2 Corinthians 1:21–22
Ephesians 4:11–13
Colossians 3:12–17
Hebrews 13:7
1 Peter 5:1–3
2 Peter 1:3–11

**524. Holy Spirit, Lord of Love**
Acts 2:1–3
1 Timothy 4:14
2 Timothy 1:6–7
Hebrews 2:4

**525. Here I Am, Lord**
Exodus 2:23–24; 3:7–8
1 Samuel 3:1–10
Isaiah *6:8;* 42:5–9, 16
Ezekiel 11:19–20
John 6:35, 51

**526. For All the Saints**
2 Samuel 22:2
Psalms 18:2; 22:4–5; 31:3; 71:3; 91:2; 144:2
Matthew 10:32
Luke 12:8
Acts 20:32
1 Thessalonians 4:13–17
1 Timothy 6:12
2 Timothy 4:7
Hebrews 2:10; 4:9 *11:13*–16, 32–34; *12:1*
James 1:12
1 Peter 1:3–5
Revelation *2:10;* 6:11; *7:2–4, 9–14; 14:13*

**527. Near to the Heart of God**
Exodus 33:14
Psalms *34:18;* 73:28
Matthew 11:28–30
John 10:28
Acts 17:27

**527. Near to the Heart of God** (cont.)
Philippians 4:7
Hebrews 4:16
James *4:8*

**528. Give Thanks for Life**
Psalms 39:49
Matthew 5:14–16
Colossians 1:3–4
Hebrews 11:32–38
Revelation 14:13

**529. Lord of the Living**
Genesis 1:1
John 11:25
1 Corinthians 15:12–28
1 Peter 1:3–4

**530. O Lord of Life, Where'er They Be**
Genesis 3:19
Deuteronomy 33:27
Psalm 103:14
Ecclesiastes 3:20
Revelation 14:13

**531. Not for Tongues of Heaven's Angels**
Matthew 17:20–21; 21:21
Romans 5:1–5
1 Corinthians 13

**532. O God, You Give Humanity Its Name**
Genesis 2:24
Matthew 19:4–6
Mark 10:6–9

**533. O Perfect Love**
Genesis *2:18, 23–24*
Joshua 24:15
Matthew 19:4–6
Mark 10:6–9
Ephesians *5:21–33*
1 Peter 3:7
1 John 4:18

**534. The Grace of Life Is Theirs**
Genesis 2:23–24
Psalm 128
Matthew 19:4–6
Mark 10:6–9
1 Peter 3:7

**535. Go with Us, Lord**
Psalms 23:3; 73:24
Romans 12:1
2 Corinthians 5:14–15

**536. Lord, Make Us More Holy**
Romans 12:9–12
Ephesians 4:1–3
Colossians 4:12–14
Hebrews 12:14
Revelation 2:10

**537. Farewell, Good Friends**
Genesis 31:49
Numbers 6:24–26

**538. Lord, Dismiss Us with Thy Blessing**
Exodus 33:14
Numbers 6:24
Psalms 3:8; 23:4; 89:15
Proverbs 14:32
Luke 2:29–30
Romans 15:13
Galatians 6:16
Ephesians 6:23–24
Philippians 1:2
1 Thessalonians 4:13–18
2 Peter 1:2

**539. Savior, Again to Thy Dear Name We Raise**
Psalms 4:8; 18:28; 29:11; 139:12; 141:3
Isaiah 26:3, 12–13; 57:2
Matthew 26:30
Luke 1:79
John 14:27
Romans 15:13
Ephesians 2:14–18; 6:23–24
2 Thessalonians 3:16
Hebrews 13:20–21

**540. God Be with You Till We Meet Again**
Genesis 31:49
Exodus 33:14
Deuteronomy 8:3; 33:27
Psalms 57:1; 73:23–24; 91:4; 95:7
Song of Solomon 2:4
Isaiah 40:11
Nahum 1:7
John 6:32–35, 48–51, 58; *10:1–18*
Acts *20:32*
1 Thessalonians 5:23–24

**541. Now the Day Is Over**
Genesis 1:4–5
Psalms 3:5; 4:8; 63:6–8; 91:5; 104:19–23
Proverbs *3:24*

**542. All Praise to Thee, My God, This Night**
Deuteronomy 33:27
Psalms 4:8; 42:8; 63:6; 92:1–2
Proverbs 3:24
Matthew 6:12
Ephesians 4:25–27
Hebrews 12:14

**543. Abide with Me**
Psalms 23:4; 72:12; 92:2; 102:25–26;
     *139:7–12;* 145:18
Malachi 3:6
Matthew 28:20
Luke *24:29*
1 Corinthians 15:54–57
Hebrews 13:8
1 John 2:28; 3:24

**544. Day Is Done**
Psalms 4:8; 42:8; 139:12; 145:18
John 1:4–5
Ephesians 4:4–5
1 Thessalonians 4:14

**545. Now on Land and Sea Descending**
Psalm 148:3
Jeremiah 31:3; 31:35
1 Corinthians 13:13
1 Peter 5:17

**546. The Day Thou Gavest, Lord, Is Ended**
Psalms 42:8; 92:2; 93:1–3; *113:1–6;*
     145:13
Isaiah 45:22–23
Lamentations 5:19
Matthew 16:18
Luke 1:33
Ephesians 3:10, 20–21

**547. When Twilight Comes**
Psalms 57:1; 61:4
Matthew 23:37; 26:17–29
Mark 14:12–25
Luke 13:34; 22:7–38

**548. O Radiant Light, O Sun Divine**
Psalms 19:1–6; 42:8; 92:2; 136:7–9

John 1:4–5; 6:40
2 Corinthians 4:6
Philippians 2:9–11

**549. O Gladsome Light**
Psalm 104:1–2
Isaiah 49:6
John *1:4–9;* 8:12
2 Corinthians 4:6
Philippians 2:9–11
Revelation 1:13

**550. O Light Whose Splendor Thrills**
Isaiah 49:6
John 1:4–9; 8:12
2 Corinthians 4:6
Philippians 2:9–11
Revelation 1:16

**551. Come, Ye Thankful People, Come**
Exodus 23:16; 34:22
Psalms *67:6–7;* 126:6
Proverbs 22:2
Matthew 9:37–38; *13:18–43*
1 Corinthians 3:13–15
2 Corinthians 9:10–14
Hebrews 13:15
Revelation 14:15; 22:20

**552. Give Thanks, O Christian People**
Proverbs 29:7
1 Corinthians 12:4–11; 15:15–18
2 Corinthians 9:6–15
Galatians 6:2
Ephesians 4:11–13
1 Thessalonians 4:16–17

**553. For the Fruit of All Creation**
Deuteronomy 26:2–3
Matthew 20:1–16; 25:37–45
Mark 4:26–29
Luke 15:31–32
Galatians 5:22–23
Ephesians 6:9

**554. Let All Things Now Living**
Genesis 1:2
Exodus 13:21
Numbers 9:16
Deuteronomy 1:33
1 Chronicles 16:31–34
Nehemiah 9:19

**554. Let All Things Now Living** (cont.)
Job 26, 38
Psalms 95:1–6; 100:3; 145
Song of Solomon 2:4
Ephesians 5:19–20
Colossians 3:16
Hebrews 1:3

**555. Now Thank We All Our God**
1 Chronicles 16:8, 34–36; *29:13*
Psalms 48:14; 71:6; 73:28; 92:1; 100:4;
       107:1, 8, 31; 126:3; 145:18
Colossians 2:7
Hebrews 13:8, 15
Revelation 1:8; 4:8; 11:17

**556. The World Abounds with God's Free
Grace**
Psalms 8:6; 95:1–6; 104:1–9; 115:16;
       136:1–9
2 Corinthians 9:8
Colossians 3:17

**557. O What Shall I Render?**
Psalms 8:4; 19:1; 95:1–2; 116:12–18; 121
Ephesians 5:1–2

**558. Come, Sing a Song of Harvest**
Genesis 1:1
Exodus 23:16
Deuteronomy 26:1–11
Matthew 25:34–40
Galatians 5:13
Hebrews 11:3

**559. We Gather Together**
Deuteronomy 31:8
Psalms 5:11; 32:8; 94:12; 119:134; 145:13
Isaiah *49:15*
Luke 12:6
John 16:33
Acts 14:22
Romans *8:31*
Hebrews 12:5–7

**560. We Plow the Fields and Scatter**
Genesis 1:11–18; 2:4–5; 8:22
Job 5:10
Psalms *65:9–11;* 103:2; 147:8–9, 16–18
Isaiah 55:10
Ezekiel 34:26
Micah 6:6–8

Matthew 6:26; 8:26; 13:37–38
Mark 4:39
Luke 12:24
Acts 14:17
Philippians 4:19
Hebrews 11:3; 13:15
James *1:17*

**561. My Country, 'Tis of Thee**
Psalm 33:12
Proverbs 14:34
Hebrews 11:13–16

**562. Eternal Father, Strong to Save**
Genesis *1:1–3*
Job *38:8–11*
Psalms 57:1; *89:8–9;* 91:2; 95:5;
       107:23–32
Matthew 8:23–27; 14:24–33
Mark 4:36–41; 6:47–52
Luke 8:26–37
John 6:16–21
2 Peter 2:9

**563. Lift Every Voice and Sing**
Psalm 33:12
Proverbs 34:14
Hebrews 11:8–16

**564. O Beautiful for Spacious Skies**
Psalms 33:12; *65:9–13*
Hebrews 11:16
James *1:17*

**565. Lord, Have Mercy**
Psalms 51:1; 57:1

**566. Glory to God in the Highest**
Deuteronomy 6:4
1 Samuel 2:2
Psalm 4:1; 6:9
Luke 2:14

**567. Glory to the Father**
Psalm 103:22
Revelation 1:5–6

**568. Holy, Holy, Holy Lord**
Exodus 15:11
Psalms 19:1; 145:8–21; 148
Isaiah 6:3
Matthew 21:9

Mark 11:9
John 12:13
Revelation 4:8–11; 5:13–14

**569. Christ Has Died**
1 Corinthians 15:3–5, 20–23

**570. Amen**

**571. Our Father in Heaven**
Matthew 6:9–13
Luke 11:2–4

**572. Lord, Have Mercy Upon Us**
Psalms 51:1; 57:1

**573. Lord, Have Mercy**
Psalms 51:1; 57:1

**574. Lord, Have Mercy Upon Us**
Psalms 51:1; 57:1

**575.** *See* no. 566

**576. Gloria, Gloria**
Luke 2:14

**577. Glory Be to the Father**
Psalm 103:22
Matthew 28:19
Revelation 1:5–6

**578. Glory Be to the Father**
Psalm 103:22
Matthew 28:19
Revelation 1:5–6

**579. Glory Be to the Father**
Psalm 103:22
Matthew 28:19
Revelation 1:5–6

**580. Holy, Holy, Holy**
Exodus 15:11
Psalms 19:1; 145:8–21; 148
Isaiah 6:3
Revelation 4:8–11; 5:13–14

**581. Holy, Holy, Holy Lord**
Exodus 15:11
Psalms 19:1; 145:8–21; 148
Isaiah 6:3

Matthew 21:9
Mark 11:9
John 12:13
Revelation 4:8–11; 5:13–14

**582. Dying, You Destroyed Our Death**
1 Corinthians 15:21–22

**583. Amen**

**584. Amen**

**585. Amen**

**586. Amen**

**587. Amen**

**588. Amen**

**589. Our Father, Which Art in Heaven**
Matthew 6:9–13
Luke 11:2–4

**590. Our Father, Lord of Heaven and Earth**
Matthew 6:9–13
Luke 11:2–4

**591. Praise God, from Whom All Blessings Flow**
Psalm 150:6
Proverbs 10:6

**592. Praise God, from Whom All Blessings Flow**
Psalm 150:6
Proverbs 10:6

**593.** *See* no. 592

**594. This Is the Feast of Victory**
Revelation 5:12–14

**595. Alleluia**
Revelation 19:6

**596. May the Lord, Mighty God**
Numbers 6:24–26
Psalm 29:11

597. **Bless the Lord, O My Soul**
Psalm 103:1–2

598. **This Is the Good News**
Matthew 16:16
1 Corinthians 15:3–7
Revelation 1:8; 22:13

599. **Jesus, Remember Me**
Luke *23:42*

600. **Song of Mary**
Luke 1:46–55

601. **Song of Zechariah**
Luke 1:68–79

602. *See* no. 601

603. **Song of Simeon**
Luke 2:29–32

604. *See* no. 603

605. *See* no. 603

# APPENDIX

## GOD: ADORATION AND PRAISE

*See also* pages 176–177 in this book.

# BIBLIOGRAPHY

Anderson, Bernhard W. *Out of the Depths: The Psalms Speak for Us Today.* Philadelphia: Westminster Press, 1983.

*Baptist Hymnal.* Edited by Walter Hines Sims. Nashville: Convention Press, 1956.

*Gather.* Chicago: GIA Publications, 1988.

Griggs, Donald L. *Praying and Teaching the Psalms.* Nashville: Abingdon Press, 1984.

Guy, Robert McCutchan. *Our Hymnody: A Manual of the Methodist Hymnal.* 2d ed. New York: Abingdon-Cokesbury Press, 1937.

*Hymnal Companion, The.* Edited by Fred Bock and Bryan Jeffrey Leech. Nashville: Paragon Associates, 1979.

*Hymnal of the United Church of Christ, The.* Philadelphia: United Church Press, 1974.

*Hymnbook for Christian Worship.* St. Louis: Bethany Press, 1970.

*Hymns for the Family of God.* Nashville: Paragon Associates, 1976.

*Hymns for the Living Church.* Carol Stream, Ill.: Hope Publishing Co., 1987.

*International Commission on English in the Liturgy: Resource Collection of Hymns and Service Music for the Liturgy.* Chicago: GIA Publications, 1981.

*Lead Me, Guide Me: The African American Catholic Hymnal.* Chicago: GIA Publications, 1987.

*Living Praise Hymnal.* Compiled by John S. Peterson. Grand Rapids: Zondervan Publishing House, 1981.

McDormand, Thomas B., and Frederic S. Crossman. *Judson Concordance to Hymns.* Valley Forge, Pa.: Judson Press, 1965.

McKim, LindaJo H. *The Presbyterian Hymnal Companion.* Louisville, Ky.: Westminster/John Knox Press, 1993.

*The Mennonite Hymnal.* Newton, Kans.: Faith and Life Press, 1969.

*The Methodist Hymnal.* Nashville: Board of Publication of the Methodist Church, 1964.

*New Church Hymnal, The.* Lexicon Music, 1976.

*Pilgrim Hymnal.* Boston: Pilgrim Press, 1958.

*Rejoice and Sing.* Oxford: Oxford University Press, 1991.

*Rejoice in the Lord: A Hymn Companion to the Scriptures.* Edited by Erik Routley. Grand Rapids: Wm. B. Eerdmans Publishing Co., 1985.

Spencer, Donald A. *Hymn and Scripture Selection Guide.* Valley Forge, Pa.: Judson Press, 1977.

*United Methodist Hymnal, The.* Nashville: United Methodist Publishing House, 1989.

*Worship: A Hymnal and Service Book for Roman Catholics.* Chicago: GIA Publications, 1986.

*Worship II.* Chicago: GIA Publications, 1975.

*Worship and Hymns for All Occasions.* Philadelphia: Westminster Press, 1968.

*Worshipbook: Services and Hymns, The.* Philadelphia: Westminster Press, 1972.